# Upgrade Your PC

In a Weekend

Sunrise · Midday · Sunset · Sunset · Evening · Sunrise

## FAITHE WEMPEN

PRIMA TECH

**A DIVISION OF PRIMA PUBLISHING**

*To Margaret*

A Division of Prima Publishing

Prima Publishing, In a Weekend, and colophon are registered trademarks of Prima Communications, Inc. In a Weekend is a trademark of Prima Publishing, a division of Prima Communications, Inc., Rocklin, California 95677.

**Publisher:** Matthew H. Carleson
**Managing Editor:** Dan J. Foster
**Acquisitions Editor:** Jenny L. Watson
**Senior Editor:** Kelli R. Crump
**Technical Reviewer:** David Plotkin
**Copy Editor:** Hilary Powers
**Interior Layout:** Marian Hartsough
**Editorial Assistant:** Rebecca I. Fong
**Cover Design:** Prima Design Team
**Indexer:** Katherine Stimson

**Important:** Prima Publishing cannot provide hardware or software support. Please contact the appropriate hardware or software manufacturer's technical support line or Web site for assistance.

Prima Publishing and the author have attempted throughout this book to distinguish proprietary trademarks from descriptive terms by following the capitalization style used by the manufacturer.

Information contained in this book has been obtained by Prima Publishing from sources believed to be reliable. However, because of the possibility of human or mechanical error by our sources, Prima Publishing, or others, the Publisher does not guarantee the accuracy, adequacy, or completeness of any information and is not responsible for any errors or omissions or the results obtained from the use of such information. Readers should be particularly aware of the fact that the Internet is an ever-changing entity. Some facts may have changed since this book went to press.

ISBN: 0-7615-1413-9
Library of Congress Catalog Card Number: 98-67620
Printed in the United States of America

98 99 00 01 02 DD 10 9 8 7 6 5 4 3 2 1

# CONTENTS AT A GLANCE

**Introduction** . . . . . . . . . . . . . . . . . . . . . . . . . . . . . . . . **ix**

**FRIDAY EVENING**
**Assessing Your Current System** . . . . . . . . . . . . . . . . . . . . **1**

**SATURDAY MORNING**
**How Much and What Kind?** . . . . . . . . . . . . . . . . . . . . . **71**

**SATURDAY AFTERNOON**
**Shopping for the Best Deal** . . . . . . . . . . . . . . . . . . . . **153**

**SUNDAY MORNING**
**Installing the Upgrades** . . . . . . . . . . . . . . . . . . . . . . . **199**

**SUNDAY AFTERNOON**
**Testing and Troubleshooting** . . . . . . . . . . . . . . . . . . . **277**

**APPENDIX**
**Post Error Beep Codes** . . . . . . . . . . . . . . . . . . . . . . . **371**

**Glossary** . . . . . . . . . . . . . . . . . . . . . . . . . . . . . . . . . **377**

**Index** . . . . . . . . . . . . . . . . . . . . . . . . . . . . . . . . . . . **385**

# CONTENTS

Introduction . . . . . . . . . . . . . . . . . . . . . . . . . . . . . . . . ix

**FRIDAY EVENING**
**Assessing Your Current System** . . . . . . . . . . . . . . . . . . . . . . 1

The Basics of a Computer . . . . . . . . . . . . . . . . . . . . . . . . . 3
What Do You Want to Do? . . . . . . . . . . . . . . . . . . . . . . . . . 5
Converting to a 32-Bit File System . . . . . . . . . . . . . . . . 42
Take a Break . . . . . . . . . . . . . . . . . . . . . . . . . . . . . . . . 43
Take a Cold, Hard Look at Your System . . . . . . . . . . . . . . . 43
Deciding What Parts to Upgrade . . . . . . . . . . . . . . . . . . . 55
The Minimums You Should Consider . . . . . . . . . . . . . . . . 67
Summary . . . . . . . . . . . . . . . . . . . . . . . . . . . . . . . . . . 70

**SATURDAY MORNING**
**How Much and What Kind?** . . . . . . . . . . . . . . . . . . . . . . . 71

How to Use This Session . . . . . . . . . . . . . . . . . . . . . . . . 73
Choosing an Operating System . . . . . . . . . . . . . . . . . . . . 73
Improving Your Processor . . . . . . . . . . . . . . . . . . . . . . . 81
My Recommendations . . . . . . . . . . . . . . . . . . . . . . . . . . 94
Adding Memory (RAM) . . . . . . . . . . . . . . . . . . . . . . . . . 94
Replacing the Motherboard . . . . . . . . . . . . . . . . . . . . . . 102

Cases and Power Supplies . . . . . . . . . . . . . . . . . . . . . . . . 110
Video Cards . . . . . . . . . . . . . . . . . . . . . . . . . . . . . . . . . . . 112
Monitors . . . . . . . . . . . . . . . . . . . . . . . . . . . . . . . . . . . . . 116
CD-ROM and DVD Drives . . . . . . . . . . . . . . . . . . . . . . . . . 122
Hard Disks . . . . . . . . . . . . . . . . . . . . . . . . . . . . . . . . . . . . 129
Removable Mass Storage . . . . . . . . . . . . . . . . . . . . . . . . . 132
Sound Cards . . . . . . . . . . . . . . . . . . . . . . . . . . . . . . . . . . 133
Printers . . . . . . . . . . . . . . . . . . . . . . . . . . . . . . . . . . . . . . 136
Scanners . . . . . . . . . . . . . . . . . . . . . . . . . . . . . . . . . . . . . 147
Special Input Devices . . . . . . . . . . . . . . . . . . . . . . . . . . . 149
Summary . . . . . . . . . . . . . . . . . . . . . . . . . . . . . . . . . . . . . 152

## SATURDAY AFTERNOON
## Shopping for the Best Deal . . . . . . . . . . . . . . . . . . . . . . 153

Understanding the Shopping Process . . . . . . . . . . . . . . . . 155
Name-Brand or Generic Parts? . . . . . . . . . . . . . . . . . . . . 156
Choosing the Brand and Model You Want . . . . . . . . . . . . . 158
Where Will You Buy? . . . . . . . . . . . . . . . . . . . . . . . . . . . . 165
Shopping the Mail-Order Vendors . . . . . . . . . . . . . . . . . . 171
Deep-Discount Shopping . . . . . . . . . . . . . . . . . . . . . . . . . 179
Take a Break . . . . . . . . . . . . . . . . . . . . . . . . . . . . . . . . . . 187
Checking Out the Retail Stores . . . . . . . . . . . . . . . . . . . . 187
Summary . . . . . . . . . . . . . . . . . . . . . . . . . . . . . . . . . . . . . 197

**SUNDAY MORNING**
**Installing the Upgrades** . . . . . . . . . . . . . . . . . . . . . . . . . . . . **199**

    How to Use This Session . . . . . . . . . . . . . . . . . . . . . 201
    Essential Precautions . . . . . . . . . . . . . . . . . . . . . . . 202
    Setting the Stage . . . . . . . . . . . . . . . . . . . . . . . . . 208
    Upgrades That Don't Involve Removing the Cover . . . . . . . . . . 210
    A Look Inside a PC . . . . . . . . . . . . . . . . . . . . . . . . 221
    Take a Break . . . . . . . . . . . . . . . . . . . . . . . . . . . 227
    Installing a Processor Upgrade . . . . . . . . . . . . . . . . . . 228
    Installing an Expansion Card . . . . . . . . . . . . . . . . . . . 234
    Installing a Drive . . . . . . . . . . . . . . . . . . . . . . . . . 239
    Installing RAM . . . . . . . . . . . . . . . . . . . . . . . . . . 254
    Replacing a Battery . . . . . . . . . . . . . . . . . . . . . . . . 261
    Installing a Motherboard . . . . . . . . . . . . . . . . . . . . . 266
    Other Installations . . . . . . . . . . . . . . . . . . . . . . . . 274
    Summary . . . . . . . . . . . . . . . . . . . . . . . . . . . . . 276

**SUNDAY AFTERNOON**
**Testing and Troubleshooting** . . . . . . . . . . . . . . . . . . . . . . . **277**

    All about the BIOS . . . . . . . . . . . . . . . . . . . . . . . . 279
    Making BIOS Changes for Your Upgrade . . . . . . . . . . . . . . 281
    Running Setup Software . . . . . . . . . . . . . . . . . . . . . . 300
    Configuring Windows 95/98 for Peer-to-Peer Networking . . . . . 312
    General Troubleshooting . . . . . . . . . . . . . . . . . . . . . 318
    Troubleshooting Video Problems . . . . . . . . . . . . . . . . . . 331
    Troubleshooting Modem Problems . . . . . . . . . . . . . . . . . 341
    Troubleshooting Sound Problems . . . . . . . . . . . . . . . . . 353
    Troubleshooting Windows 95/98 Network Problems . . . . . . . . 363
    New Device Works but System Crashes Frequently . . . . . . . . . 365
    Getting Help from the Manufacturer . . . . . . . . . . . . . . . . 366
    Protecting Your Warranty Rights . . . . . . . . . . . . . . . . . . 368
    Defective Merchandise: What to Do? . . . . . . . . . . . . . . . . 370
    Summary . . . . . . . . . . . . . . . . . . . . . . . . . . . . . 370

**APPENDIX**
**Post Error Beep Codes** . . . . . . . . . . . . . . . . . . . . . . . **371**
    Awards BIOS . . . . . . . . . . . . . . . . . . . . . . . . . . . . . . . 372
    AMI BIOS. . . . . . . . . . . . . . . . . . . . . . . . . . . . . . . . . . 372
    Phoenix BIOS. . . . . . . . . . . . . . . . . . . . . . . . . . . . . . . . 373

**Glossary** . . . . . . . . . . . . . . . . . . . . . . . . . . . . . . . . **377**

**Index** . . . . . . . . . . . . . . . . . . . . . . . . . . . . . . . . . . **385**

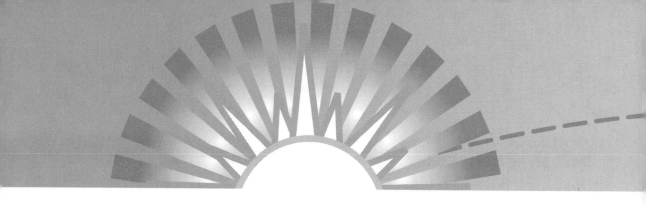

# ACKNOWLEDGMENTS

Thanks to the wonderful Prima editors who made this a fun project to work on. Jenny Watson handled contracts and payments; Kelli Crump managed the editing process; Hilary Powers cleaned up my grammar and spelling; David Plotkin made sure I had my facts straight; and Bill Grimes drew the artwork. Great job, everyone!

I also had a lot of help among my friends and family on this project. Thanks also to Rea Rae Sears for letting me take her computer apart and put it back together, Jane Washburne for taking photos for the illustrator to draw from, Judy Braswell and Janet Bailey for accepting "Sorry, I have to work on the book" as an excuse for not going out, and Margaret Colvin, as usual, for everything.

# ABOUT THE AUTHOR

FAITHE WEMPEN operates Your Computer Friend, a PC troubleshooting and training business in Indianapolis that specializes in helping beginning home users with their PCs. She is also the author of over 25 computer books, including Prima's *Learn Word 97 In a Weekend*, *The Essential Excel 97 Book*, and *The Essential PowerPoint 97 Book*.

# INTRODUCTION

You've probably been saying to yourself for months, maybe even years, "I've got to do something with that old computer." Maybe you've run out of hard disk space or that snazzy new game you just bought doesn't run properly. Or maybe you just want a faster modem or a bigger monitor. Whatever your complaint, you've come to the right place.

*Upgrade Your PC In a Weekend, Revised Edition* gives you a crash course in PC upgrades—it explains how the pieces fit together, how to tell which piece is causing your performance bottleneck, and how to buy and install a replacement piece. I won't try to make you an all-around expert or confuse you with technical terms, but you'll have enough information to get that old PC running in top shape.

Why a weekend? Because that's when most people have some free time. This book is structured so that the average reader can go from decision making to a typical installation before it's time to dress for work on Monday morning, but you are free to take as much time as you want to actually complete the process. In some cases, in fact, you won't be able to complete the entire upgrade in a weekend. If you decide to order a part from a mail-order supplier, for example, you may have to wait a week for it to be delivered.

# Why Upgrade?

You've probably heard the old saying "A chain is only as strong as its weakest link." That adage holds true for your computer, too. Suppose, for example, that you have a state-of-the-art computer system except for the video adapter, which is five years old. Your system won't perform very well at all, even though every part but one is top notch. The video card, the weak link, will hold it back.

The theory behind upgrading, then, is that if you can identify and replace your system's weakest link, all the other components can work to their full potential. (Upgrading one component is a lot cheaper than buying a new PC, too!)

Upgrading works best when you have an unbalanced system—that is, when some parts are better than others. If the entire system is old and weak, you might not have any big performance bottlenecks—the entire system might just be anemic. In a case like that, you're better off buying a whole new system. (Don't worry; you don't have to make that determination alone! I'll help you in the Friday Evening session.)

Upgrading can also involve adding a brand-new component to your system that you've always wanted, like a scanner, a digital camera, or a color printer. These new toys can bring old life to your dull computer setup! I'll talk about how to select and install these extras in detail in this book.

# How to Use This Book

This book is divided into five sessions that you should complete in roughly the order in which they appear. If you are further along in the process and already know what to do, however, you can skip certain sessions.

- ✪ **Friday Evening: Assessing Your Current System.** The first session covers upgrading in general and explains how to identify the bottlenecks in your system.

- ✪ **Saturday Morning: How Much and What Kind?.** This session concentrates on hardware. You may decide to skip the sections that are

not relevant to your upgrade. (For example, if your hard drive is just fine, you don't have to read the "Hard Drives" section.)

✿ **Saturday Afternoon: Shopping for the Best Deals.** Here you start looking for the best prices. Now that you know what you want, you can choose the manufacturer and model that presents the best balance of features, reliability, and cost, and then find the best price for it.

✿ **Sunday Morning: Installing the Upgrades.** It's time to do the installation. You can start here if you bought the upgrade part before you bought this book. This session explains the basics of computer assembly and disassembly. Get ready to dive into your upgrade—tools first.

✿ **Sunday Afternoon: Testing and Troubleshooting.** After you install the new part, you need to tell the rest of the components that it's there; you also need to test the new part to make sure it's working properly.

For the best all-around education, read the entire book from cover to cover; for the most efficient use of your time, skip around and read only the parts that pertain to your upgrade situation.

# Conventions

Several special elements in this book will help you on your way:

**TIP** *Tips* offer insider information about a technology, a company, or a technique.

**NOTE** *Notes* provide background information and insight into why things work the way they do.

**CAUTION** *Cautions* warn you of possible hazards and point out pitfalls that typically plague beginners.

## SIDEBARS FOR CHECKLISTS AND SIDE TRIPS

These special sections offer checklists for organizing your upgrade project, plus stories, techie digressions, and anecdotes about other people's real-life upgrade situations.

# Assessing Your Current System

- ✿ Identifying the Parts of Your Computer
- ✿ Analyzing Your Current Setup
- ✿ Streamlining Your Current System
- ✿ Deciding Which Parts to Upgrade

When you go to a doctor, he or she determines what is wrong with you before prescribing drugs or recommending surgery, right? It's the same thing with your computer. You can't know what parts need upgrading until you do an examination and make a diagnosis. In this evening's session, it's exam time.

## The Basics of a Computer

Before you can think about what you need to upgrade, you need to know at least a little bit about the innards of your PC. Throughout this weekend you'll read about the components that make up your computer and how one or the other of them presents a bottleneck to peak performance. Here's a brief summary of these important components. (You learn how to actually identify them inside your computer later in the weekend.)

- **Processor**. The processor is the "brain" of your computer. The types include 286, 386, 486, Pentium, Pentium Pro, and Pentium II. Your processor has a speed—given in megahertz (MHz)—at which it operates. As I write, this speed can be anywhere from 10MHz (for a slow 286) to 450 MHz for a high-end Pentium II—and there'll be 500MHz chips and maybe even faster ones out there before the book goes into a third edition. If you have an old processor, some programs may not run. If you have a slow processor, programs run slowly.

- **Memory (RAM)**. Memory is the workspace in which your computer operates. The more memory you have, the more and bigger programs you can run at the same time. If you don't have enough memory, your programs may run more slowly or not at all. (I explain this concept in more detail later.)

- **Motherboard**. The motherboard is the big circuit board inside the case that everything else plugs into. The motherboard you have determines the processor (or processors) you can use, the type and amount of memory, the video card type, and more. If you don't have the right kind of motherboard for the upgrade you want to do, you may have to get a whole new system, or at least replace the motherboard.

- **Case**. The case is the metal container that holds the innards. It must have enough bays (storage compartments) for all the drives you want to use (hard, floppy, CD, and so on). It also must have a power supply with enough wattage to supply all the innards with power.

- **Video card**. The video card is the interface between your PC and your monitor. The card interprets the PC's instructions and sends codes that tell the monitor which pixels (dots) to light up with which colors. If you have an old, slow video card, your screen might not refresh quickly. For example, in a drawing program you might experience a delay between drawing a line and seeing it appear on the screen.

- **Monitor**. The monitor shows you what's going on. Monitors vary in their screen size, clarity, and refresh rate. A big monitor with a high refresh rate can help prevent eyestrain.

- **Hard drive**. The hard drive is where you store most of your files. If you run out of hard disk space, you have to delete something before you can install a new program.

- **CD-ROM drive**. This drive reads CD-ROM discs. Most programs come on CD-ROM these days, so a CD-ROM drive is almost a necessity for any computer. Some CD-ROM drives have extra features, like the ability to play DVD movies or hold more than one disc at a time.

- **Sound card**. The sound card plugs into the motherboard and enables you to hear sound through speakers (typically sold separately). If you don't have a sound card, you miss out on the sound effects associated with most games and also on the audible warnings your computer issues from time to time.

- **Multimedia**. A "multimedia system" usually has a sound card, speakers, and a CD-ROM drive.

You can refer to this list as you read about the various components of your computer system; you might want to place a sticky note on the page so you can turn back to it quickly. (I give you a lot more detail about each component later!)

# What Do You Want to Do?

One philosophy of computing is that there are no good or bad computers—only computers that are appropriate or not for the task at hand. And in a sense that adage is true. For example, a tiny, simple computer on the first *Apollo* mission did nothing but calculate trajectory. That computer was not nearly as powerful as the PC you have on your desktop right now (even if you have an old clunker). But was it a bad computer? Nope, it was a great computer if you happened to need to calculate a trajectory.

So the first question for you tonight is, "What do I want to do that my old computer can't handle very well?" not "What's wrong with my old computer?" The following sections aren't here to give you quick answers or to help you make snap decisions; you'll arrive at the right answers as you work through this evening's session. These questions are just guidelines to get you started in the right direction. Take some notes if you want, or just mull over the questions as you go along.

## Do You Want to Run Programs That You Can't Run Now?

If software manufacturers would stop releasing new programs and new versions, hardly anyone would ever need to upgrade. The program that worked fine on your old computer yesterday will likely work fine today and tomorrow and the next day. Unfortunately (or fortunately), new versions of your favorite software packages are always appearing on the store shelves, with the vendors touting features that you "absolutely must have."

For example, seven years ago, my favorite word processing program was Microsoft Word 5.0 for DOS. It ran like lightning on my computer at the time, which had a 386 processor and a whopping 2 megabytes of RAM. (Don't worry if that last sentence had some terms in it you don't understand;

I explain them later.) If I had stayed content with that old word processor, I might still be happy with that old 386 computer.

Nowadays, however, I'd have trouble finding new software that would run on that computer. Software manufacturers can turn higher profits by making software that runs only on more powerful computers. (After all, who is more likely to have money to buy a new program: the person who has an old computer or the person with a new one? The person with the new computer has already proved that she or he has expendable income.)

**NOTE** Something to think about: if you never need to buy and use new software, you will never need a new computer, at least as long as nothing breaks. Suppose your computer is now 10 years old and that you can no longer find, say, a spreadsheet program that runs on it. If you had bought a spreadsheet program when your computer was new and you were still happy with that program, you would not need to upgrade now. Buying lots of software for your PC when it is new, then, can actually help stave off obsolescence. Of course, it's a fine balance—you might spend more money buying a lot of programs that you might never need than you would spend on a whole new computer. But it's a tradeoff to consider if you want your current computer to be the last one you will ever buy.

## Windows 95/98 Programs

There has been a major shift in the PC world in the past 10 years. It used to be that everyone used DOS as their operating system. Companies writing software for PCs needed to create only one version: a DOS one. Then along came Windows 3.0 and then 3.1 in the early 1990s, and many programs were written to run with those operating systems. In those days, you could go to the store and find two versions of almost everything: one for DOS and one for Windows.

Nowadays, nearly all the cool new programs are written for Windows 95 or Windows 98 only. You can continue to use your old software as long as you like, but when you want to buy a new program, you may be forced to buy Windows 95 or Windows 98 too in order to run it. (Throughout this book, I'll say Windows 95/98 whenever I mean either or both. These two operating systems are very similar, and the hardware requirements for them are nearly identical.)

**NOTE**   Windows 95 and Windows 98 can both run "legacy" programs—that is, programs designed for earlier versions of Windows and for MS-DOS. So if you are using DOS and Windows 3.1 now, and you have some programs that you want to continue to use, they will probably continue working just fine under Windows 95/98.

The main impediments to running Windows 95/98 are the processor and the amount of memory it requires. You may read other minimum or recommended requirements for Windows 95/98, but here's my take:

- ✪ **Processor**. The 286 won't work at all, and the 386 will barely creep along. A 486's performance will seem very sluggish. Pentium or Pentium II is what you really want.

- ✪ **Memory (RAM)**. Windows 95/98 requires at least 4 megabytes to run at all, but this is woefully inadequate. Sixteen megabytes will suffice (barely), but 32 or more is best. If you play a lot of graphics-intensive games or do graphics editing, you will want more: 64 or even 128 megabytes.

- ✪ **A CD-ROM Drive**. Windows 95/98 comes on CD, so you'll need a CD-ROM drive to install it. You can order a special version on floppy disks, but this version is rarely sold in stores.

Because Windows 95/98 is the standard on which most programs you want to run are built, you should, at minimum, upgrade your system to run Windows 95/98. Or you can scrap your old system and buy a new one if upgrading it in all the required ways gets too pricey.

## The Latest Games

Many exciting graphical games are now on the market, and most of them are designed for Windows 95/98. Besides the minimum requirements for Windows, some games require other special hardware for best performance.

**NOTE**   When a game needs something "for best performance," it means that if you don't have the right hardware, the game may run too slowly; the video clips may be choppy; and the sound may be poor quality, garbled, and out of sync with the video.

Always check the recommended requirements listed on the game's box. Depending on the game, you may need any (or all) of the following:

○ **An MMX-capable processor**. This graphics-processing capability is built into all Pentium and Pentium II processors sold today, but older Pentiums (usually the ones that run slower than 133MHz) may not have it.

○ **A sound card and speakers**. If you have a multimedia system, you probably have these already. You usually can't hear a game's sounds and music without them. (And you can't plug in the joystick or game pad, either—the port needed to do so usually comes on the sound card.)

○ **A video card capable of supporting at least 256 colors**. This feature is not a big deal; nearly all the cards made in the last several years support millions of colors.

○ **A joystick or game pad**. If you don't have one of these, you can use a keyboard or mouse to play the game, but it will be harder to play well and win.

## Graphics-Intensive Programs

I have a photographer friend who has an older PC, and she recently bought a program called Adobe Photoshop that retouches scanned photos (among other things). Her PC needed an upgrade because programs that display and make changes to complex graphical images need extras like the following:

○ **More RAM**. Graphics-intensive programs for Windows 95/98 may make it worthwhile to buy more than the 32 megabytes of RAM that I recommended earlier. Sixty-four or 128 megabytes can make a difference in the speed at which images load and image alterations appear.

○ **A high-quality local-bus graphics card**. Your graphics card is the interface between the computer and your monitor. If your monitor needs to show frequent changes to a complex image, a good graphics card with a local bus connection to the motherboard can improve the speed at which altered images appear on the screen. (*Local bus* includes VLB, PCI, and AGP video card connections. I explain more about local bus later.)

○ **A bigger monitor**. All monitors work the same way, so a larger monitor won't really improve performance. However, a larger monitor can help you see your work and can make your computing experience more pleasant. When you are working with fine details on a graphic image, a large viewing area is especially important.

## Do You Want to Make Your Computer Stop Running Out of Memory?

Do you get Out of Memory messages in Windows 3.1 or Windows 95/98, or does your system start running very slowly when you have more than one or two programs open at once? If so, your system may benefit from more RAM. Windows 3.1 is happiest when it has 16 megabytes of memory or more. Windows 95/98 likes to have at least 32 megabytes. If you have less than that and you try to open several programs at the same time, you may sometimes get Out of Memory error messages telling you to close some programs, or everything may slow to a crawl.

Ironically, if you get Program Too Big To Fit In Memory or Insufficient Memory messages at a DOS prompt, adding more RAM to your system is not likely to help. The first message is usually the result of a defective program file. You can usually clear up this problem by restarting your computer and then reinstalling the software. Other messages from the DOS prompt, such as those that say you do not have enough free memory, refer to a lack of *conventional memory*—that is, the available memory below the 640K mark. Later in this session I explain how to fix this problem, but adding more memory to such a computer will not help.

If you get a message that your printer is out of memory, that's still another story. Adding more memory to your computer will not fix that, either. You must add memory to your printer (if it is possible; not all printers can accept memory upgrades), or consider investing in a new printer altogether.

## Do You Want to Make Your Existing Programs Run Faster?

Even if all the programs that you need will run on your current computer, they may not run as well or as fast as they should. For example, in your word processing program, do you have to wait for several minutes for a long document to repaginate? When you search for a record in your database program, do you have time to make a cup of coffee while you wait?

Slow program performance is a symptom of one (or both) of the following problems:

- ✿ Your processor is too old and slow.
- ✿ Your PC needs more memory.

One exception: If the program is slow only when repainting the screen (for example, if you draw a line in a drawing program and it doesn't show up on the screen right away), your video card might be inadequate. (However, a slow video card doesn't eliminate the processor and memory as possible co-culprits.)

**TIP**   Here's an easy way to determine in Windows whether the problem is the processor speed or the lack of memory. When you are waiting for a program to do something (like perform a search), watch the hard disk indicator light. Does it flash on and off a lot? If so, it's a memory deficiency. Is the PC eerily quiet with no lights flashing? If so, it's the processor maxing out. (Note that starting up the program does not count as "doing something" for this test, because the hard disk indicator always flashes as a program is starting up.)

# Do You Want to Connect to the Internet or Speed Up Your Online Connections?

To enjoy the Internet, along with the several million other people who have already discovered it, you will need a modem. Modems are an easy and relatively inexpensive upgrade.

Already on the Internet, but stuck in low gear? If you get impatient waiting for information online, you might consider a faster modem. Anyone who uses the Internet for more than a few minutes a month should have a 56K modem. (The number is the modem's maximum data transmission speed, as you'll learn in detail tomorrow morning.) You can pick up a 56K modem for $100 or so at any computer store. Modems that run at 33.6K are even cheaper, and work almost as well.

However, a new modem may not be the panacea that you dreamed it would be; other factors also contribute to delays in your online communications. In fact, most of the time when you're waiting for something while online, your modem is not the bottleneck—the Internet itself is. I explain more about this situation in "What's Your Modem Speed?" later in this session.

**NOTE** Some modems are "voice modems," which means that in addition to their regular capabilities, they can run voice mail software, so your computer can answer the phone and take messages.

## Do You Want to Create Your Own Web Site?

The big fad in Internet living these days is to create your own Web site that tells the world about yourself or your business. It's surprisingly easy to create such a site with any of the very good programs available today, such as Front-Page 98 or HotDog Pro.

The hardware you need to go along with it is minimal: you need to be able to run the page-creation software (the best stuff is for Windows 95/98 only), and you need a modem to transfer your pages to your Internet Service Provider's computer.

## Do You Want to Capture Photos or Video to Use on the Computer?

Another easy and fairly cheap computer upgrade enables you to scan photos and other pictures, much like a copy machine does, so that they end up as files on your computer. You can then e-mail them to other people, use them on your Web pages or in your word processor, or just admire them privately.

To get those images into your PC, you need a scanner or a digital camera. A scanner works like a copier and picks up images off flat pieces of paper; a digital camera can actually take pictures of real-life objects.

## Do You Want to Play Audio CDs as You Work?

Many people don't realize it, but computer CD-ROM drives also can play audio CDs. All you need is a CD-ROM drive (natch), a sound card, and some speakers or headphones.

# Do You Want to Decrease Eyestrain?

When you work at your computer for a long time, do your eyes start to hurt? Several factors, each of which you can fix with an upgrade, can cause this problem:

- **The monitor may be too small**. If you find yourself leaning forward and squinting to read the tiny print on the screen, you might get relief from a larger monitor.

- **The refresh rate may be too low**. *Refresh rate* refers to how often the video card sends updated instructions to the monitor. If you have ever seen a videotape of someone working at a computer and the computer screen seemed to be blinking or flickering, the computer screen's refresh rate was lower than the videotape's frame rate. Even if you don't directly see the flickering when you look at a screen, it can still give you a headache over time. Both monitors and video cards can be bottlenecks to improving refresh rates.

- **The monitor suffers from glare**. You can usually eliminate the glare problem with a no-cost fix; just reposition the computer so the lamp or sunlight does not bounce off it.

# Do You Want to Make More Professional-Looking Printouts?

If your old printer isn't giving you the output you need, you can try several fixes:

- **Add memory to the printer**. This upgrade helps if you are frequently getting an Out Of Memory or The Printer Does Not Have Enough Memory error message when you print a graphics-intensive page on a laser printer. (Not all printers can take extra memory, though.) It doesn't improve print quality.

- **Add more fonts**. In earlier days adding fonts meant buying a cartridge or circuit board to plug into the printer. Nowadays, if you use Windows, you can just buy a CD full of extra fonts to install on your PC.

- **Buy new toner or ribbon**. If your printouts don't have crisp, sharp blacks or if the colors are off, you may need some new supplies. These supplies are called *consumables* in techno-jargon because your printer "consumes" them.

✿ **Buy a new printer**. Unfortunately, this upgrade is probably the only one that is going to make an appreciable difference in the quality of your printouts. Fortunately, however, a good color ink-jet printer costs only about $250.

# Tweaks You Can Do for Free

Some quick fixes that can make a PC run better don't cost a penny! That's good news, isn't it? Before you start evaluating your PC in earnest, you should try all the freebies so that you can evaluate your equipment in the best possible light.

# Checking the Disk for Errors

Sometimes drives get errors on them, and those errors can affect your system's performance. (See the following sidebar for details on why and how these errors occur.) The primary cause of these errors is abnormal program termination, which most often results from shutting off the computer's power or restarting the system while it is in use. (Unexpected shutdowns aren't always your fault; power outages are frequent culprits, or sometimes your computer locks up and you have to shut it off to restart.) Disk errors sometimes manifest themselves in odd ways—I have seen these errors cause everything from missing files to out-of-memory errors. Fortunately, a single cure is available: a disk repair program.

If you have DOS 6.0 or above or Windows 95/98, you have a program called ScanDisk that does a great job checking for and repairing errors. (If you have a version of DOS earlier than 6.0, your computer is probably so old that you should consider scrapping it and buying a new one.)

---

### THE TECHIE SCOOP ON DISK ERRORS

Think of your hard disk as a grid of little compartments, like a wall of post-office boxes. Each compartment holds a piece of data, and each compartment has a unique address.

Your computer maintains a big chart that identifies the content of each compartment; it's called the File Allocation Table (FAT). The FAT is so important that your system maintains two identical copies of it, lest one get damaged.

When the FAT copies get out of sync with each other, or when the actual content of the disk gets out of sync with the FAT, a disk error occurs. The kinds of disk errors you might encounter include:

✪ A file's size being reported by the FAT does not match its size on the disk. (This error is called an *allocation error*.) Allocation errors can cause the file to not open correctly because the FAT may not completely retrieve the file from all its address compartments.

✿ An address contains data, but the FAT does not know to which file the data belongs. (This error is called a *lost cluster*.) This data may be important and belong to a file, but it also might just be junk that should have been deleted.

✿ A conflict in the FAT keeps the system from knowing which of two files an address belongs to. (The files involved in the dispute are *cross-linked*.) Of course, the data rightfully belongs to only one of the files, so when the wrongful owner is opened, it becomes corrupted because it contains data not its own. If that owner is a program file, the inappropriate data may prevent it from running correctly in the future.

✿ The copies of the FAT do not agree because one of them has been damaged or is in error. This situation can happen if the computer loses power in the middle of a change being made to the FAT, and it can result in a file not appearing on a file list when you know it should be there.

✿ A physical error on the disk causes it to be unreadable and unwritable at a certain address. Whatever was stored there is probably lost. This situation can happen when you bump or jostle your computer's case while it is on. The head that reads the hard disk is like a needle on a phonograph, and the needle can come crashing down, scratching the hard disk at whatever address it happens to be at when the trauma occurs. You can also have physical errors on a hard disk that is slowly going bad—or *dying*, in techie talk.

## Checking for Errors with DOS 6.0 or Later

Because many people who are now upgrading their systems don't have Windows 95/98 yet, here's the information you need to use to check for disk errors in DOS 6.0 and its successors:

1. Type the drive letter you want to check and a colon (for example, **c:**) at the DOS prompt and press Enter.

◆ ◆ ◆ ◆ ◆ ◆ ◆ ◆ ◆ ◆ ◆ ◆ ◆ ◆ ◆ ◆ ◆ ◆ ◆ ◆ ◆ ◆ ◆ ◆ ◆ ◆ ◆ ◆ ◆ ◆ ◆ ◆ ◆ ◆ ◆ ◆ ◆ ◆ ◆ ◆

**CAUTION**    Use this procedure *only* at the real DOS prompt—not the one you can get while Windows is running. If you run the DOS version of ScanDisk under Windows, you may corrupt your hard disk. ScanDisk checks before it runs to make sure Windows is not running, so in theory, you should not be able to do this anyway.

◆ ◆ ◆ ◆ ◆ ◆ ◆ ◆ ◆ ◆ ◆ ◆ ◆ ◆ ◆ ◆ ◆ ◆ ◆ ◆ ◆ ◆ ◆ ◆ ◆ ◆ ◆ ◆ ◆ ◆ ◆ ◆ ◆ ◆ ◆ ◆ ◆ ◆ ◆ ◆

2.  Type **SCANDISK** and press Enter. ScanDisk starts immediately, checking your drive.

    If ScanDisk finds any errors, it reports them to you in a Problem Found box, like the one in Figure 1.1.

3.  Type **F** for Fix It.

4.  Accept or decline ScanDisk's suggestion to create an Undo disk. This step is a precaution in case correcting the error causes some horrible problem on your computer (very unlikely) and you need to return to the uncorrected state. You can either pop a floppy disk into drive A: and type **A** for Drive A: or you can type **S** for Skip Undo. (Personally, I always skip.)

5.  Respond to any more problems by typing **F** for Fix It (as you did in step 3). When ScanDisk has finished checking the structure, it prepares to do a surface scan.

6.  Answer Yes to perform the surface scan when prompted.

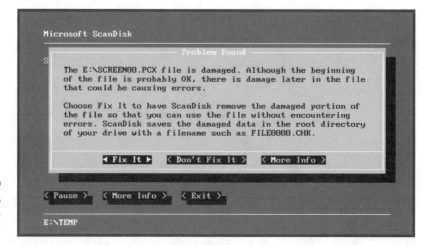

**Figure 1.1**

ScanDisk reports each problem that it finds.

7. Respond to any more error messages that appear by pressing **F** for Fix It.

   ScanDisk ends the process by either telling you that you had no errors or telling you what it fixed.

8. Press Enter to return to the DOS prompt.

If you have more than one hard disk, you should run ScanDisk on each of the drives. You can do them all at once by adding /ALL at the end of the command you type at the DOS prompt, like this: **SCANDISK /ALL**.

## Checking for Errors with Older DOS Versions

If you don't have at least DOS 6.0, you won't have access to ScanDisk. Instead, you'll need to use a program called Chkdsk. It's cruder, but it works. To start this program, type **CHKDSK /F** at the DOS prompt, and then press Enter.

✿ If Chkdsk does not find any errors, it displays some information about your computer on the screen, and then the DOS prompt returns.

✿ If Chkdsk finds an error, it asks you whether you want to repair the error. Type **Y** for yes. Repeat this response for each error Chkdsk finds until you see the DOS prompt.

## Checking for Errors with Windows 95/98

If you are lucky enough to already be using Windows 95 or Windows 98, you can use a special Windows version of ScanDisk. Follow these steps:

1. Click on the Start button; then point to Programs, Accessories, System Tools.

2. Click on ScanDisk. The ScanDisk program starts, as shown in Figure 1.2.

3. Click on the drive you want to check on the drive list at the top. If you want to check more than one drive at once, hold down the Ctrl key while you click on more than one drive.

4. Click on the Thorough option button to run the full test.

5. Click on the Automatically Fix Errors check box to avoid having to deal with dialog boxes (especially if you're a beginner).

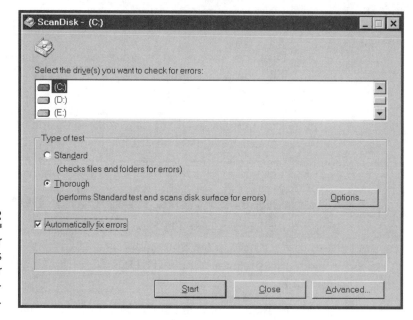

**Figure 1.2**

ScanDisk for Windows makes checking your drives a click-and-shoot operation.

6. Click on Start.

7. Wait for the checking to finish. A message box reports whether or not ScanDisk found and corrected errors on the drive.

8. Click on Close to close the message box. Then click on Close in the ScanDisk window to close the program.

## Defragmenting Your Drive

Over time, a drive becomes fragmented, and this condition affects your hard disk's performance. (See the sidebar that follows for a techie explanation of this term.) Compared to an unfragmented drive, a fragmented drive needs more time to retrieve a file (for example, when you issue the command in your word processor to open a document), and it sometimes takes longer to save a file, too. Therefore, for best performance, you should defragment your disk regularly (say, once a month). This procedure won't turn a slow and old system into a powerhouse, but it may result in a modest speedup.

There are two versions of the disk defragmenter program: one that came with DOS versions 6.0 and higher (a.k.a. 6.x), and one that comes with Windows 95/98. The versions in Windows 95 and Windows 98 are slightly different,

## TECHIE TALK ON DEFRAGMENTING

Earlier I told you about the way your disk is arranged with compartments, each holding a piece of data and each with its own address. The storage system on your hard disk is not sequential, which is why FAT has such a big job of keeping it organized. For example, suppose you had a word processing document that took up 18 compartments on the disk. Those compartments are not necessarily adjacent to each other; they may be scattered all over the disk. The FAT keeps a record of which 18 compartments that file uses, and when you open the file, the disk's read/write head hops around gathering up the pieces so they can be assembled into a whole file in your word processor.

When a file is not stored in adjacent compartments, it's considered *fragmented*. As you can imagine, hopping all over the disk to pick up the fragments takes time, which is why fragmentation slows down your system's performance.

How does fragmentation happen? Well, when your hard disk is empty, files are written to it in sequential compartments. Suppose, for example, that you saved a word processing file that used five compartments. Then perhaps you installed another program. The new files were written right next to your word processing file. Now you reopen the word processing file and type more pages, and it ends up needing a total of nine compartments. No compartments are available next to the original five, so the additional four compartments' worth of data must go to another location. Over time, your file may be split into many different locations over the disk.

When you defragment, a special program rearranges the content of your hard disk so that all files are stored in sequential slots. That way, when you open the files, the disk read/write head reads from a single location rather than having to hop around, so it is able to read faster.

but they work the same way. (You do not have the program at all if your DOS version is less than 6.0. However, you can buy applications such as Norton Utilities or PC Tools that offer equivalent programs.)

## Defragmenting with DOS 6.x

To defragment your disk under DOS, use a program called DEFRAG. It works like this:

1. Type **DEFRAG** at the DOS prompt and press Enter.

   The program asks which drive you want to optimize.

2. Type the drive letter of your hard disk, followed by a colon. Then press Enter.

3. Wait for the recommendation to appear, as shown in Figure 1.3.

4. Choose configure. You want to do a full defragment, regardless of the recommendation. A box appears with your choices.

5. Choose Optimization Method. A list of choices appears.

6. Choose Full Optimization. The optimize choices reappear.

7. Select Begin Optimization, and DEFRAG goes to work.

8. Press Esc to leave the program when DEFRAG displays the Optimization Complete message.

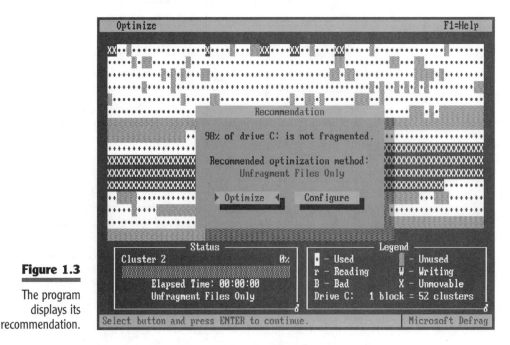

**Figure 1.3**

The program displays its recommendation.

## Defragmenting with Windows 95/98

As with ScanDisk, you can defragment your drives from within Windows 95 and 98 through a special system tool—Disk Defragmenter. Here's how to do it:

1. Click on the Start button, and then point to Programs, Accessories, System Tools.

2. Click on Disk Defragmenter. The Select Drive dialog box asks which drive you want to defragment. (You can choose only one at a time.)

3. Select your hard disk from the list. (If you have more than one hard disk, repeat Steps 3 through the end for each one.) Then click on OK.

   If you are using the Windows 95 version, a message box tells you how defragmented the drive is and suggests a course of action. For example, in Figure 1.4, the drive is only 5 percent defragmented; the program suggests that it may not be worth the time. You won't see this with the Windows 98 version.

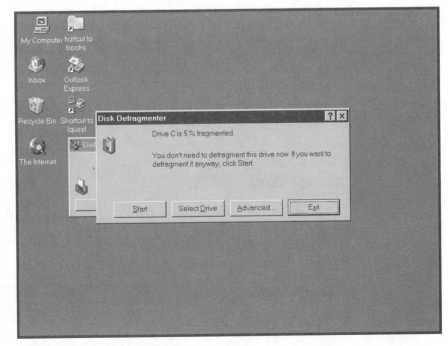

**Figure 1.4**

The Disk Defragmenter in Windows 95 presents its evaluation of the hard drive's fragmentation condition.

4. Click on Start (in Windows 95) or OK (in Windows 98) to start the defragmentation process. Wait for the drive to be defragmented. To entertain yourself while you're waiting, click on Show Details and watch a graphical representation of the proceedings, as shown in Figure 1.5.

**TIP**

If Disk Defragmenter (or ScanDisk) displays a message like Disk Contents Changed, Restarting, even when you haven't touched the computer, programs running in the background may be interfering. Close all other open programs. If the problem continues and you have Microsoft Office installed, open the Control Panel (Start, Settings, Control Panel) and double-click on the Find Fast icon. Open the File menu and choose Pause Indexing. Resume the indexing when you finish defragmenting or checking for errors, or just leave it turned off; it doesn't help your system performance very much anyway.

5. When it finishes, the program asks if you want to quit. Click on Yes if all your drives are done, or on No to choose another drive and return to Step 3.

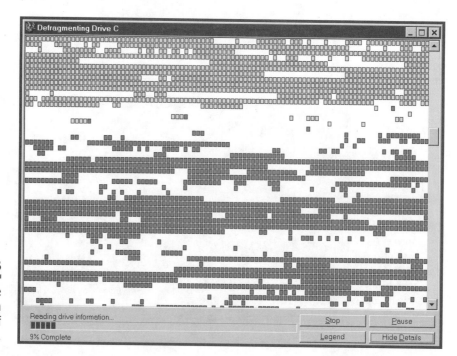

**Figure 1.5**

You can watch the defragmentation take place if you want.

# Making Better Use of Your Memory in DOS

As I mentioned earlier, when DOS tells you that your computer does not have enough memory to run a program, the message usually means that you are short on conventional memory. A memory upgrade is not the solution to this problem. (See the following sidebar "How Your Computer Uses Memory" if you're interested in the different memory designations.) To enable the program to run, you need to make some changes to your start-up files.

## Creating an Emergency Startup Disk

Before you start altering your computer's startup files, buy yourself some peace of mind: Create a startup disk. This disk will save you if any of the changes you make to your startup files accidentally disable your computer. To create the startup disk:

1. Place a blank disk in your A drive. Make sure it contains nothing that you need to save.

2. Type **FORMAT A: /S** at the DOS prompt and press Enter. Then wait for the disk to format and for the DOS prompt to return. (This puts enough of DOS onto the disk to allow the system to start (*boot* in techie-talk) from it instead of from your hard disk.)

3. Type the following lines at the DOS prompt, pressing Enter after each line. (This puts copies of your current startup files—before you start playing with them—onto both the startup disk and your hard disk.)

   **COPY C:\CONFIG.SYS A:\CONFIG.SYS**
   **COPY C:\CONFIG.SYS C:\CONFIG.SAV**
   **COPY C:\AUTOEXEC.BAT A:\AUTOEXEC.BAT**
   **COPY C:\AUTOEXEC.BAT C:\AUTOEXEC.SAV**

4. Remove the startup disk from your drive.

If you run into trouble as you're working through the next few sections and your computer won't start, do the following:

1. Insert the emergency disk into your A drive and press Ctrl+Alt+Del. Your computer will start from the disk, with whatever settings you had before you got into trouble.

## HOW YOUR COMPUTER USES MEMORY

Every personal computer (well, except for the really old ones) has at least 1 megabyte of memory (RAM). That's 1,000 kilobytes, or K for short. Of that, 640K is designated *conventional memory*, or the memory that's used by DOS programs. The rest (approximately 360K) is called *upper memory*. Upper memory is set aside for system use, but it's mostly wasted because the system does not need all of it. Any additional memory you may have (for example, the other 15 megabytes in a 16-megabyte system) is called *extended memory*, and most DOS programs don't use it. (Of the programs that do use it, most are games.)

When you start your DOS-based computer (I'm not talking about Windows 95/98 systems here), two files—Autoexec.bat and Config.sys—automatically load certain terminate-and-stay-resident (TSR) programs into your computer's memory. So, for example, if you start out with 640K of free memory, after you've loaded a mouse driver and a CD driver, you may have only 590K left. Then if you try to run a DOS program that requires 600K, DOS displays an insufficient memory message.

In DOS 5.0 and above, you can load certain helper programs in your Autoexec.bat and Config.sys files that force all the other programs loaded there to place themselves in upper memory rather than in conventional memory. This configuration can free up enough conventional memory to enable you to run a program that you otherwise could not. When I talk about optimizing memory in DOS, I'm talking about setting up these helper programs to do their stuff.

2. Type the following lines at the DOS prompt, pressing Enter after each line:

COPY C:\CONFIG.SAV C:\CONFIG.SYS
COPY C:\AUTOEXEC.SAV C:\AUTOEXEC.BAT

**3.** Remove the disk from your drive and press Ctrl+Alt+Del again to restart your computer from the hard disk. This will confirm that the system has been restored to the way it was before you started meddling.

## Trimming Your Startup Files

Installing various DOS-based programs often adds commands to your computer's startup files (Config.sys and Autoexec.bat). If you remove one of these programs from your computer or you don't use it anymore, its commands continue to load anyway, hogging your precious memory. You can go on a cleaning spree in your startup files by editing them with the MS-DOS Editor. This text-editing program is really a very simple word processor, and it comes free with DOS 5.0 and above.

**NOTE** Users of DOS versions below 5.0 do not have Edit; they have a hard-to-use editor called Edlin. Beginners should forget about even trying to use it. You are better off using a word processing program (such as WordPerfect or Word) that can save files in text-only format to edit your Config.sys and Autoexec.bat files. If you use a word processor on these files, remember to save them as plain ASCII text—you'll need that startup disk if you forget and let the word processor save them in its own mode.

To start the editor, change to the drive and directory on which your startup files reside. Type **C:** and press Enter; then type **CD\** and press Enter. Then type **EDIT**, a space, and the name of the file:

**EDIT AUTOEXEC.BAT**

or

**EDIT CONFIG.SYS**

The editor displays the file you chose. Look for lines that contain references to programs that you know you no longer use. For example, suppose you had a scanner once, but it is now broken. You know that it was a Logitech scanner, and you see a line in your Config.sys like this:

DEVICE=C:\LOGITECH\PGSCAN.SYS

It's a good bet that you can disable this line without changing the way your system works. To disable the line, type **REM** and then a space before the rest of the line, like this:

**REM** DEVICE=C:\LOGITECH\PGSCAN.SYS

Look through your startup files for other lines that you can safely "REM out." For example, DOS has a utility called DOSKey that enables you to create keyboard macros. Most people never use this file, so there is no reason to load the driver. The line looks something like this:

DEVICE=C:\DOS\DOSKEY.EXE

If you're not sure about a line, REM it out and restart your computer. If everything continues to work fine—great. If you find that some particular device doesn't work anymore, go back in, remove the REM, and restart. You can always use your startup disk to get out of a hopeless mess.

## Freeing Up Conventional Memory in DOS 6.x

If you have DOS 6.0 or above, run a program called Memmaker. Just type **MEMMAKER** at the DOS prompt and press Enter; then follow the self-explanatory prompts. If you don't know what to pick for a particular option or setting, pick the default. Memmaker automates the process of setting up the proper commands in your startup files (Config.sys and Autoexec.bat) so that more conventional memory is free.

## Freeing Up Conventional Memory in DOS 5.0

If you have DOS 5.0, you can still optimize your memory, but you don't have a handy program like Memmaker to help you—you have to do it by hand. (You can also do this with DOS 6.x, but Memmaker is handier.) Here's what to do:

1. Check to see how much free conventional memory you currently have by typing **MEM /C | MORE** at the DOS prompt and pressing Enter.

**NOTE** The | symbol is probably on the same key as \. The | MORE part stops the screen from scrolling and displays the message MORE to indicate that not all the information can fit on your screen at once. When you see MORE, press any key after you have read what's on the screen to see the rest.

**TIP** What's the "Any" key? Almost anything will do, except perhaps Shift, Ctrl, or Alt. It's useful to get in the habit of using the same key every time—the spacebar or the letter Z, for example, as they're harmless and easy to remember—that way if something strange happens, you'll at least be able to explain what you did.

The system will reply with a chart showing which programs are loaded into conventional and upper memory, like this:

```
Conventional memory:

Name        Size in Decimal        Size in Hex
--------    ----------------       -----------
MSDOS       59280    ( 57.9K)      E790
ANSI         4192    (  4.1K)      1060
MOUSE       17072    ( 16.7K)      42B0
COMMAND      5472    (  5.3K)      1560
DOSKEY       4128    (  4.0K)      1020
MIRROR       6512    (  6.4K)      1970
FREE           64    (  0.1K)        40
FREE          176    (  0.2K)        B0
FREE       558240    (545.2K)      884A0


Total FREE:  558480     (545.4K)

Total bytes available to programs:   558480 (545.4K)
Largest executable program size: 558240 (545.2K)

    3145728 bytes total contiguous extended memory
    3145728 bytes available contiguous extended memory
```

All the programs on the list are taking up space in conventional memory, with the result that you only have 545K of a possible 640K available to run programs. (Check the Largest Executable Program Size.) If a program needs more memory, it won't run. You can also see by the last two lines that your system has a total of 4 megabytes of memory (the standard 1 megabyte plus these 3 million bytes, or 3 megabytes, of extended memory).

2. Write down the names of programs taking up space in conventional memory, in order from the largest to the smallest, ignoring the MSDOS line and the COMMAND line. For example, here's my list:

MOUSE

MIRROR

ANSI

DOSKEY

3. Change to the root directory of your main hard disk by typing **C:** and pressing Enter. Then type **CD\\** and press Enter.

4. Type **EDIT CONFIG.SYS** and press Enter. The DOS Editor opens and displays the contents of your Config.sys file.

5. Make sure the following lines are in the file, in this order, at the beginning of the file. If they aren't there, add or move them as needed. (If you have Windows 3.1, substitute C:\\WINDOWS for C:\\DOS in these lines.)

DOS=HIGH,UMB

DEVICE=C:\\DOS\\HIMEM.SYS

DEVICE=C:\\DOS\\EMM386.EXE NOEMS

◆ ◆ ◆ ◆ ◆ ◆ ◆ ◆ ◆ ◆ ◆ ◆ ◆ ◆ ◆ ◆ ◆ ◆ ◆ ◆ ◆ ◆ ◆ ◆ ◆ ◆ ◆ ◆ ◆ ◆ ◆ ◆ ◆ ◆ ◆ ◆ ◆ ◆ ◆

**CAUTION**  If you think you need to get rid of a line in your Config.sys or Autoexec.bat, don't delete it; just type **REM** and a space at the beginning of its line. REM disables the line without deleting it. If you find out that one of your programs needs the line to run, you can restore it simply by removing the REM and space.

◆ ◆ ◆ ◆ ◆ ◆ ◆ ◆ ◆ ◆ ◆ ◆ ◆ ◆ ◆ ◆ ◆ ◆ ◆ ◆ ◆ ◆ ◆ ◆ ◆ ◆ ◆ ◆ ◆ ◆ ◆ ◆ ◆ ◆ ◆ ◆ ◆ ◆ ◆

6. Locate any lines that look like they belong to a program on the list you made in Step 2. For example, you might see a line like this that belongs to MOUSE:

DEVICE=C:\\MOUSE\\MOUSE.SYS

7.  Rearrange the lines in the file so that any lines that belong to programs on your list from Step 2 are in order from largest to smallest; also change DEVICE to DEVICEHIGH. For example, I would arrange my lines like this:

    DEVICEHIGH=C:\MOUSE\MOUSE.SYS

    DEVICEHIGH=C:\DOS\ANSI.SYS

    You probably won't find corresponding lines for everything on your Step 2 list, because some of them will be in Autoexec.bat, the other startup file.

8.  Press Alt+F and then X to close the editor. When asked whether you want to save your changes, type **Y** for Yes.

9.  Type **EDIT AUTOEXEC.BAT** at the DOS prompt and press Enter.

10. Locate any lines that correspond to the rest of the items on your Step 2 list and reorganize to start with the largest.

11. Add **LH** and a space before each of the lines that corresponds to something from Step 2. (LH stands for Load High, by the way.)

12. Press Alt+F, and then X to close the editor and save your changes when asked.

13. Press Ctrl+Alt+Del to restart your computer.

14. Type **MEM /C | MORE** at the DOS prompt. This time you should have two lists: one for conventional memory and one for upper memory.

```
Conventional Memory:
    Name        Size in Decimal        Size in Hex
    ____.       _____            _____.

    MSDOS       12304     ( 12.9K)        3010
    HIMEM        1072     (  1.0K)         430
    EMM386       3232     (  3.2K)         CA0
    COMMAND      3392     (  3.3K)         D40
    FREE           64     (  0.1K)          40
    FREE       635104     (620.2K)       9B0E0

    Total FREE:  635168     (620.3K)
```

```
Upper Memory:
Name         Size in Decimal         Size in Hex
----.        ----------              -----.
SYSTEM       183856    (179.5K)      2CE30
MOUSE         17072    ( 16.7K)      42B0
ANSI           4192    (  4.1K)      1060
DOSKEY         4128    (  4.0K)      1020
MIRROR         6512    (  6.4K)      1970
FREE            176    (  0.2K)        B0
FREE          46080    ( 45.0K)      B400
Total FREE:   46256    ( 45.2K)
Total bytes available to programs (Conventional+Upper):
681424 (665.5K)
Largest executable program size: 634928 (620.0K)
Largest available upper memory block:  46080 ( 45.0K)

     3145728 bytes total contiguous extended memory
           0 bytes available contiguous extended memory
     2891776 bytes available XMS memory
             MS-DOS resident in High Memory Area
```

Notice that the largest executable program size is now much higher (620K) than it was before. Your mission is accomplished.

# Improving Windows 3.1 Performance

If your primary complaint with your computer is that Windows 3.1 and its programs run too slowly, the fixes explained in this section might provide some relief. None of these upgrades will make your system zip along like a Pentium, but they might speed up a sluggish system by about 10 percent.

## Using a Better Video Driver

Some motherboards have special slots called *local bus* slots, for example, VLB slots (common on 486 systems), PCI slots (common on Pentium systems), and AGP slots (common on newer Pentiums and Pentium IIs). Specially designed circuit cards plugged into these slots work faster and more efficiently than regular circuit cards in regular slots because their pathway to the processor is fast and direct.

In Windows 3.1 you can maximize the performance of a local bus video card plugged into a local bus slot by using a special video driver that is designed to take advantage of the superior connection. (This special driver can also enable you to see more colors in Windows 3.1 than the default 16 at once.) By default, however, the normal, generic VGA video driver is loaded in Windows 3.1.

To load a video driver specific for your video card in Windows 3.1, follow these steps:

1. Open the Main program group. Double-click on Windows Setup.

2. Open the Options menu and choose Change System Settings.

3. Open the Display drop-down list and select your exact video card and a particular combination of resolution and colors. For example, if you have an STB Vision card, you might select STB Vision 640×480 256 Colors.

   If you don't see your video card on the list but have a disk of drivers that came with your video card (check the box that your computer came in), insert that disk in your floppy drive, choose Other (Requires Disk from OEM), and load the correct driver from that disk.

4. Click on OK to save your changes. When prompted, agree to restart Windows. When Windows restarts, your new driver will be in place.

**CAUTION** ✦✦✦✦✦✦✦✦✦✦✦✦✦✦✦✦✦✦✦✦✦✦✦✦✦✦✦✦✦✦✦✦✦✦✦✦✦
When trying to squeeze the fastest performance out of Windows 3.1, you should stick to 640×480 resolution (no higher) and no more than 256 colors. Other resolutions and colors make an attractive display but cause slower performance.
✦✦✦✦✦✦✦✦✦✦✦✦✦✦✦✦✦✦✦✦✦✦✦✦✦✦✦✦✦✦✦✦✦✦✦✦✦

If Windows 3.1 won't start anymore or the display is garbled, do the following:

1. Type **CD\WINDOWS** at the DOS prompt, and press Enter.

2. Type **SETUP** and press Enter. A DOS-based Windows setup program opens.

3. Use the arrow keys to highlight the Display line, and press Enter to open a list of drivers. Choose VGA from the list and press Enter.

4. Choose Accept the Configuration Shown Above. When the DOS prompt returns, Windows is using the original standard VGA driver; everything should work fine.

**5.** Try another video driver, or give up, depending on your persistence level.

Several factors could cause problems with different video drivers:

- ✿ Some older monitors do not support more than 16 colors and more than 640×480 resolution. They won't work with different selections.

- ✿ Some old video cards do not support more than 16 colors or more than 640×480 resolution. (However, if you are choosing a video driver especially for your video card, this should not be a problem.)

- ✿ You may not have chosen the correct driver for your video card. Some manufacturers make many different cards with similar names, and you need to use the specific driver that is compatible with your card.

■ ■ ■ ■ ■ ■ ■ ■ ■ ■ ■ ■ ■ ■ ■ ■ ■ ■ ■ ■ ■ ■ ■ ■ ■ ■ ■ ■ ■ ■ ■ ■ ■ ■ ■ ■ ■ ■ ■ ■

If you have a video card that you think should support more than standard VGA (for example, 640×480 resolution and 256 colors instead of the generic 16 colors), but you don't have a driver for it, try to download a generic driver from the Internet.

I found a good generic driver on America Online that works with almost all video cards, even ones from obscure manufacturers. Click on the Software Search icon on the AOL toolbar, and then type in the keywords **SVGA Generic Video Driver**. The file is called SVGA.EXE. Copy it to a new directory and run it to decompress the files. When Windows 3.1 asks for the location of the OEM driver, instead of A:, type in that directory; Windows will find the drivers.

■ ■ ■ ■ ■ ■ ■ ■ ■ ■ ■ ■ ■ ■ ■ ■ ■ ■ ■ ■ ■ ■ ■ ■ ■ ■ ■ ■ ■ ■ ■ ■ ■ ■ ■ ■ ■ ■ ■ ■

## Creating a Permanent Swap File

A swap file can improve the performance of Windows 3.1 dramatically. By default, Windows 3.1 uses a temporary swap file, but if you have 10 megabytes or so of extra space on your hard disk, you can improve Windows performance by creating a permanent swap file instead.

To check your swap file in Windows 3.1 and make it permanent (if it isn't already), follow these steps:

1. Defragment the drive on which you plan to place the swap file. (You learned about defragmenting earlier in this session.)

2. In Windows, open the Main program group and double-click on the Control Panel.

## What Is a Swap File?

Swap files began as a way to make a computer with very little memory think that it has more when it's running Windows, and therefore be able to run programs in Windows that it normally wouldn't have enough memory to run. (We're talking about total memory here, conventional plus extended, not just the conventional memory of DOS programs.)

For example, suppose you have a new DOS-based word processor that requires 2 megabytes of memory to run (620K of conventional plus 1 megabyte of extended). If your old DOS computer has only 1 megabyte total, you are out of luck.

Now look at the same situation in Windows. Suppose you have a Windows program that uses 5 megabytes of RAM when it runs, but your system has only 4. If you have a swap file set up, Windows makes part of the hard disk pretend that it is memory, which enables the program to load.

With a temporary swap file (the default), whenever Windows 3.1 encounters a situation that needs more than the available memory, the program claims a piece of the hard disk to serve as memory on the spot. When the program finishes, it releases its claim on that piece. The program runs, but it runs very slowly because the hard disk is hundreds of times less efficient than real memory, and Windows needs extra time to select and claim a part of the hard drive.

With a permanent swap file, Windows always keeps part of the hard disk for itself. The program still runs slowly—but less so, because you avoid the time needed to select and claim the space on the hard disk for each run.

3. Double-click on the 386 Enhanced icon and click on the Virtual Memory button in the next dialog box.

4. Notice the current virtual memory (a.k.a. swap file) settings at the top of the box.

5. Click on the Change button. At the bottom, you'll see the recommended swap file settings.

6. Choose the drive for the swap file from the Drive drop-down list.

**CAUTION**

◆◆◆◆◆◆◆◆◆◆◆◆◆◆◆◆◆◆◆◆◆◆◆◆◆◆◆◆◆◆◆◆◆◆◆◆◆◆◆◆◆◆◆

If you have DoubleSpace or DriveSpace running to increase the capacity of your hard disk, do not create a permanent swap file on the compressed hard disk. Instead, create it on the host drive (probably G: or H:). Choose the host drive from the list in Step 6.

◆◆◆◆◆◆◆◆◆◆◆◆◆◆◆◆◆◆◆◆◆◆◆◆◆◆◆◆◆◆◆◆◆◆◆◆◆◆◆◆◆◆◆

7. If you don't have a permanent swap file, choose Permanent from the Type drop-down list.

8. If the New size is not the same as the Recommended size, enter that number in the New box.

9. Click on OK. When prompted, restart your computer.

# Improving Windows 95/98 Performance

Windows 95 and 98 are great operating systems, but they require more system resources than Windows 3.1. If you have an old or slow computer, you may want to stick with Windows 3.1 until you get it upgraded! If you have already upgraded to Windows 95 or 98 and are unhappy with the speed at which things happen, try some of these tricks.

## Keeping the Display Simple

Windows 95/98 operates at peak speed when you are using a 32-bit video driver (in other words, a driver file designed to work with your specific video card under Windows 95/98) and when you use only the resolution and number of colors that you need. For people with 14-inch monitors, that would be 640×480 resolution and 256 colors. For 15-inch and 17-inch monitors, the most you would want to use if you're looking for extra speed is 800×600 resolution and 256 colors. (This is not to say that other video resolutions and numbers of colors don't look great and have practical uses, but we're talking about wringing maximum speed out of your existing stuff right now.)

To check out your video setup, follow these steps:

1. Right-click on the desktop and choose Properties from the shortcut menu that appears.

2. Click on the Background tab.

3. Select None as the background to achieve the fastest video.

4. Click on the Settings tab. Figure 1.6 shows it for Windows 98; it looks almost exactly the same in Windows 95.

5. Set the Color palette to no more than 256 colors to achieve the fastest video.

6. Set the Desktop area to no more than 800×600.

7. Click on the Advanced button. (It's called Advanced Properties in Windows 95.)

8. Click on the Adapter tab if it is not already displayed.

9. Make sure that the correct video driver for your video card appears on the Adapter tab. If you aren't sure, click on the Change button and reselect your video card from the list of Windows 95/98 drivers.

10. Make sure that the Refresh Rate is set to Optimal.

11. Click on the Monitor tab.

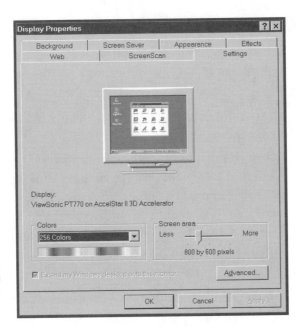

**Figure 1.6**

Choose the video mode from here.

**12.** Make sure that the correct name for your monitor appears; if it doesn't, click on the Change button. Click on Show All Devices, and then choose your monitor from the list. If it isn't there, pick a monitor of the same size from the same manufacturer.

**13.** Click on the Performance tab.

**14.** Make sure the Hardware Acceleration slide bar is set to Full (unless you have a history of video problems that you corrected by changing this setting).

**15.** Click on OK to close the Properties box.

**16.** Click on Yes if you are prompted to restart the computer.

Other ways to speed up your video performance in Windows 95/98 include:

- Choosing None for the Background. To do this, right-click on the desktop and choose Properties. Then on the Background tab, choose None.

- Disabling the Active Desktop (Windows 98 only, or Windows 95 with the Internet Explorer update installed). Right-click the desktop and choose Active Desktop. If the View As Web Page command has a check mark next to it, select it to remove that check mark.

## Removing Programs You Are Not Using

You can save some hard disk space and perhaps slightly improve Windows' startup speed by uninstalling any programs that you no longer use. Follow these steps:

**1.** Choose Start, Settings, Control Panel and double-click on the Add/Remove Programs icon.

**2.** Scroll through the list of installed programs on the Install/Uninstall tab. If you find a program that you no longer use, select it and then click on Add/Remove. The program's setup program starts and you can uninstall it. (Depending on the program, you may have to reinsert the program's CD or floppy disk to perform the uninstall.)

**3.** Repeat Step 2 until you have uninstalled every program that you don't use.

**4.** Click on the Windows Setup tab. A list of installed Windows 95/98 components appears.

5. Click on a category, and then click on the Details button to see the choices for that component.

6. Click to remove the check mark and deselect any component that you never use; then click on OK to return to the list of categories.

7. Repeat Steps 5 and 6 for each category until you have examined them all.

8. Click on OK to apply all your program changes. Depending on what you removed, you may have to reinsert the Windows 95/98 CD-ROM to complete the process.

## Checking for Compatibility Mode

If you have certain DOS-mode programs loaded in your startup files when you install Windows 95/98, Windows runs in a special DOS compatibility mode so that those programs will continue to function. Perhaps you don't need those programs anymore, but Windows has no way of knowing. DOS compatibility mode can make Windows run much slower than normal.

To find out whether your system is running in DOS compatibility mode, follow these steps:

1. Right-click on the My Computer icon and choose Properties. The System Properties dialog box appears.

2. Click on the Performance tab. It should say "Your system is configured for optimal performance." If it doesn't, you will see an explanation about what is forcing the system to run in DOS compatibility mode.

3. Make a note of the recommended change and change your startup files accordingly. (You learned to edit them earlier in this session.)

4. Restart the computer and return to the Performance tab to see if it now says your system is optimally configured. If it doesn't, repeat Step 3.

## Tuning System Performance

Here are a few nit-picking fine adjustments that will make your computer run just a little bit better under Windows 95/98:

1. Right-click on the My Computer icon and choose Properties. The System Properties dialog box appears.

2. Click on the Performance tab.

3. Click on the File System button. A File System Properties dialog box appears with its own tabs: Hard Disk, CD-ROM, and Troubleshooting, as shown in Figure 1.7. (The Windows 98 version is shown here; the Windows 95 version is nearly identical.)

4. Open the drop-down list and select Network Server for the Typical role of this machine. Don't worry if the computer isn't a network server; this option sets the disk buffer settings to maximum.

5. Make sure the Read-ahead buffer slide bar is set to Full.

6. Click on the CD-ROM tab.

7. Make sure the Supplemental cache size slide bar is set to Large.

8. Open the Optimize Access Pattern For drop-down list and select the appropriate setting for your CD-ROM drive.

9. Click on the Troubleshooting tab.

10. Make sure that no check boxes are marked, unless you have previously marked one of them to eliminate a problem with your system.

11. Click on OK to close the dialog box.

12. Click on the Graphics button.

13. Make sure that the Hardware Acceleration slide bar is set to Full (unless you have set it to something else for a reason). Then click on OK.

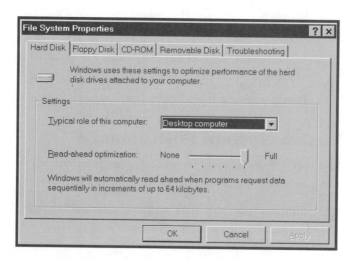

**Figure 1.7**

You can make some minor system adjustments from the File System Properties dialog box.

> ### FOR TECHIES ONLY!
>
> **On the Windows 98 CD, in a folder called Tools\ResKit, you'll find some utilities from the Windows Resource Kit. Run the setup program you find there, and a Tool Management Console will be installed that explains and helps you run many interesting Windows 98 system utilities. Some of these can be dangerous in the hands of a novice, but they're great fun for those who are very familiar with Windows 98 and are looking for some opportunities to tweak how the system works.**

**14.** Click on the Virtual Memory button.

**15.** Make sure that the Let Windows Manage My Virtual Memory Settings option button is selected; then click on OK.

**16.** Click on Close to apply your changes.

**17.** If prompted that you must restart your system, click on Yes.

## Deleting Unneeded Files on Your Hard Disk

Be careful! It's tempting to try to make more room on your hard disk by deleting programs and other files that you don't use, but you can really mess up your system if you delete important files.

In general, you can safely delete any file that ends in .CHK, .TMP, or .BAK, as long as you're not in Windows. You should not delete .TMP files while in Windows because Windows may be using the temporary files as it operates. You can also delete any files in the Windows folder (called a *directory* in Windows 3.1) that end in .BMP and any files that begin with a tilde character (~). Never delete any files that end in .DAT, .SYS, .DLL, or .DRV unless you are sure you know what they are and that you don't need them. You can also delete files in other directories that end in .CHK or .TMP or that begin with ~.

If you have installed a new version of DOS over an older one, you may have a backup of your old version on the computer. You can get rid of it by typing **DELOLDOS** at the DOS prompt and pressing Enter. If you don't have an old version, this command has no effect.

**NOTE** Windows 98 has a program called Disk Cleanup that can help you remove unneeded files. To get to it, choose Start, Programs, Accessories, System Tools, Disk Cleanup.

# Increasing Your Hard Disk Capacity

Is your hard disk full? You have two choices: you can buy a new one, or you can stave off that day by using a disk-compression program.

Disk-compression programs such as DoubleSpace and DriveSpace all have the same effect. They approximately double the capacity of your current hard disk, while slightly degrading its performance. (See the accompanying sidebar if you're curious about the mechanics of how these utilities work.) The trade-off is that your hard disk may work a bit more slowly and that utility programs like ScanDisk and Disk Defragmenter (DEFRAG) will take at least twice as long to run.

A free utility to compress your drive comes with DOS versions 6.2 and above (except version 6.21) and with Windows 95/98. If you have an earlier version of DOS, you can buy a program to compress your disk, but it would be cheaper for you to simply buy a DOS upgrade.

Before you use any compression program to alter your drive, you should back up any important files onto floppy disks. The drive compression process is fairly reliable but not 100 percent safe; disk problems have been known to occur occasionally during compression. Better safe than sorry.

## Compressing Your Hard Disk with DOS 6.2x

DOS comes with either DoubleSpace or DriveSpace, depending on the version. DOS 6.2 has DoubleSpace (DBLSPACE), DOS 6.21 has nothing, and DOS 6.22 has DriveSpace (DRVSPACE). To run the program, type **DBL-SPACE** or **DRVSPACE** at the DOS prompt and press Enter. Friendly screens prompt you through each step of the process.

**TIP** If you don't know what version of DOS you have, simply type **VER** at the DOS prompt and press Enter.

## How Disk Compression Works

Hard disks store data very reliably, but there is often lots of wasted space between files. Disk compression removes all the wasted space in the disk storage system by storing the files using a different filing method, so that your old disk can store more data.

The way it works is kind of tricky. The disk compression program essentially fools your system into thinking that a file is a disk, and it puts all your files from the hard disk into that big disk-like file. Because it's really a file, it isn't constrained by the inefficient filing system on a real disk, so it can store your hard disk content more efficiently.

Say your hard disk is drive C. The disk compression program creates a big file on C and calls it H. The operating system treats this file like an extra hard disk. Then one by one the program moves your files from C to H, gradually increasing the size of H until H takes up almost all the space on C. So now this massive file is consuming your C drive, and within that file is drive H and all the programs that used to be on C.

There is one last step: All your programs are expecting to be on C. If they're on a drive called H, they might not work properly. So the compression program swaps the letters; that is, your original C drive is renamed H and the new H drive is called C. Now all the programs are happy again, because they think they are still on C. This process is all completely automatic; you don't have to worry about swapping anything yourself.

## Compressing Your Disk with Windows 95/98

Windows 95/98 comes with a disk-compression program that is actually DriveSpace in disguise. To run it, follow these steps:

1. Choose Start, Programs, Accessories, System Tools, DriveSpace. A dialog box lists the drives on your system.

2. Click on the drive you want to compress, open the Drive list, and select Drive, Compress (in Windows 98) or click on the Compress button (in Windows 95).

3. Follow the self-explanatory prompts to finish the process.

■ ■ ■ ■ ■ ■ ■ ■ ■ ■ ■ ■ ■ ■ ■ ■ ■ ■ ■ ■ ■ ■ ■ ■ ■ ■ ■ ■ ■ ■ ■ ■ ■ ■ ■ ■ ■ ■ ■ ■

If you use Windows 98, or Windows 95 plus the Windows 95 Plus Pack, you have an additional program called Compression Agent (Start, Programs, Accessories, System Tools, Compression Agent). You can use it for greater control over your compressed drive (for example, to specify some files for additional compression or make other files uncompressed.)

■ ■ ■ ■ ■ ■ ■ ■ ■ ■ ■ ■ ■ ■ ■ ■ ■ ■ ■ ■ ■ ■ ■ ■ ■ ■ ■ ■ ■ ■ ■ ■ ■ ■ ■ ■ ■ ■ ■ ■

## Converting to a 32-Bit File System

This is for Windows 98 users only. If you have upgraded your system to Windows 98 and you have a very large, nearly full hard disk, you may be able to get some benefit from converting your file system from 16-bit to 32-bit with a free utility that comes with Windows 98. I won't get too techie about this, but basically, a 32-bit file system is more efficient and eliminates some of the wasted space on your hard disk so it can store more. You won't see as dramatic an improvement with the conversion as you will if you use Drive-Space. However, converting to a 32-bit file system is actually good for your system and makes it run better, while using DriveSpace slows some aspects of the system down somewhat.

To run the converter, choose Start, Programs, Accessories, System Tools, Drive Converter (FAT32). Then follow the self-explanatory prompts to perform the conversion.

• • • • • • • • • • • • • • • • • • • • • • • • • • • • • • • • • • • • • • • •

Some later OEM releases of Windows 95 include support for 32-bit file systems, but there is no conversion program included, so you have to completely wipe out and repartition and reformat your hard disk to set it up. And for most people, that's too much trouble. (An OEM release, by the way, is a release of a program that is distributed only with new PCs, and not available in stores.)

• • • • • • • • • • • • • • • • • • • • • • • • • • • • • • • • • • • • • • • •

# Take a Break

That's it! You've now wrung every last drop of performance out of your old system. If you're still unhappy with it, you know for sure that it's time to upgrade.

In the next section, I'll teach you how to assess your current system to find out what you have. But first, why don't you take a little break? Stretch your legs and take the dog for a walk—clear your head a little before starting the next section.

# Take a Cold, Hard Look at Your System

So far I've talked about what kinds of upgrades are possible and how to make the best of your current system. Now it's time to dive in and see what you actually have there on your desk.

## How Much Memory Do You Have?

One easy way to find out how much memory your computer has is to watch as it starts up. Most systems "count up" the memory as it is being tested at startup. If you watch carefully, you may see the count, up to a number like 4096K (4 megabytes), 8192K (8 megabytes), 16384K (16 megabytes), and so on.

Why doesn't it count in rounded numbers like 1, 2, or 3? Well, 1 megabyte of memory is actually 1024 kilobytes. The extra 24K isn't a significant amount, so the whole 1024 is commonly referred to as 1 megabyte. When you have many megabytes, the extra bits begin to add up, until at 32 megabytes, you actually have 32768K, or closer to 33 megabytes. A nice little bonus, but nothing to focus on too intently.

Another way to find out how much memory you have is the MEM command (which you saw at work earlier in this session). At the DOS prompt, type **MEM** and press Enter. If you use Windows 95, you can open a DOS window with Start, Programs, MS-DOS Prompt. (Type **EXIT** to return to Windows when you finish.)

Windows displays a report of your memory situation, and toward the end you will see a total amount of extended, XMS, and EMS memory, as shown in the following mini-table. (The following report is from a DOS prompt opened from within Windows 95.) Look on the Total Memory line in the Total column for the amount of memory in your computer.

```
Memory Type       Total      Used       Free
– – – – – – –     – – –.     – – –      – – –.
Conventional       640K       175K       465K
Upper                0K         0K         0K
Reserved           384K       384K         0K
Extended (XMS)  64,512K       224K    64,288K
– – – – – – –     – – –.     – – –      – – –.
Total Memory    65,536K       783K    64,753K

Total under 1MB    640K       175K       465K

Total Expanded (EMS)    63M (66,551,808 bytes)

Free Expanded (EMS)     16M (16,777,216 bytes)

Largest executable program size    465K (475,952 bytes)
Largest free upper memory block      0K (0 bytes)
MS-DOS is resident in the high memory area.
```

### EXTENDED, XMS, AND EMS MEMORY

What's all that about extended, XMS, and EMS? They are simply three ways that DOS can use extra memory (above the first megabyte).

In its "raw" state, this extra memory in 386, 486, Pentium, and Pentium II systems is called *extended*. You can make extended memory pretend that it is any of several kinds of memory, depending on what the DOS program you are running needs. Most DOS programs that can take advantage of memory over 1 megabyte like it to be in eXtended Memory Specification (XMS) format, but some need the Enhanced Memory Specification (EMS) format. For DOS programs, commands in your startup files determine which kind, if any, your extended memory will pretend to be. Windows 95/98 provides the correct memory format to each program as needed.

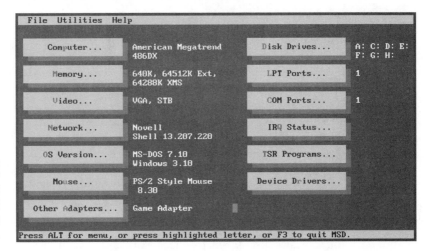

File   Utilities   Help

| | | |
|---|---|---|
| Computer... | American Megatrend 486DX | Disk Drives...   A: C: D: E: F: G: H: |
| Memory... | 640K, 64512K Ext, 64288K XMS | LPT Ports...   1 |
| Video... | VGA, STB | COM Ports...   1 |
| Network... | Novell Shell 13.207.220 | IRQ Status... |
| OS Version... | MS-DOS 7.10 Windows 3.10 | TSR Programs... |
| Mouse... | PS/2 Style Mouse 8.30 | Device Drivers... |
| Other Adapters... | Game Adapter | |

Press ALT for menu, or press highlighted letter, or F3 to quit MSD.

**Figure 1.8**

You use the MSD program several times during this session.

Still another way to check out your memory, if you have DOS 5.0 or above, is to use the Microsoft Diagnostics (MSD) utility. At the DOS prompt, type **MSD** and press Enter. The new screen looks like the one in Figure 1.8. The number next to Memory is how much memory your computer has.

In Windows 95/98, you can check the memory like this:

1. Right-click on the My Computer icon and choose Properties.
2. Click on the Performance tab. The line at the top of the dialog box tells you how much total memory your system has.
3. Click on Close to close the dialog box.

## What's the Video Situation?

First of all, do you even have a VGA monitor and card? Unplug the monitor from the back of the PC and look at the plug. If you have three rows of pins on the plug (some may be missing; that's OK), you have VGA or SuperVGA (SVGA). If you see only two rows of pins, you have either EGA (an old type of color monitor) or monochrome (all one color; you'll know already if you have this). If you have either EGA or monochrome, you will definitely need a new video card and monitor, and probably a whole new computer, too. Manufacturers stopped producing these items at least eight years ago, and you will have a hard time finding software that will work with them.

## Brand, Model, and Memory

OK, assuming you have VGA, what kind? If you are very alert, you can see the video card's identity information briefly onscreen when you turn on the computer. For example, it might say something like

```
STB Nitro 3D GX
Bios Ver. 1.0
1996 STB Systems
4096 Video Memory
```

If you saw that, congratulations! You would know that you have an STB Nitro video card with 4 megabytes of video memory. (You would be very fortunate! That's a good card, and 4 megabytes is plenty of video memory.)

You can also use MSD to check your video card type and memory. Start MSD from the DOS prompt (type **MSD**), and then click on the Video button (or press V if your mouse isn't working in MSD) to see a display like the one in Figure 1.9.

Windows 95/98 does not have a tool through which you can directly check the exact video card type you have, but you can find out what Windows *thinks* you have. (Windows might be right, or it might be wrong.) Right-click on the desktop and choose Properties. Click on the Settings tab, and then click on the Advanced (or Advanced Properties) button. At the top of

**Figure 1.9**

Here is the MSD analysis of your video capabilities.

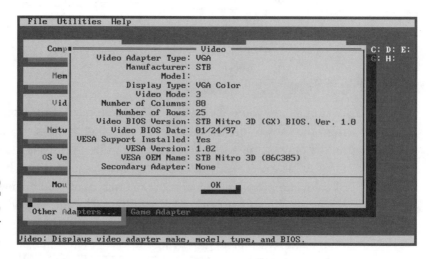

```
 File  Utilities  Help

   Comp                        Video                         C: D: E:
            Video Adapter Type: VGA                           G: H:
                  Manufacturer: STB
                         Model:
                  Display Type: VGA Color
                    Video Mode: 3
   Mem        Number of Columns: 80
                Number of Rows: 25
            Video BIOS Version: STB Nitro 3D (GX) BIOS. Ver. 1.0
   Vid          Video BIOS Date: 01/24/97
            VESA Support Installed: Yes
                  VESA Version: 1.02
   Netw          VESA OEM Name: STB Nitro 3D (86C385)
             Secondary Adapter: None

   OS Ve

   Mou                          OK

 Other Adapters...   Game Adapter
Video: Displays video adapter make, model, type, and BIOS.
```

the dialog box Windows tells you what driver is installed for your video adapter. Click on the Change button, and then click on Show Compatible Devices. Windows does its best to guess what type of video card you have. Click on Cancel when you finish checking the list. (Don't change the type right now.)

**NOTE**  Windows 98 has a sophisticated utility called System Information that provides detailed information about your installed hardware (Start, Programs, Accessories, System Tools, System Information). However, it doesn't actually read the information from the hardware itself; it reads it from your Windows configuration. That means that if you have configured your video driver as Generic VGA, that's the kind of video card it thinks you have, even if you have some whiz-bang special card actually installed.

## Is It a Local Bus?

The other information you need to know about your video card is how it connects to your motherboard. If you have a local bus motherboard—that is, one with Vesa Local Bus (VLB), Peripheral Connection Interface (PCI), or Accelerated Graphics Port (AGP) slots, you want a video card that takes advantage of that feature. If you're using a regular old Industry Standard Architecture (ISA) card on such a system, you're wasting your motherboard's capability.

To find out what you have, you need to remove the cover from your PC. First, however, shut down your computer and unplug the power. You don't need to remove any connectors right now from the back of the computer. Just unscrew the Phillips-head screws that hold the cover on your case and then slide back or pull off the cover. This step doesn't require any special skill or knowledge; at most it just needs the ability to be observant and figure out which screws are holding the cover on and which way to slide it back to remove it. And if you have a really modern case, there may be a couple of levers you can turn to release the cover—no screws involved—so look carefully before you reach for the toolbox. Check out the detailed discussion of removing the case in the Sunday Morning session if things don't go smoothly.

♦ ♦ ♦ ♦ ♦ ♦ ♦ ♦ ♦ ♦ ♦ ♦ ♦ ♦ ♦ ♦ ♦ ♦ ♦ ♦ ♦ ♦ ♦ ♦ ♦ ♦ ♦ ♦ ♦ ♦ ♦ ♦ ♦ ♦ ♦ ♦ ♦

**CAUTION** Static electricity can fry your system. See the detailed warnings in the Sunday Morning session for more information, but for the time being, try not to touch anything inside your PC. If you must touch something, touch your PC's power supply first (the big gray metal box to which the power cord connects).

♦ ♦ ♦ ♦ ♦ ♦ ♦ ♦ ♦ ♦ ♦ ♦ ♦ ♦ ♦ ♦ ♦ ♦ ♦ ♦ ♦ ♦ ♦ ♦ ♦ ♦ ♦ ♦ ♦ ♦ ♦ ♦ ♦ ♦ ♦ ♦ ♦

When the cover is off, follow the cord from the monitor to the connector. The circuit card that it connects to is your video card. Notice that the circuit card is plugged into one of probably about eight *expansion* slots. The removable metal plates at the back of the computer enable you to slide new cards into the slots.

Notice also that the motherboard has several kinds of slots. Some slots have either one or two plain black slots in a line. These are ISA slots. Some motherboards have only this kind. Depending on your motherboard, you may see one of the following local bus slot types:

- Several regular-looking black slots with a smaller brown slots at the end. These are VLB slots. If you have a 486-based PC or a very old Pentium system that runs at less than 100 MHz, you probably have this.

- Several small white or cream-colored slots, smaller than the regular black ones. These are PCI slots. If you have a newer Pentium PC, you probably have this.

- Several PCI slots, plus a single small slot that is slightly smaller than and positioned a little differently from the PCI slots. This is an AGP slot. If you have one of these, congratulations! It's the newest and is found mainly in Pentium II systems.

If you see one of these types of local bus slots and your video card is plugged into it—great. Your video card is taking advantage of the local bus, which is what you want. If you are using the video card that originally came with your system, and your system has a local bus, chances are very good that it's the appropriate local bus type card. (Why would a PC manufacturer not take advantage of all the system's capabilities, after all?)

If you see one of the local bus slots but the video card isn't using it (unlikely but possible), you can probably benefit from a new video card.

If you don't see any local bus slots at all, your motherboard is probably fairly old. You might need a new motherboard as well as a new video card. (In systems of this age, buying a whole new computer is often more cost-effective than trying to upgrade what you have.)

If you don't see a video card at all, perhaps your system has integrated video, with the video card built into the motherboard. Compaq Presario and HP Pavilion systems are especially noted for this. On some such systems you can disable the built-in graphics and add your own; on others you are stuck with the video that you've got. Consult your computer's manual for details.

## Is the Monitor Up to Snuff?

The best video card in the world can't help you if you have a bad monitor. *Bad* is a subjective term—if it bothers you, it's bad. For now, just decide the following:

- Are you happy with the monitor size? Most people these days like at least a 15-inch monitor for a computer that they use occasionally, or a 17-inch monitor for a computer that they use a lot.

- Are you happy with the monitor's picture sharpness and clarity? (By the way, have you cleaned the dust off the screen recently? A good shine can do wonders for the clarity.)

- Would you be willing to settle for what you have if it cost a substantial amount of money to get a new one? You can't buy a good monitor for less than $150 these days, and that's for a basic 15-inch model. Nice 17-inch models cost upwards of $400.

## Is Your Hard Disk Full?

If your hard disk is full, you have probably already encountered a message to that effect when trying to save something. You have probably already been through the frustrating process of deleting other files on your hard disk to make room for the new ones you want to save. I won't make you rehash that nightmare again.

To find out how much free hard disk space you actually have, and how much is free, you can use either Windows 95/98 or a DOS prompt. In Windows 95/98, you can open My Computer, right-click on a drive, and choose

Properties to display a window that tells you how big your drive is and how much space is left on it.

To find out the same information at a DOS prompt, you must use two different commands. To find out how much free space you have, change to the drive you want to check (**C:** for example), type **DIR,** and press Enter. After the list of files, look for a message that gives the drive's free space, like this:

```
27 directories 24,498,394 bytes free
```

You can ignore the directories part. This message tells you that you have approximately 24 megabytes free on your drive.

To find out how big the hard disk is at the DOS prompt, type **CHKDSK** and press Enter. Chkdsk is an error-correction program, but it also reports on your disk's capacity. The following report describes a 2 gigabyte hard disk:

```
2,138,243,072 bytes total disk space
26,869,760 bytes in 297 hidden files
16,089,088 bytes in 491 directories
1,048,870,912 bytes in 7,512 files
1,046,357,776 bytes available on disk
```

That last line—the bytes available on disk—is the important one. This disk still has more than 1 gigabyte of free space (that's 1,000 megabytes), so this computer does not need a new hard disk. If your computer has less than 100 megabytes available, you might consider a hard disk upgrade. With less than 20 megabytes left, you need to upgrade *now.*

## What Kind of Processor?

You can use several different approaches to find out what kind of processor you have. Here's a rundown, from easiest to the most "pain-in-the-butt" way:

○ Look on the outside of your computer's case. If you haven't upgraded the computer since you bought it and you bought it new, any sticker on the outside that lists the computer's processor and speed is probably correct. For example, one of mine says P5-90 on the outside; that means it's a Pentium (P) at 90MHz. Another says GP6-400; it's a Pentium II running at 400MHz. Sometimes you have to pick the specifications out of a long string. For example, your sticker might say 486DX4-100XLS, which means it's a 486 processor running at 100MHz.

✿ Watch for a message that tells what kind of computer you have when your computer starts up. For example, you might see a message like this:

```
386 Processor 25 MHz
```

or

```
CPU: Pentium (tm)
```

✿ If you have a DOS system, run the MSD program from the DOS prompt. You should see what kind of processor you have on the Processor line. However, if you have a Pentium or better, this program doesn't reliably detect it; it might report the chip as a 486DX instead. That's because this program was written at about the same time Pentiums were introduced.

✿ If you have a Windows 95/98 system, right-click on the My Computer icon and choose Properties. Click on the General tab. You should see the name of your processor and the amount of memory you have at the bottom of that tab.

✿ On a really old computer, you can remove the computer's cover (see the warnings and instructions earlier) and look for a big square chip on the motherboard, about two inches in diameter. It may have writing on it that identifies the model and speed, such as AMD 486-40 or Pentium 90MHz. This doesn't work on newer computers because there are cooling fans or heat sinks attached to the processor that obscure the label. (But then, on a newer computer, you can probably use one of the aforementioned methods instead.)

## Are You Happy with Your Printer?

People have three kinds of gripes about their printers: they don't print good enough quality, they don't print fast enough, or they don't print certain things at all. Which category does yours fall into?

✿ If the quality of your printer's output is not good enough, it's time to get a new printer. You can't do much to fix this situation. The only exception is if the print is too light or lines or splotches appear on the page. Too-light printing means it's time to change the ribbon or toner; lines and splotches mean your printer needs to take a trip to the repair shop.

○ If the printer doesn't print fast enough for you, your only recourse is to get a new printer.

○ If the printer doesn't print color but you want it to, check your printer's manual. Color upgrade kits are available for some ink-jet printers. But in most cases you're back to buying a new printer.

○ If your laser printer conks out with an Out of Memory error message when you try to print complex graphics, you need more memory for your printer. Printers vary on the type of memory they will accept; most of them require special, rather expensive memory that you purchase directly from the printer's manufacturer. Call the toll-free number in your printer's documentation and find out.

**TIP** Most printers have a self-test mode where they spit out a print sample that may include a spec sheet. Check your printer's documentation to find out how to run the test. It usually involves holding down certain buttons on the printer's control panel while you turn it on, but every printer is a little different.

## What about Multimedia?

If you don't have a sound card and CD-ROM drive right now, you don't have "multimedia." If you already have these gadgets, you need to decide whether they are working well enough for you.

As you learned earlier in this chapter, you need a CD-ROM drive to read CDs—and almost all new programs sold today come on CD. If you already have a CD-ROM drive but you experience delays when playing games that read information from the CD, you may need a faster one. For example, if you play a game that includes video clips and the clips are choppy with bad sound that doesn't match the speakers' lips, a faster CD-ROM drive can help.

If you already have a sound card that works, chances are good that you don't need a new one. Almost all programs (especially Windows 95/98 ones) can work with even the oldest sound card. A good reason to consider a new sound card might be compatibility—if your current sound card is not a

SoundBlaster or 100 percent SoundBlaster compatible, not all your programs may work with it. The new speech-recognition programs available today are a prime example; many of these are picky about the sound card they will accept.

You might also consider a new sound card if you are a musician who wants to record music by attaching a keyboard to your PC. If you have a very old sound card, it might not support this. Still another reason to get a new sound card would be if your current one doesn't produce good enough quality sounds in the latest games.

## Do You Have a Good Backup System?

If you keep important data on your PC—and who doesn't, these days?—you need to safeguard it by periodically copying it to a removable disk (or tape cartridge) and storing it in a safe place. You need a plan for doing this.

You can back up using floppy disks, but for even a medium-size system, it can take hundreds of disks. A better solution is a drive that can hold more than a normal floppy. Any of the following will work:

- ✿ A ZIP or Jaz drive or other removable mass storage. These removable cartridges work just like miniature hard disks.

- ✿ A SuperDisk (L-120) floppy drive replacement. This drive uses normal floppies and also special 120-megabyte floppies.

- ✿ A tape backup drive. This unit reads to and writes from special tape cassettes that store data.

Such a backup drive isn't necessary, if you don't mind backing up to floppies, but if you have the extra $100 or so, it can certainly be worth the money. You'll learn more about each of these in tomorrow morning's session.

## Do You Need Video Input?

By *video* input, I mean picture input, either still or moving. There are dozens of reasons why you might want to put your own pictures into your PC, from e-mailing a photograph to a friend to including a video of your CEO in a computerized presentation.

If you need still video input, consider a scanner. You'll learn about scanners in tomorrow morning's session; they work like copiers to *digitize* (convert to computer format) text and pictures.

A scanner requires you to have the photos or other pictures already developed; if you plan to take a lot of pictures and use them directly in your PC, consider a digital camera. These work like regular cameras, but instead of saving to film, they save to a computer disk. You can take as many pictures as you want without paying a cent for film or developing.

If you need moving video input, there are a variety of handy little video devices that you can attach to your PC. One of them, the Connectix camera, is a little round "eye" that captures an image of whatever you point it at. Other devices include the Snappy video capture box, which helps you record and compress video. You'll learn about at these tomorrow morning too.

## Is Your Internet Connection Satisfactory?

If you experience delays when working online, the fault might not lie with the modem. The Internet and online services can sometimes have delays and bottlenecks too, and a faster modem on your end isn't going to help one iota.

**TIP**    ■ ■ ■ ■ ■ ■ ■ ■ ■ ■ ■ ■ ■ ■ ■ ■ ■ ■ ■ ■ ■ ■ ■ ■ ■ ■ ■ ■ ■ ■ ■ ■ ■ ■ ■ ■ ■
You can use a shareware program called the Modem Doctor to figure out why a modem isn't working right. The program is available for download on the Internet; search for it at **http://www.shareware.com**. But of course, if you were able to connect to the Internet, you wouldn't need the program—Catch-22.

To find out if your modem is the bottleneck causing the delays, watch the modem lights when you experience a delay. If they continue to flash frantically, the modem is either downloading a file (in which case it's natural that you have to wait) or it's struggling to keep up with the data being sent. If no lights flash, the delay is not the modem's fault.

If you have an internal modem, you can't really look for lights, unless the program you are using provides onscreen lights that simulate modem lights. (Windows 95/98 shows red and green lights in the bottom-right corner of the screen when your modem is communicating with another modem.) You can also download freeware or shareware programs that simulate modem lights.

**TIP**  A good utility that simulates modem lights is WMPLUS, which you can download from America Online. Just do a software search for the keywords MODEM and LIGHTS. It is also available at other sites on the Internet; search for it at **http://www.shareware.com**.

# Deciding What Parts to Upgrade

Now that you know what you have to work with and have an idea of where the problems lie, you need to make some decisions. Obviously, you're not made of money; there's a limit to the amount you want to spend to upgrade this computer. At some point buying a whole new system makes more sense than upgrading—and might even cost less.

## Finding the Weakest Link

You can use the following guidelines to figure out which components are probably slowing down your system. If you discover that more than two components are "weak links," you should consider buying a whole new system.

Your processor is a weak link if:

❏ The whole system is generally slow.

❏ A command that uses the processor heavily, like repagination or sorting, causes long waits during which no lights are flashing on the computer—nothing, just dead waiting time.

❏ It is not a Pentium or a Pentium II.

Your memory is a weak link if:

❏ The computer runs slowly in Windows when you have more than one program open.

❏ The computer starts out running at an acceptable speed but slows down the more you use a program.

❏ Your hard disk light flashes and you hear the drive churning frequently, even when you are not saving or opening a file.

❏ You are running DOS programs (only) with less than 4 megabytes of RAM.

❑ You are running Windows 3.1 with less than 16 megabytes of RAM.

❑ You are running Windows 95/98 with less than 32 megabytes of RAM.

Your hard disk is a weak link if:

❑ You are constantly trying to figure out what you can delete so that you can squeeze new programs and data files onto your hard disk.

❑ You have already used a disk compression program on your drive (DriveSpace, DoubleSpace, and so on), and you are out of room again.

Your video card is a weak link if:

❑ The screen does not refresh itself immediately when you change something on it. If you notice the screen being refreshed (for example, if you can see the top portion of the screen refresh before the bottom is refreshed), it is being refreshed too slowly. You should not be able to see the screen refresh itself.

❑ You see a noticeable flicker when you look at the screen, and the software that came with the video card does not enable you to change the refresh rate to a higher setting.

❑ You cannot display as many colors or as high a resolution in Windows as you would like because the video card won't support it.

❑ Games with 3-D effects (such as Doom) have slow or choppy video.

The following components are somewhat separate from the rest of the system. If any of these is weak, you can upgrade it individually without affecting the main system. You should not use these weaknesses to calculate whether or not you should buy a whole new system, because vendors usually don't include them in the system bundle and you still have to buy them separately.

Your monitor is a weak link if:

❑ You would like to use a higher-resolution display, but it makes everything too small for you to see comfortably.

❑ The monitor display is fuzzy and of poor quality.

❑ You do not have a color monitor.

❑ Your monitor is not at least VGA quality.

Your printer is a weak link if:

- ❏ You cannot print in color, but want to.
- ❏ You are embarrassed to use your current printer's output for business.
- ❏ You need faster output.
- ❏ The printer will not print some of your complex documents.

Your modem is a weak link if:

- ❏ You experience long delays online while the modem lights furiously flash.
- ❏ You download many files, and the download times are unacceptably long.
- ❏ You have less than a 33.6K modem.

A lack of extras is a weak link if:

- ❏ You don't want to have to back up using floppies, but you don't have a removable mass storage device of some sort.
- ❏ You want to import still or motion video into your PC, but you don't have a scanner, digital camera, or video import device.
- ❏ You want to do something else with your PC but you don't have the right add-ons.

## Does Your Computer Have Room for Additions?

A lack of components can also be a weak link. For example, if you don't have a CD-ROM drive, you probably should get one. Other desirable components include a joystick, a ZIP drive, a CD recorder, a scanner, a digital camera or video camera, and a trackball. When evaluating these additions, you must think not only of the device you want to add but also how you are going to plug it into your existing system.

New components generally require one or more of the following: an open expansion slot, a serial port, a PS/2 port, a parallel port, a USB port, a drive bay, or a power connector.

## An Open Expansion Slot

Upgrades that come on circuit cards must plug into expansion slots. Such devices include sound cards, internal modems, and SCSI or other proprietary cards that run external devices like scanners, tape backup units, and external CD-ROM drives. A special kind of mouse called a *bus mouse* also plugs into a circuit card.

**NOTE** The industry seems to be moving away from using circuit cards such as SCSI cards to drive external devices. The latest external CD-ROM drives, tape backups, and even scanners are mostly the kind that run on either a parallel or serial port, or on a USB port.

You saw the slots in the motherboard when you removed the computer's cover to look at the video card connector. Motherboards have different kinds of expansion slots into which you can plug expansion cards; you need to have one free slot of the right kind. Most devices require either an 8-bit or a 16-bit ISA slot. Those are the regular black slots. Some devices require a PCI or VLB slot; your motherboard has one or the other of these, but not both. Generally speaking, 386s have regular ISA slots only, 486s have ISA and VLB, and Pentiums and higher have ISA and PCI. (Some Pentium and Pentium II systems also have an AGP port, but that is already taken by the video card.)

**NOTE** Eight- versus 16-bit slots? The 8-bit slots are single, short slots; the 16-bit slots consist of two 8-bit sections running end to end. Sixteen-bit cards have two sets of connectors so they can plug into both parts of the slot.

In the newest systems—high-end Pentium IIs—the trend is toward more PCI slots and fewer ISA slots. This can be a problem because you can run out of ISA slots. (My newest system had only two, which I quickly filled with my old internal modem and sound card.) That's why it's important not to assume that just because your system is fairly new, it has the type of slot open that you will need.

Many internal devices that require a slot come in multiple versions, so you can choose which type of slot to plug it into. For example, sound cards come in both ISA and PCI interfaces, so you can buy one that matches the type of slot you have available.

# A Serial Port

Most computers have two serial ports: COM1 and COM2. Computers that also have a PS/2 port (see the following section) sometimes have only one serial port.

You can plug various devices into a serial port—for example, a serial mouse, an external modem, a palmtop PC, or a serial printer. (Serial printers are rare; most printers plug into the parallel port. However, some special-purpose printers, such as those that print labels, are generally serial devices.) A serial port can accept only one device, so if your serial ports are already taken, you're out of luck. If you want to add a serial device to such a system, you have these choices:

- Look for a different version of the device. For example, instead of buying a serial mouse, look for a PS/2 mouse if you have an open PS/2 port or a bus mouse if you have an extra expansion slot. (The bus mouse comes with a circuit card that creates its own dedicated serial port.) Instead of an external modem, look for an internal one if you have an open expansion slot.

- Buy a circuit card containing an extra serial port. These *I/O cards* are usually inexpensive (less than $50). However, if you have too many extra ports, you may run into IRQ conflicts.

---

### WHAT ARE IRQs?

IRQs are interrupt addresses. Your system has 16 of them (0 through 15), but most are already taken by other devices. For example, your parallel port gets one, each serial port gets one, your keyboard gets one, and so on. Most systems have three or four free IRQs, but if you have already added a few devices to your system, you might have used them all. The MSD program (DOS) can tell you about your IRQ situation (although it is known to sometimes report inaccurately), as can the System dialog box in Windows 95/98. You'll look at IRQs in more detail later.

✪ Buy a serial port switch that lets you share the serial port with up to 4 devices. These are cheaper still (around $15), but have several disadvantages. You have to remember to flip the switch whenever you want to change the device being used, and you can use only one of the connected devices at once.

## A PS/2 Port

IBM introduced the PS/2 style connector with its PS/2 line of computers about ten years ago. The PS/2 computers are long gone, but the connectors caught on and most computers today have them. They're essentially just a different kind of connector for plugging in serial devices. The most common device plugged into a PS/2 port is a mouse. In fact, PS/2 ports are sometimes called "mouse ports." If you have a PS/2 port, you should try to use a PS/2 mouse, rather than a serial one, so you can free up your serial port for some other use. Most systems have only one PS/2 port. Depending on the type of motherboard you have, your keyboard port may also look like a PS/2 port. But the keyboard port can't really be considered "available," because you can't use your PC without a keyboard, and the keyboard can't be attached through any other means.

**NOTE** My laptop has a special PS/2 port that accepts either an external keyboard or a PS/2 mouse. The computer determines which device I've plugged in and acts accordingly. On regular desktop PCs, though, you can't interchange the keyboard and the mouse plug-ins, even if they have the same kinds of connectors.

## A Parallel Port

The parallel port is almost always used for a printer; in fact, many people call their parallel ports "the printer port." However, several new brands of scanners also plug into the parallel port. And their manufacturers were smart enough to devise connectors that didn't interfere with your printer. For example, I have an old (circa 1996) Logitech PageScan Color scanner with a parallel connector. I can plug it directly into my parallel port, or I can use a special adapter that enables both the scanner and my printer to share one parallel port. As long as I'm using just one of the devices, everything works fine.

If you want a second printer, you have three choices:

⚙ You can purchase an I/O card with an extra parallel port on it, provided you have an open expansion slot and an IRQ available for it. If you go this route, make sure the card you purchase will work with one of your open IRQs—some of them can use only a limited range of IRQs. More about IRQs in tomorrow morning's session.

⚙ You can purchase a switch box, which is essentially a square box with one knob in the middle. You plug both of your printers into the switch box and plug the switch box into the computer. Then you flip the switch to the A or B position depending on which printer you want to use. Some laser printer manufacturers warn against the use of these devices, but I have used one quite a bit with a laser printer and have not experienced any problems.

⚙ You can plug in the correct printer to your PC whenever you want to use it, leaving the other printer unplugged. This technique works well if you rarely use the other printer.

There are also other devices that want a parallel port to operate from, such as some models of ZIP drives and some scanners. Some of these devices come with port-sharing adapters, however, that enable you to "pass through" the parallel port so that both devices can be plugged into it at the same time. Then, as long as only one of the devices is in use at a given moment, everything works fine. (If both devices try to use the port at the same time, special software manages the conflict.) Sharing a port in this manner can sometimes cause frustrating problems such as lockups and error messages, depending on the PC, so be prepared to fall back to one of the other solution methods if you experience problems.

## A USB Port

USB stands for Universal Serial Bus, a new kind of connector that PC manufacturers began including on their systems in mid-1997. USB promises to be a really cool technology, because you can plug several USB devices into a single USB port (chaining them together) and you don't have to do any special configuring for them.

If you have a USB port in your system (it looks like a small—about one inch wide—flat rectangle on the back of your PC, and there are usually two), by all means look for USB devices when you shop for new peripherals. Currently available USB devices include mice, keyboards, scanners, and digital cameras. However, at this point USB devices are not quite mainstream, because so few people have a system with a USB port. Also, the built-in USB port may not provide enough power for a scanner; in addition to the USB port, users need to get a separate device called a *self-powered hub* that plugs into the wall and provides independent power to anything plugged into it.

## A Drive Bay

Take a look at the floppy disk on your PC. It sits in a drive bay. Other drives, like a CD drive, sit in their own bays. If you have any blank panels, you have open external drive bays. If all the panels are filled with drives, you don't. They're called external because they provide access to the drive from outside the case. All drives that use removable disks must be in external bays.

You can add a floppy drive to a system with no open drive bays, but it has to be an external model. At present, one of the few choices for an external floppy for a desktop system is an LS120 drive, which lets you use both regular floppy disks and special 120-megabyte cartridges called *superfloppies*. These devices are rather expensive, need access to a parallel port, and take up space on your desk.

You can't see the internal bay situation without removing the computer's cover. Internal drive bays look like shelves; you can put hard disks on them. Most computers have at least two internal drive bays, so if you have only one hard disk right now, you are probably safe in assuming that you have room for another.

If you run out of internal drive bays but still have an open external bay, you can use the external bay to house an internal device. Simply don't remove the blank panel over that bay from the front of the computer.

You can also buy a new case for your computer, and transfer all the innards to a new "box." This project is a very ambitious undertaking, however, and I don't recommend it for beginners. (I don't even like to do it myself unless I have a whole day to troubleshoot the inevitable problems.)

## Power Connectors

If you still have the cover off your PC, look for a big silver box with colored wires coming out of it. That's your power supply. The power supply has a tangle of colored wires arranged in groups of four. Each group of four wires runs to a specific device in the system: to a floppy disk, a hard disk, the motherboard, and so on.

You should also see several loose groups of wires with dangling plastic connections at the end. These wires are spare power connectors, and you will need them if you add any drives (hard, floppy, or whatever). No extra connectors means no new drives.

If you are out of power connectors, you can buy a splitter, which plugs into one of the connectors and divides it so two devices can plug into it. This solution is like using an extension cord to increase the number of electrical outlets in your room. It works fine—to an extent. Then you start having problems with lack of power because you have split the available current among too many devices.

The alternative is to replace the power supply with a bigger one. Generally, bigger power supplies have more connectors. Your power supply may say what wattage it is; common wattage values are 150, 175, 200, 230, and 250. Most computers run out of drive bays before they run out of connectors, so replacing the power supply does not become an issue.

# How Much Can You Spend?

Do you have an idea now of the constraints of your current system and what you might like to buy? You have probably formulated a "wish list" for your system and perhaps you have also prioritized that list. Here's a ballpark estimate of what you can plan to spend for your upgrades: this information should help you narrow down your list to the components you really need.

- ⚙ **Hard disk.** Plan on about $40 to $50 per gigabyte. (You'll figure out how many gigabytes you need tomorrow morning, but for now plan on at least 4 gigabytes if you want to add a hard disk.)

- ⚙ **Memory.** Plan on about $3 a megabyte—a bit more if your system requires a special kind of memory, such as full parity or SGRAM. (More on the different types in tomorrow morning's session.) Memory prices fluctuate quite a bit, though, so you may pay much more or much less. (You'll do some price shopping tomorrow afternoon.)

○ **Video card**. You can pick up a video card that will do nicely on most systems for $100 or less, but really fancy cards go for up to $250.

○ **Monitors**. A cheap 14-inch color Super VGA costs about $150; a nice 15-inch is $250; and the 17-inch models go from $350 to $1000. If you're feeling rich, 21-inch models are $1000 and up, and are absolutely gorgeous (but require a lot of front-to-back desk space). There are also flat-screen LCD panels that take up very little room but are outrageously priced at the time of this writing (over $1000 for a 15" model).

○ **Motherboards**. Without a CPU, you'll pay from $100 to $300.

○ **CPUs and CPU Upgrades**. Anywhere from $100 to $1000 depending on the model.

○ **Modems**. A cheap 33.6K model is less than $100; top-of-the-line 56K modems can cost more than $200.

○ **Printers**. You can get a decent color ink-jet printer for $200; laser printers (black and white) start at $400. I have seen printers that cost as much as $10,000. You can find a printer for any price you want to pay.

# The Dollars-to-Obsolescence Ratio

You can pay almost any price for any component. In other words, if you want to spend $50 on a printer, you can find someone who will sell you a $50 printer. Unfortunately, it will probably be several years old and well on its way to becoming obsolete. And don't expect to find a replacement ribbon or toner cartridge for it at your local computer superstore.

According to my dollars-to-obsolescence ratio, the more dollars you spend on a component, the longer you stave off that component's obsolescence. For example, I can walk into a store right now and buy computers for $999 and $1,999, either of which will do what I want to do today. However, the $999 computer is last year's technology. It will be obsolete a year earlier than the $1,999 machine. Given that a computer has about three to four years before it is obsolete, an extra $1,000 buys me one year's worth of technology readiness.

I'm not saying that the $999 computer won't be usable after two years. On the contrary—as I told you at the beginning of this session, if you never need to run new software or have new capabilities, you never need a new computer. It's just that two years from now, some of the new programs you'll see in the computer stores might not run on that $999 computer without an additional upgrade or two.

This same principle applies to upgrade components. By buying state-of-the-art parts, you buy yourself an extra year or so before the next upgrade. For example, if you are buying a replacement motherboard and CPU, you could buy a Pentium (or off-brand equivalent) right now for a very attractive price and get a lot of use from it. Or you could buy a Pentium II motherboard and CPU for a higher price and get yourself another year or two of compatibility with the rest of the computing world.

Parts that use older technology are not necessarily a bad buy. In fact, they make some of the best upgrade values. Face it: When you are upgrading an old computer, you aren't trying to make it last for three or four more years— you just want it to last another year or two until you can afford a brand-new system. In another year or two, some other parts of the computer are going to need replacing, and then a few other parts, until you will have built a new system one part at a time. So when choosing upgrade components for an existing PC, you may find that last year's model is just right. I'll tell you more about the hot new features in each component technology in tomorrow morning's session.

## Maybe You Should Just Scrap It?

I don't want to discourage you from upgrading your computer, but sometimes upgrading just isn't the best value. As I told you earlier, the cost of upgrading three or more components approaches the cost of buying a new system (if you figure in the price you would get for selling your old one). Don't believe me? Here's some math to consider.

Say you have a 486 computer with a 120 megabyte hard disk and 4 megabytes of RAM. It has an older ISA video card and an older VGA monitor. It has no CD or sound card, both of which you would like to have. (You want to be able to run Windows 95/98 and Microsoft Office applications.) You could probably sell your system in the local classified ads for about $100.

Here are the parts and approximate costs to upgrade your old system to the level you need:

| | |
|---|---:|
| New motherboard (Pentium II): | $150 |
| Pentium II 333MHz processor: | $500 |
| CD-ROM drive: | $80 |
| Memory (new motherboard requires different kind): | $120 |
| New hard disk (old one is too small): | $200 |
| AGP video card: | $100 |
| 15-inch SuperVGA monitor: | $250 |
| Windows 98: | $90 |
| Microsoft Office software: | $220 |
| Total: | $1,710 |

For about $1,600, you can buy an equivalent new, brand-name system that comes with at least a one-year warranty (probably more like two or three years). Plus, you don't have to fiddle with any tools or shop for parts. So it actually costs more to do it yourself in this situation! Why? Because computer manufacturers, who buy large quantities of parts, can get a better price than you can as an individual buying single items.

The situation is a little less clear when you have a computer that comes closer to being what you want. Suppose, for example, that you have a 90MHz Pentium computer with 16 megabytes of memory and a 1 gigabyte hard disk, which is almost full. You have a PCI local bus video card and an average-quality SuperVGA monitor. You have a 4X CD-ROM drive that works, but won't play the latest games very well. You would like to upgrade to Windows 98 and play games. Here are the upgrades you would need:

| | |
|---|---:|
| Pentium MMX upgrade chip for motherboard: | $150 |
| Faster CD-ROM drive: | $80 |
| Bring memory up to 32 megabytes: | $50 |
| Additional hard disk: | $200 |
| Windows 98: | $90 |
| Total: | $570 |

In this case you can upgrade your computer to the level you need at a substantially lower cost than a new computer. Because so many of the components are salvageable for the new system (the monitor, the video card, the old memory, and the old motherboard), upgrading makes great sense.

# The Minimums You Should Consider

I'd like to end this session the way I started it: by reiterating that there are no bad computers—only computers that are inappropriate for the tasks you need to accomplish. If your needs are very simple, you may be happy with a very simple upgrade, or none at all. Or you may be able to buy someone else's old system through your local classified ads and get something better than what you have but still not fancy and expensive.

The following sections consider what kind of computer setup would be appropriate for people involved in four typical scenarios.

## Scenario #1: Just a Glorified Typewriter

Some people want a computer just to type letters and reports. It's just a typewriter to them, albeit one with a spell-check and a Save feature. My mother, for example, doesn't love computers the way I do. Rather, she sees them as a necessary evil because her typewriter no longer works, and she can't buy a typewriter to replace it that doesn't beep mysteriously and insist on feeding in its own paper.

If you want to use the computer primarily for word processing, you don't need much in the way of computing power. The only quirk is that the best word processor (in my opinion), Word 97, runs only on Windows 95/98, so you need to have a computer capable of Windows 95/98 to use it. Other word processors are available for Windows 3.1 and even for DOS, although they are becoming harder to find.

Word processing users need to spend their upgrade money on the following components:

✿ A computer capable of running the operating system (DOS, Windows 3.1, or Windows 95/98) that your word processing program of choice requires.

✪ A good printer (black and white will do) capable of printing several pages per minute. Low-end laser printers are ideal.

✪ A clear, crisp monitor in a large enough size to see your work clearly. A 15-inch monitor would do nicely.

✪ (Optional) A scanner with character-recognition ability if you frequently have to retype items from hard copies or you want to include photos and drawings in your writing.

## Scenario #2: My Kids Want to Play Games

You would think that games, being "kid stuff," would not be too taxing on a computer. Wrong. Most of the popular games today require state-of-the-art computer equipment for best play. If you're a game player, look to the following:

✪ An MMX-capable processor or an upgrade chip to make your current processor MMX-capable. (MMX stands for Multimedia Extensions, which are special program codes written into many of the latest games that make them display video clips efficiently.) This item will be your biggest expense, because MMX technology is found only in newer Pentiums and the new (expensive) Pentium II.

✪ A local-bus video card that supports 3-D imaging. (More on this tomorrow morning.)

✪ A fast CD-ROM drive (at least 16X; 32X or more is better).

✪ A 16-bit sound card. Wavetable synthesis is a plus. (I'll talk about this more tomorrow morning.)

✪ Lots of hard disk space (at least 500 megabytes free), for storing game files. (If you have a CD-ROM drive that is fast enough to play the game directly from the CD, this requirement eases a little.)

✪ A good joystick or game controller.

## Scenario #3: I Want to Start a Home Business

A home business needs good office-management software, a big hard disk to store business data, and a reliable backup system. It also needs phone and fax capabilities and a way to produce professional-looking printouts. Consider these minimums:

- *At least* a 486 processor—Pentium or Pentium II would be better. The more you use the computer, the more time you waste waiting for things to happen if you have a slow processor.

- Enough memory to run your operating system of choice speedily (16 megabytes for Windows 3.1 or 32 for Windows 95/98).

- A big enough hard disk to store your records. If you keep inventory on the PC, you will need at least 2 gigabytes (to allow your business to grow over time); if you store only names and addresses, you can manage with a smaller hard disk.

- A good-quality printer that won't keep customers waiting for their receipts and that produces professional-quality business reports and letters.

- A fax modem or stand-alone fax machine. If you have to buy a printer, too, consider a multifunction machine that combines faxing, scanning, copying, and printing.

- A tape backup or a removable hard drive such as an Iomega Jaz or ZIP drive on which you can regularly back up your data. If your data files (for example, your inventory database) will ever be more than 100 megabytes, avoid small-capacity removable drives like the ZIP drive, which have a 100 megabyte capacity limit. One hundred megabytes may seem like a lot, but I have a friend who runs an auto parts business and his database of more than 50,000 parts takes up more than 150 megabytes on his hard disk.

- An uninterruptible power supply. This device is essentially a big battery that kicks in when the power goes off. It prevents the loss of valuable data and enables you to finish critical transactions without interruption.

## Scenario #4: I Surf the Internet a Lot

If your passion is the Internet, you will want the best modem you can get (and maybe a special phone line). You will also want a monitor large enough to comfortably display at least in 800×600 resolution, a decent amount of memory, and lots of hard disk space. Consider these features:

- A good enough system to comfortably run Windows 95/98. The best and newest Web browsers are written for Windows 95 and higher. In addition, setting up and maintaining dial-up connections is easier in Windows 95/98 than in Windows 3.1 or DOS.

- The fastest modem you can afford. The new 56K modems don't cost much more than older 33.6K models and offer greater performance potential.

- A good, static-free phone line. Complain to your phone company if you don't have this. You won't be able to take advantage of your 56K modem's highest speeds if your line is weak.

- (Optional) An ISDN phone line and ISDN modem, cable modem, ADSL (Asynchronous Digital Subscriber Line), or satellite PC system. These technologies cost a bit more per month than a regular Internet connection, but they make your online experience much faster.

- Enough hard disk space to store all the temporary Internet files that your browser generates. (When you visit a Web page, your browser caches it in a temporary file in case you want to return to it. These temporary files can take up tens of megabytes of space.)

- A big enough monitor and powerful enough video card that you can run your system in 800×600 resolution with at least 256 colors. The higher the resolution you use, the more of a given Web page you will be able to see onscreen without scrolling. And most Web pages contain graphics that won't look right unless your display uses at least 256 colors.

## Summary

In this evening's session you learned how to tweak and evaluate your old computer. You also made some broad decisions about the upgrades you might want to undertake, based on your priorities and budget. Are you excited yet? Not too excited to sleep, I hope, because tomorrow is a big day. Tomorrow morning you'll learn more about the components you need to purchase, and in the afternoon and evening you'll go shopping for them.

# How Much and What Kind?

- Choosing an Operating System
- Do You Need a new Processor?
- Understanding Memory Types
- Evaluating Video Cards and Monitors
- Options for Adding Storage
- Multimedia Upgrade Choices

**A**rmed with the decisions you made last night, you're ready to start finding out what replacement parts are available—and what they're going to cost. Shopping is an all-day affair. This morning's goal is to provide the technical information you need to decide which components to buy. Then this afternoon and evening, you learn how to shop for the best values.

# How to Use This Session

This session contains a lot of detailed information about computer parts—so much that you might not be able to get through it all and absorb the information fully before lunchtime. Don't worry; I'm not expecting you to read every word. Instead, skip around to the sections that pertain to the upgrades you've decided to do. For example, if you want to run Windows 95/98 and have decided to get memory and a CPU upgrade, just read those three sections.

# Choosing an Operating System

The operating system you choose is important because its requirements determine the kinds of hardware upgrades you'll be doing. For example, if you want to move up to Windows 95/98, your computer may need more upgrading than if you decided to stay with Windows 3.1 and DOS.

You have very few choices (realistic ones, that is) for a home or office PC operating system. You can stay with your current version of DOS (with or without Windows 3.1), or you can go for Windows 95 or Windows 98.

**NOTE** You may have heard about another operating system, OS/2 Warp. At one time this IBM product seemed like it might be a serious competitor to Windows 95. However, OS/2 Warp never caught on, and although it can run some Windows programs, few developers have written Warp-specific applications. Unless you have a special reason for using OS/2 (such as for compatibility with your company's systems), you should avoid this product.

## Windows 95/98

If your hardware is good enough, or is going to be after you have upgraded, Windows 98 is the best choice for your operating system. Figure 2.1 shows a Windows 98 display.

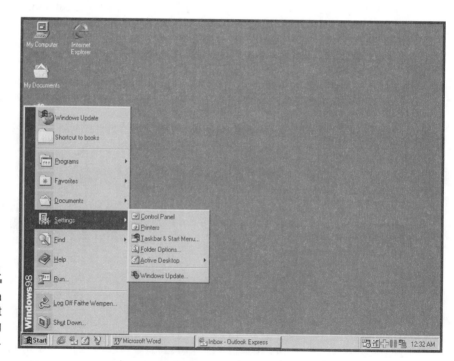

**Figure 2.1**

Windows 98 is a powerful yet friendly operating system.

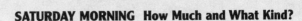

Windows 98 is the current version, the one sold in stores. However, if you bargain-shop on the Internet (as I'll teach you to do this afternoon), you might be able to get an excellent deal on a new or used copy of Windows 95, and save yourself $50 or more.

**CAUTION**

If you buy a copy of Windows on the Internet, make sure that it comes with a certificate of authenticity and a CD Key number. You will need the CD Key number to install the program, and the certificate of authenticity proves that it is a "legal" copy, not a bootleg.

For home use, Windows 95 is almost as good as Windows 98, and should work just fine for most people. If you see your situation in one of the following scenarios, upgrading to Windows 98 is definitely worth your while. Otherwise, either Windows 95 or Windows 98 will do equally well.

Upgrade to Windows 98 if:

- You are a techie who really enjoys having all the latest features and software.

- Your system has the latest USB or DVD equipment, an ISDN terminal adapter, or a television tuner. Windows 98 supports these latest technologies better than Windows 95.

- You need support for using multiple monitors at once (not very likely on a home system). Windows 98 supports this.

- You have vision, hearing, or mobility problems that could benefit from the enhanced accessibility features in Windows 98.

- You have a really buggy Windows 95 system that keeps crashing all the time. Windows 98 might help.

**NOTE**

As in the preceding chapter, I'm going to refer to Windows 95 and Windows 98 as a single product here, Windows 95/98, whenever I'm talking about features that they share. I'll explain the differences whenever there are any.

With adequate hardware Windows 95/98 runs very well, and it has all kinds of wonderful beginner-friendly utilities and features, such as:

○ **Plug and Play**. If your motherboard and a new device are both Plug and Play–compatible, when you add your upgrade components to the system, Windows 95/98 detects and configures them automatically. No messing around with jumpers and switches on the circuit board! In this regard, Windows 98 is superior to Windows 95; it handles Plug and Play more gracefully and painlessly, especially for off-brand components.

○ **Easy-to-use interface**. According to Microsoft, beginners can learn to use Windows 95/98 faster than they can learn Windows 3.1. (You can't be 100 percent sure that this research is objective, but Windows 95/98 is pretty darned easy to use.)

○ **Built-in connection program for the Internet**. If you use Windows 3.1, you have to struggle with a separate Winsock program, but Windows 95/98 makes dialing into an Internet Service Provider painless. Windows 98 has a multi-link feature that works with ISDN lines and multiple modems to create faster Internet connections; Windows 95 doesn't. However, not many people have ISDN lines or multiple modems, so this is not an issue for most people.

○ **Thirty-two-bit programs**. With Windows 95/98 you can run software that has been enhanced to take advantage of the 32-bit capability of Windows 95/98, such as Microsoft Office 97. Windows 3.1, on the other hand, still uses the older versions of most popular software. You cannot run software designed for Windows 95/98 on Windows 3.1, but the reverse is true—Windows 95/98 will run Windows 3.1 software.

○ **New program compatibility**. Increasingly, the coolest new programs are being released for Windows 95/98 only. If you don't upgrade to Windows 95/98, within a few years you might not be able to buy new software for your computer.

Windows 95/98 has very few drawbacks. The only major one is that if you don't have a powerful enough computer, Windows 95/98 runs very slowly or may not install at all. Microsoft claims that Windows 95/98 will install on all 386DX or better computers. (Sorry, 386SX users, that doesn't include

you.) However, in my opinion, if you have less than a 66MHz 486, the sluggish performance will make you sorry you ever heard of a Windows upgrade.

Memory is also an issue. Microsoft claims that Windows 95/98 will run with 4 megabytes of RAM, but I wouldn't wish that on my worst enemy—performance would be at a crawl, because the system would have to rely so heavily on its swap file (explained in last night's session). In my opinion, 16 megabytes is the absolute minimum you need to survive with Windows 95/98. You should also have a CD-ROM drive, because Windows 95/98 comes on a CD-ROM.

 **NOTE** You can order a disk version of Windows 95/98 by mail, so the CD-ROM drive is not an absolute requirement; however, you will find that most new programs you buy in stores come on CD-ROM, so you will soon wish you had a CD-ROM drive.

## Windows 3.0 or 3.1

If you are using Windows 3.*x* (that is, 3.0 or 3.1 or 3.11; see the explanation later in this section), your *operating system* is actually DOS, which I get into momentarily; your *operating environment* is Windows. What's the difference? Your operating system starts the computer and keeps it running. That's DOS's job; Windows 3.*x* just provides an easy-to-use interface. (In contrast, Windows 95/98 handles both functions together.) Figure 2.2 shows a typical Windows 3.1 screen.

If you are not planning to make your computer into at least a 486 with 16 megabytes of RAM, you should probably stick with one of the versions of Windows 3.*x*. Windows 3.*x* runs fairly speedily on 386 and 486 computers.

What are those version numbers all about? Here's a quickie explanation:

✪ **Windows 3.0**. The oldest viable version. With this version you can run most Windows 3.*x* software, but somewhat less efficiently than with Windows 3.1. If you have this version, consider upgrading to Windows 3.1.

✪ **Windows 3.1**. This version will serve you well. It is the most recent major version.

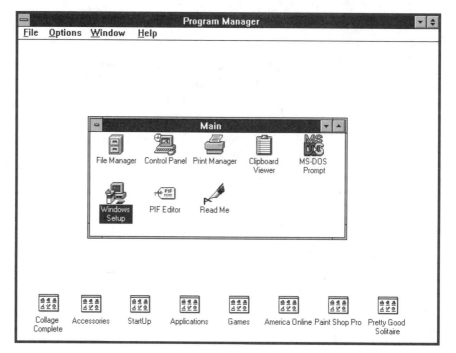

**Figure 2.2**

Windows 3.1 is a good choice for an old system because it requires less system resources to run.

O   **Windows 3.11**. This was an incremental upgrade to Windows 3.1 that added some networking extras plus a few other minor features. It's not worth upgrading from 3.1 to 3.11 unless you can't upgrade to Windows 95/98 for some reason and peer-to-peer networking is extremely important to you.

**NOTE** *Peer-to-peer networking* is where you hook up two computers with a simple cable instead of having to buy a network card and network operating system.

## DOS

DOS is the other piece of a system that runs Windows 3.*x*. It runs beneath and supports Windows 3.*x*, and when you exit from Windows, you can type DOS commands at a prompt. (You learned last night that you can find out your DOS version number by typing **VER** at the DOS prompt.)

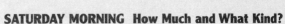

---

### DIFFERENCES IN DOS 6.x VERSIONS

The differences in MS-DOS versions 6.0, 6.2, 6.21, and 6.22 are very minor, and they center on disk compression. There was no MS-DOS 6.1. (IBM came out with PC-DOS 6.1, which confuses things somewhat.)

MS-DOS 6.0 and 6.2 are practically identical except that 6.2 comes with DoubleSpace. Recall from last night's session that DriveSpace or DoubleSpace are DOS utilities that compress your hard disk so it will hold more data. However, the company that made Stacker, a competing disk compression program, sued Microsoft, claiming that Microsoft had stolen the compression algorithm. Following a big court case centering around whether a mathematical formula could be copyrighted, Microsoft had to pay damages to Stacker's manufacturer and remove DoubleSpace from DOS. Version 6.21 is the same as version 6.2 without DoubleSpace; it's virtually identical to DOS 6.0. Microsoft a few months later developed its own version of disk compression and put it back into DOS as DriveSpace in Version 6.22.

---

If you are going to stick with DOS and Windows 3.1, you should upgrade to the latest version of DOS (it costs less than $50) if you have a DOS version of 5.0 or less.

DOS 6.0 and above comes with some handy utilities that can help you manage your system; I told you about some of these in last night's session. They include ScanDisk, DEFRAG, and DriveSpace. (See the sidebar above for the skinny on DriveSpace and DOS 6.x.) These aren't absolutely essential, but they're nice.

## What to Shop For

You can buy Windows 98 at almost any mail order or retail store. It comes on a CD-ROM, but you can sometimes find a floppy disk version for sale through mail order. You can also buy the CD version and then contact Microsoft with your new serial number to request floppy disks.

Windows 95 is harder to find, since it has been replaced by Windows 98. But unless you happen to find a great deal on a copy of 95, there is no real reason to want it instead of Windows 98. Windows 98 is equal to it or better in every way.

If you are buying Windows 3.x, you may have to shop a bit, but you should be able to find it by mail order. The version for sale will probably be 3.11, but either 3.1 or 3.11 will do.

**TIP** You may be able to pick up a copy of Windows 3.1 or 3.11 very cheaply from an online auction site; see this afternoon's session for more information. You might also be able to find a recent version of DOS (6.0 and above).

When you upgrade your DOS version, you upgrade to the most recent version available, no matter what version you currently have. (That's because the most recent one is the only one you can find in stores.) At this writing, it's DOS 6.22. Microsoft has stopped releasing new versions of DOS, so 6.22 will probably continue to be the latest version for the foreseeable future.

# Hardware Limitations

I have already told you about hardware limitations for Windows 95/98: Regardless of what the box says, you will not be happy with this product with less than a 486 and 16 megabytes of RAM.

Windows 3.0 will run on any computer made in the last 10 years (that is, an XT or higher). Windows 3.1 will run on a 286 or better with 1 megabyte of RAM, but you won't be happy with Windows 3.1 unless you have at least a 386 and 4 megabytes of RAM. (You'll be even happier with more, of course.)

DOS, for all practical purposes, has no hardware limitations. It is designed to run on virtually every IBM-compatible PC ever made. (An exception might be a really old computer with no hard disk, but if you had such an antique, you wouldn't be upgrading it; you'd be scrapping it and buying a new computer!)

# My Recommendation

If you are going to invest enough in your computer to upgrade it, you might as well have the best operating system for your hardware. If you are upgrading to a level that will support Windows 98, buy that. If not, at least buy Windows 3.11 and DOS 6.22.

# Improving Your Processor

If you have determined that your processor is a bottleneck (see the Friday Evening session), the next step is to figure out what kind of processor improvement your system will accept.

## Understanding the Processor-Motherboard Connection

The motherboard and the processor are integrally connected. The processor provides the raw brainpower; the motherboard supplies the power and circuitry to distribute the processor's brainpower to all the other parts of the system.

Because these two components work as a team, you must select one with the other in mind. Most motherboards work with only a short list of processors. That means if you want to get a different processor, you must often get a new motherboard as well. Keep this in mind for later, when upgrading motherboards is discussed.

## Examining Your Current Processor

Take a moment now and locate your current processor on your motherboard. Depending on the age of your system and the type of processor it has, your processor might also have a cooling device.

✪ The processor may appear as a big square chip (the biggest chip) on the motherboard and probably has writing on it that indicates its type (such as Intel 486DX). This type of processor is common on 486 and older systems.

- The processor may be hidden under a heat sink, which is basically a grid of black spikes like porcupine quills. (The heat sink helps keep the processor cool.) Such heat sinks are common on newer 486 and older Pentium systems.

- The processor may be hidden under a cooling fan. This small round fan (probably no more than two inches in diameter) sits flat on top of a square chip. The fan does an even better job than a heat sink of keeping the processor cool. You'll find this arrangement mostly on newer systems.

(If your processor is a big rectangular plastic cartridge with a fan strapped to its side, it's a Pentium II. If that's the case, you can skip the rest of this section. You do not need to upgrade your processor. You already have a really good one.)

If you have a processor with no heat sink or cooling fan, you have the best view of the writing on the chip. You can probably read the processor type on the chip, and you can also see how the processor is fastened to the motherboard.

- **Permanently attached**. This method is common on old 286 and 386 computers. You can clearly see that the processor is soldered down. It has little splayed-out "legs" on all sides that fasten into the motherboard. Such systems are not worth upgrading.

- **Low-insertion force (LIF) socket**. This method is common on 486 computers and some newer 386 models. The processor looks like it is just sitting on the motherboard, but in fact it has little pins on its bottom that are wedged tightly into corresponding little holes. You can pry the processor out with a special tool and replace it. It may have loops of wire in each of the four corners, which are supposed to help you grab the processor and lift it out.

- **Zero-insertion force (ZIF) socket**. This method is common on newer 486 computers and all Pentiums and Pentium-equivalent computers. The processor appears to be sitting on a small platform (usually white) with a handle alongside it. You lift the handle, and the chip then lifts easily out of the socket. Figure 2.3 shows a processor in a ZIF socket.

**Figure 2.3**

In a ZIF socket, you can just lift the handle and lift out the processor.

**NOTE** By the way, the type of socket shown in Figure 2.3 is called Socket 7. The Pentium II cartridges fit into a socket called Socket 1. A motherboard has one or the other, but not both, so you can't use a Pentium chip in a Pentium II motherboard, or vice versa.

If you want a better processor in your computer, you can either replace the processor you have with a better one or get an upgrade processor. *Replacement processors* are normal processors, just like the ones that people who build new computers buy. *Upgrade processors* are special processors that are designed to increase the capabilities of existing computers. There is no single answer as to which is best—it all depends on what your existing system can accept and what bargains you are able to find.

## Replacement Processors

Replacement processors are ordinary processors, just like the ones that you would buy if you were assembling computers from scratch. To be able to use one of these, your current motherboard must be able to accept a better processor than the one it currently has. (For example, perhaps your motherboard supports up to a 200MHz Pentium and yours is 120MHz.)

On 286 and 386 systems, replacement processors are not worth it. They usually are not even an option. That's because the processor is probably soldered permanently into place. And even if the processor is not soldered down, the motherboard is probably designed to accept only the one particular processor that it already has.

Starting with the 486 line, you can find motherboards that accept a range of processor speeds and brands. For example, one of my clients has a system that accepts any of the following processors:

| Cyrix | AMD | Intel |
|---|---|---|
| 486DX2 (66 to 80MHz) | 486DX (33 to 40MHz) | 486SX (16 to 50MHz) |
| 486DX4 (100MHz) | 486DX2 (50 to 80MHz) | 486DX (20 to 50MHz) |
| 5x86 (100 to 120MHz) | 486DX4 (100MHz) | 486DX2 (50 to 66MHz) |
| | 486SX (33 to 40MHz) | 486DX4 (75 to 100MHz) |
| | 486SX2 (50 to 66MHz) | 486DX2 OverDrive (66MHz) |
| | AM5x86 (133MHz) | 486DX4 OverDrive (100MHz) |
| | | Pentium 63 OverDrive (63MHz) |
| | | Pentium 83 OverDrive (83MHz) |

If you have this type of system and you have one of the lower-speed processors installed now, you can upgrade the system with a higher-speed processor.

**TIP**

■■■■■■■■■■■■■■■■■■■■■■■■■■■■■■■■■■■■■■■■■■■■

Upgrading a slow 486 to a fast 486 with a replacement processor would not be my first choice for that machine. Upgrade processors (discussed in the next section) are available for less than $100 that will take such a machine almost up to the Pentium level. I would replace a slow 486 chip with a fast one only if I got a phenomenally good deal on the newer chip (like $25 or less). Such bargains can sometimes be found in online auctions, which you'll learn about this afternoon.

■■■■■■■■■■■■■■■■■■■■■■■■■■■■■■■■■■■■■■■■■■■■

When choosing a replacement chip, you must also pay attention to the voltage. Processor chips are either 3 or 5 volts. You must either buy the same voltage chip as the old one, buy a separate voltage regulator adapter, or have a motherboard that can accept either 3 or 5 volt processors. (Some motherboards require different jumper or switch settings to enable the different voltages.)

## 486s and Clock Speeds

Many 486 motherboards can handle such a large range of processors because of clock-doubling (or quadrupling) technology. These motherboards can handle standard, doubled (DX2), or quadrupled (DX4) versions of the same chip.

*Clock-doubling* doesn't refer to the clock inside the computer that keeps the actual time of day; rather, it refers to the metronome-like clock that tells the processor how fast to operate. The computer processes a certain number of bits of data (for example, 32 on a 32-bit system) with each tick of the clock. There are millions of ticks per second, but the ticks are at very precise intervals. DX2 or DX4 processors start with the same 486 chip, but they speed up the ticking of that clock by two or four times.

Pentium systems and above do not have doubled or quadrupled clock speeds.

The documentation that came with your computer should tell you which chips and speeds your motherboard accepts. If you don't have the documentation, you have three options:

- Go with an upgrade processor instead (see the next section in this chapter, "Upgrade Processors").
- Search for information on the Internet (as described in the following sidebar).
- Remove the processor from the motherboard (explained in the Sunday Morning session) to see whether any writing on the motherboard indicates what processors it can take, as shown in Figure 2.4.

# Upgrade Processors

Most systems can't take a replacement processor because the motherboard is already "maxed out" with the most powerful processor it can accept. Are you stuck, then? Not at all.

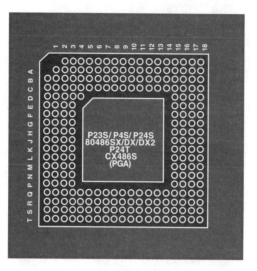

**Figure 2.4**

Some motherboards list the replacement processors they will accept in the space under the processor socket.

---

### GETTING INFORMATION ABOUT OLD MOTHERBOARDS

Suppose you have a motherboard with no documentation. Now what? You'll need to do some detective work if you want to keep it, and the best way is to use the Internet. (If you don't have a modem, you can try to find the manufacturer's phone number and call the company for a replacement manual, but the Internet method is basically free, so use that first if you can. Your local library may offer free access to the Internet—see if you can sign up for a session there.)

First, examine the motherboard carefully, looking at all of the writing. Try to find a brand name and a model number. If you find several strings of characters and are not sure which is the model number, write them all down.

Now use an Internet search engine (such as http://www.lycos.com) to search for the manufacturer name. A good resource listing is available at http://www.motherboards.org. You are looking for the manufacturer's home page, or, alternatively, an archive that lists motherboard information. If you can find a site that talks about that motherboard, sometimes you can find information about jumper settings, what kinds of processors it can use, and so on.

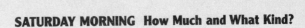
*Upgrade processors* are designed to improve existing systems. They trick the motherboard into thinking that they are a compatible kind of processor, when in fact they perform much better than any of the processors the motherboard has been built to accept.

With an upgrade processor, you can jump the system's performance quite a bit. Some upgrade processors, for example, can make a 486 perform almost as well as a Pentium, and some can make slow Pentiums into much faster Pentiums.

Two kinds of upgrade processors are available: processors that go into an OverDrive socket on the motherboard (a second processor socket that some motherboards have) and processors that fit into the original processor's socket. Therefore, in order to use an upgrade processor, at least *one* of the following conditions must be true:

- ✿ Your current processor is removable (ZIF or LIF socket).
- ✿ Your motherboard has an OverDrive socket, and you are able to locate an upgrade chip that will work in it.

## Upgrading a Removable Processor

If your current processor is removable, you have many choices for buying upgrade processors. Many good brands and types are available from companies like Intel, Cyrix, AMD, and Evergreen. You'll learn how to shop for them this afternoon.

For now, though, you need to know whether your processor socket has three or four rings of holes so that you can buy the correct kind of processor.

- ✿ **Socket 6**. Three rings of holes (168 or 169 in total): This socket is the smallest, oldest kind. You may not be able to find an upgrade processor for this motherboard. Intel no longer makes one, and other companies are phasing out theirs too. It is a 5-volt socket.
- ✿ **Socket 7**. Four rings of holes (237, 238, or 235 in total): This socket is the standard 486 and Pentium size. Its voltage varies depending on the number of pins: 238 holes means 5 volts, 237 means either 3 or 5 volts, and 235 means 3 volts.

### ALL ABOUT OVERDRIVE SOCKETS

The first upgrade processors were Intel OverDrive chips for 486 computers. Intel encouraged motherboard manufacturers to make "upgradable" motherboards including a special OverDrive socket that could accept user-installable OverDrive chips. The OverDrive sockets looked a lot like regular processor sockets, but they had a different number of holes so nobody assembling a PC would get them confused. If your motherboard had an OverDrive socket, you could buy an Intel OverDrive chip to put into it.

However, competitors such as Cyrix and Evergreen eventually began releasing their own upgrade chips. These companies' chips not only worked in other PC models (such as older 286 and 386 machines) but also could be placed directly in the original processor socket. These rival upgrade chips could be used in a motherboard that didn't have an OverDrive socket. More people began buying these non-Intel upgrade chips, not only because they were cheaper than Intel's but also because they worked in more systems.

In response to the competition, Intel changed its OverDrive processors so they too could work directly in the original processor socket, and if you buy an OverDrive processor from Intel today, that's how it will work. Motherboards are no longer made with OverDrive sockets, because the sockets are no longer needed.

Here's an easy way to tell whether you have a socket 7 (230+ hole) capable machine. If you can see a ring of extra holes around the existing processor, as shown back in Figure 2.3, you definitely have socket 7.

Most processor upgrades work with both 3- and 5-volt systems, so you don't have to use that as a buying criterion. For now, just be aware of the voltage issue, which you'll learn about later in the section that describes how to do the actual upgrading.

# Upgrading a Nonremovable Processor

If your system requires an upgrade processor that fits in an OverDrive socket, you probably have a 386 system. (Almost all 486s and above have removable processors.) You need to be extremely careful to find a processor that exactly matches the existing motherboard and processor speed.

The really bad news is that Intel and most of the other upgrade manufacturers are no longer making upgrade chips for 386 computers. Your best bet is either to find a used chip or to get a whole new motherboard.

# Processor Upgrading Advice for Specific Models

Now that you know something about processors in general, it's time to look at your specific situation.

## Upgrades for 386 Computers

As I mentioned earlier, unless your budget is extremely tight, I don't recommend upgrading a 386 computer. It's just not worth the hassle.

If you are determined to upgrade, you have several options. Your only problem might be finding the upgrade chips you need for sale. Like the chips themselves, upgrades for 386s are no longer manufactured.

**NOTE**  Back when 386 computers were new, you could buy math coprocessors for them (a.k.a. 387 chips) that boosted their ability to perform math calculations. Almost all 386 motherboards have a math coprocessor socket for this upgrade. However, you will be hard-pressed to find a 387 chip for sale today, because you can upgrade the entire processor to a 486 (with a built-in coprocessor) for about the same cost as the old 387 chip. The coprocessor socket has three rings of holes; don't confuse it with a usable OverDrive socket, which has four rings of holes.

First of all, do you have a 386, a 386DX, or a 386SX? The tests you ran on your system last night should have determined this. (Type **MSD** at the DOS prompt to run the utility that tells you what processor you have.) A 386 and a 386DX are exactly the same thing; I'll refer to them as 386DX throughout the book for consistency.

If you have a 386DX system, you have a 32-bit chip and a 32-bit external data bus. What does that mean? Picture a busy highway that goes into a tunnel. Both the highway and the tunnel have 32 lanes, so even when traffic is at a maximum, no delays occur.

On a 386SX system, in contrast, you have a 32-bit chip and a 16-bit external data bus. This configuration is like having a tunnel with 32 lanes but only 16 lanes of highway leading to and from it. When traffic is light, you don't notice any difference, but if you run a program that taxes the system's abilities fully, traffic will have to slow down when it exits the tunnel, and the overall system performance will be slower.

If you have a 386SX system, don't bother upgrading it. Your processor probably isn't the bottleneck: The 16-bit external data bus is, and to upgrade that you must buy a new motherboard.

A 386DX system, however, could conceivably be worth salvaging with an upgrade chip, if you can find one and depending on the capacity of the other components. For example, if you have a 386DX with a big hard disk, 8 megabytes of memory, and a VGA monitor and video card, and you don't plan on using Windows 95/98, you may be able to wring another year of life out of the system with an upgrade chip. If, however, you have a 386DX with an overloaded small hard disk and not much memory, you may find it more economical in the long run to buy a whole new system.

Personally, I would never try to upgrade a 386 computer. I would save my money for a new system.

## Upgrades for 486 Computers

Upgrading a 486 to a 586 (basically, Pentium quality) can be a very good investment for the casual home user because, in general, 486 motherboards have enough RAM capacity and data bus speed to avoid further bottlenecks.

Depending on your motherboard (see the documentation), you may be able to use either a replacement or an upgrade processor. If your motherboard's documentation shows a range of processor speeds, you may be able to get a replacement processor. (These are typically very cheap, especially if you can get a used one that someone has taken out of a system to make way for an

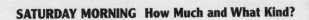

upgrade processor.) However, unless cost is your overriding factor, you may be happier with an upgrade chip that turns your 486 into a Pentium or 586, because the performance gain will be greater.

**TIP**

The speed in MHz is not the only measure of a processor; the processor type is the other half of it. Generally, Pentiums and 586s (generic Pentiums) are better performers than 486s, even if the speed rating is lower. For example, a 75MHz Pentium will outperform a 100MHz 486.

Intel and Evergreen are leading manufacturers of 486-to-586 (or Pentium) processor upgrades; Kingston and Cyrix are two other well-respected vendors. Both Cyrix and AMD have a 486 upgrade called 5x86; it isn't a true 586 (Pentium) processor, but the 5x86 offers improvements on normal 486 processors.

In general, Intel's OverDrive upgrades are fussier about what systems they'll run on than the competitors' upgrades. Intel has lots of different models, each designed for a different kind of original system. If you have Internet access, you can visit Intel's upgrade Web page, which walks you through the OverDrive selection process with a series of questions. It's at **http://www.intel.com/overdrive/upgrade/index.htm**.

## Upgrades for Pentium or 586 Computers

Pentium is a brand name that refers to an Intel brand processor; the other brands (such as AMD or Cyrix) call their versions 586. They're all approximately the same level of performance.

**CAUTION**

In general, any chip that says it is a 586 is Pentium class. However, any non-Intel chip that begins with 5x, such as 5x86, is not really Pentium class. These are basically 486-class processors with some improvements that make them work better than the average 486. AMD and Cyrix are two makers of these faux-586 models. They are better than a 486, but do not mistake them for real 586s.

If you have a Pentium or 586 computer, why upgrade? There are two good reasons:

- To get MMX capabilities
- To improve overall speed, especially in Windows 95/98

*MMX* stands for multimedia extensions. This feature, which is built into the processor, helps multimedia programs—especially 3-D graphics–intensive ones—run faster and better. All Pentium processors that you can buy now include this technology, but earlier Pentiums did not.

For MMX to help a program run better, that program must be written specifically to take advantage of MMX; in other words, MMX does not improve the performance of your existing programs. However, if you buy new programs that can use MMX, they will run very well on an MMX-capable computer.

MMX began turning up on Pentium computers that ran at 166MHz and higher in late 1996. Now just over two years later, you would have trouble finding a new computer without MMX. However, if you have an older system, for example, a 90MHz or 120MHz Pentium, you don't have this capability. An upgrade chip can provide it.

You might also want to upgrade your Pentium system to a higher speed just for speed's sake. You can buy an OverDrive chip (Intel's upgrade processor for Pentiums), for example, to boost a 90MHz Pentium to 180MHz.

## Pentium II and Its Competitors

As of this writing, Intel has stopped producing Pentium chips; it's making only Pentium II chips. Other chip manufacturers like AMD and Cyrix, however, are still making their Pentium-equivalent systems, so you can still buy that class of new computer if your budget says no to a Pentium II.

The Pentium Pro, which is no longer being made, was essentially a souped-up Pentium with no MMX. It required a special motherboard designed just for it. When Pentium II came out with MMX built in, the Pentium Pro went the way of the dinosaur.

Today's standard for new PCs is Pentium II. Pentium II is better and faster than the original Pentium. It has MMX capability built in, as well as a built-in cache for faster operations. The Pentium II chip comes in a large rectangular plastic casing that looks nothing like any previous-generation computer chip. It fits into a slot in the motherboard known as Slot 1. It requires a special Pentium II motherboard that has such a slot on it.

Meanwhile, Intel's competitors are producing chips that are supposedly just as good as Pentium IIs, but these chips fit into old-style Pentium slots (Socket 7). Nevertheless, you can't just plop them down in a regular Pentium motherboard and expect them to work, even if they will physically fit in the processor socket; as you have learned already in this chapter, motherboards are picky about what processors they will accept. These Pentium II equivalent processors must have motherboards with sockets designed to take advantage of them.

## What to Shop For

When shopping for a replacement or upgrade processor, the primary determining factor is your motherboard: What will it accept? Do you need an upgrade that fits into the coprocessor socket, or can you replace the processor chip that's already there? Read your computer's manual carefully and examine your motherboard.

The next shopping decision is how fast you want to go. You are limited, obviously, by your current setup, but you may have some leeway. For example, if you have a 40MHz 486 and your motherboard supports a 120MHz DX4 chip, you could buy that chip, if you could find one for sale, or you could go with a 486-to-586 upgrade chip or a genuine Intel OverDrive processor (both of which you can easily find).

Finally, you'll need to pick a brand. They are all basically alike; they either work or they don't, and if they don't, you can take them back for a refund. With other components, you must shop carefully for particular brand names to get quality, but with an upgrade processor, you will be happy with Cyrix, AMD, Intel, Kingston, or Evergreen, and probably a few other brands that I haven't named.

> ## PROCESSOR CHECKLIST
>
> **My current processor is (circle one):**
>
>     386    486    586/Pentium    686/Pentium II
>
> **My current processor speed is _____.**
>
> **My processor is (circle one):**
>
>     Removable    Nonremovable

# My Recommendation

Here's my (biased) opinion on processor upgrades. If you have a 286 or 386, donate it to charity. Don't waste your time upgrading it, unless you really can't afford anything better. If you have a 486, let the other components dictate your options. If you are happy with the monitor, hard disk, case, and so on, upgrading the processor (and probably adding some RAM too) can make sense.

If you have a Pentium, you are probably fine as-is with your processor. The only exceptions are if you want to play games that require MMX and can't, or if you are generally displeased with your system's overall processing speed. In either of those cases, consider a Pentium OverDrive chip with MMX capabilities from Intel or a comparable processor from another manufacturer.

# Adding Memory (RAM)

Lack of adequate memory is one of the most common reasons that a computer runs more slowly than it should, especially in Microsoft Windows. As I explained last night, when you don't have enough real memory in your computer, Windows tries to create fake memory out of sections of your hard disk to run the programs that you ask it to run. This fake memory is very slow and inefficient, and it's probably why your computer runs so slowly, especially if the slowness occurs after you have been using the computer for a while and you hear whirring sounds coming from your hard disk when the system slows down.

The most important part of memory shopping is making sure that you know what kind of memory your system needs before you make the purchase.

# Types of RAM

Several types of RAM are available, and you need to make sure you get the right kind.

Single inline memory modules (SIMMs) are found in 486 and some Pentium systems. SIMMs come in 72-pin or 30-pin sizes, as shown in Figure 2.5. The pins are the little metal strips along the bottom. You will know right away if you try to put a SIMM with the wrong number of pins into a memory bank on your motherboard—it won't fit. The SIMMs are different lengths.

The 72-pin size is the most common, and it comes in three varieties:

- **True parity memory**. This memory is for systems that require parity memory. Many older 486 systems require true parity memory. Look for a *36* in the specifications for parity memory, as in 16×36-60ns.

- **Fast page mode (FPM) memory**. FPM is generic memory. It works in just about any system that requires "non-parity" memory and doesn't mention anything about EDO. Look for a *32* in the specifications for this, as in 16x32-60ns.

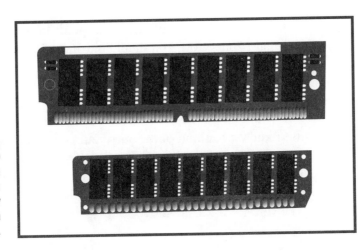

**Figure 2.5**

SIMMs are the most common memory type; they come in 72-pin and 30-pin models.

✪ **Extended data out (EDO) memory**. EDO is a newer, better kind of non-parity memory. Many of the Pentium-class systems use it.

The second type of SIMM is the 30-pin SIMM. This type of memory is older, and you may not find it in high denominations. A recent check at my favorite memory vendor's Web site showed that only 4-megabyte pieces were in stock. Thirty-pin SIMMs are available in only one variety: true parity.

Last on the list are 168-pin dual inline memory modules (DIMMs). One variety called *S-DRAM DIMM* is the latest rage in new systems because it is faster and better than SIMM. You'll find DIMM slots in newer Pentium-class motherboards and in all Pentium II systems. (Some motherboards support both SIMM and DIMM memory, so you can reuse memory from an older system if you have it. A nice touch!) If your motherboard happens to support S-DRAM DIMMs, great.

**CAUTION** ◆◆◆◆◆◆◆◆◆◆◆◆◆◆◆◆◆◆◆◆◆◆◆◆◆◆◆◆◆◆◆◆◆◆◆◆◆◆◆◆◆◆
Memory for Apple computers also comes in the form of 168-pin DIMMs. Make sure you are buying the type for IBM-compatible PCs if you are buying S-DRAM DIMMs.
◆◆◆◆◆◆◆◆◆◆◆◆◆◆◆◆◆◆◆◆◆◆◆◆◆◆◆◆◆◆◆◆◆◆◆◆◆◆◆◆◆◆

RAM also comes in different speeds, measured in nanoseconds (ns). A lower number is faster, and faster is better. Most RAM you buy today is 60ns, but you can sometimes buy 70ns or even 80ns at a discount. You must buy RAM that is at least as fast as your system requires. A faster speed won't help, but it won't hurt either. So, for example, if your system needs 70ns RAM, you could use 70ns or 60ns equally well—but if it needs 60ns, it won't work with anything slower. You should not mix speeds in the same computer; if you already have 70ns RAM, you should buy more 70ns RAM to go with it, or replace all the RAM.

## Determining the Type of RAM You Need

If you don't know what kind of memory your computer uses, that's actually a good thing—it means you're not a total computer geek, and you have better things to do than remember such trivia. Besides, you can always look it up if you have to.

There are lots of ways to figure out what kind of RAM your computer needs. Some ways are easier than others.

## Look on the Motherboard

You'll be adding RAM into empty memory banks on your motherboard—if you have any empty banks, that is. If you don't have any empty banks, you will have to take out some of the RAM that's already there and replace it with RAM of a higher denomination. For example, suppose you have four banks, and each one already has a 4-megabyte SIMM in it. If you want more memory, you must remove at least two of the SIMMs (they usually work in pairs) and replace them with 8- or 16-megabyte SIMMs. (This advice assumes that your motherboard can take the higher denomination SIMMs; I address that issue momentarily.)

Therefore, before you buy RAM, take a look at your motherboard and find out whether you have any open memory banks. If so, which ones are they and what size? Look on the motherboard for a small circuit board propped up at a 45-degree or 90-degree angle to the motherboard. You might find one, two, four, or eight of these small boards, all lined up in a row. You should also see at least four slots for RAM—and with luck, some of them will be empty. Figure 2.6 shows a motherboard with four memory banks.

Many newer computers have a four-bank setup, as shown in Figure 2.6, or a four- or eight-bank setup plus a few DIMM slots for S-DRAM, but some 486 computers have a more complex setup. One computer I worked on recently had two 72-pin SIMM banks and four 30-pin SIMM banks. The theory, I believe, was to enable you to recycle your old 30-pin SIMMs. Because 30-pin SIMMs come in low denominations only, the computer contained four 30-pin slots so that you could get a decent amount of memory in it. Two of the slots looked like the ones in Figure 2.6 and there were four shorter slots lined up beside them.

Make a note of which banks are full and which are empty. Also look for any writing on the chips on the SIMMs. Sometimes they contain decipherable code; sometimes not. If you're lucky, you'll see something that indicates the size (for example, 4MB for 4 megabytes) and speed (for example, 60ns).

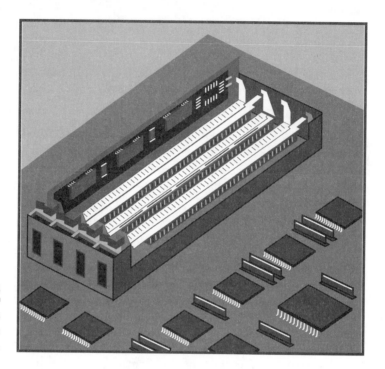

**Figure 2.6**

Here's what SIMMs look like on a motherboard.

**CAUTION**

You may see SIMM converters for sale; these are circuit boards that plug into SIMM slots. Each circuit board holds four or more SIMMs, so you can put more memory in each slot. That's the theory, anyway. In practice, these don't always work with every system, and they're only a good value if you have lots of extra low-denomination memory lying around. I don't recommend SIMM converters for beginning upgraders.

## Check the Documentation

Look in the manual that came with your computer. You should find a chart that shows what kind of RAM you already have and what kind you need. A warning, though: these charts are sometimes hard to decipher.

The chart in Figure 2.7, for example, is for the motherboard with two 72-pin SIMM slots and four 30-pin SIMM slots that I described in the preceding section. (The chart in Figure 2.7 is an abbreviated version; the real

chart went all the way up to 64MB.) Your motherboard's chart will likely be different from this one; I'm using this example only for chart-reading practice.

---

### DRAM Installation

DRAM Access Time: 80ns, page mode

DRAM Type:   256KB/1MB/4MB/16MB SIMM Module (30 pin)
         1MB/2MB/4MB/8MB/16MB/32MB SIMM Module (72 pin)

| Memory Size | Bank 2 (30 pin) | Bank 0/2 (72 pin) | Bank 1/3 (72 pin) |
|---|---|---|---|
| 8M | 1M x 4 | 4M x 1 | --- |
| 8M | 1M x 4 | --- | 4M x 1 |
| 8M | --- | 4M x 1 | 4M x 1 |
| 8M | --- | 8M x 1 | --- |
| 8M | --- | --- | 8M x 1 |
| 9M | 256K x 4 | 4M x 1 | 4M x 1 |
| 9M | 1M x 4 | 4M x 1 | 1M x 1 |
| 9M | 1M x 4 | 1M x 1 | 4M x 1 |
| 10M | 1M x 4 | 4M x 1 | 2M x 1 |
| 12M | 1M x 4 | 4M x 1 | 4M x 1 |
| 12M | 4M x 4 | --- | 8M x 1 |
| 12M | --- | 4M x 1 | 8M x 1 |
| 12M | --- | 8M x 1 | 4M x 1 |
| 16M | 4M x 4 | --- | --- |
| 16M | --- | 16M x 1 | --- |
| 16M | --- | --- | 16M x 1 |
| 17M | 256K x 4 | 16M x 1 | --- |
| 17M | 256K x 4 | --- | 16M x 1 |
| 17M | 4M x 4 | 1M x 1 | --- |
| 17M | 4M x 4 | --- | 1M x 1 |
| 18M | 256K x 4 | 1M x 1 | 16M x 1 |
| 18M | 256K x 4 | 16M x 1 | 1M x 1 |
| 19M | 256K x 4 | 16M x 1 | 2M x 1 |
| 20M | 1M x 4 | 16M x 1 | --- |
| 20M | 1M x 4 | --- | 16M x 1 |
| 20M | 4M x 4 | 4M x 1 | --- |
| 20M | 4M x 4 | --- | 4M x 1 |
| 21M | 256K x 4 | 4M x 1 | 16M x 1 |
| 21M | 256K x 4 | 16M x 1 | 4M x 1 |
| 24M | 1M x 4 | 4M x 1 | 16M x 1 |
| 24M | 1M x 4 | 16M x 1 | 4M x 1 |
| 32M | 4M x 4 | 16M x 1 | --- |
| 32M | 4M x 4 | --- | 16M x 1 |
| 32M | --- | 16M x 1 | 16M x 1 |
| 32M | --- | 32M x 1 | --- |
| 32M | --- | --- | 32M x 1 |

**Figure 2.7**

Excerpt from a memory configuration chart from a 486 computer manual.

Suppose I know that the system in Figure 2.7 has 8 megabytes of RAM: two SIMMs in long slots, and four empty shorter slots.

From Figure 2.7 I can see that the motherboard has six slots altogether. Each of the two 72-pin slots constitutes one individual bank, named 0/2 and 1/3, respectively. (See the *x1* next to each entry in the corresponding columns.) The four 30-pin slots form a single bank collectively. (See the *x4* next to each entry in that column.)

If I have SIMMs in both 72-pin slots, and I have 8 megabytes in total, I can conclude that each module is a 4-megabyte SIMM. Only one of the 8MB rows in the table (the third row) shows something in each of the 0/2 and 1/3 banks and nothing in Bank 2. That row lists 4MB x 1 in each of those two columns.

From the information at the top of the chart in Figure 2.7, I can also conclude that the RAM in the system is at least 80ns, which is what the system requires, and that it is "page mode," which is short for Fast Page Mode, or FPM.

Suppose I want to upgrade this PC to 16 megabytes of RAM. What are my options? Well, looking at the table in Figure 2.7, I can see three possible configurations for 16 megabytes: I can put a single 16MB SIMM in either of the two 72-pin banks (Bank 0/2 and Bank 1/3, respectively, in Figure 2.7), or I can fill up Bank 2 (the four 30-pin SIMM slots) with four 4MB SIMMs. Either way, I can't reuse my existing 4MB SIMMs.

What if you bought a 16MB SIMM for one of the 72-pin banks and reused a 4MB SIMM in Bank 2 for a total of 20MB of RAM? According to the chart, the only possible configurations for 20MB are one 16MB 72-pin SIMM and four 1MB 30-pin SIMMs. For some reason, this particular motherboard won't let you have two different kinds of SIMMs in banks 0/2 and 1/3 unless Bank 2 is also full. Good thing you checked.

Well then, what if you put some SIMMs in Bank 2? Check out the 21M line on the chart. You could put 256KB SIMMs in Bank 2 and then use one of the old 4MB SIMMs in Bank 1/3 or 0/2 along with the new 16MB SIMM that you plan to buy. Look at the 24MB line, too: You could also put 1MB SIMMs in Bank 2 for a total of 24MB. Is this a good idea? Only if you happen to have old 30-pin SIMMs lying around already. You wouldn't want to buy them just for this purpose. If you need more memory than 16MB, just buy a second 16MB SIMM. As you can see on the 32MB line of the chart, you can have 16MB in both banks 0/2 and 1/3 for a total of 32.

If you were following this chart to make a purchase decision for this motherboard, you would buy one 16MB Fast Page Mode SIMM of at least 80ns.

Now look at another example: a Pentium-class system with two 72-pin SIMM banks and two 168-pin DIMM banks. The information it came with looks much simpler than on the 486 system. However, in some ways it is harder to understand. Figure 2.8 shows it in its entirety.

From this you can tell that the system has a great deal of flexibility; it can take either FPM or EDO SIMMs and either S-DRAM or EDO DIMMs. It does not specify what speed of RAM to use, so assume 60ns (the current standard). You also know that the system can't handle two DIMMs and four SIMMs at the same time.

Suppose you look on your motherboard and you see two SIMMs. You know that your computer has 8MB of RAM in total, so you can deduce that they are 4MB SIMMs. You can add two more SIMMs (always in identical pairs), or you can add one DIMM or two DIMMs, or you can add two SIMMs and one DIMM. The only thing you can't do is add two DIMMs plus two more SIMMs. If you want a system with 32MB in total, and you want to be able to reuse your existing SIMMs, you could add one 16MB DIMM and two 4MB SIMMs.

**Figure 2.8**

Some computer manuals may not have a chart; there may be only skimpy information like this.

```
                          Memory:

Up to 256MB in two banks using four SIMMs of 8, 16, 32, or
64 with support for FPM and EDO DRAM and two DIMMs of 8,
16, 32, or 64MB with support for S-DRAM and EDO DRAM.

SIMM 3,4 and DIMM1 cannot be used at the same time.

When using S-DRAM, JP6 must be set to 3.3V position (A).
```

## Gold or Tin?

While the computer's cover is off, take a look at the SIMMs you have already. Are the little metal tabs (the pins) silver colored or gold colored? The silver-colored ones are tin; the gold-colored ones are gold plated.

Why does this metal matter? It depends on who you ask. Some computer experts will tell you that it doesn't matter. But there are apocryphal stories floating around among computer folk about dissimilar metals causing corrosion. If you put tin-pinned RAM in gold-lined SIMM banks, the dissimilar metals in time will corrode and cause problems—so it is said. Ditto for putting gold-pinned RAM in a tin bank.

In my opinion you really don't have to worry. Your computer will be in the junkyard many years before the corrosion, if any, becomes severe enough to cause a problem. However, if you're a perfectionist, check your computer's existing RAM and try to buy RAM with the same color connectors (assuming that the original RAM in the system matches the metal in the motherboard's banks).

## My Recommendation

Check your system's documentation, now that you understand how to read the chart, and determine what type of RAM you need to buy. Then fill out the following checklist.

If you can afford it, you will be happiest with at least 16MB for a DOS/Windows 3.1 system or 32MB for a Windows 95/98 system. My home system has 64MB.

RAM is a "generic" component. It either works or it doesn't. If it doesn't work, you send it back for a refund. Therefore, when I buy RAM, price is my primary consideration. I don't bother with name-brand RAM.

## Replacing the Motherboard

Replacing the motherboard is a big, hairy job, and not one to be lightly undertaken. It's also rather expensive, because the motherboard is one of the priciest parts of your computer, next to the processor and monitor. If the

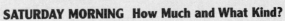
## RAM CHECKLIST

**I need at least (circle one):**

80ns / 70ns / 60ns

**My system has these memory banks:**

| Bank # | Type | # of slots in the bank | Empty? |
|---|---|---|---|
| _____ | _____ | _____ | Yes/No |
| _____ | _____ | _____ | Yes/No |
| _____ | _____ | _____ | Yes/No |
| _____ | _____ | _____ | Yes/No |

**Here is what I plan to buy:**

**Quantity:** _____

**Type (circle one):**

non-parity (FPM) / EDO / True Parity / S-DRAM

**Size:**

72-pin SIMM / 30-pin SIMM / 168-pin DIMM

**Denomination:**

4MB / 8MB / 16MB / 32MB / 64MB / 128MB

**Connector metal:**

tin / gold / doesn't matter

other components (hard disk, monitor, video card, and so on) are not top performers, replacing the entire computer might make more sense than attempting a motherboard transplant.

If you still want to give it a try, you need to consider the following information when looking for a motherboard.

## Motherboard Size and Orientation

Motherboards come in different sizes, and not all sizes fit into all cases. If you are keeping your current case, the size and form factor of the replacement should be your first concern.

The ads usually give the measurement for the board (for example, 8.66" × 13.25") and describe the size as either ATX or AT form factor. *Form factor* refers to whether the expansion slots point toward the long or narrow edge of the motherboard. Figure 2.9 illustrates the difference.

**NOTE**   A smaller version of the AT form factor, called *Baby AT,* is the same shape as an AT, but smaller. If your present computer has a small case, you may need this kind rather than a full-size AT. Luckily, most AT motherboards made these days are Baby AT size, so they will fit in any case.

A computer case is designed to hold either an AT or ATX motherboard. A quick look at your current motherboard can tell you which your system is. (Just compare it to one of the pictures in Figure 2.9.) AT is the older specification. In an AT motherboard, the expansion slots point toward the narrow

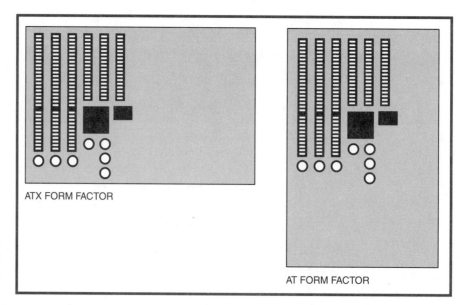

**Figure 2.9**

AT versus ATX motherboards

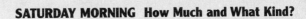
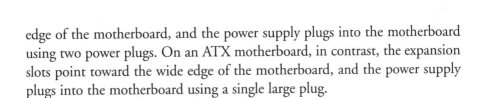

edge of the motherboard, and the power supply plugs into the motherboard using two power plugs. On an ATX motherboard, in contrast, the expansion slots point toward the wide edge of the motherboard, and the power supply plugs into the motherboard using a single large plug.

The power supply built into your current case contains the right kind of plug to plug into its current motherboard. That's another reason why you must make sure to get the right form factor. Even if you manage to wedge an ATX motherboard into an AT case, for example, you could not hook up the power supply to it because the plug would be wrong.

If you have to buy a new case anyway, choose an ATX case and motherboard. On an ATX motherboard, the processor is located near the fan on the power supply, so it stays cooler. ATX motherboards also offer some special features that AT ones don't, such as Wake Up on Ring, which turns the computer on when the modem's telephone rings so it can answer it.

## What Processors Will It Support?

If you're buying a new motherboard, it should support the very latest processors. This very competitive market offers lots of choices:

- **Intel Pentium with MMX**. This processor is no longer cutting edge, even though it is less than two years old at this writing. Consequently, you can find it at bargain prices. The Intel Pentium with MMX is a perfectly good processor that will serve most people very well. It comes in speeds ranging from 166 to 233MHz.

- **Intel Pentium Pro**. The Pentium Pro was the original successor to the Pentium. It fits in a different size socket from the one the regular Pentium uses, so you need a new motherboard if you want a Pentium Pro. It is optimized for 32-bit operating systems like Windows NT; if you are an NT user, the Pro will boost your system's performance. However, this chip has been phased out and is no longer being produced because the Pentium II (see the following entry) is better. The Pentium Pro comes in speeds from 166MHz to 200MHz.

- **Intel Pentium II**. This processor is an improved Pentium with both MMX capability and features from the Pentium Pro. It is a good choice for Windows 95/98 and Windows NT power users. It also has a different kind of socket from the regular Pentium and requires a special motherboard. The Pentium II is expected to be around for a while, so it is a good investment if you have to buy a new motherboard anyway. It comes in speeds ranging from 233MHz to 400MHz, with 450MHz due out soon. Intel has also recently introduced variations on it called Celeron (cheaper than a regular Pentium II and not quite as good) and Xeon (more expensive than a regular Pentium II and better).

✿ **AMD K6 and K6-2.** The AMD K6-2 is the Advanced Micro Device processor that competes with the Pentium II. (Its earlier relative, the K6, is still available also.) It fits in a regular-size Socket 7, but your motherboard must support it. It includes MMX technology. The K6-2 has a built-in 3-D technology called 3DNow! that supposedly gives it an edge over a Pentium II.

✿ **Cyrix 6x86MX and M-II.** The 6x86MX is Cyrix's MMX technology processor; it competes with the Pentium MMX. It is usually a good choice for a high-speed, low-cost system. It includes MMX technology. The Cyrix M-II competes with a low-end Pentium II, but is cheaper, and works in a Socket 7 motherboard (like the AMD K6-2).

✿ **Digital Alpha 21164 and 21664PC.** This Digital product is an ultra-fast, rather high-cost chip that operates at speeds up to 600MHz. It's a good choice for high-end computers that run Windows NT, but top performance is available only with native Alpha versions of NT and applications. It comes in speeds from 366 to 600MHz. This processor is not a good choice for most users because of its questionable compatibility with ordinary software.

Many, but not all, motherboards support more than one type or brand of processor. For example, Pentium Pro and Pentium II motherboards use only those specific processors. You need to make your processor selection first and then choose from among the motherboards that support it.

## What Kind of Memory Does It Need?

The memory section earlier in this session covered the various kinds of memory available. If you are buying a new motherboard, you can choose the one that supports the type of memory you want to have. The best choices are:

- ✪ **Non-parity EDO SIMMs**. These 72-pin SIMMs are readily available and not too expensive. They offer improved performance over the older fast page mode SIMMs of the same type. Most motherboards support at least 128 megabytes through four banks that each will hold a 32-megabyte SIMM.

- ✪ **S-DRAM DIMMs**. This newer, faster kind of memory comes in a 168-pin package. The performance is great, but the cost per megabyte may be higher than it is for non-parity EDO SIMMs.

◆◆◆◆◆◆◆◆◆◆◆◆◆◆◆◆◆◆◆◆◆◆◆◆◆◆◆◆◆◆◆◆◆◆◆◆◆◆◆◆

There have been some recent compatibility issues with S-DRAM SIMMs. Some high-speed motherboards (supporting 350 and 400 MHz Pentium IIs) will not support every kind of S-DRAM, so it is best to check with the motherboard manufacturer to find out which brands and specs of S-DRAM they recommend.

◆◆◆◆◆◆◆◆◆◆◆◆◆◆◆◆◆◆◆◆◆◆◆◆◆◆◆◆◆◆◆◆◆◆◆◆◆◆◆◆

Many motherboards support both kinds of RAM, for extra flexibility. When shopping for a motherboard, you need to consider not only what kind of SIMMs it uses but also what its maximum RAM capacity is. For example, the first Pentium systems that used S-DRAM DIMMs (way back in 1997) could handle only 64MB of RAM. You may think that 64 megabytes sounds like more memory than you will ever need, but computing power expands exponentially every year; I remember when everyone thought that 20 megabytes was an obscenely large hard disk.

Some motherboards have more than one type of bank for memory, so you can reuse some of the memory from your existing system. For example, the board might have two slots for 72-pin SIMMs as well as four slots for S-DRAM DIMMs. Reusing some of your memory means you have to buy less of the new stuff.

■■■■■■■■■■■■■■■■■■■■■■■■■■■■■■■■■■■■■■■■■■■

Some memory vendors will give you a trade-in allowance on your old memory. It doesn't hurt to ask.

■■■■■■■■■■■■■■■■■■■■■■■■■■■■■■■■■■■■■■■■■■■

# Slots and Ports Supported

Nowadays, almost every motherboard supports the PCI local bus standard. The only question is how many PCI slots and how many ISA slots it has. If you want to reuse your old ISA devices (for example, your old sound card and modem), make sure the motherboard has enough slots for them. A new motherboard should also have an AGP slot to plug in an AGP video card. This is the fastest, best kind of video card on the market.

You should also have at least two EIDE interfaces. These are the connectors where you plug in your hard drives and other devices like IDE CD-ROM drives. Your motherboard should also support a PS/2 mouse port and an ECP/EPP parallel port. (ECP/EPP is a standard for parallel ports that makes for better communication with your parallel devices; *ECP* stands for extended capabilities port.)

Any new motherboard you buy should also support the Universal Serial Bus, or USB. USB is a new standard for connecting devices to computers that promises to be better and easier to use than the standard ways of connecting through parallel ports, serial ports, monitor ports, and so on. The only trouble is that there are very few USB devices on the market yet! A few scanners, keyboards, and mice will work with a USB port, but this technology hasn't really hit its peak yet. Still, it never hurts to plan for the future. Make sure the motherboard you buy supports USB connectors.

# Other Motherboard Features

You should also look for a motherboard that has at least a 256KB cache— 512KB is better. A *cache* improves CPU efficiency by storing recently used bits of data for quick reuse. On Pentium Pro and Pentium II motherboards, you will see the cache advertised as *on CPU.* This means that there is a 32K cache that is actually built into the CPU. Chips of Pentium quality and below do not have this.

A system may also have an L2 cache, which is also known as *a pipeline burst cache.* This is an external cache because it is not contained within the CPU chip. In the Pentium Pro and Pentium II, this cache is housed in the

cartridge that contains the CPU. In Pentium (and compatible) systems, the cache comes on a small circuit board that plugs into a slot on the motherboard. The most common kind of cache is *COAST,* which stands for Cache On A STick. (Odd name, isn't it?)

The bus speed is also important. The latest and best motherboards have a 100MHz bus, which is the "highway" that carries the data to and from the processor, as I explained earlier. Earlier systems had 66MHz or slower buses. If you are putting together a Pentium II or equivalent system that will run at 350MHz or higher, look for a motherboard with a 100MHz bus; stick to the older (and cheaper) 66MHz bus for slower systems.

Almost all motherboards sold today have a Plug and Play flash BIOS, but check the specifications to make sure. Plug and Play works with Windows 95/98 to automatically detect your hardware. A flash BIOS can be updated with special software when it becomes outdated; you don't have to change a chip on the motherboard to update it, as you do with nonflash BIOS.

## My Recommendation

You'll find a mind-boggling number of motherboards available, and most have about the same features. Here are some shopping tips:

❖ Don't go with the cheapest generic motherboard, but don't go for the most expensive, feature-laden model either. Try to balance price with the features that you really believe you'll use.

❖ Stick with a well-known manufacturer. (Not sure which are the well-known brands? Thumb through a magazine like the *Computer Shopper* and see which brands are consistently carried by the majority of motherboard vendors.)

❖ Make sure you choose a motherboard that is the correct size and orientation for your case, or you will be in for a rude surprise when you try to install it.

❖ A large cache is never a bad investment. Cache is one of the few motherboard features that actually improves system performance in a significant way.

---

**MOTHERBOARD SHOPPING CHECKLIST**

**Type of motherboard (circle one in each line):**

    **Pentium or Equivalent / Pentium II**

    **ATX / AT / Baby AT**

**Cache size desired (circle one):**

    **256KB / 512KB**

**The motherboard must support _____ megabytes of memory.**

**The memory must be (circle one):**

    **72-pin SIMMs / 168-pin S-DRAM DIMMs**

**Other features desired: _____**

---

# Cases and Power Supplies

Most of the time, you will not need to replace the case. It has no electronic parts to go bad. You might have a bad power supply to replace, but in my experience, the power supply usually outlasts the other major components.

The main reason to replace these components is to get more capability than you currently have. If your case does not have any free drive bays, you will not be able to add internal drives (such as a CD-ROM drive or a ZIP drive) to your system. You must either buy external models of these products or buy a new case.

**CAUTION**

Swapping cases is a big job, almost as big as replacing the motherboard. It's not easy, especially for beginners, and should not be undertaken lightly.

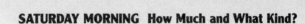
## Sizes and Types

Cases vary in their size and orientation. Desktop cases (the ones that sit flat on the desk) used to be the most popular type of case; they have the fewest drive bays. Tower cases are tall and thin and generally have lots of drive bays. Mini- and midtower cases are smaller versions of the tower case with fewer drive bays and are the most popular cases on new systems. Cases also vary in their construction—heavy steel cases are much more attractive than flimsier metal cases with sharp, unfinished edges.

Besides picking a case with room for all the goodies you want to put into it, probably the most important thing to consider is how difficult it is to get the case open. Some cases still use many screws, but others simply pop open by unclamping a couple of clamps. If possible, look at the available cases at a supplier and choose one that opens easily—and closes easily as well.

As I mentioned earlier, there are two sizes of motherboards: AT and ATX. You must match the case style with the motherboard type. You can't put an ATX motherboard into an AT-style case, for example. Typically, AT cases are cheaper (about half the cost of an ATX) but ATX cases offer better processor cooling, which becomes more important the faster the processor you use.

## Power Supply Capacity

The power supply must match the case and motherboard type (AT or ATX). And power supplies vary in their capacity, from 100 watts in really old systems to 250 or more watts in the newest and most powerful systems. You can buy replacement power supplies separately or buy a case with power supply already installed.

## My Recommendation

Don't replace the case unless you are completely out of drive bays. If that's your problem, buy a new case with a minimum of two more drive bays than you currently need.

If you buy a new case, buy one with the power supply preinstalled; you can throw away your old case and power supply or donate them to a charity that builds computers out of old parts.

If the power supply on your old computer is nonfunctional, buy a replacement power supply (of at least 200 watts) only if you are happy with your current case and it has at least one empty drive bay. If it doesn't, you might as well replace the entire case and power supply combo because the next bottleneck you encounter might be the case. It is typically cheaper to buy a case with a preinstalled power supply than to buy the case and power supply separately.

# Video Cards

The stores are full of great video cards, but most of them have far more capability than the average home user will ever need. Therefore, you don't need the most expensive and feature-laden video card to be happy. All you need is a good medium-priced card with a local bus (preferably AGP, if your motherboard supports it) connection to your motherboard.

## Evaluating a Video Card

You should gather the following information about any video cards you might buy:

- What kind of connector does it use to plug into the motherboard (ISA, VLB, PCI, or AGP)?
- How much RAM does it have?
- Does it use video RAM (VRAM), or the slower type, dynamic RAM (DRAM)?
- How many colors can it display?
- At what resolution can it display various numbers of colors?
- At what refresh rate can it display a given combination of colors and resolution?
- Does it have built-in support for 3-D features?
- If it's an AGP card, which specification does it support (1x or 2x)? The newest cards run faster, supporting the 2x specification.

The following sections examine some of these criteria individually and evaluate how critical they really are (or aren't).

## Making the Local Bus Video Connection

The most important reason to upgrade your video card is to take advantage of your system's local bus, if it has one. (I talked about this technology in last night's session.) If you have an AGP slot on your motherboard, a video card should be plugged into it—period. The same goes if you have no AGP but if you have a VLB or PCI slot. There's no excuse not to use a local bus slot for a video card if you have one available. If you use a video card that plugs into a regular ISA slot, you're wasting your system's capabilities. Not using an existing VLB or PCI slot is the number one good reason to buy a new video card.

So assuming that you're going to buy a video card to work with your system's local bus, the only question is whether it is a VLB or a PCI.

Look at your motherboard. You'll see a series of black plastic slots that circuit cards can plug into. Some of them may be short and have only one compartment; these are 8-bit slots. Others are longer and have two compartments; these are 16 bit. If those are the only two kinds of slots you see, you do not have a local bus motherboard.

If, however, you see another kind of slot, it's likely a local bus slot. If you see an extra slot (probably brown or a different color than black) at the end of one of the 16-bit slots, you're looking at a VLB slot. If you see a short white slot, shorter than the regular 8-bit slots, you're looking at a PCI slot. It doesn't matter which kind you have; both are good. You just have to make sure that you buy a video card that matches.

## Video RAM

Video cards have their own RAM because they do quite a bit of processing independently of the rest of your system. This RAM is usually VRAM (expensive, faster video performance) or DRAM (cheaper, ordinary performance). Let your budget be your guide. Other variants include EDO RAM (about 10 percent faster than DRAM), WRAM (a modified, cheaper form of VRAM), MDRAM (special DRAM designed for graphics), and SGRAM (expensive and very fast).

You also have a choice of how much RAM comes on the video card. You will see cards with everything from 1MB to 8MB of RAM on them. (Old ISA video cards may have as little as 256KB of RAM on them, but the stores don't carry them any more.)

The amount of video RAM has nothing to do with how well a video card works. It pertains only to the maximum colors and resolution your video card can display on your monitor.

The next few sections cover colors and resolution. Both features take up RAM; for example, a 2MB video card might be able to display 16.7 million colors at a 800×600 resolution, but only 256 colors in 1280×1024 resolution. A video card with 4MB would handle more colors at higher resolutions. Be aware, however, that higher resolutions make everything on the screen appear smaller. If you do not have at least a 17" monitor, you might find a resolution higher than 800×600 to be too tiny. If you don't think you will use a very high resolution for your display, it doesn't make sense to pay more for a video card with more RAM.

## Colors

The number of colors your video card can display at once at a given resolution is wholly dependent on the amount of RAM it has. As I mentioned in the preceding section, resolution combined with the number of colors, determines the amount of RAM required. Casual users may be satisfied with a 256-color display in Windows. Yet people who spend a lot of time in front of their PCs, especially people who do graphics editing, will be happier in the highest-color mode, true color (16.7 million distinct colors).

## Resolution

Resolution refers to the number of individual dots that make up the display. The higher the numbers, the smaller the dots and the sharper the image (and also the smaller the image).

## Refresh Rate

The monitor and the video card work as a team to give you a decent refresh rate, which is the rate at which the dots on the screen are updated with the latest information from your computer. (You can learn lots more about refresh rate in the "Monitors" section that follows this one.) Look for a video card that supports at least 70Hz to 72Hz. Higher is better.

## 3-D Features

Graphics-intensive programs like 3-D games (Doom, Quake, and so on) and graphic editing programs like Adobe Photoshop require a lot of graphics manipulation. Ordinarily, your computer's processor handles this work, but certain video cards (the 3-D ones) have special built-in 3-D accelerator features that take some of this load off of the processor. These features speed up your overall system performance for working (or playing) with programs that are heavy on the 3-D graphics.

Do you need 3-D capability? It's a nice feature to have, but I wouldn't go out and buy a new video card just to get it—unless, of course, you're a heavy-duty game player or graphic artist. If you have to buy a new video card anyway, go ahead and get a 3-D one if the price difference is not great.

# My Recommendation

Stick with name brands when shopping for video cards. Matrox, Diamond, STB, and Paradise are well-known brands; a sales clerk can point out the best-selling brands in a particular store. Do not buy a generic video card. Even if it comes with drivers for Windows, a future version of Windows may require newer drivers, and a fly-by-night generic video card manufacturer may be out of business by then.

---

**VIDEO CARD SHOPPING CHECKLIST**

**The type of connector I need is (circle one):**

   **VLB / PCI / AGP / ISA**

**I want ___ of memory on the video card, of this type:**

   **DRAM / VRAM / WRAM / Doesn't matter /**
**Other: _____**

**Other features desired:** _____

For a basic home system, 2 megabytes of video RAM (either VRAM or DRAM) should be fine. You don't need a fancy and expensive video card unless you have a huge monitor that you need to run with millions of colors.

Look for a video card that advertises its compatibility with Windows 3.1 or 95/98, whichever you use. If you enjoy 3-D games, or if the price is about the same either way, consider a card with 3-D features.

# Monitors

When shopping for a monitor, appearance is (almost) everything. You're going to be looking at that monitor for hours on end—how does the picture look to you? If the monitor has a great picture, everything else will probably be OK. The features that make up a good monitor all feed into this central goal: making a great picture.

## Size

Size refers to the diameter of the screen. Monitors come in sizes ranging from 14 inches (the standard no-frills model) to 21 inches and up. If you are not sure what size you have, it is probably 14 or 15 inches because that's what is sold with most computer systems. The size is measured diagonally, just like on a TV.

Large monitors make a lot of sense for people who sit at their computers all day and want to avoid eyestrain. Be warned, however, that a big monitor is not necessarily a sharp, crisp one, and you can get a worse headache from looking at a big fuzzy picture than a smaller, sharper one.

Large monitors are also good for people who need to run their video display at a very high resolution so they can fit lots of information on the screen at once. A very high resolution makes everything on the screen tiny and hard to read unless you have a big monitor.

When you see the size listed, you may see two different numbers. For example, you might see: 15-inch monitor (13.9-inch viewable). This differential is because, like TV manufacturers, monitor manufacturers try to wring every

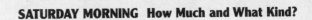

last centimeter out of the system for advertising purposes. Most monitors advertised as 15-inch actually do have a 15-inch piece of glass in them, but the plastic frame around the edges covers part of it, so that area is not viewable. When comparing two monitors of the same alleged size, you should also compare the viewable areas; one 15-inch monitor may have a 13.4-inch viewable area, while another may have a 14.1-inch viewable area. That's more than half an inch difference—which makes a big difference in real estate on the screen.

**TIP**  Lately there has been a push in the computer industry to convince users that 17 inches is the minimum bearable size for a monitor and that the new 19-inch models are the best balance of cost and size. If you want to splurge on a big monitor, go for it, but don't let all this propaganda convince you that your current 14-inch or 15-inch monitor is unusable.

## Maximum Resolution

A monitor's maximum resolution refers to the maximum number of separate dots it can display horizontally and vertically. Many small monitors (14 inches and 15 inches) can display up to 1024x768—that is, 1024 dots across and 768 dots down. If you combine the monitor with a video card that has enough memory to handle that resolution, you have a well-matched set. Larger monitors display much higher resolutions; the better quality the monitor, the higher its maximum resolution. Almost all monitors can display an infinite number of colors. The color limitation is a function of the video card and its memory.

## Monitor Technology

Your video display is made up of tiny dots. The *dot pitch* is the measurement of how close together they lie. A dot pitch of .28 is considered the minimum adequate amount. Lower dot pitch is better; I have a monitor with a .25 dot pitch that I use most of the time. You can find inexpensive monitors in large sizes, but they usually have higher dot pitch (like .31 or .32), making their pictures less crisp.

The most common kind of monitor is called *dot trio shadow mask.* With this technology, three colored guns (red, green, and blue) shine light through a grille of round holes to form the picture. These monitors deliver clean edges and sharp diagonals, which is important for showing text onscreen.

Another kind of monitor has an aperture grille rather than dots. (Trinitron monitors fall into this category.) These monitors use an array of stretched wires to create images. Their performance is measured in *stripe pitch,* rather than in dot pitch. Look for a stripe pitch of .25mm or less. These monitors have superior brightness and contrast, but their poorer horizontals make them less suited for displaying text.

**CAUTION** Monitors with an aperture grille have two faint horizontal lines running across them, at approximately one-third and two-thirds of the way down the screen. These never go away; they're caused by the wires that run across the back of the monitor glass. You get used to them eventually, but they are noticeable, especially on a white background, if you look for them. Some people decide not to get an aperture grille monitor because they find these lines so annoying.

A third kind of monitor is a *slot mask.* NEC invented this hybrid that combines the attributes of shadow mask and aperture grille. It uses a .25mm mask with elliptically shaped phosphors.

The final kind of monitor, LCD, is found mostly on laptop computers. Some manufacturers are beginning to use LCD in large desktop monitors with stunning results. The monitors can be nearly flat (no more unwieldy monitor casings!), and the displays are beautiful. Unfortunately, desktop monitors of this quality sell for more than $1,000, so they are out of the reach of most people.

## Interlacing and Refresh Rate

To understand these two factors, you need to know a bit about how monitors work. The screen is made up of tiny dots that contain particles that glow when a light hits them. A light gun (or a set of three guns: blue, red, and green) moves very quickly over the monitor, dot by dot, making each dot

glow with the appropriate color. Without being "refreshed" by the light gun, the particles in each dot fade quickly, so the light gun must refresh each particle hundreds of times per second. The rate at which the particles are refreshed with the light gun is the *refresh rate*. You have probably seen some monitors that are hard to look at because the display appears to flicker; the flicker is a result of a low refresh rate. Because each particle begins to lose its charge before the gun returns to it, the display appears to flash on and off. A higher refresh rate means that each particle is refreshed more frequently, so there is little or no noticeable flicker.

On some cheaper monitors, the light gun simply can't keep up; to compensate, they use a scheme called *interlacing* to keep the display readable. With interlacing, the light gun scans alternate horizontal lines, rather than every line, on each pass, so the gun can make twice the number of passes in a given amount of time. Because the horizontal lines are so close together, your eye can't pick up on the fact that every other line is not refreshed. However, your eye probably does notice a faint flicker or fuzz on an interlaced display.

**CAUTION** ◆◆◆◆◆◆◆◆◆◆◆◆◆◆◆◆◆◆◆◆◆◆◆◆◆◆◆◆◆◆◆◆◆◆◆◆◆◆◆◆
Non-interlaced monitors are the standard these days, and they are very affordable, so there is no reason why you should settle for an interlaced model.
◆◆◆◆◆◆◆◆◆◆◆◆◆◆◆◆◆◆◆◆◆◆◆◆◆◆◆◆◆◆◆◆◆◆◆◆◆◆◆◆

The best monitors are ones capable of noninterlaced operation and a high refresh rate. Look for a monitor with a maximum refresh rate of at least 85KHz. My monitor supports up to 120KHz, and I am very happy with it. (Of course, your video card has to support the same high resolution or you won't be able to take advantage of it.)

**TIP** ■■■■■■■■■■■■■■■■■■■■■■■■■■■■■■■■■■■■■■■■■
Even though your monitor supports a high refresh rate, your software might not automatically use the highest refresh rate. In Windows 95/98 you can choose the refresh rate from the Display Properties dialog box. (Right-click on the desktop and choose Properties.) Windows 3.1 uses different versions of the video driver for different refresh rates. Consult the documentation that came with your video card.
■■■■■■■■■■■■■■■■■■■■■■■■■■■■■■■■■■■■■■■■■

# Other Monitor Features

Some extras are nice to find in a monitor, but not necessary. Here's a rundown:

- **Speakers (a.k.a. multimedia)**. Some monitors have speakers built into them, eliminating the need for desktop speakers.

- **USB connectors**. Some of the very newest monitors have an extra cable that lets you hook up to the main USB port and relay it to a pair of unpowered USB ports on the front of the monitor. Such a monitor is an investment in the future, when presumably many devices will run on USB ports. If you've got a bunch of alternative devices on hand, you won't want to have to crawl around behind the main case every time you want to use one.

- **Calibration controls**. Some monitors provide built-in calibration setup programs that let you match printer output to screen image color precisely.

- **Other adjustment controls**. Look for easy-to-use monitor controls located on the front of the monitor.

- **Dual connectors**. Having both a standard VGA and a BNC connector enables you to attach two computers simultaneously to the same monitor and switch between them.

- **Clean back**. For corporate reception areas, it is nice to have a plain back on the monitor, with no unsightly cables sticking out. (On such monitors the cables come out the bottom instead.)

- **Cable length**. If you are going to put the computer case on the floor and your monitor on a table, a 6-foot cord works better than the shorter 3-foot cord that comes on some bargain monitors.

- **Footprint**. If space from back-to-front is an issue on your desk, look for a monitor with a shorter depth. In general, most monitors are the same depth as they are inches in diagonal display: a 17-inch monitor is about 17 inches deep.

# What to Shop For

The best way to shop for a monitor is to go to a store and look at lots of them. You don't have to buy from that store; just use the store display to

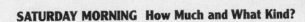

compare brands and models. Decide on one that looks good and then shop for it by mail order. The mail-order company has the same monitor, in the same box, for probably $50 less—plus you might not be charged sales tax if you're not in the same state as the company. (However, the shipping costs can more than counteract the mail-order discount on a large monitor.)

When shopping for a monitor, first decide on what size you want. I wouldn't buy a replacement monitor with less than a 17-inch display for my own use. Then, within that size, decide how much you are willing to spend, given that the more you spend, the better the picture will look. The lower the dot pitch and the more features the monitor has, the more it will cost.

Beware the generic bargain mail-order monitor! It's one thing to buy a cheap monitor in a store, after you've seen it perform, but quite another to buy a cheapie sight unseen—especially if it doesn't have a reputable brand name to back it up. Here's a quick way to learn the big brand names in monitors: Buy a *PC Magazine* (or some other computer magazine) and flip through the ads. If a monitor company has a full-page ad, it's a big-name company. My favorite brand is ViewSonic, but Mag Innovision, Princeton, CTX, and Sony are also very good.

### CHECKING CONVERGENCE

If you are looking at an off-brand or used monitor, you need to pay attention to additional issues—especially convergence. (With a high-quality, brand-name monitor, you can usually assume that the convergence will be OK.) Convergence refers to how well the three "guns" inside the monitor—red, blue, and green—align to paint the color onto each dot. If one of the guns is misaligned, the colors will not be true. The best way to check convergence is to display a pure white screen. (Open a Windows-based word processor and start a new document; it displays a nice expanse of whiteness.) Do you see a blue, green, or red tint to the white? If so, the monitor has convergence problems.

---

### MONITOR SHOPPING CHECKLIST

**Monitor size desired:**

   14" / 15" / 17" / 19" / 20" or 21"

**Must be non-interlaced?**    Yes / No

**Resolution I plan to use most:**

   640×480 / 800×600 / 768×1024 /   Other: _____

**Minimum refresh rate needed at the above resolution:** _____

**Other features desired:** _____

---

## My Recommendation

If you are going to go to the expense of a new monitor, get a good one. If you get a good-quality 17-inch monitor, you can keep it for many years, saving money on your future computer purchases. I use a 17-inch ViewSonic PT775 monitor, which I bought for about $700 last year. It has a .25 aperture grille and supports high refresh rates and noninterlaced display.

 **TIP**  If you happen to have a Gateway 2000 system, you might consider buying a new 19-inch monitor from Gateway as an upgrade. These monitors have been getting good reviews and are reasonably priced. The only catch is you have to be a Gateway customer (that is, you have to already have one of the company's computers, or at least be registered in its system as owning one).

## CD-ROM and DVD Drives

In my opinion every computer needs a CD-ROM drive, because most of the good software now comes on CD-ROM. But which drive should you buy? Or should get a DVD drive instead? Here are some suggestions.

# Deciphering the Xs

The most obvious feature that manufacturers advertise for a CD-ROM drive is its speed. You'll see 8X, 16X, 24X, 12X/16X, and so on. It's important to know what this means.

When CD-ROM drives first came out, they were basically just big read-only floppy disks, used to transfer large amounts of data onto your system. You could buy programs to install or large collections of literature, fonts, or clip art. The CD-ROM was just a data warehouse.

Then manufacturers got the idea of running programs right from the CD-ROM drive. The original CD-ROM drives were too slow to make this idea viable, so vendors introduced 2X drives. They were capable of reading information from the disc approximately twice as fast as the original CD-ROM drives. From there, the race to be the fastest has spiraled ever upward—now there are 24X drives and even faster ones on the horizon.

The higher speeds make a big difference when it comes to loading programs and looking things up in an encyclopedia, but they won't do a lot for your older games. Game manufacturers tailor their video clips for the CD-ROM drive speed they expect most users to have, and spinning the drive faster than the expected rate won't improve them. The faster drive won't do any harm to the game video; it just won't do any good, either. So if games are your goal, it probably isn't worth springing for a drive faster than about 4X at this time—save your money for your new system, a couple of years down the road.

Software manufacturers develop their products knowing that most people don't have the latest and greatest equipment, so most software in the stores today requires only a 4X or 8X CD-ROM drive. If you go to a store to buy a CD-ROM drive, however, you will be hard-pressed to find anything less than 12X for sale. Consequently, you really don't need to worry about buying the highest *X* drive you can find, because packaged software won't require such a drive for many years, if ever.

The exception is if you are a serious PC game player buying the latest games on a regular basis. Games will be the first arena to require the higher drive speeds because they are so heavy on graphics and sound. If you plan on buying and playing all the latest games in the next few years, get a 24X drive.

**NOTE** Sometimes you may see a drive advertised with two speeds, such as 12x/16x or 12X min/16X max. This type of statement is "truth in advertising." Many CD-ROM drives read more quickly from the center of the disc than from the outer edges. Even though a drive says it is a 16X drive, it can actually read only the data near the center of the disc at 16X speed. The outer part of the disc is read at a much slower speed (say, 12X). If you see a drive advertised with two speeds, you can probably compare it fairly to other drives advertised at the greater of those two speeds. (Some drives do have motors that vary the rotation speed depending on where the read head is working, so they can actually read the whole disc at a constant speed.)

## Choosing an Interface

When CD-ROM drives first came on the market, the most popular models were Small Computer Systems Interface (SCSI) drives. You hooked them up to a special SCSI circuit card that you placed in one of your computer's expansion slots. So in addition to buying the CD-ROM drive, you had to buy a SCSI interface card if you didn't already have one.

The next wave of drives came with their own special interface cards. These were SCSI cards, but they were cheap models that could run only one device: that particular CD-ROM drive. Consumers liked this approach because they didn't have to buy and set up a SCSI card.

Then someone got the bright idea of building special capabilities into sound cards so that they could be used as CD-ROM controller cards. This was the birth of the "multimedia kit," which was usually a sound card, a CD-ROM drive connected to it, and a set of speakers.

All these interface methods were well and good, and they are still fine methods. However, the dominant type of interface today for CD-ROM drives is IDE. This is the same interface that your computer's hard drives hook into, so it's already in place—nothing extra to buy. Most motherboards let you have up to four IDE devices, so unless you have four separate hard disks already, you probably have an open IDE connector. IDE CD-ROM drives are also very fast; the IDE connection is used to handling the heavy data load from the hard disk, so it handles the CD-ROM's data easily.

> ### CHECKING YOUR SYSTEM'S IDE INTERFACE FOR VACANCIES
>
> One way to find out whether you have any IDE interfaces left on your system is to check the startup screen. It may tell you "Hard Disk 1 Detected," "Hard Disk 2 Detected," and so on. Most computers can have up to four hard disks, and any of these spots not taken can support a CD-ROM, ZIP drive, or other drive. So if four hard disks aren't listed, chances are good that you have some IDE acreage free.
>
> Another way to check the IDE status is to enter your computer's BIOS setup program, as you'll learn Sunday afternoon. As the computer is starting, watch the screen for a message like "Press F1 for Setup." Then do it. In this program, it'll list your primary and secondary IDE interfaces and what's plugged into them. If any of them say "available," or "empty," you're OK. (To exit the BIOS program, press Esc.)
>
> Yet another tactic is to use the MSD program at the DOS prompt, which you learned about Friday evening, to get system information.
>
> And finally, you can remove the cover on your PC and check out the ribbon cable that runs from your hard disk to your motherboard (or to a card in one of your motherboard's slots). If the only device on the cable is your hard disk, but you see an extra connector somewhere along the cable, you can plug your IDE CD-ROM drive into there.
>
> I'm telling you all this now just for shopping and planning purposes; you'll get into the actual installation in the Sunday Morning session.

## Compatibility

A few years ago when you bought a CD-ROM drive, you needed to worry about it adhering to a minimum standard for multimedia called MPC-3. This standard consisted of a certain speed of CD-ROM and a certain quality of sound card. However, today's drives far outstrip MPC-3; you cannot buy a CD-ROM drive in any store that does not meet or beat the standard. Therefore, you don't have to worry about it.

The same goes for a multitude of other drive standards, such as XA, Kodak Photo CD, and so on. A few years ago, you needed to check to make sure the drive you bought supported all the technologies you wanted to use. Nowadays, all drives support everything, so compatibility isn't an issue.

## Internal or External?

Your choice of an internal or external CD-ROM drive should be based on your current computer's situation. If you have an available externally accessible drive bay, internal is better, because it doesn't require a separate power cable and it doesn't take up extra space on your desk. However, if you are going to be sharing the drive with someone else, an external model might make sense. Each of you could have a SCSI card in your computer, and whoever needs the CD-ROM drive that day could simply plug it into the card before turning on the computer.

If you can find an external CD-ROM drive, it will probably be SCSI, though you may also find a CD-ROM drive that works with an external parallel port. All the other possible interfaces for a CD-ROM are inside the computer's case, and an external drive can't be attached to them.

## DVD: The Wave of the Future

DVD drives are like super CD-ROM drives. They can read not only regular CDs but also special DVD discs, which can hold as much as 8.5 gigabytes. That's 133 minutes of video; you could store an entire full-length movie on one of them. That's a lot of data. DVD drives can also function as regular CD-ROM drives (at about 13X speed, unless you find one of the old ones, which run at 4X).

The original DVD drives that came out had a few quirks. For one thing, they couldn't read CDs created with a PC CD-ROM writer. They also couldn't play audio CDs. But the newer DVD drives, called DVD-II, can do both of these things, so you should have no problems using a DVD drive to do all the same things you do with a regular CD drive.

The only thing that might give you pause about buying a DVD drive right now is the price. They cost more than $200, while a regular CD-ROM drive can be had for about $60. And as of this writing, besides playing movies,

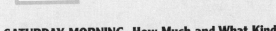

there aren't a lot of reasons to spend the extra money. If you do want movies on your computer, you'll need a special MPEG decoder card along with your DVD drive—another $200 on top of the drive, and you should be sure to buy the card and the drive as a set, because installing the parts separately can be a real nightmare.

I just bought myself a brand-new computer with all the bells and whistles, but I opted not to get a DVD drive. Why? Because I couldn't think of a good reason to buy one now, and if I wait till I actually need it, by that time the prices will have come down and the technology will be better.

## CD-ROM Changers

Some CD-ROM drives can hold several discs at a time in a multidisc cartridge. They can still only read (play) one disc at a time, though, so it's not really like having an extra CD-ROM drive. It's more like having a stereo system that lets you load several CDs together, so you don't have to keep returning to the stereo to put another disc in.

You have to pay extra for this neat feature; drives like this cost more than their single-disc counterparts. In my opinion, it's not worth the extra dough.

## Recordable CD-ROM Drives

Recordable CD-ROM drives act just like regular CD-ROM drives, except you can create your own CD-ROMs with them. If you get one of these, you will almost certainly also want a regular CD-ROM drive, too, so you can make copies of both audio and computer CDs.

I have a recordable CD-ROM drive, and I have lots of fun with it. I also use it to create CDs that contain archive copies of the final manuscript files for books that I write. These files would fill up many floppy disks, but I can put an entire book on a single CD-ROM.

There are two kinds of recordable CD-ROM drives: CD-R, which stands for CD recordable, and CD-RW, which stands for CD rewritable.

CD-R is an older technology. You can record to a disc only once. (An exception is a multisession setup, which I explain in the following note.) And if an error occurs while you're recording, you've just wasted a disc. You must record everything that you want to put on the disc in a single operation. You can't put one file on it, then another, and so on; you must choose all the files for the CD-ROM in advance and then issue a single command to copy them all as a group. Blank recordable disks are rather expensive—about $1.50 each for a pack of 10 is the going rate.

**NOTE** Some CD-ROM recorders are *multisession capable*. This feature enables you to write to a blank CD-ROM, and then write to the same CD-ROM later in a new session. This capability is good for backing up data. For example, say you have 100MB of data to back up once a week. A typical recordable disc holds about 600MB, so you could have six sessions on the CD-ROM. When you finish recording the last session in the sixth week, you would file the disc away. As long as each week's file had a separate name, you could go back and read any of them later. If each backup used the same file name, however, you could read only the most recent version even though the older data would still be on the disc.

CD-RW is the latest thing. With it, you can record multiple times on the same disc, like you can a floppy. CD-RW drives are expensive (the cheapest I've seen was $450), and their discs are expensive, too.

Generally speaking, with any type of recordable CD-ROM drive, you get much less $X$ for your money. My current recordable drive cost more than $300, and it writes at 2X speed and reads at 4X. That's not very fast. It takes about 20 minutes to record a CD-ROM on my system.

## My Recommendation

The average computer user doesn't need a special DVD or recordable drive, just like the average driver doesn't need a touring bus with a built-in kitchen and bathroom. Sure it would be cool, but why spend the money on that when you can put it to better use elsewhere?

CD-ROM drives are fairly generic—they either work or they don't. For that reason, I wouldn't spend much extra money on a brand name. If you have a spare drive bay and IDE connection, buy a plain 24X or faster IDE internal model. It'll be under $100, and it'll serve you just fine.

```
┌─────────────────────────────────────────────────────────┐
│                                                         │
│              CD-ROM SHOPPING CHECKLIST                  │
│                                                         │
│     Minimum speed I will accept is: _____X            │
│                                                         │
│     Internal or External? _____                     │
│                                                         │
│     IDE or SCSI? _____                             │
│                                                         │
│     Recordable?  Yes / No                               │
│                                                         │
│     Multi-disk?  Yes / No                               │
│                                                         │
│     DVD-capable?  Yes / No                              │
│                                                         │
│     Other: _____             │
│                                                         │
└─────────────────────────────────────────────────────────┘
```

# Hard Disks

Most people don't pay any attention to their hard disks until they become full. Then suddenly the hard disk is a big issue.

Hard disks are distinguished from one another in several ways: the interface they use, their capacity, and how quickly they can read and write data. The following sections look at each factor individually.

## Choosing an Interface

Your current hard disk is probably an IDE of some variety. These drives offer decent performance at a very good price, and they run on almost any computer. Your computer probably has built-in support for at least two—and possibly four—IDE devices, so you can probably add another IDE drive without buying anything extra except the new drive. The most common types of IDE-compatible drives are EIDE (the *E* stands for enhanced) and ATA-2. There is also a new IDE type, UltraDMA (UDMA) IDE, which offers improved performance over other types of IDE drives.

You can also get SCSI hard disks. These hook up to SCSI interface cards, so if you don't already have a SCSI interface card in your system, you need to buy one if you want to use a SCSI hard disk. SCSI hard disks are usually more expensive than IDE drives, too. However, many computer experts consider SCSI hard disks superior, and under some conditions they do perform better and more efficiently. (Personally, I have never been able to tell much difference.)

## Deciding What Capacity to Get

When choosing a new hard disk capacity, always overestimate. Decide how much space you think you want for all the programs you can ever imagine buying, and then double that amount. For example, I bought a 6.4 gigabyte hard drive in the new computer I got earlier this year. It seemed huge at the time, but it's more than half-full already.

You don't want to have to buy yet another hard disk a year from now, so buy the largest capacity drive that you can possibly afford. You can buy anything from 1.2 gigabytes to more than 15 gigabytes these days—and maybe more by the time you read this—so let your pocket be your guide.

CAUTION    ◆ ◆ ◆ ◆ ◆ ◆ ◆ ◆ ◆ ◆ ◆ ◆ ◆ ◆ ◆ ◆ ◆ ◆ ◆ ◆ ◆ ◆ ◆ ◆ ◆ ◆ ◆ ◆ ◆ ◆ ◆ ◆ ◆ ◆ ◆ ◆ ◆

In addition to capacity, you also need to consider physical size. Most hard disks are called *half height* or *third height.* This designation refers to the portion of an old-style full-height drive bay that they consume. (In the old days of computing, hard disk technology was so primitive that hard disks had to be very large in physical size. To get an idea of how tall a full-height drive was, picture two CD-ROM drives stacked.) Some ultra-high-capacity drives, such as Quantum's Bigfoot drive, have larger than average physical dimensions. (The Bigfoot, for example, is a "full height" drive.) If you have limited space for your upgrade, ask about the dimensions of a drive before you buy it.

◆ ◆ ◆ ◆ ◆ ◆ ◆ ◆ ◆ ◆ ◆ ◆ ◆ ◆ ◆ ◆ ◆ ◆ ◆ ◆ ◆ ◆ ◆ ◆ ◆ ◆ ◆ ◆ ◆ ◆ ◆ ◆ ◆ ◆ ◆ ◆ ◆

## Ways to Evaluate Performance

Hard disks have two critical measurements:

✿ **Average access time.** This measurement is the time it takes for the drive head to reach and read the average bit of data. It's measured in milliseconds (ms). The lower the number, the faster the drive. A decent speed is 10 to 12ms.

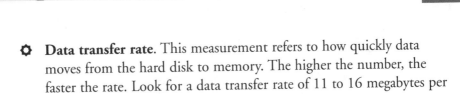
✪ **Data transfer rate**. This measurement refers to how quickly data moves from the hard disk to memory. The higher the number, the faster the rate. Look for a data transfer rate of 11 to 16 megabytes per second.

Most ads for hard disks give these two measurements. If this information is missing, call the supplier and ask.

## My Recommendation

Of course, all the factors are important, but here is my order of priority for a hard disk:

1. I eliminate all the drives that have the wrong interface. If I'm shopping for IDE, I ignore SCSI drives.

2. I look at the available drives in the capacity I want.

3. From that narrowed list, I look to see which drives have the best data transfer rates and average access times.

4. Of the drives with the best performance measurements, I go with the cheapest one, provided it is a brand I have heard of before.

Popular hard disk brands include Maxtor, Western Digital, Seagate, Quantum, and JTS.

---

### HARD DISK SHOPPING CHECKLIST

**Interface desired (circle one):  IDE or SCSI**

**Minimum size I will accept:** _____

**Minimum data transfer rate:** _____

**Maximum access time:** _____

**Other features or notes:** _____

# Removable Mass Storage

Besides the standard hard disks, you can buy drives that have removable disks, like floppies, but that hold lots of data, like hard disks.

## Super Floppies

There are now floppy drive replacements called SuperDrives (LS-120) that read and write regular 3.5" floppy disks, but also special SuperDisks that hold 120 megabytes each. If you want removable mass storage but you don't have an extra drive bay in your system, you might consider replacing your current A: drive with one of these. However, not all motherboards have a system BIOS that would allow you to boot from this type of drive, so check with your PC's manufacturer to make sure you can use one with your system. You can put a SuperDrive in as the B: drive—an extra floppy drive that you're never going to try to boot from—without worrying about the BIOS.

## Removable Hard Disks

The most popular types of removable mass storage devices right now are Iomega's ZIP and Jaz drives. They accept floppy-like cartridges that hold 100 megabytes (ZIP) or 1 or 2 gigabytes (Jaz). Competitors such as Sparq (which competes with the Jaz) are also worth considering.

The cartridges cost a bit more than a regular hard disk with that capacity (about $10 for a ZIP cartridge, $30 for a Sparq, or $100 for a Jaz), so you're basically paying the $100 to $300 for the drive itself and the extra amount for the cartridges as surcharges for the extra convenience.

Although several competing brands are available, Iomega's drives seem to be winning the market-share war. ZIP drives are standard equipment on many new PCs, so if being able to transport data to another computer is important, the ZIP drive may be the best choice.

Iomega makes four kinds of ZIP drives: SCSI internal, SCSI external, IDE, and parallel. The IDE version runs off the same IDE interface as your hard disk; if you buy a new PC with a ZIP drive installed, you'll probably get this type because it's the least expensive to produce.

The SCSI internal version runs off your existing SCSI card if you have one; it also comes with a special limited-use SCSI card, which you can use if you don't already have a SCSI card. Its performance is about the same as that of the IDE version.

The SCSI external version requires a SCSI interface that can be accessed from outside your computer—that is, a SCSI card that you can plug into the drive. This version is a good choice if you need high performance plus the capability to share the drive among several PCs.

The parallel version runs off your computer's parallel port, but can be extremely slow compared to the other versions, and I don't recommend it.

## Tape Backup Drives

Tape backup units have been around for a long time. They are primarily used for backups, as their name implies, because they are slow. They store data in a sequential order, like the songs on a cassette tape, so you can't jump easily from the beginning to the end as you can with an audio CD. Therefore, tape backup drives are best used for storing data that is infrequently needed. The oldest computers used tape drives before hard disks were invented, so the technology has a very long tradition in computers.

Today's tape drives are much faster than their predecessors and hold hundreds of megabytes on each tape. If you need to do regular backups, you may like having a tape drive because you can eliminate swapping floppies in and out. However, if you don't have much data to back up (less than 100 megabytes, for example), you might be better off backing up to a ZIP drive. An internal tape drive takes up a precious drive bay in your computer; an external one requires its own power supply and takes up space on your desk.

## Sound Cards

Sound cards have come a long way in the last several years. Creative Labs started out and remains the industry leader, with everyone else imitating its products—its SoundBlaster is the standard. The current technology in sound is wavetable synthesis. Unless you plan on composing your own music, however, you really don't need a fancy sound card; one that simply plays your audio CDs and makes your games sound good is probably plenty. Here's the lowdown on sound-card features.

## Number of Bits

Sixteen bit is the standard for today's sound cards. A 16-bit sound card can process 16 bits of data at once. The more bits, the higher fidelity the sound. You may find a very old 8-bit sound card for sale somewhere, but you don't want that.

## Wavetable Cards

Wavetable cards have prerecorded, built-in sounds, such as the sounds of different instruments playing different notes. (Regular FM synthesis sound cards don't have wavetables; they simulate these notes instead, which doesn't sound as good.) You can use wavetable cards to simulate great-sounding music, playing dozens of instruments at once without having lots of recorded sound files taking up space on your hard disk. These cards are really useful for music enthusiasts who are trying to write their own music using the computer's *MIDI interface* (basically, an interface that can accept input from a keyboard or other instrument or export musical data to a synthesizer). Wavetable cards commonly have 32, 64, or 128 voices that they can play at once. (Naturally, more voices means more money.)

**NOTE**  If you hear of a sound card that has the number 16 in its name, it is probably referring to 16 bits, and it probably does not contain wavetable synthesis. If, on the other hand, there is 64 or 128 in the name, the numbers probably refer to the number of wavetable voices.

Unless you are serious gamer or a music composer, a wavetable card isn't necessary—but if the capability comes built into your sound card, it certainly doesn't hurt anything. You can also buy an add-on card that adds that capability to your existing sound card.

# Input and Output Jacks

The important question about input and output jacks is this: Does the card have the jacks you want? Jacks come in many varieties, depending on the sound card, and not everybody needs every kind.

- ✪ **Speaker output**. All sound cards have a speaker output jack. You plug in speakers so you can hear the sounds. Some cards, especially those that advertise themselves as 3-D, provide two sets of output jacks so you can have four speakers.

- ✪ **Joystick port**. Some sound cards double as joystick controller cards. With these, you can plug in a joystick to play games.

- ✪ **MIDI input**. This port enables you to plug in a keyboard or other instrument to put sounds into the computer for manipulating or saving.

- ✪ **Auxiliary input**. This is an extra port that can accept input from a variety of sources. For example, you might connect your voice-mail modem to your sound card so that you can hear your voice-mail messages through your sound card.

- ✪ **CD-ROM support**. Some sound cards can also double as controller cards for some CD-ROM drives.

- ✪ **Microphone**. This lets you record your own sounds through an auxiliary microphone.

- ✪ **Line in and line out**. A line in jack provides a way to route sound from another amplifier, such as your home stereo system or a boom box headphone jack. The line out jack provides a way to route the sound card output to an amplifier, such as your home stereo system.

# My Recommendation

Business users don't need sound cards, although they may enjoy them. Practically the only reasons you *need* a sound card are to play games, to listen to downloaded sound or music files from the Internet, or to listen to audio CDs as you work at your computer.

---

**SOUND CARD SHOPPING CHECKLIST**

**Wavetable? Yes / No**

**Interface: IDE / PCI**

**MIDI Interface? Important / Not Important**

**Support for 4 speakers? Important / Not Important**

**Game port? Important / Not Important**

**SoundBlaster Compatibility? Important / Not Important**

---

Of those who need a sound card, most need only a very basic 16-bit card that is SoundBlaster or SoundBlaster Pro compatible. Almost all games use those standards, so it is important to have this compatibility. Some newer motherboards have sound support built into them, so you don't even have to buy a sound card to have basic sound support.

Very few people, mostly musicians, need a high-end sound card with wavetable synthesis. The Creative Labs SoundBlaster AWE-64 is a very popular sound card with this audience and goes for about $160, but before making the investment, you might check with some computer music professionals.

# Printers

Look back to last night's notes. What did you determine is wrong with your current printer? Are you looking for more speed? Higher quality? Color printouts? Whatever your priorities, you can find a printer out there to fit your needs.

## What Makes One Printer Better Than Another?

The price of a printer reflects its balance of these qualities:

- ✿ **Technology**. The newer the technology and the better the output of that technology, the higher the price. For example, a laser printer is more expensive than a dot matrix printer.

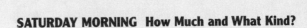

- ✿ **Speed**. More pages per minute costs you more.
- ✿ **Color**. You always pay more for a printer that can print in color than the equivalent black-and-white model.
- ✿ **Print quality**. Print quality is measured in dots per inch (dpi). For black and white, the higher the dpi, the nicer the output and the higher the price. For color printers, dpi is a factor but dot size and number of ink colors can make more of a difference in photographic color quality—and price.
- ✿ **Fonts**. Higher-cost printers, especially laser printers, often have lots of built-in fonts.
- ✿ **Memory**. Printers that compose the entire page at once (notably laser printers) need enough memory to hold the entire page. More memory means a higher up-front cost, but you will probably pay even more to add extra memory later. Memory is not an issue with ink-jet and dot matrix printers.
- ✿ **PostScript**. The capability to print PostScript fonts and images adds to the printer's price.

You need to base your purchase decision on the balance that is right for you. For example, you might want the best possible output regardless of the speed while your neighbor opts for speed (for example, for draft manuscripts) at the expense of quality.

## Printer Technologies

Three technologies dominate the printer market: dot matrix, ink jet, and laser. Each technology has its hybrids and subtypes, but almost all printers fall into these categories.

**NOTE**  You might come across a few other kinds of printers, such as dye sublimation, thermal wax transfer, and pen plotter, but these are expensive and not practical choices for the casual user. They are designed for professional-quality color graphic arts work.

## Dot Matrix

The low-end printer technology is dot matrix. It works by striking the paper with a series of little pins against a ribbon (like a typewriter ribbon). In many ways a dot matrix printer is like an automated typewriter except that, instead of letter-shaped hammers, a group of small pins changes position to form each letter.

Most dot matrix printers sold today have 24 pins, which gives nearly the same quality as a typewriter when the printer is operating at its maximum quality setting. Older dot matrix printers have only 9 pins, which results in less desirable output.

Dot matrix printers and their replacement ribbons are inexpensive. However, they are noisy and slow, and you can't print in more than one color. (You can get a colored ribbon to print in a single color instead of black for some printers.)

I don't recommend that you buy a new dot matrix printer unless you absolutely have to print on multiple-part forms or use tractor-fed paper, or both. If you don't need those features—which only a dot matrix printer will give you—you can have a faster, quieter ink-jet printer for just a little bit more money. On the other hand, if you can buy a dot matrix printer used, it might be a good solution for a tight budget even if you're only making single copies.

**NOTE**   Don't pay more than $50—$75 at the max—for a used dot matrix printer. It's not worth it, no matter how fancy the printer.

## Ink Jet

Ink-jet printers are the current favorite for home and office use because they are inexpensive, produce nearly laser quality output, print fairly quickly (three or more pages per minute), and can print in color. Their only drawback is the high cost of the replacement ink cartridges, which can run $20 or more depending on the model.

If you are sure you want only black-and-white output, you can get a great deal on an ink-jet printer. Because almost everyone wants color, stores are

almost giving away black-only models. I saw one for $100 in a retail store the other day. You don't need a fancy ink jet with color and a high dot per inch (dpi) count if all you ever print is text.

On the other hand, if you want a color printer that can produce greeting cards, banners, T-shirt transfers, and the like, you'll want to splurge on a printer with a high dpi and photorealistic quality printing. Some color printers advertise that they print photographic quality out of the box; others require an upgrade kit. (Sometimes the so-called "upgrade kit" is just a special ink cartridge.)

If speed is important, you should also look for a printer that has a decent pages per minute (ppm) rating. For an ink-jet printer, 6 ppm for black and white and 3 ppm for color is pretty good. The ppm rating is a lot like reported gas mileage for a new car, though—yours may vary and probably will, and not in your favor. It's a good idea to time the printer as it produces something comparable to the work you have in mind before you decide you can live with the speed. Despite the ratings, complex color output can run into minutes per page rather than pages per minute!

You should also consider the ink cartridge system when choosing an ink-jet printer. Ink-jet printers work in one of the following ways, listed from most to least preferable.

- Four separate cartridges: one for each of the three colors that make up all other colors: magenta, cyan, and yellow, and one for black ink. All four cartridges can be loaded into the printer at once.

- Two cartridges: one color cartridge that contains each of the three colors in separate compartments, and one black cartridge. Both cartridges can be loaded into the printer at the same time.

- Two cartridges: one color cartridge and one black and white, but only one or the other is in the printer at any given time. When you want to switch between black-and-white and color printing, you must manually switch the cartridges.

The advantage of having separate ink cartridges for each color, of course, is that you don't waste ink. If you print a lot of red, for instance, the magenta may run out long before the cyan. With a separate cartridge system, you can replace just the colors you use up.

Low-cost ink jets usually use the two-cartridge method of color printing, while more expensive ones give you four cartridges. Printers using the cartridge-switching method are mostly available only in used-computer stores. They probably aren't worth the price, no matter how cheap they are—in addition to the extra work of switching the cartridges, they give you very poor copies of photographs. They have to simulate black while printing in color by combining the three colored inks, and the result is a sort of nasty brown. I would not buy a model like this.

The cost and availability of the ink cartridges is the final factor to consider. If you buy a well-known printer brand, like Canon, Epson, or Hewlett-Packard, you will be able to buy cartridges at almost any office supply store. If you go with an off-brand printer, make sure it can use the same cartridges as a brand-name unit.

## Laser

Before ink-jet technology got the kinks worked out of it, laser printers were the only choice for serious business users. They are still very popular in business because of their razor-sharp text output and fast, quiet operation.

With a laser printer you are stuck with black-and-white output only—unless you want to spend more than $2,000 on a color model. Upgrading laser printer technology for color was not a simple matter of revising the ink delivery system by adding some extra cartridges, as it was for ink-jet printers. The innards of a color laser printer are completely different than those of a black-and-white one.

When shopping for a laser printer, you are interested in several factors:

- ✪ **Print quality**. The minimum you should consider is 600 dpi.
- ✪ **Maximum memory**. Many low-end laser printers come with only 512KB of memory, but you will run into problems printing full-page graphics unless you have at least 1MB of memory in the printer. Personally, I wouldn't buy a laser printer with less than 2MB of memory, and even then I'd make sure I could add more memory later.
- ✪ **Maximum print speed**. The minimum you should accept is 6 ppm; some of the better lasers print 12 or even 20 ppm.

You should also check the price of a toner cartridge, and whether your local office supply or computer store keeps the cartridge in stock. For example, I made an expensive mistake when I bought my laser printer a few years ago; I bought a Texas Instruments MicroLaser Pro 600 because it was rated highly in computer magazines. I didn't know it then, but the replacement toner cartridges cost more than $100, and I have to order them by mail because no local stores carry them. Ouch.

## Hybrids

Several manufacturers have recently introduced a new breed of printer that is designed mainly for small and home offices. The unit combines a printer and some other device or devices, for example, a fax machine, a copier, a scanner, and so on. They go by different names: one manufacturer calls its model a Mopier; another is an OfficeJet. Others simply call them multi-function printers.

These multifunction devices can seem like great values—you get all the functions of several devices for the price (and footprint) of one. The thing to keep in mind is that you're not getting a top-quality unit in any of its categories. It may print, but it won't print as well as a dedicated printer of the same price as the multifunction unit. It may scan, but not as well as a dedicated scanner. You get the idea. They also break down more disastrously than single-function units—the parts aren't unreliable, but when the scanner goes out it's apt to take the printer with it, which wouldn't be the case if they were in two separate boxes.

I'm not telling you to avoid these hybrids, but keep in mind that you are trading performance for size and price when purchasing one of these units.

## Speed

The printer's speed depends heavily on the technology that it employs. Dot matrix is the slowest, followed by ink jet, with laser at the top of the heap.

If you pay enough money, you can have a printer that prints at incredible speeds like 24 ppm. Most people have better things to do with their money, though; home users will probably be happy with a modest 6 to 8 ppm.

Keep in mind that when a printer is advertised at 6 ppm, that's its maximum speed—your results will be lower. The 6 ppm is the speed that the printer could print—in theory—if it didn't have to process any graphics or wait for the computer to send it any data. In reality, whenever you print a page that contains fonts that are not resident in the printer, or graphics, you will have to wait for the page to come out of the printer. Sometimes you may wait 30 seconds or even a minute or more for the printer to begin to print a page. This operation is normal; don't take your printer back for a refund if it happens.

## Color

Nearly all ink-jet printers sold today are color-capable, and nearly all laser printers aren't. So your choice of a color or black-and-white printer is already made for you when you decide on the printer technology you want.

If you plan on printing photographs, get a photographic-quality printer such as the Epson Stylus Photo 700 (or any other ink-jet with "photo" in its name). These printers produce photos exceptionally well, with vivid colors.

 **CAUTION**

Some ink-jet printers require special paper to produce the highest dpi images. If you pick up a stunning color printout sample at a store, notice whether it is printed on glossy paper. If it is, you won't be able to duplicate that result at home unless you buy some of that special, expensive paper. Such paper can cost over $1 a sheet!

The photo-quality ink-jets are for those who need the highest quality of photo printing, not for casual home and business users. If you will mostly be printing spot colors (for example, colored clip art), a regular ink-jet printer is fine. Most regular color ink-jet printers can reproduce photos fairly well, certainly well enough for home use.

To evaluate color printing, nothing works better than taking a trip to a big computer store and actually seeing and handling the printouts from various models. You don't have to buy the machine at that store; just look at the samples and then buy the printer wherever it is cheapest.

# Print Quality

Print quality on a dot matrix printer is not measured very precisely. Printers are either 9 pin (and the output is euphemistically called "near letter quality," which, in fact, it isn't) or 24 pin (where the output is called "letter quality").

On ink-jets and laser printers, quality is measured in dots per inch. The higher the number, the finer the quality of the image. Note that in most cases, you worry about dpi only for the sake of the graphics quality; text looks good no matter how many dpi you have.

Most home and casual business users will be happy with anything over 600 dpi, the common quality of low-budget laser printers. Most ink-jet printers offer at least 720×720 dpi. On ink-jet printers, dpi is given in two separate measurements: vertical and horizontal. You might have an ink-jet printer that prints 1440×720, for example, which means that the printer's vertical resolution is better than its horizontal. (You don't notice the difference; all you notice is that the printout looks a little better than one from a 720×720 printer.)

Some printers offer resolution enhancement, which means they use one trick or another to make the printout seem like it has a higher dpi than it actually has. One such is technology is Hewlett Packard's PhotoRET, which varies the inkjet dot size to make sharper images. These technologies can make a huge difference in image quality, so don't let the dpi be your only determining factor. Look at sample printouts if possible to decide which unit has the best quality.

# Fonts and PostScript

Different people will tell you that different things are important about printer fonts, depending on what time period in history they are stuck in. In other words, over the last 10 years, different font-handling schemes have been popular, and various shopping schemes for printers have been appropriate. The sidebar "Whatever Happened to PostScript?" explains the whole gory story.

The bottom line is this: Windows 3.1 or Windows 95/98 puts dozens of TrueType fonts at your disposal, so you don't need a printer that supports PostScript, comes with lots of built-in fonts, or has cartridge slots. Some wily

## WHATEVER HAPPENED TO POSTSCRIPT?

Back in the days when all programs were DOS-based, each program had its own font files. For example, I used Ventura Publisher for DOS in 1988, which came with two typefaces: Dutch (similar to today's Times New Roman) and Swiss (similar to today's Arial). When I installed the program, it asked me what sizes I wanted of these typefaces. It then generated font files for each size and variant that I wanted, with separate files for each combination of typeface, size, and attributes (like bold, italic, and bold/italic). These font files took up a lot of space on my hard disk! When Ventura Publisher was ready to print, it first sent the appropriate font files over to the printer, and then sent the document to be printed using them.

Besides using these fonts on disk, you could also use any fonts that were built into your printer. For example, if your printer came with two extra fonts besides Swiss and Dutch, you could also use them in your documents. You could buy cartridges that plugged into your printer and added more fonts to it. I had a 72-font cartridge for my old printer back then, but because each combination of typeface, size, and attribute was considered a separate font, I probably had only three additional typefaces to work with. During this era in printer history, it was important to have a printer with slots that accepted these cartridges.

During the same time, if you had $1,000+, you could have had a *PostScript* printer. A PostScript printer had lots of built-in typefaces (I think there were about 35 of them), so you didn't need the cartridges. You could also print PostScript format graphics—a format popular with professional graphic artists—with a PostScript printer. Best of all, the printer used outline-font typefaces, which meant you could use them at any size without having a separate font file on your hard disk for each one. The printer kept an "outline" of what each letter should look like, expanded or contracted that outline, and then filled in the middle to form the letters.

Then along came Windows 3.1, which introduced TrueType fonts. What a revolution! These TrueType fonts were outline fonts (like PostScript) that could be resized to any size you wanted. They also worked generically with whatever Windows printer driver you installed, so they worked on any printer, not just a PostScript one. Sales of PostScript printers dropped dramatically because the primary reason people needed them (to have more fonts) went away.

salesclerk may try to tell you that you need these features, but 99 percent of the time they're a waste of money as long as you will be using only Windows programs.

## Printer Memory

Printer memory serves different functions, depending on what kind of printer you have.

On dot matrix and ink-jet printers, the printer prints one line at a time on the page, as the paper moves through it. Therefore, the printer needs only enough memory to hold one line at a time. That's not much! Any additional memory the printer has serves as a buffer. When the computer tells the printer what to print on the upcoming line before the printer has finished the current line, the extra information waits in the buffer. The larger the buffer, the more data can wait in line. More memory doesn't help the printer function any better for the most part, so the memory amount in an ink-jet or dot matrix printer is not important.

In contrast, the memory in a laser printer is very important. A laser printer composes the entire page in its memory and then spits it onto the paper in one pass. Consequently, the printer needs enough memory to hold the entire page. Sadly, most laser printer manufacturers cut corners and provide only 512KB of memory with their printers. You have to buy memory upgrades to get more. That 512KB is not even enough to hold a single full-page graphic. If you get out-of-memory error messages when printing large graphics, your printer is probably memory deficient. You should have at least 1MB of printer memory in a laser printer—and more is better. Why? Because the memory also has to hold any fonts that the computer sends to the printer. If you are printing a page with lots of different fonts and lots of graphics, you may need more than 1MB of memory for the printer to print it.

## Paper Handling

A good printer should be able to accept at least 100 sheets in its paper tray so that you don't have to constantly be restocking the paper supply. Nicer models accept up to 250 pages, and some have more than one paper tray.

Models with two paper trays are good when you use two kinds of paper, such as regular and letterhead or first-page letterhead and subsequent-page letterhead. Special trays are often available for legal-size paper or other nonstandard sizes. You can also get special envelope feeders (usually at additional cost) for many laser printers.

## My Recommendation

If you are buying for home use, especially if you have kids, get a color inkjet printer. My current favorite models are the Epson Stylus Color 600 (for casual home use) and the Epson Stylus Color 850 (for more rigorous use). Both models offer photographic-quality printing at 14,400 dpi. The biggest difference is speed. The 850 prints at about 9 ppm (pages per minute) in black and white and 8 ppm in color. The 600 prints at 6 ppm in black and white and 3 ppm in color.

If you are buying a printer primarily for business, where professional-looking correspondence and reports are a priority, get a laser printer. The

---

### PRINTER SHOPPING LIST

**Type of printer: Dot Matrix / Ink jet / Laser**

**Minimum resolution I will accept:** _____ x _____

**Minimum amount of RAM printer should have:** _____

**Color? Yes / No**

**Minimum speed:** _____ pages per minute color

_____ pages per minute b/w

**Postscript?    Yes / No**

**Paper tray must hold at least** _____ **sheets**

**Envelope feeder attachment needed? Yes / No**

**Legal size paper tray needed? Yes / No**

**Other special features desired:** _____

output will be basically the same quality for almost all the models and brands you look at, so look instead at speed, features, cost of supplies, and the amount of memory that comes with it. There are lots of good laser printers, but I like the Hewlett-Packards, partly because it is usually easy to find their toner cartridges in local stores.

# Scanners

If your business requires you to take photos and insert them into computer documents or Web pages, you can legitimately justify a scanner. Otherwise, it's just a toy. But what a fun toy! And at under $200 for a home-quality one, why not?

A scanner digitizes pictures so that you can use them in your computer. Some scanners also come with optical character recognition (OCR) software, which allows you to scan text and then translate the picture of the text into real text in a word processor. This feature sounds great, but in practice the OCR software that comes with most scanners makes so many mistakes, you may spend as much time correcting the typos as you would have spent retyping the entire article. If you really need OCR, you can usually upgrade to a professional version of the software—which will be good enough to be preferable to retyping the original, though still not perfect.

## Colors and Resolution

The resolution of a scanner's scanned image is measured in dots per inch, or dpi, just like printer output. You want a scanner that can scan in at least 300 dpi. (This should not be a problem to find.)

Scanners used to come in both black-and-white and color models, but nowadays it's hard to find anything but color for sale. You may hear the quality of the scanner expressed as a number of bits—low-end scanners are 30 bit, while higher-end models are 33 or 36 bit or more.

## Type

You can buy hand scanners (the cheapest), sheet fed, or flat bed. A hand scanner is like a big mouse that you drag across the image to be scanned. It doesn't take up much space and can be removed and stored easily. However, you may have trouble dragging it at the right speed across the image, and you can't scan an entire 8.5×11" page in one pass. These are getting harder to find, as the trend is moving toward flat-bed models.

Sheet-fed scanners work the way fax machines or ATM card slots work— you feed in your paper; the machine scans it and feeds it back to you. These scanners don't take much room, and because they are self-propelled, you don't have to worry about dragging the document at the right pace. However, you can't scan things out of books without tearing out the page.

Flatbed scanners are like copy machines. You lay the image down on glass, put the cover over it, and click the button on the screen. It makes a copy of the image and sends the copy over to your PC. These scanners are usually the best quality ones and the most flexible. However, they take up an enormous amount of desk space. Flatbed scanners are the most common type sold nowadays, for better or worse; recently when I went to a CompUSA looking for a scanner, there were 12 different flatbed models, one sheet-fed, and no hand scanners.

## Interface

Some scanners come with their own interface cards; others require you to have a SCSI card. A third category attaches to your parallel port, which means that you don't need an extra interface card. (It provides a pass-through for your printer, so you can connect your scanner and printer at the same time.) It's also becoming possible to find scanners that hook up to a USB port—the wave of the future, if your system has one.

## My Recommendation

For home use, you will not be able to tell much difference in quality among the various scanner models, so go with one of the cheaper ones. The fancy, expensive ones are primarily for business use, such as for producing professional-quality brochures, magazine layouts, and so on. You probably won't have much choice in the type—flatbed has all but overrun the market. For interface, if you are planning to use it a lot, get a SCSI; if it is going to be an occasionally-used toy, get a parallel or USB interface.

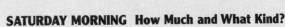

# Special Input Devices

Devices in this category help you get input into your computer. They include keyboards, mice, and scanners. You may already have a mouse, and you certainly already have a keyboard, but you may find that spending an extra $20 to $100 for a special input device will make your computing experience more pleasant.

# Multimedia Input Devices

There is a wide array of devices available these days to help you put sound and video into your PC. You can buy all kinds of microphones, and even digital video and still cameras. Microphones plug into your sound card; digital video cameras typically come with their own interface cards.

## Video Capture and Digital Cameras

Video capture refers to hooking up a video camera of some sort to your PC and capturing live motion video. You can buy a number of different devices that do this in varying degrees of quality. Once such device is a Connectix (or other brand) camera. It's a little round ball with a camera lens in the middle and a cord that attaches to your PC. You can point it at whatever you want to record. You can also get interface cards or external adapters that you can attach your home video camera to, and feed the video into the PC.

A digital camera, in contrast, captures still images and feeds them into your PC. Unlike the video capture devices, digital cameras are not attached to your PC, so you can take them out into the world with you, just like a regular camera. Then you bring them back to your PC and transfer the pictures you have taken. Some digital cameras (notably the ones in the Sony Mavica line) hold diskettes that you can pop out and insert in your PC; others have interface cards that they hook into via a cable.

Both of these can be a lot of fun, but the models that are priced so that most home users can afford them are not professional-quality, and you may be disappointed if you are planning to use the data for business. For example, the images taken by a digital camera are fairly low resolution compared to the much sharper images you get when you use a regular camera to take a picture and then scan in the results.

## Mouse Variants

Besides a normal mouse, you can use various untraditional devices for pointing on the screen. Just go to any computer hardware store and take a look at the vast display of options!

- ✪ **Cordless mouse**. The cordless mouse is a regular mouse that communicates with your PC through an infrared beam or radio waves (or other technology) so you don't have to deal with the unsightly and awkward mouse cord. Some people swear by them; personally, I don't think they're worth the money.

- ✪ **Trackball**. Trackballs are like upside-down mice. The base stays stationary, and you roll a ball with your thumb or hand to move the mouse cursor on the screen. My favorite models are the Kensington ExpertMouse and the Logitech TrackMan Marble. You really need to try out the model you want to buy to make sure it feels comfortable in your hand before you decide on it.

- ✪ **Touchpad**. These small rectangular pads are built into many laptop computers, but you can also buy them to plug into a desktop computer's mouse port. You just glide your finger across the pad to move the mouse pointer and tap the pad to click or double-click. I have one of these on my laptop and I like it a lot.

- ✪ **Light pen**. These devices never really caught on, but the general idea is that you move a pen across a grid of wires, and light from the pen shines on the grid to indicate a position on the screen. Light pens are supposedly good for drawing, but not many applications support them.

## Special Keyboards

Special keyboards fall into two categories: those with extra keys and those with unusual shapes that supposedly prevent wrist problems. Some models have both features.

My favorite special keyboard is the Microsoft Natural keyboard. It has some special Windows 95/98 keys that open menus with a touch of the key, but the best part is that the keyboard is slightly split so that your hands can come in at a natural angle to type. It also has a built-in wrist rest at the bottom. Generic keyboards with the same features cost slightly less, but if the price difference is small, I prefer to go with the name-brand product.

You can also get keyboards with cordless mice, keyboards with trackballs attached, and keyboards with touchpads. There are keyboard that are split into two pieces and keyboards that slant up or down—walk through a computer store's keyboard aisle sometime and marvel at the variety.

## TV and Radio Cards

As if productivity hadn't slipped enough in the American worker, now you can watch TV right on your computer screen. A TV card is an interface card that enables you to open a window in Windows 95/98 and watch your favorite TV shows. I don't own one of these, so I can't attest to how well they actually work, but it sounds like an interesting idea.

**CAUTION**

◆ ◆ ◆ ◆ ◆ ◆ ◆ ◆ ◆ ◆ ◆ ◆ ◆ ◆ ◆ ◆ ◆ ◆ ◆ ◆ ◆ ◆ ◆ ◆ ◆ ◆ ◆ ◆ ◆ ◆ ◆ ◆ ◆ ◆ ◆ ◆ ◆ ◆

If you're shopping for a TV card, read the box carefully. Another kind of interface card—also sometimes called a TV card—does not contain a TV tuner. Instead, this card enables you to use your TV set as a computer monitor, an entirely different concept. You won't be happy with it if you went shopping for a card for watching TV on your monitor.

And remember that although Windows 98 touts its support for TV cards, it currently supports only the ATI All In Wonder Pro. When you shop for a TV card for Windows 98, check carefully to be sure that it will run when you get it home.

◆ ◆ ◆ ◆ ◆ ◆ ◆ ◆ ◆ ◆ ◆ ◆ ◆ ◆ ◆ ◆ ◆ ◆ ◆ ◆ ◆ ◆ ◆ ◆ ◆ ◆ ◆ ◆ ◆ ◆ ◆ ◆ ◆ ◆ ◆ ◆ ◆ ◆

## Joysticks and Game Controllers

If you're a serious game player, you can rack up higher scores in your favorite games with the right equipment. All kinds of game controllers are available—from simple game pads to complex steering wheels and gas pedals for driving games, flight yokes for flight games, and rapid-fire joysticks for shoot 'em-up action. By the time you read this book, you may also be able to buy virtual reality gloves and helmets at your local computer store, along with games to play with them.

If you're just beginning to explore the world of games, don't overbuy. I bought a simple joystick for under $20 six months ago, and I have yet to find a game that requires a fancier controller.

On the other hand, if you play a particular type of game—say, a flight simulator—all the time, you owe it to yourself to have a good controller. Go to stores where these devices are available for demonstration and see which ones feel the best to you.

## Summary

You covered a lot of ground this morning! I hope you didn't try to read everything, but rather skipped around to the subjects that pertained to your upgrade.

This afternoon's session builds on your newfound general knowledge of hardware by doing some specific shopping for the components you want. You'll come away with a realistic idea of the brand and model you want and how much you should expect to pay for it.

# Shopping for the Best Deals

- ✪ Brand-Name or Generic?
- ✪ Choosing the Brand and Model
- ✪ Finding the Best Stores
- ✪ Working with Mail Order Outlets
- ✪ Going on a Retail Shopping Expedition

Now that you understand the technical side of the components you need, it's time to learn about the market side. There are probably 50 models of every component, and 200 vendors who want to sell them to you, and they all seem approximately the same—at least on paper. This session shows you how to weed out the garbage from the good stuff and how to shop for the best prices.

I ask you to do a lot of research and running around in this chapter. You may need to make a trip to a newsstand or library, to a computer store or two, or to a friend's house to use an Internet connection if you don't have one, so you can visit Web sites to research models and get prices. You don't have as much to read this afternoon as you had this morning, but you have a lot to accomplish.

## Understanding the Shopping Process

No matter what you shop for, the process is the same. For example, here's a look at the shopping process for something everyone can relate to: grocery items.

Suppose you want peas for dinner. First you decide on the peas you want (canned versus fresh, creamed versus packed in water); you choose canned in water. You did the same thing in terms of computer parts in this morning's session: You learned what varieties were available and decided what you wanted.

The next step is deciding what brand you want and how much you are willing to pay. Suppose your favorite brand of peas is VeggieFresh, which is also

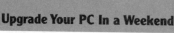
the most expensive brand at about $1.50 per can in most supermarkets. Other brand names are available, too, for anywhere from $1.00 to $1.40 per can. A generic product is also available at about $.80 per can. All the cans contain 12 ounces of peas packed in water and the same nutritional values. Are you willing to pay the extra price for the name-brand peas? That's up to you to decide. You need to make that decision about your computer upgrades too: Are you willing to pay extra for the name-brand component with the attractive box (and perhaps the better quality), or are you willing to accept the functional but plain (and perhaps inferior quality) generic components?

Sometimes the best idea is to postpone the final brand selection until you have done some shopping. You might find, for example, that the Quick-EE-Mart has a sale on VeggieFresh peas that make them almost the same price as the generic. Similarly, you might find a top-quality computer part on sale for the same price as a lesser-known brand. You might decide to make the VeggieFresh 64 sound card your first choice, but only if it is no more than $20 more expensive than the other brands. Or you might say to yourself, "I want the cheapest CD-ROM drive possible, and I don't care if it's generic. However, if generic is less than $10 cheaper than the name brands, I might as well go with a name brand." You need to decide which trade-offs to accept.

After you decide on the brand and model you want (or have a list of brands and models you will accept), you can start price shopping to find out the lowest price. You'll need to make phone calls, visit stores, browse computer magazines, surf vendor sites on the Web, and so on. The place with the best price will probably not be the most convenient source! Local stores are usually more expensive than mail-order suppliers because the former have more overhead expenses. But the mail-order store will make you wait several days, maybe even a week, for delivery and will make you pay shipping costs. On the other hand, with a local source you can install the new component within hours of your purchase.

That's the big picture. Now let's get down to doing!

## Name-Brand or Generic Parts?

Name-brand parts are going to cost more than generics, just like name-brand canned peas cost more than their generic equivalents. You might be able to find a great sale and pick up a really good name-brand component at a

discount, but it doesn't always work out, so leave that what-if out of your thinking for now.

When you buy a name-brand part, what are you getting for the extra money that you spend?

- **Higher quality**. Name-brand parts are usually (but not always) made from better-quality materials. For example, a name-brand computer case may be made of a higher-grade, thicker metal than a generic one. Depending on the component, the quality difference may be small or great from one brand to another.

- **Fewer defective units**. In general, name-brand parts are manufactured under stricter quality control, resulting in a smaller percentage of returns due to defects. Generic parts are apt to come from some unregulated foreign factory.

- **Advertising**. A name brand becomes that way through advertising. By buying the product, you are helping to pay for that advertising.

- **Customer support**. A name-brand company usually provides more service after the sale, perhaps a toll-free number that you can call with questions. Generics do not.

- **Warranty**. Even if a generic part comes with a warranty, you may find it hard to contact the company and get it to honor the warranty. Large name-brand companies have well-established systems for honoring warranties.

Are all those factors worth paying for? Usually. Every time I buy cheap generic parts, I end up regretting it and telling myself not to be such a penny-pincher the next time. Ultimately, the decision is up to you. Perhaps your budget won't allow you to go with name-brand parts. But if you have the extra money, you can save yourself some headaches by buying name-brand quality parts.

A quick scan through a computer magazine can give you an idea of the big, successful brand names. First, leaf through the first 100 pages or so, looking at the full-page ads for a particular product. These are ads placed by the manufacturers for a particular model or line of component, such as sound cards, hard disks, and monitors. If a company has placed a full-page ad in the front of the magazine, chances are good that it's a well-known and successful name-brand company.

Now look at the vendor ads in the back. These are ads for mail-order stores that sell components. You'll recognize them by the prominently displayed toll-free number and the long columns of tiny type listing the parts they sell. Look for the brand names that appear in these ads. Mail-order vendors carry only the most popular brand names, so if several vendors advertise a particular brand name, you can be sure it is among the most popular.

# Choosing the Brand and Model You Want

If you have decided to go with whatever is cheapest, you can skip this section because the only pertinent quality you are looking for is price. (I urge you to reconsider, though.)

The rest of you, however, are looking for the best component for your money. The strategy I use to pick a component is to ask the following questions:

1. What is the overall best brand and model available today, regardless of price? What makes it the best?
2. Which features of the best model can I do without?
3. Which alternative models offer the features I care about without the features I don't need?
4. Of the products from question 3, which can I afford?

If my answer in question 4 is "None of them," I go back to question 2 and try to reduce the list of features I care about until I can find a product I can afford.

To tackle question 1, you'll need to educate yourself about the market for the component. From this morning's session, you know all the pertinent measurements for the component (for instance, that hard disk performance is measured in access time in milliseconds). So get out there and shop the specifications.

# Read Magazine Articles

Computer magazines are the single best source of information about components. These magazines are hot off the presses; the information is very current, and the article authors typically are experts in computer hardware.

**TIP** My favorite magazines include *PC World, PC Computing, PC Magazine* (for experienced users), and *PC Novice* (for beginners).

Computer magazines offer three benefits for the shopper: manufacturer ads, vendor ads, and feature articles. For your first task, which is educating yourself, you'll be primarily concerned with the feature articles. Therefore, when facing the magazine stand, choose the magazine that has a cover story on the component you are shopping for. For example, if you are shopping for a new monitor, the one that says "Forty Great 17-inch Monitors" would be a good choice. If none of them do, look at some of the tables of contents to try to find at least one good article on your component.

When computer magazines do in-depth reviews of various brands of a particular component, they usually choose one or two outstanding models as their Editor's Choice. You can rely on these picks as being at least at the Good level in quality and features. The primary audience for these magazines is computer professionals, who typically have more demanding hardware requirements than the average person. So if the editors have chosen a particular model as suitable for the "geeks," it will probably work fine for non-geeks too.

It pays to look at more than one magazine. Three different magazines evaluating the same component may pick three different winners. If one particular model wins an award in more than one magazine, you should certainly consider it.

**CAUTION** The computer world frequently debates the objectivity of the reviews in computer magazines. These magazines rely on hardware manufacturers to buy ads and supply free parts for their tests, so the publications don't want to anger the manufacturers with bad reviews. The editors of these magazines walk a difficult line between serving their readers and maintaining friendly relations with the manufacturers. In general, though, they do not give their Editor's Choice awards to total dogs. Although you can't be certain that the award-winning model is the absolute best, you can be assured that it is at least in the top half of the group in quality.

Take a trip to your local newsstand—now is as good a time as any—and peruse the magazine racks. Bring home the top two or three magazines that look like they have articles pertinent to your search. Then take an hour or so to read.

**TIP**   Later this afternoon take a look at those mail-order vendor ads in the backs of the magazines. The big-daddy magazine of vendor ads is *Computer Shopper*, an oversize publication (more like the size of a book of wallpaper samples than a regular magazine). It has ads from hundreds of vendors. Even though it doesn't have the best articles, you may want to buy a copy for your research.

## Request Literature from the Manufacturer

If a company can afford a full-page ad in a magazine, chances are good that it also has some nice literature to give away. Most of the ads in the magazines have a toll-free number that you can call for more information. Call the companies and ask for their product literature. (It should be free. After all, you've got the power—*you* have the dollars to spend.)

In a hurry? Call that toll-free number and ask questions. What is the maximum refresh rate on that monitor? How much would it cost to add more memory to that video card? Don't be shy—the operator on the other end of the phone is paid to know these things, or to find out.

## Visit Web Sites

Almost all hardware manufacturers have Web sites—it's becoming almost a requirement for being taken seriously in the computer industry these days. Visiting Web sites can help in two ways. You can get an impression of a company by checking out its Web presence. You can also find out a lot about the company's product offerings and identify the model numbers that you want to shop for.

Most manufacturer advertisements in computer magazines include a Web site address. These addresses usually begin with http:// and then have a string

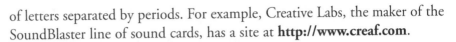

of letters separated by periods. For example, Creative Labs, the maker of the SoundBlaster line of sound cards, has a site at **http://www.creaf.com**.

Most manufacturer sites include descriptions (sometimes very detailed) of each model the company makes. For example, the Web page shown in Figure 3.1 from the Creative Labs site lists the models of sound card and explains their appropriate uses.

Many manufacturer Web sites have automated systems to help you choose the right model for your needs. The example in Figure 3.2 shows the user information form from the ViewSonic Web page. You submit the form, and ViewSonic uses that information to tell you which ViewSonic monitor is right for you, as shown in Figure 3.3.

If you have an Internet connection, go ahead and spend about an hour right now investigating Web sites for the companies that make the component you need to buy.

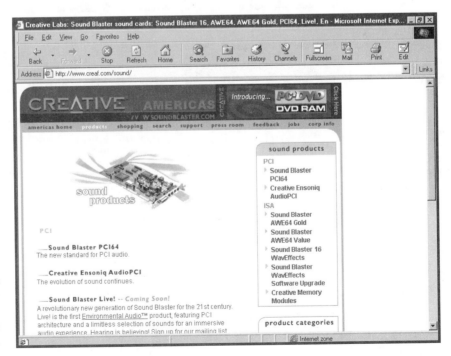

**Figure 3.1**

Manufacturers are eager to help you learn about each model they make.

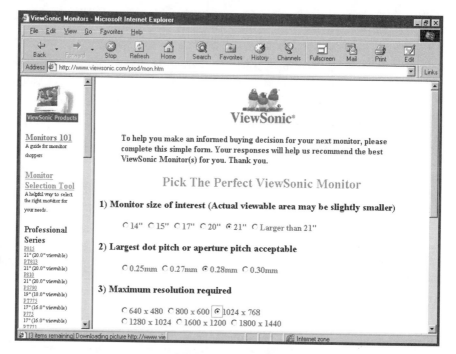

**Figure 3.2**

Some manufacturers use a questionnaire to help you choose a model.

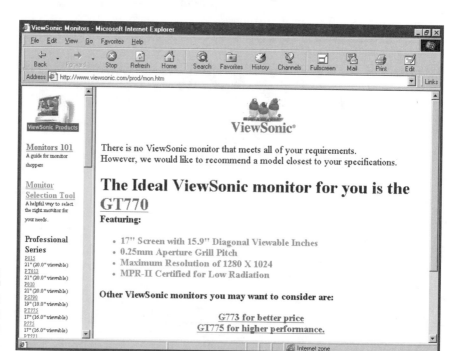

**Figure 3.3**

ViewSonic's response to the questionnaire in Figure 3.2.

# Read USENET Newsgroups

You get the official scoop on a manufacturer's products at the corporate Web site, but on USENET newsgroups you can find out what the average guy on the street thinks of the products. Both perspectives are valuable, of course, for different reasons.

If you have a news reader program, check out the newsgroups in the **comp.sys.ibm.pc.hardware** hierarchy. You can find newsgroups devoted to every kind of hardware component. For example, for video cards, check out **comp.sys.ibm.pc.hardware.video**.

If you don't have time to wade through all those newsgroups, you can use a Web site like DejaNews to search all the USENET newsgroups for a particular keyword. Here's a quick example to show you how it works:

1. Open your Web browser and go to this address:
   **http://www.dejanews.com**
2. Type your keywords in the text box provided. Be as specific as possible, including a model number if you have one. In Figure 3.4, for

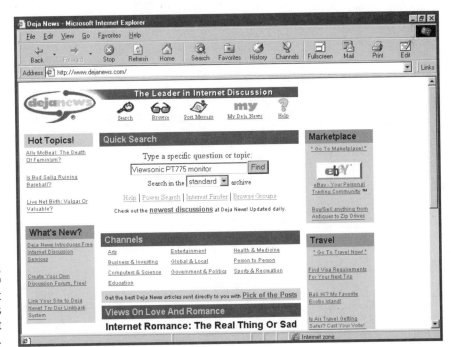

**Figure 3.4**

Use the most specific keywords possible for best search results.

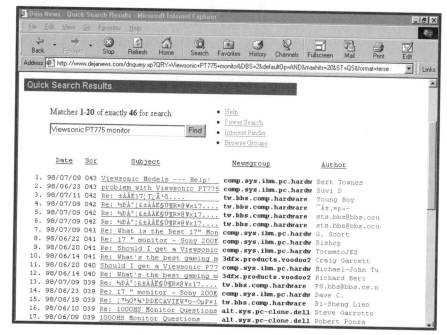

**Figure 3.5**

DejaNews displays
a list of articles
that contain the
words you entered
as keywords.

example, I entered keywords for information about the ViewSonic
PT775 monitor, which is the monitor I currently use.

3. Click on the Find button. A list of messages appears, as shown in Figure 3.5. You can tell from the name of the newsgroup they came from whether they'll be of interest. For example, unless you want to buy a used item, you won't want to look at articles from the "forsale" groups.

4. Click on the hyperlink for the message you want to read. Use the browser's Back button when you're finished to return to the list.

Take a half-hour or so and investigate the USENET newsgroups, either with
your regular newsgroup reader or DejaNews.

# Talk to Salesclerks

Most salesclerks in computer stores are computer buffs themselves and have
very definite ideas about the best hardware for your money. Just ask! You

may not want to make a special trip out right now, especially because later in this session you'll focus on store expeditions. But keep it in mind that you can always ask the clerks what they think.

Be warned, however, that many salesclerks work on commission and are sometimes told by their managers to push certain overstocked items. Therefore, the advice you get from a salesclerk may not be completely objective.

## Ask Your Friends

If you have any friends who are computer enthusiasts, now would be a good time to give them a call. Find out what brands and models of components they have and whether they are happy with them.

Don't have any computer enthusiast friends? Ask around at work. Surely someone there has been through the upgrade process and would be willing to tell you all about how a particular brand and model behaved.

## Where Will You Buy?

After you decide how much extra you are willing to spend for high-quality parts versus inexpensive ones, you need to decide how much extra you are willing to spend for a full-service sales experience.

You make decisions like this every day in real life—it's no different with computer equipment. Say a coffeemaker costs $55 at the fancy Luxoor department store in the mall. The identical coffeemaker costs $42 at the local X-Mart. Some people are willing to pay the extra $13 at the mall for the privilege of shopping in a carpeted store with classical music playing and having a polished, well-dressed saleswoman say, "Thank you, Mr. Brown, and have a pleasant day!" as she hands you a colorful shopping bag with your purchase. Other people would rather keep the $13; they don't mind dodging screaming children with a plastic shopping cart and having their purchase rung up by a gum-chewing teenager in a polyester uniform.

You can buy computer equipment at any of the following places, depending on how much you want to pay for the extra services you receive along with your purchase.

## BRAND/MODEL DECISION WORKSHEET

Use the following worksheet to help you make your decision. Fill it out for each component you are buying. (Use a blank sheet of paper to answer the questions if you have already used up the blanks given here.)

For the component I want to buy, the big-name brands are:

_____    _____    _____

_____    _____    _____

The features that are important to me are:

_____    _____    _____

_____    _____    _____

I don't need these extra features if I have to pay more for them:

_____    _____    _____

_____    _____    _____

From my research, these products seem like the most appropriate models for me:

_____    _____    _____

_____    _____    _____

After researching the companies and products through the Internet, magazines, books, and other opinions, my first choice is:

_____

If that is not available, or if others are available for a better price, I am willing to accept any of these instead:

_____    _____    _____

# Locally Owned Computer Store

If you go to a real computer store, one that employs professionals who love and know about computers, you will probably pay close to the manufacturer's

suggested retail price (MSRP). These "Dwayne and Gilbert" operations (kind of like mom-and-pop stores, except it's two computer geeks instead) are too small to make large-quantity buys from the distributor, so they're forced to pay higher prices. They must, in turn, pass these prices along to their customers.

Although you won't find many discounts at your local store, you will find knowledgeable, helpful clerks who can confirm that you're purchasing the right part for your upgrade. You can also expect quick and painless returns and exchanges, and possibly some advice on installation. Some local shops have their own on-site repair and installation facilities where you can have someone else install your upgrade if you chicken out.

**CAUTION** Be a decent human being. Don't go into a locally owned computer store, pick the guy's brain for an hour, and then go across the street and make your purchase at the MegaSuper Warehouse. You might save $20, but you've just done a crummy thing to the local store owners who are trying desperately to compete with the big chain. If you are going to use the knowledge found in a local store, pay for it by making your purchase there.

## National Chain Computer and Electronics Stores

In the last five years, a whole lot of computer and electronics stores have sprung up in the big cities. Some of them, like CompUSA, sell only computer hardware and software. Others, like Best Buy, sell a variety of things— not only computers, but also appliances, TVs, and so on. Given the choice, I prefer the computers-only stores, because the sales staff seems to be more knowledgeable and the selection seems better than in a general electronics store.

You can expect to find some decent bargains in these national chain stores because they buy in bulk and pass some of the savings on to you. You will also find a fairly knowledgeable sales staff (typically computer-techie teenagers who like their jobs) and a well-established policy on returns and exchanges. Some of these stores also have on-site repair and upgrade facilities. You may have to hunt for someone to help you, though; these stores are sometimes understaffed.

You may also have a hard time finding the exact brand and model you want here unless you are looking for one of the most popular products in the category. These stores cater to the low-end user and carry mostly the economy models from name-brand manufacturers.

## Office Supply Stores

Increasingly, national chain office supply stores have begun offering computer equipment. Their salespeople are usually not computer focused, although they are normally friendly and mature. Their prices vary, usually on the high side except for special sales, which can be very good.

I have noticed that office supply stores typically cater to the nonexpert. They assume that their customer is a busy person who just wants a piece of hardware that can do the job and is not picky about models or features. In keeping with this philosophy, these stores usually carry older models, rather than the latest thing. A recent trip to a local office superstore, for example, turned up six laser printers, four of which I knew were last year's models and on sale at clearance prices at most computer stores. However, this office supply store was selling the printers at full price, as if they were still the latest thing. The newer models that replaced them in the manufacturer's lineup were not on the shelves.

## Department Stores

Big department stores in malls, like Sears, J.C. Penney, Marshall Fields, and so on, sometimes have computer departments. They are usually small and stuck in the corner of the TV and VCR department. You will seldom find components for sale; these departments deal mainly in new systems.

I would avoid these types of stores for buying computer hardware components. The prices are typically not very good, and the salespeople are usually not computer experts. They don't sell enough computers to compete with the computer superstores.

## Discount Stores

Discount stores—Target, Wal-Mart, K-Mart, and so on—do not usually have a wide selection of computers or parts. However, if you happen to find

what you want, and it is on sale, you may get a great deal. I got some inexpensive speakers, for example, for my nephew's computer. There was only one model for sale, but it was $10 less than the same model at the local computer superstore. Watch the weekly ads and circulars for bargains, but don't expect to walk into the store cold and find exactly what you want.

## Direct from Manufacturers

Can't find the product for sale in any store? You can order it directly from the manufacturer. Most manufacturers have toll-free sales lines; some manufacturers also take orders on their Web sites.

The telephone salesperson should be extremely knowledgeable about that brand and may even be able to suggest a model that is better for your needs than the one you had in mind. This type of buying experience is usually very pleasant. However, you probably won't get any kind of discount—you can expect to pay the full MSRP (plus shipping).

 **TIP** If you can't find the product in stores, visit the manufacturer's Web site and look for a page called Where To Buy or Vendor List. Manufacturers often provide lists of stores that carry their products, and you may be able to get a better price from a retail source than you would from the manufacturer.

## Mail-Order Vendors

Mail-order companies deal in deep discounts. The best price will almost always come from a mail-order source. They can afford to offer the best prices because they buy large quantities from the distributor and have very low overhead (no showroom or well-dressed salesmen).

Drawbacks? You won't get much advice here; you need to know exactly what you want before you call. Luckily, you already have this information. Also, if the merchandise is damaged, you have to mail it back; you can't just drive over to the store like you can with a local vendor. Most vendors require you to call first and get a special return-authorization code to put on the package. (I explain returns more thoroughly in the Sunday afternoon session.)

I make most of my purchases through mail-order vendors, simply because the prices are so good. Rather than calling on the phone, I usually shop from their Web sites. Appendix A lists the Web sites and phone numbers of lots of mail-order vendors.

## Summing Up

Table 3.1 lists the relative pros and cons of the various upgrade sources. Of course, each category has exceptions—you may find a locally owned store with lousy service, for example, or an office supply store with a very knowledgeable sales staff. Table 3.1 merely reflects my own biased opinions, based on my own experiences.

### TABLE 3.1 COMPARISON OF SHOPPING SOURCES

| Store Type | Low Price | Salesclerk Availability | Salesclerk Knowledge | Repair and Exchange Policies |
|---|---|---|---|---|
| Locally owned computer store | Fair | Excellent | Excellent | Excellent |
| National chain computer store | Good | Fair | Good | Excellent |
| Office supply store | Fair | Fair | Fair | Good |
| Full-service department store | Poor | Good | Fair | Excellent |
| Discount department store | Good | Poor | Poor | Good |
| Manufacturer | Poor | Excellent | Excellent | Good |
| Mail-order vendor | Excellent | Poor | Fair | Varies |

# My Recommendations

❂ If you are uncertain as to whether you are buying the right thing, pay the higher price to get the part from a friendly local computer store. The extra service will be worth it.

❂ If you know exactly what you want and you need it right away, go to your local computer superstore chain.

❂ If price is the most important factor and you know what you want, buy through mail-order.

❂ If you have shopped and shopped and cannot find the part you want for sale, call the manufacturer and ask where it is sold.

# Shopping the Mail-Order Vendors

Even if you have decided not to buy from mail-order vendors, you still need to check them out. Why? Because their prices are the lowest. By shopping mail-order vendors, you get a baseline low price for the item. Then if you decide to pay extra by buying somewhere else, you at least know how *much* extra you are paying.

For example, suppose you have decided on a Creative Labs SoundBlaster AWE64 sound card. You go to your local computer superstore. It is regularly $120 there, but it is on sale for $100. Is that a good price? You probably have no idea.

But what if you shopped a few mail-order vendors first? A flip through the vendor ads in several computer magazines will tell you that the mail-order price is between $80 and $110. Now you can make an informed choice: you can buy it locally for $100 and have the convenience and immediate gratification, or you can take the time to investigate and buy from the vendor who has it for $80.

**TIP** When figuring out mail-order prices versus retail, don't forget that you have to pay shipping on mail-order purchases! That usually adds from $5 to $30 to the price, depending on the weight. However, if the vendor is in a different state, you may not have to pay sales tax, so the extra charge may come out as a wash.

Mail-order buying isn't for everyone, and the low prices come with some drawbacks. In the following sections, I show you how to check out a mail-order company, step by step.

# Finding the Best Mail-Order Prices

Mail-order vendors want to make it very easy for you to shop with them, so they typically have several contact methods:

- Magazine ads
- Catalogs
- Telephone inquiries
- Web-based shopping

## Magazines

If you are ready to shop the ads, the best magazine to get is *Computer Shopper*. It's an oversized whopper of a publication with very little *except* ads. Some big vendors have minicatalogs of 8 to 10 pages in here, rather than just single-page ads. You can really get a feel for the big-name mail-order vendors by flipping through an issue.

**CAUTION**    The ads in computer magazines are great, but sometimes they aren't accurate. Those ads are submitted to the magazine publishers over a month in advance, and the vendor may have changed the price by the time you see the ad. You should always call and verify a price if you are going to use it as the basis for your comparison. Memory prices are especially volatile; never trust a published price on memory to be the currently available price.

## Catalogs

After you buy something from a mail-order company, you will begin to receive their catalogs, and will probably continue getting them for many years. (These companies don't give up on you easily.) You can also call the toll-free number in the ad to request a free catalog. Catalogs are more reliable than ads because the company publishes them on a tighter schedule, so the prices are less likely to have changed. (And some companies will *always* honor a catalog price as a matter of principle.)

## Phone Calls

If you don't have any catalogs or ads, you can still find out a vendor's price on an item. Just call a vendor and ask for a price. Then say "Thank you" and hang up. Don't let anyone pressure you into buying the item on the spot.

**TIP**  When you call for a price on an item, the telephone representative may ask for your name, address, and phone number. You do not have to provide this information. Some companies sell their contact lists to other advertisers, so say no if you want to; don't feel pressured. The worst that can happen is the company won't give you a price. Their loss.

## Vendors' Web Sites

Finally, you can visit the vendor's Web site to get current prices. Many vendors have online ordering, so you don't even have to talk to a salesperson. When the time comes to make the purchase, you just fill in a form with your Web browser, enter your credit card number, and click on Send. Some systems are set up for secure ordering, which means your credit card number is encrypted so it can't be stolen easily. But in reality, the chance of someone stealing a credit card number you send online is extremely remote (less than being hit by a car in the next five minutes), so personally I never worry about it.

Here's an example of a Web site shopping excursion. If you're not interested in Web shopping or already have experience with it, you can skip this section.

1. Start your Internet connection and point your Web browser to a vendor's site. This example uses MicroWarehouse (**www.warehouse.com**).

2. Suppose you are looking for a Hayes Accura 56K modem. Type that string in the Search box, as shown in Figure 3.6.

3. Click on Submit. A list appears of the items for sale that match your criteria, as shown in Figure 3.7.

4. Jump back to the MicroWarehouse home page by clicking on the Back button.

5. Click on the Blowouts button to see what is on sale. Even if your first choice is not on sale, it's worth looking. You may be able to find a better model on sale for the same price as that of your first choice. If you

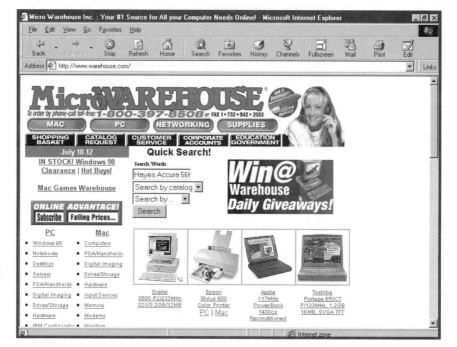

**Figure 3.6**

Look for a Search
text box and
type your search
criteria into it.

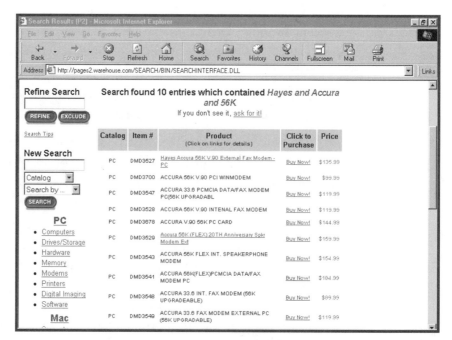

**Figure 3.7**

The results of the
search for Hayes
Accura 56K.

see something on sale that you want, click on it; otherwise click on Back to return to the home page.

**NOTE**  If you want to buy something, click on the Click Here To Order link while you're looking at the description. The next screen will prompt you for the information it needs to process your order. (You probably don't want to buy right now, though; you're just looking.)

6. Click on the Customer Service button for information on shipping terms and return policies. Click on the links on that page that refer to shipping, returns, and so on.

7. Repeat the process for several other vendors.

## Multiple-Vendor Shopping Sites

Besides visiting the Web sites of individual vendors, you can also check out sites that cull price information for many vendors and present it in a compare-and-contrast format. Follow these steps to check out PriceWatch, one of my favorite such sites:

1. Point your Web browser to this address:

   **http://www.pricewatch.com**

   A list of hardware categories appears along with a search box, as shown in Figure 3.8. This example uses the Search box; later this afternoon you will return to this site and browse by category.

   Say you've decided on a Matrox Mystique video card.

2. Type **Matrox Mystique** in the Search box, and then click on Find It. A list appears of all the companies that sell the part, sorted from least to most expensive, as shown in Figure 3.9.

**CAUTION**  When viewing PriceWatch results, keep in mind that not everything listed is the actual item you want. These are just items with the words you searched for in their description. They might be, for example, an add-on part for that item, as are many of the first few items shown in Figure 3.9.

**Figure 3.8**

Type your search
criteria in the
Search box or click
on a type of
hardware.

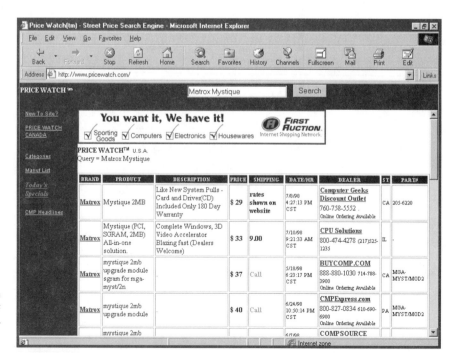

**Figure 3.9**

The results of
searching for
Matrox Mystique.

3. Read the description for each item carefully to make sure it is the actual item you want. Then make a note of the company name and telephone number to call.

4. Call the vendor and verify the price. Prices on PriceWatch are sometimes out of date; the vendor may not have the item for sale at that price anymore.

## Checking the Shipping Terms

You can check a vendor's shipping terms on its Web site (usually in the customer service area); you can also check the terms by reading the fine print in the catalogs or ads and by calling on the phone.

Shipping terms are really important because some companies gouge you in a big way. They'll charge $15 or more to ship a tiny part that doesn't weigh more than six ounces. Only about half of that money goes for postage; the rest pays for their shipping operations. You shouldn't have to pay for that! I try to find companies that make a big deal out of their inexpensive and fast shipping; one vendor, as I write this section, is offering to ship any item that costs $200 or less for $2.99. That's a great deal, especially if you buy something heavy.

## Checking Return and Warranty Policies

You should also try to find the company's policy on accepting returns, both defective and nondefective.

For nondefective returns (for example, if you realize you bought the wrong thing after you get it), you will probably have to pay for the return shipping. That's only fair. However, avoid companies that charge a 10 percent or more "restocking" fee. Although a restocking fee isn't particularly unfair, plenty of companies don't charge it, so you don't have to do business with a company that does.

Almost every company will take back defective goods within 30 days of purchase, but do you have to pay the shipping to send them back? You shouldn't have to—after all, it's not your fault that the part is defective.

After the first 30 days, you can't return defective goods to the vendor; you must deal with the manufacturer instead. Most products are covered under

the manufacturer's warranty for one year or more. The manufacturer's warranty is the same regardless of your source. Each manufacturer has its own system for handling warranty repairs and replacements. You usually have to mail in the part and pay the shipping yourself. Look for the details on the warranty card that comes with the product.

# Evaluating Reliability

When you deal with a big-name mail-order vendor like MicroWarehouse, CDW, Insight, or PC Zone, you automatically get a certain measure of reliability. These big companies have well-oiled procedures in place for order processing, shipping, customer service, and returns. You don't need to investigate these companies too closely. They're not going to go out of business and run off with your money.

However, with the smaller mail-order companies, you might want to do a background check before you give them a big order. Here are some ways to investigate a company:

○ Call the Better Business Bureau in the city in which the company is located. (Use directory assistance to find the number.) Ask about the company's rating.

○ Call the company's customer service phone number (not the sales number) and see how long it takes to get through to a real human being. This length of time is how long you will probably have to wait if you have a problem with your order. Avoid companies that simply patch you through to a customer service voice-mail system, with no opportunity to talk to a real person.

○ Search for the company's name in USENET newsgroups with DejaNews, as described earlier in this session. See what, if anything, people are saying about the company. If this company has ripped off someone, the irate consumer may have shared the gory details in a newsgroup article.

○ Call the sales phone number and ask about a price. Do representatives answer the phone in a professional manner? Is the person who answers the phone pleasant and knowledgeable? While you've got someone talking, ask about their return policy.

# Deep-Discount Shopping

This section is for those of you who have decided, against my recommendation, that price is your motivating factor. Because you've already made up your mind, I won't discourage you; instead, I'll show you where to go to find some incredible bargains on used, overstock, or unknown-quality parts.

Most of the deep-discount shopping experiences are available only through the Internet, so if you don't have an online connection, you won't get much out of this section. If you're really interested, you may want to use a friend's Internet connection for an afternoon.

## Price-Comparison Sites

In Figures 3.8 and 3.9 you saw the PriceWatch Web site, which compares prices for many different vendors. In addition to searching that site for the specific brands and models, you can also use it to look for the cheapest products. Here's how:

1. Point your Web browser to **http://www.pricewatch.com**.
   PriceWatch displays a list of types of hardware (refer to Figure 3.8).
2. Click on the link for the hardware you want. For this example, click on Monitors. PriceWatch displays a page containing a series of keywords.
3. Click on 17-inch. PriceWatch displays a list of all 17-inch monitors, sorted from least to most expensive, as shown in Figure 3.10.
4. Make a note of the vendor and phone number of the cheapest model. There's your product!

Of course, even if rock-bottom pricing is your priority, you will probably want to check out the vendor's reputation before you buy, as described earlier in this session. You should also ask a few questions about the item for sale to make sure it meets your minimum requirements. The 17-inch monitor that costs only $201, for example, probably has an unacceptably high dot pitch (like .38mm for the cheapest one in Figure 3.10) or lacks features like a tilt/swivel base and antiglare coating. Remember, in the end *you get what you pay for.* You should settle for less than the best only when the features it lacks are features that you don't care about. With rock-bottom-priced merchandise, the lacking features are usually semi-important ones.

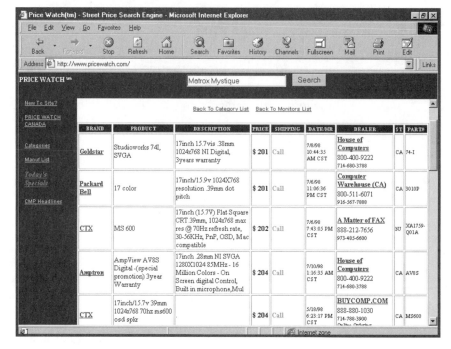

**Figure 3.10**

By browsing
PriceWatch's
categories, you can
find the lowest
priced components.

The same folks who publish *Computer Shopper* magazine also maintain a price-comparison site. It's called NetBuyer, and you can find it at **http://www.netbuyer.com**. You can use it basically the same way as you use PriceWatch to search for vendors who sell the parts you want to buy.

## Commercial Auction Sites

Commercial auction sites are springing up all over the Internet. Here's how they work.

Distributors sell overstocks, last year's models, or factory-refurbished parts to vendors at a deep discount. The vendors then make a contract with an auction site.

The auction site lists the items for sale at a ridiculously low starting price, and then people go to the Web site with their browsers and place bids on the merchandise, usually with a credit card to secure their bids.

At the end of the bidding period (somewhere between 22 hours and seven days, depending on the site), the high bidder is notified by e-mail that she

or he won. The winner's credit card is charged for the purchase, and the vendor ships the product directly to the winner's home. The auction site takes a cut of the profit from the vendor.

◆◆◆◆◆◆◆◆◆◆◆◆◆◆◆◆◆◆◆◆◆◆◆◆◆◆◆◆◆◆◆◆◆◆◆◆◆◆◆◆◆◆◆

Unless the description explicitly says *new,* you can assume that products sold on a commercial auction site are refurbished. That means they are formerly defective units that have been repaired. By law, these products cannot be sold as "new," so they are sold at a discount as *refurbished.*

*Factory refurbished* is the best kind because the manufacturer has performed the repairs. Factory-refurbished equipment usually carries a manufacturer's warranty of at least six months. If the description doesn't say factory refurbished, you can assume that the component is *vendor refurbished,* which means the vendor has fixed it. Such parts usually have a short warranty (like three months) that the vendor honors, and the quality depends on the individual vendor's repair capability.

◆◆◆◆◆◆◆◆◆◆◆◆◆◆◆◆◆◆◆◆◆◆◆◆◆◆◆◆◆◆◆◆◆◆◆◆◆◆◆◆◆◆◆

My favorite auction site is Onsale.com. You can take a tour of this site right now:

1. Point your Web browser to **http://www.onsale.com**.

2. Click on the Computer Products Supersite button at the top of the next Web page that appears.

3. Click on the category you want from the list of categories on the left. For this example, choose Printers. A list of the printers for sale appears, broken down into categories, as shown in Figure 3.11.

4. Scroll down to the category you are interested in (for example, Ink Jet Printers), and click on one of the item numbers to see more information about the item.

5. Scroll through the page to see the description and current bids. Pay special attention to the shipping costs and the return policies. Figure 3.12 shows a description for a printer for sale.

If you want to bid on the item, click on the Place Bid button and follow the prompts that guide you through the registration and bid-placing procedure. You will be notified by e-mail when someone outbids you, or when the auction is over and you have won.

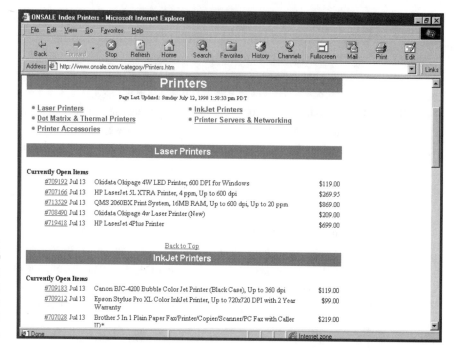

**Figure 3.11**

An auction site gives you a chance at snagging a decent item at a really good price.

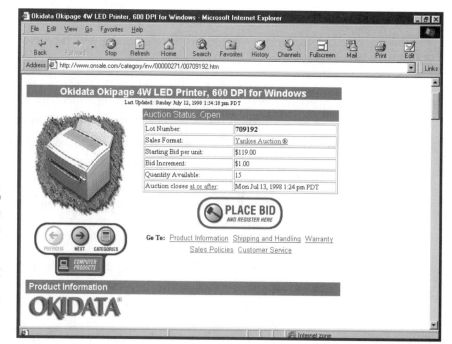

**Figure 3.12**

The item's page typically includes a picture, bidding information, and a product description (which you could see by scrolling down on this page).

I have had good luck buying some items through a commercial auction site; I have also had some extremely bad luck. In general, anything that is advertised as new and is a brand name is a safe buy. I have bought several non-computer items this way (a rice cooker, a cordless phone), and they've worked fine.

**CAUTION**

◆◆◆◆◆◆◆◆◆◆◆◆◆◆◆◆◆◆◆◆◆◆◆◆◆◆◆◆◆◆◆◆◆◆◆◆◆◆◆◆◆◆◆◆

I really like shopping at Onsale.com, but I have two gripes with it. One is the shipping costs. They are usually outrageous, over twice the actual postage. By the time you pay the shipping costs in some cases, you might as well have bought a brand-new unit. Watch for these costs; they're listed at the bottom of each item's description page.

The other gripe I have with this site is that if you need to contact the seller about changing or canceling your order, or to find out why it is late in arriving, you must go through Onsale's customer service department. They won't give you the phone number of the actual vendor so you can contact them directly. They say they will pass along messages to the vendor, but they don't put any pressure on that vendor to respond, so you may end up waiting weeks for an answer to a simple question about your order. Very frustrating!

◆◆◆◆◆◆◆◆◆◆◆◆◆◆◆◆◆◆◆◆◆◆◆◆◆◆◆◆◆◆◆◆◆◆◆◆◆◆◆◆◆◆◆◆

Refurbished equipment works well sometimes; other times the unit is a lemon with a propensity for problems. I had bad luck with a vendor-refurbished name-brand monitor I bought through an auction, but the vendor was good enough to ship me a replacement and pay for the shipping. (Not all vendors will pay for shipping; check the shipping terms.) Unfortunately, the replacement unit was also a lemon. I went through four monitors before the vendor sent me one that worked perfectly.

If you are going after rock-bottom generic components, the auction site is a good way to find and buy them. However, as I have mentioned before, personally I have had bad luck many times when I tried to cut corners this way.

# Consumer-to-Consumer Auction Sites

Another kind of auction site is one where individual people like you and me can list things for sale as well as buy.

For example, suppose Joe in Sacramento has an extra monitor that he doesn't need. He lists it for sale on the auction site. The site takes a listing fee from

Joe's credit card and also a percentage of the final selling price. Glenn in Seattle sees Joe's item for sale and places a bid on it. The auction lasts three days; Glenn wins. Then Joe contacts Glenn by e-mail and congratulates him. He provides an address for Glenn to send his money order to. (The payment method is up to the individuals involved; most people prefer money orders.) Joe also calculates the shipping costs to Glenn's house and asks Glenn to include that extra amount with his payment. Glenn sends Joe his payment, and Joe boxes up the monitor and sends it to Glenn.

Assuming both Joe and Glenn are men of honesty and integrity, and nothing happens to the monitor during shipping, this system works very well. But if anything goes wrong, it can be a nightmare. The problem is that you never know who you're dealing with. Either party might be a con artist. The monitor might get damaged during shipment, in which case both parties will claim that the other party is responsible for the repair. The list of potential headaches is long.

Nevertheless, a lot of people sell (and buy) a lot of merchandise at consumer-to-consumer auction sites (also called personal auctions). I have successfully sold many computer books that I didn't need and have bought a used modem and an upgrade processor without problems.

**NOTE** Consumer-to-consumer auctions have one advantage over commercial auctions: The sellers have usually used the equipment personally, so they can answer detailed questions about it. Also, the seller of a computer part probably removed the item recently from his or her PC to replace it with something newer and better, so you have a reasonably good chance that the item isn't a lemon.

My favorite consumer-to-consumer auction site is AuctionWeb, partly because it includes a system whereby users can leave feedback about one another. You can read what other people have said about someone before you choose to do business with that person. This information gives you a bit of extra assurance that the seller is not going to take your money without shipping you the item. You can find lots of other auction sites by using a search engine (like **http://www.lycos.com**) to search for the keywords *Computer* and *Auction*.

To check out AuctionWeb, follow these steps:

1. Point your browser to **http://www.ebay.com**.

2. Click on the View Listings link on the page that appears.

3. Scroll down past the Featured Auctions to the eBay Categories section and click on a category (for example, Hardware under the Computers heading). A list of subcategories appears.

4. Click on the subcategory you want (for example, Video). A list of items for sale appears.

5. Click on the hyperlink for an item that sounds like what you want. The item description appears, as shown in Figure 3.13.

**TIP**

You can click on the Search hyperlink at the top of the page to open a form where you can search by keyword. For example, if you want to know if anyone has a used Canon BJ620 printer for sale, you could type **Canon BJ620 printer** as a keyword string.

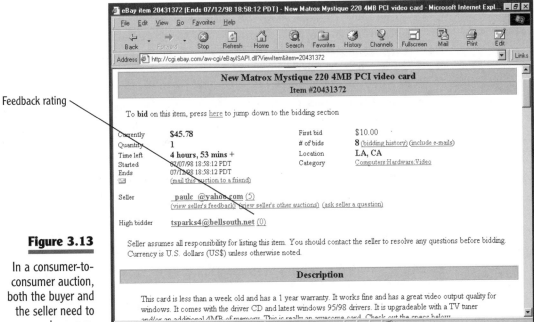

Feedback rating

**Figure 3.13**

In a consumer-to-consumer auction, both the buyer and the seller need to be aware.

# Places to Buy Refurbished and Overstock Equipment

If you want refurbished goods but don't want to play the auction game, you can find many Web sites for companies that will gladly sell you refurbished, overstocked, or slightly out-of-date equipment.

Hundreds of companies sell this way, and you can get a good list of them by using your browser's Search feature (or the one at **http://www.lycos.com**) to look for the keywords *Refurbished* and *Computer*. Here are a few to get you started:

- NetBuyer has a special area called the NetBuyer Basement that show-cases refurbs and overstocks. Go to **http://www.net-buyer.com/** and click on the NetBuyer Basement button.

- Maxim Technology has lots of refurbished equipment for sale. Some is factory refurbished, and some is done by Maxim. Its site is at **http://www.maximtechnology.com**.

- Computer Discounters, Inc. (at **http://www.computerdiscounters. w1.com/**) specializes in used and refurbished equipment.

- Yahoo!'s list of used computer parts dealers (which includes vendors who also sell refurbished and overstock) can be found at **http://www.yahoo.com/Business_and_Economy/Companies/Computers/Retailers/Hardware/Used/**.

**NOTE** A *pull* is a piece of equipment that has been removed from an old system. Buying one is like going to a junkyard to buy a part from a wrecked car. Suppose that the Acme Company buys 100 nonworking computers. Acme removes all the parts and sells them to the public. Acme may or may not test the parts to weed out the bad ones; testing is rather time-consuming and the sales manager may figure that it's cheaper to simply allow buyers to return non-working parts for exchange. Acme's goal is to make a profit after subtracting the money it paid for the computers. When you buy a pull, you can't be sure what you're getting or what shape it's in; that's why pulls are really cheap.

The preceding list just scratches the surface. If you search the Web for *computer* plus various combinations of the terms *refurbished, overstock,* and *used,* you will find hundreds of vendors.

## Take a Break

After an afternoon of shopping research, you're probably ready for a time-out. Have a bite of dinner and get dressed up in your "going to town" clothes, because you're going on a shopping expedition in the remainder of this session.

## Checking Out the Retail Stores

Now that you've seen all the great prices available through mail-order or the Internet, you may be tempted to pick up the phone and place an order without even shopping the local stores. If price is your primary consideration and you don't care that you won't have your part to install until next weekend (or maybe later), go right ahead. However, if you still aren't sure what you want or you want immediate gratification (that is, you want the part in your hands *today*), you should plan a shopping expedition for this evening.

### Planning Your Shopping Stops

Where ya gonna go? Let's make a plan.

1. Find last Sunday's newspaper and look for any ads that show the item you want on sale. Make a note of the nearest store.

2. Go through the Yellow Pages and find all the stores in your area under *Computers, Sales.* Weed out the ones that are too far to drive to or that aren't open on Saturday evenings (unless you want to spread the shopping out over more time).

If you aren't familiar with the locations of some of the stores, use a city map to plan your shopping route. A free online mapping program is available at **http://www.mapblast.com**. Enter the address and city to display a map of the area, as shown in Figure 3.14.

**Figure 3.14**

Online mapping
programs can help
you find the
computer stores in
your area.

# What to Take with You

You should also assemble a shopping toolkit to take with you, consisting of these items:

- A pad of paper for note taking
- A pen or pencil—and a spare one
- Lists of model numbers and prices you found on the Internet or through mail-order shopping
- Your map, if you aren't sure how to get to the various stores

# Your In-Store Shopping Strategy

Your goal is to spend as little time in each store as possible while still gathering the information you need. You can try two different strategies, depending on whether you are interested in talking to salespeople or not.

## Strategy 1: Quick In and Out

Enter the store and scan the landscape to locate the component you are looking for. Don't stop and browse the software displays; march purposefully to the hardware.

Check the price and availability of the models you are interested in. If a salesperson tries to talk to you, be polite but say firmly that you are just looking, thanks.

When you find the item you want, verify that the model number on the box is the same as the one on the price tag. Write down the price, including whether or not it is on sale. (If the item is on sale, call that salesperson back over and ask when the sale ends.)

When you have recorded the information you need, turn around and march out. Don't let yourself get sucked into browsing for anything else.

## Strategy 2: Information Gathering

This strategy is good when you aren't sure you have made the right decision yet. With this strategy, you should take your time in each store, browsing all available models on the shelves and chatting with the salespeople.

When you first enter the store, amble over to the rebates board, where the store keeps pads of rebate coupons. Find out what brands and models of the component have rebates right now. If you can find a rebate coupon worth $50 for a better model than the one you had picked out, you may be able to get the better model and still stay within your budget.

Next go to the section containing the parts you want. Look at the brands and models on your list and also look at some of the others. Take notes on all of them. If you see a brand and model that you hadn't considered, write down all the information you can about it.

In time, a salesperson may come by and ask if you need any help. If one doesn't show up, go looking for somebody. Then start asking questions. The following section provides a template for that conversation.

# How to Talk to a Salesperson

Salespeople vary wildly in their knowledge level and pleasantness to deal with. You may find a real gem, or you may find an obnoxious, pushy creep. You can evaluate the situation quickly and react appropriately by following the guidelines below.

## Start With a General Question

When the salesperson says, "Can I help you?" you say:

> *I'm thinking about buying a <fill in the blank>, but I haven't completely decided which model yet. Can you explain the differences between some of these?*

This broad, open-ended query will show what your salesperson knows—or doesn't know. You'll get one of these kinds of responses:

- **A vague, obvious answer.** If your salesperson doesn't know much, you will get an answer that would satisfy only a complete novice. Luckily, you've done your homework, and you can pick up on it. For example, if you ask about a group of CD-ROM drives and the only difference the salesperson can point out is that some of them are faster than others, you've got a sales dud on your hands.

- **An ultratechie rundown of the features.** This type of answer can be helpful, especially because you'll understand it (after all the study and research you did this morning). You may learn some hidden drawbacks to the model you were most interested in or discover a feature you didn't know you wanted.

- **A request for more information.** The salesperson who asks for more information is the best kind of salesperson. He or she wants to get a better idea of your level of expertise so as to tailor an answer to your needs. For example, the salesperson may ask "What kind of system are you going to use this in?" or "What features are the most important to you?"

If the salesperson asks you for more information about your needs, don't get defensive and huffy about privacy—he or she is just trying to be helpful.

## Be Honest about Your Priorities

If you get a good, knowledgeable salesperson, it can really benefit you to be honest about your shopping situation. Let the salesperson know what your primary motivating factor is. Are you shopping for price? Performance? A particular model at the best price? The salesperson may be able to suggest a brand that you had not considered. (You should go home and research that new brand.)

## Ask Advice—but Don't Believe It

You can ply the salesperson with all kinds of questions and probably learn quite a bit from the answers. But don't take those answers as the gospel truth. The salesperson may not be as knowledgeable as he or she pretends to be, or may receive a higher commission for selling one brand over the other. Still, take notes on the answers and compare them to the answers given by the salespeople at other stores. Eventually a pattern will emerge that approximates the truth.

Here are some good questions to ask:

*Price is my primary consideration, but I also want it to be a reliable brand. Which brands do you think are the best?*

(Looking at two different models by the same manufacturer) *What's the difference between these two?*

*What features do I get with the top-of-the-line model that I don't get with a cheaper one?*

*Which model do you use at home?* (Computer salespeople almost always have computers at home.)

*How do I install it?* (You'll be getting advice on this in tomorrow morning's session, but getting another perspective never hurts.)

*Do I need to know anything special to use one of these?* (You're fishing for advice and tips.)

You don't have to rely on any of the advice you get, but don't completely discount it either. You might learn something valuable about a particular brand or model that you otherwise would never have known. Consider any good advice you get from a salesperson to be a free bonus.

## Ask about Returns and Exchanges

Quiz the salesperson about the store's policies. Does the store accept nonde-fective returns and exchanges after you open the box? Do you need your receipt? (Probably.) How many days do you have to bring something back?

What about defective merchandise? Can you bring it back within 30 days for an exchange, or do you have to send it to the manufacturer?

Personally, I wouldn't do business with a store that doesn't offer a 30-day no-questions-asked return policy on hardware. (Software is a different story; most stores will take it back only if it is still in its original shrink-wrap or defective.) I also look for a store that offers in-store warranty repair service so I don't have to ship a broken part to the manufacturer for repair. (You are going to pay extra anyway if you buy retail as opposed to mail-order, so you might as well get a perk like in-store repair for your money.)

## Cool Off a Pushy Salesperson

If you get a salesperson who tries to shove a particular model down your throat—or stuff it into your hands and point you toward the cash register— force the salesperson to calm down. These people usually work on commis-sion. Their primary motivation is *not* to help you find the best merchandise for your needs, but to push the highest-priced merchandise that they think you will buy. The best thing to say to them is:

> *I'm not ready to buy yet; I'm still deciding what I want.*

You can also deflect the attention onto the merchandise itself by asking ques-tions like these:

> *Which of these two is a better model?* (pointing to two units of about the same price)

> *Which model sells best?*

> *What's the newest technology for devices like this?*

> *Have you heard anything in the news about new products that will be coming out soon?*

You can make it clear to the salesperson that you are not going to close the sale today by saying these things (which, technically, are lies, but you don't owe any allegiance to this pushy dude).

*Do you have a card? I'll be sure to ask for you when I come back ready to buy.*

*I'm shopping for a friend who will be making the actual purchase; I'm just researching the options.*

If all else fails and you're really getting mad, here are some nice ways to say, "You're a jerk; leave me alone."

*Thank you, I'll let you know if I need any more help from you.*

*I need some time to shop by myself.*

*I need some more time to think about it; I'm not ready to buy today.* (Repeat this over and over, no matter what the clerk says. Eventually, even the thickest-skinned salesperson will get frustrated and leave you alone.)

## Your Final Selection

By now you are probably tired out from running around to various stores and making phone calls. But all the research you've done is going to pay off because you're going to make the absolute best purchasing decision.

You can go through this final analysis at home, or if you've decided to buy at a local store, you can do it in your car in the parking lot so you don't have to drive all the way back out there.

# Evaluating Your Notes

If you have taken good notes, you know exactly what models are available and how much they cost at various stores. You know how much money you'll save by buying mail-order, and you know what the exchange and return policies are at every vendor that you looked at.

At this point you might want to summarize your notes on a grid like the one for modems shown in Figure 3.15. It doesn't have to be fancy or neat; you can draw it out on a sheet of notebook paper. Down one side, list the items you have been considering, and then list the vendors that sell them across the top. At the row-column intersections, write the price and any pertinent information.

| | MAIL ORDER | | | LOCAL | | USED/REFURBISHED | |
| --- | --- | --- | --- | --- | --- | --- | --- |
| | CompuZone | MicroShip | CompWarehaus | Best Club | PC-USA | AuctionSite | Basement |
| Hayes Accura 56k | $102 plus $15 shipping | $125 plus $3 shipping | $135 (free next-day shipping) | $140 plus $8.75 tax) | n/a | n/a | n/a |
| US Robotics Sportster 56K | $99 plus $15 shipping | $95 plus $3 shipping (on sale till 12/1) | $129 (free next-day shipping) | $133 plus $8 tax | $159 plus $9.05 tax | n/a | n/a |
| Zoom 56K | $88 plus $15 shipping | $95 plus $3 shipping (backordered) | $110 (free next-day shipping) | n/a | $125 plus $7.75 tax | n/a | n/a |
| New off-brand 56K | n/a | n/a | n/a | $88 plus $6.60 tax | n/a | $75 plus $12 shipping | $89 plus $15 shipping |
| Used US Robotics 56K | n/a | n/a | n/a | n/a | n/a | $55 plus $12 shipping | n/a |

**Figure 3.15**

A grid can help you organize your notes.

# Balancing Cost, Quality, Convenience, and Service

As I told you at the beginning of this session, low cost is important, but it's not everything. Maybe low cost is not even the most important thing. You need to make your decision based on your own priorities:

- Is it important that you be able to install the component tomorrow morning? If so, go with a local vendor.
- Is low cost the overriding factor above all else? If so, go with a used or refurbished model.
- Do you mind waiting a week or so in order to save a few dollars? If not, mail-order is for you.

After you select the type of vendor, you must choose the specific vendor. For mail-order, ask yourself these questions:

- Who has the best price, including shipping costs?
- Does the company seem well-known and reliable?
- Are you comfortable with its exchange and return policies?
- Have you heard anything bad about the company through news-groups or the press that would make you hesitate to buy from it?

For local vendors, these are the factors to consider:

- Who has the best price?
- Does the store have a liberal exchange and return policy?
- Does it do in-store warranty repairs?

For auctions and refurbished/overstock vendors, ask these questions:

- Who has the best price?
- Are you comfortable with the level of risk associated with buying from this source?
- What will you do if the item you buy turns out to be a lemon?

When you have considered carefully all these factors, the correct answer for you should be clear.

## Making the Purchase

After all this fuss, the actual purchase may seem anticlimactic. Still, keep your wits about you; something could still go wrong.

### Purchasing in Person

When buying in a retail store, make sure the box you pick up off the shelves is sealed with its original factory shrink-wrap. If there's no shrink-wrap, look for a plastic seal over the box opening that shows it has not been tampered with. You don't want to get a box that someone else has bought and returned—it might be missing some parts.

**TIP**

If you are buying on a Saturday night, it might pay to check your mailbox to see whether part of the Sunday paper has arrived yet. If it has, you might find an ad showing that the item is going to be on sale starting Sunday morning. You wouldn't want to buy the item for $20 more tonight than you would pay tomorrow morning. Some stores offer a price guarantee that refunds the extra money you paid, but most do not.

When the clerk rings up your purchase, make sure that the cash register shows the same price that was marked on the display. Keep your receipt in a very safe place in case you have to return the item.

On your way out of the store, check the rebate board for any coupons or rebates for the item you bought. You can sometimes get up to $50 or more cash back if you bought an item that has a rebate.

## Purchasing by Phone

All mail-order companies accept orders by phone. When you are ready to buy, call the toll-free number. Have a major credit card ready; most companies won't accept cash or C.O.D.

■ ■ ■ ■ ■ ■ ■ ■ ■ ■ ■ ■ ■ ■ ■ ■ ■ ■ ■ ■ ■ ■ ■ ■ ■ ■ ■ ■ ■ ■ ■ ■ ■ ■ ■ ■ ■ ■ ■ ■

**TIP**  If you don't have a credit card, you may be able to place an order by mail and include a check with it. Call the toll-free number and ask about this possibility.

■ ■ ■ ■ ■ ■ ■ ■ ■ ■ ■ ■ ■ ■ ■ ■ ■ ■ ■ ■ ■ ■ ■ ■ ■ ■ ■ ■ ■ ■ ■ ■ ■ ■ ■ ■ ■ ■ ■ ■

Have the model number ready and, if possible, the catalog item number. Ask the salesperson to confirm the item name and model number and make sure the price quoted is the price you expected. If it's not, ask why.

You will be asked for your name, address, and phone number. It's OK to give it out. However, many of these mail-order businesses sell their mailing lists to telemarketing companies. If you don't want your name to be sold, tell the salesperson specifically to keep you off all mailing lists.

Ask when and how the item will be delivered. You may have a choice of shipping methods and costs. Let the urgency of your need be your guide. I have paid $20 to have a $10 part shipped overnight when I needed it that fast, but that's certainly not a normal situation.

Jot down the salesperson's name and extension and the order ID number. That way, if you need to call in and change or cancel the order, you have a chance of getting back to someone who might remember you—and whoever answers will be able to find you in the system.

Mark on your calendar the day you made the purchase and the day that you expect the delivery. If the package doesn't arrive on the expected date, call the vendor and make sure it was shipped. Don't wait for weeks without checking.

When the package arrives, open it immediately and inspect it for shipping damage. Then install it promptly (as explained in tomorrow morning's session) and test it to make sure it works. Many mail-order companies will not exchange defective goods unless you report the problem within seven days.

## Purchasing on the Internet

Many mail-order vendors let you place orders through their Web sites. Many of the same caveats from phone purchasing apply here, too. Make sure the price and shipping charges are what you expected; make sure you jot down your order number. Don't be afraid to give out your address and phone number, but include a note that you don't want to be added to any mailing lists.

Many Web sites offer "secure ordering," which means your credit card number is encrypted for extra safety. This feature is nice, but I would not hesitate to order from a system without it. The chances of your credit card number being stolen are extremely remote, much more remote than when you use a credit card at a local store.

## Summary

You're done for the day—go get some sleep! If you made your purchase locally, you'll be tackling the installation first thing in the morning. If you have to wait for a mail-order delivery, you can either read ahead to get a preview or set the book aside until your package arrives.

# Installing the Upgrades

- ✿ Essential Precautions
- ✿ Looking Under the Hood
- ✿ Setting Jumpers and DIP Switches
- ✿ Installing Your New Component
- ✿ Replacing a Battery

**N**ow comes the scary part—or at least it always seems that way to me. No matter how many hardware installations I do, I always feel a moment of panic when I face the new project and say to myself, "What if I don't do it right?"

In this chapter you'll learn how to do it right, no matter what part you are upgrading. I take you through the ins and outs of internal and external installations, memory, hard disks, and even motherboards. I can't promise to take away that panicky feeling altogether, but at least you'll know what you're doing.

# How to Use This Session

You need not read every single word in this session. If you're not installing a hard disk, for example, skip the hard disk section unless you have some latent geek curiosity about the subject. (That's not a bad thing; in my opinion, the geeks will eventually inherit the Earth. Bill Gates is just the beginning.)

Before you start skipping around, though, you should definitely read the following sections, which apply to all upgrades:

✪ Essential Precautions
✪ Setting the Stage

# Essential Precautions

All computer parts have the same basic elements: circuit boards, plastic casing, and metal supports. Each part is susceptible to the same kinds of hazards, and they're not necessarily the same hazards that face human bodies. A zap of static electricity, for example, is merely annoying to a person, but it can spell death to a circuit board. Here's how to protect your system against various threats as you work on the upgrade.

## Beware of Static Electricity

Static electricity presents the greatest potential hazard to computer innards. Electronic circuitry is extremely sensitive to static electricity. A zap that is too mild for you to feel can destroy a microchip and, by association, the entire circuit board to which it's soldered. (If that circuit board happens to be your motherboard, say good-bye to at least $100.)

The professional way to avoid static electricity is to wear a special grounding strap. One end wraps around your wrist, and the other end clamps to the air vent on the PC's power supply. The strap effectively grounds your whole body, so it is incapable of conducting static electricity. If you are going to be doing a complex upgrade like replacing the motherboard, I recommend that you buy an antistatic wrist strap. The straps cost about $10 at any computer store.

If you don't want to bother with the wrist strap, you can simply touch the computer's power supply box every minute or so to ground yourself, so static electricity does not build up in your body. This method is not as effective as the wrist strap, but it's better than nothing. Taking your shoes and socks off also helps, as does working in an uncarpeted room. The worst way to work on computer equipment is on carpet in your stocking feet on a cold, dry day. The best way to work is either barefoot or with rubber-soled shoes on a stone or tile floor on a hot, humid day.

**CAUTION** ◆◆◆◆◆◆◆◆◆◆◆◆◆◆◆◆◆◆◆◆◆◆◆◆◆◆◆◆◆◆◆◆◆◆◆◆◆◆◆◆
Some upgrades need an antistatic wrist strap more than others do. You can probably get away with installing a circuit board or a drive without one, but do not attempt "unprotected" motherboard, memory, or processor installation.

◆◆◆◆◆◆◆◆◆◆◆◆◆◆◆◆◆◆◆◆◆◆◆◆◆◆◆◆◆◆◆◆◆◆◆◆◆◆◆◆

# Watch Out for Magnets

Magnets are another natural enemy of computer parts. And unfortunately, magnets are everywhere, even in locations that wouldn't occur to most people:

- Most of the screwdrivers in your toolbox probably have magnetic tips. Don't use these tools when working on your PC; get special, nonmagnetized screwdrivers. The tip of a magnetized screwdriver that accidentally touches a chip or circuit can destroy it. You can buy a computer tool kit containing several nonmagnetized screwdrivers for about $10 at a computer store.

- Your PC probably has a small speaker mounted on one wall of the case. This speaker contains a powerful magnet; keep all circuit boards well away from that speaker. If you are removing the motherboard, you might want to remove the speaker first so that the motherboard does not have to squeeze past it.

- Your telephone probably has a magnet in its ringer. Don't set a part down on top of the phone. If the phone rings, the magnet could harm the part. (Some people consider this warning to be computer geek folklore, but don't take the chance.)

# Avoid Temperature Extremes

Computer components are generally comfortable in the same temperatures as human beings, except that the computer parts prefer it a little cooler than you might. In the "olden days" of computing, when large mainframes filled entire rooms, those rooms were air-conditioned almost to the point of discomfort for the humans to keep the computers cool and comfortable.

If you are too hot, the component is too hot, too. Don't leave your upgrade parts in a hot car. They can withstand hot temperatures to an extent, but why take the risk?

If you are too cold, the component is probably happy unless it is really freezing (literally, below 32 degrees Fahrenheit). In that case, nobody is happy—not you, not the circuitry.

When moving from one temperature to another (for example, bringing a component into a warm house from your cold car), don't try to install it right away. Wait until the component reaches room temperature. If you don't, it may not work properly and condensation on the component could cause it to short out.

**CAUTION**   Here's a true story. I once took a used laser printer to my aunt's house—several hours' drive (in the middle of winter). As soon as I walked through her door, I set up the printer and tried to demonstrate how wonderful it was. The print quality was horrible—big strips were missing ink entirely on each page. I panicked, because I had just paid $200 for the printer in "as is" condition. An hour later, however—after the printer had reached room temperature—I tried printing again, and the thing worked perfectly. Apparently, the toner didn't spread evenly when cold.

## Always Turn Off the Power

Before you start working on a piece of computer equipment, make sure that the power is off. In my opinion the best way to protect yourself is to unplug the thing completely. That way you don't have to worry about accidentally bumping the power switch. Some experts disagree, claiming that you should leave the computer plugged in (with power off) while working on it, especially if you do not have an antistatic wrist strap. Can you guess why? When you touch the power supply to ground yourself, it works because any static electricity in your body passes through the power supply and runs to the wall outlet through the three-prong (grounded) power cable of the PC. If you unplug that cable, touching the power supply doesn't ground you nearly as efficiently.

The ultimate decision is up to you. The safest possible solution is to use a wrist strap and unplug the computer. Personally, I always unplug everything, wrist strap or not.

## Don't Touch the Electronics

Always handle circuit boards by their edges. Never put your fingers on the flat part. That's because you could crush one of those delicate little resistors or knock loose some important bit of soldering. If you haven't grounded yourself, you could also zap whatever you touch with static electricity.

◆ ◆ ◆ ◆ ◆ ◆ ◆ ◆ ◆ ◆ ◆ ◆ ◆ ◆ ◆ ◆ ◆ ◆ ◆ ◆ ◆ ◆ ◆ ◆ ◆ ◆ ◆ ◆ ◆ ◆ ◆ ◆ ◆ ◆ ◆ ◆ ◆

**CAUTION**   Most circuit boards have resistors and capacitors. They look like little logs with a leg at each end. Each leg is soldered to the circuit board. If a leg looks like it's been bent, don't attempt to straighten it. You'll only make the problem worse. The appearance of the resistor doesn't matter in the least; all that matters is that both ends are securely soldered to the circuit board. Any attempt to straighten the legs only increases the chance of one of them coming loose.

◆ ◆ ◆ ◆ ◆ ◆ ◆ ◆ ◆ ◆ ◆ ◆ ◆ ◆ ◆ ◆ ◆ ◆ ◆ ◆ ◆ ◆ ◆ ◆ ◆ ◆ ◆ ◆ ◆ ◆ ◆ ◆ ◆ ◆ ◆ ◆ ◆

# Back Up Your System Files

Before you turn off the computer and open the case, take a moment to imagine the worst possible scenario: Something happens that destroys your hard disk or affects the computer's ability to start. Got it in mind? Good. Now prepare for that possibility.

Copy all your important data files to floppy disks and store them somewhere out of the way. The list may include word processing files, your checkbook register from Quicken or Microsoft Money, any artwork you have downloaded from the Internet, and so on. If you have the time and enough disks (or a tape backup drive), performing a full system backup is the safest and most thorough plan. If not, at least preserve your most critical data files.

# Make a Boot Disk

The next step is to make an emergency boot disk. You can insert this disk in your floppy drive to start the computer if your hard disk won't boot. An emergency boot disk is a simple thing and takes only a few minutes to make, but having one can mean the difference between fixing a problem yourself and paying a technician $75 or more to fix it for you.

## Making a Boot Disk in Windows 95/98

If you have Windows 95 or 98, making a boot disk is simple. Follow these steps:

1. Find an empty disk or one that contains nothing that you want to keep.
2. Label it "Windows Startup Disk."
3. Choose Start, Settings, Control Panel.

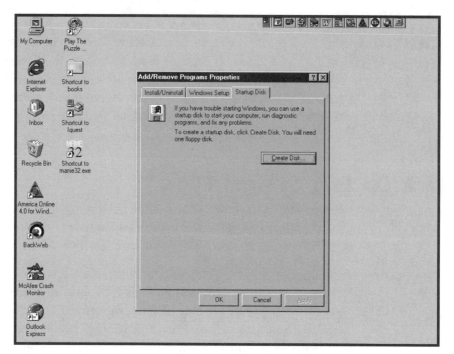

**Figure 4.1**

The Create Disk command on the Startup Disk tab automates the process of creating a startup disk.

4. Double-click on Add/Remove Programs.

5. Click on the Startup Disk tab (see Figure 4.1).

6. Click on the Create Disk button.

7. Insert the Windows CD into your CD-ROM drive (if prompted) and click on OK to continue.

8. Insert your disk into the disk drive when prompted and click on OK to continue.

9. Wait for Windows to copy the appropriate files to the disk. It may take several minutes.

10. Wait for the progress bar to disappear and the Startup Disk tab to return to view.

11. Shut down the computer (Start, Shut Down) and test the disk to make sure the computer starts correctly with it.

12. Remove the boot disk from your disk drive and turn off the power. You are ready to upgrade.

## Making a Boot Disk in DOS

If you do not have Windows 95 or 98, you can make your own boot disk in DOS, although it takes a little more effort. Follow these steps:

1. Find either an empty disk or one that contains nothing that you want to keep.

2. Label it "DOS Startup Disk" and place it in the A: drive.

3. Type **FORMAT A: /S** at the DOS prompt and press Enter. Then wait for the formatting to occur.

 **TIP** If the disk you are using has already been formatted, you can save some time by adding the /Q (for Quick) switch to the command in Step 3, like this: **FORMAT A: /Q /S**.

4. Press Enter when DOS prompts you to enter a volume label. (This label isn't necessary.)

5. Type **N** for No when DOS asks whether you want to format another disk.

6. Change to the DOS directory by typing **CD\DOS** and pressing Enter.

7. Type the following commands at the DOS prompt, pressing Enter after each one:

    **COPY CHKDSK.EXE A:**

    **COPY SCANDISK.\* A:**

    **COPY ATTRIB.EXE A:**

    **COPY EDIT.COM A:**

    **COPY QBASIC.\* A:**

    **COPY FORMAT.COM A:**

    **COPY FDISK.COM A:**

    **COPY SYS.COM A:**

    **CD\**

    **COPY AUTOEXEC.BAT A:**

    **COPY CONFIG.SYS A:**

**TIP**  If you are using a DOS version earlier than 6.*x*, you may get a File Not Found error message when attempting to copy the ScanDisk files. Ignore it.

8. Leave the disk in the A: drive and press Ctrl+Alt+Del to restart the computer. If it boots and you see a DOS prompt (A> or A:\>), the boot disk worked.

9. Remove the boot disk from your drive and turn off the power. You are ready to upgrade.

# Setting the Stage

Most upgrades require a clean, roomy place to work and good tools. After you have prepared such an area, you can unpack your new equipment, read the instructions, and prepare for the big installation event.

The work area should be a clean, well-lit table with plenty of room. Don't try to work on a card table (too shaky), or worse, on your lap (no room) or on the floor (where dogs and children can interrupt). If you plan on testing your upgrade in the same location, make sure to have an electrical outlet nearby. (The outlet is not a necessity; you can always move the computer back to its original location to test it.)

**CAUTION**  If the table you choose is made of finished wood, you might want to cover it with a piece of cardboard or some newspapers. Computer cases sometimes have sharp edges that can mar the finish on a wooden table.

# Assembling Your Tools

Here are the minimum tools you will need:

- ✪ A pad of paper and a pencil for taking notes
- ✪ The emergency startup disk you made earlier in this session
- ✪ A small, nonmagnetic Phillips-head screwdriver
- ✪ Any available manuals for the computer

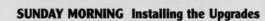

❂ An antistatic wrist strap (recommended but not essential)

Depending on the upgrade you're performing, you may also need the following items:

❂ A small, nonmagnetic flat-head screwdriver

❂ A large pair of nonmagnetic tweezers (in case you drop a screw inside a component and need to fish it out)

❂ A chip-removal tool (usually provided with upgrade processors that require chip removal)

## Unpacking the New Component

I know it probably seems like Christmas morning, with the excitement of the purchase, but try to restrain yourself. Don't rip the package open and toss packing materials every which way. Unpack the item as if you are doing so on the sly and want to be able to put it all back in the box later with no evidence of it having been unpacked.

Save all packing materials and make a note of how any Styrofoam supports fit around the item. Don't throw away anything! If the component is defective and you need to return it, the vendor may not take it back unless you include every last little slip of paper that came in that box.

◆ ◆ ◆ ◆ ◆ ◆ ◆ ◆ ◆ ◆ ◆ ◆ ◆ ◆ ◆ ◆ ◆ ◆ ◆ ◆ ◆ ◆ ◆ ◆ ◆ ◆ ◆ ◆ ◆ ◆ ◆ ◆ ◆ ◆ ◆ ◆ ◆ ◆ ◆

If the component is memory or a circuit board, don't remove it from its antistatic plastic bag until you are ready to put it into the computer. The longer the part is exposed, the greater the chance of something bad happening to it.

◆ ◆ ◆ ◆ ◆ ◆ ◆ ◆ ◆ ◆ ◆ ◆ ◆ ◆ ◆ ◆ ◆ ◆ ◆ ◆ ◆ ◆ ◆ ◆ ◆ ◆ ◆ ◆ ◆ ◆ ◆ ◆ ◆ ◆ ◆ ◆ ◆ ◆ ◆

Locate the instructions and place them in your work area. You will need to follow them closely. If the product box contains extra pieces, like a cable or a knob, place them in your work area. The instructions will probably explain what to do with them.

## Reading the Instructions

This step is the simplest of all, and the most essential; yet it's the one most often skipped. *Don't skip it.*

Each upgrade component you buy comes with instructions for its installation. Read them carefully. Any special instructions that came with the component supersede anything written in this book. Those instructions apply to the specific model you bought, and that model's installation procedure may be different from the general instructions presented here.

Here's an example: I was installing an off-brand internal modem for a friend a few weeks ago, and it wasn't working properly. I have installed dozens of internal modems and I thought I knew exactly what to do, so I skipped reading the instructions. When I finally went back and did so, I found out that I was supposed to run a special program before the installation and use the numbers it gave me to set jumpers on the circuit card. When I read and followed the instructions, everything worked beautifully.

The moral of this story is not to assume that you know how a device works. Always, always, *always* read the instructions. Most of the time they will match what you read in this book, but if they're different, you'll be glad you checked.

You should also read the instructions that came with your original computer; the manufacturer may have some tips for upgrading the particular component that you have bought. For example, if you are upgrading the memory, the computer manual probably lists which banks must be full or empty and which jumpers need to be set, if any. (Refer to Figure 2.7 in the Saturday Morning session for a detailed example of a memory chart in a computer manual.)

# Upgrades That Don't Involve Removing the Cover

Some upgrades are easy—you can just plug the new item into the back of your PC and be running in no time. Look at the easy jobs first so that if you have only this kind of installation to do, you can finish early this morning. These include:

♦   Monitors

♦   Printers

- External modems
- Parallel port devices

## Connecting a New Monitor

New monitor? Just unplug the old one from the back of the PC and plug the new one into the same socket. Make sure to turn off the power on both the old monitor and the PC before you start.

Your old monitor's plug may be fastened to the PC by plastic screws that you can turn with your fingers (the more modern way) or with actual metal screws that require a screwdriver. In the latter case you will probably need to use a flat-head screwdriver. (Almost every other screw in your computer has a Phillips head.) Loosen the screws enough to free the connector (no need to remove them from the connector completely) and then gently pull the connector away from the PC (see Figure 4.2).

■ ■ ■ ■ ■ ■ ■ ■ ■ ■ ■ ■ ■ ■ ■ ■ ■ ■ ■ ■ ■ ■ ■ ■ ■ ■ ■ ■ ■ ■ ■ ■ ■ ■ ■ ■ ■ ■ ■ ■ ■

**TIP**   The monitor always plugs into the short socket with three rows of holes (adding up to 15 in total) on the back of the PC. All the other sockets have only two rows.

■ ■ ■ ■ ■ ■ ■ ■ ■ ■ ■ ■ ■ ■ ■ ■ ■ ■ ■ ■ ■ ■ ■ ■ ■ ■ ■ ■ ■ ■ ■ ■ ■ ■ ■ ■ ■ ■ ■ ■ ■

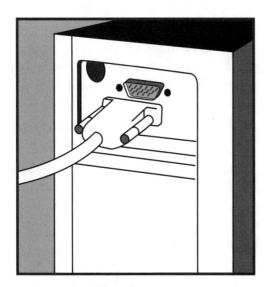

**Figure 4.2**

Loosen the connector's screws and pull it out of the socket.

When plugging in the new monitor, take note of the connector direction; the connector is wider on one side than the other (six holes/pins on one side and four on the other), so it plugs in only one way. Plug the new connector into the PC and tighten the screws to secure it. Don't worry if some pins appear to be missing from the new monitor's connector; not all monitors use all pins. Variations in this configuration are normal.

After you connect the monitor to the PC, connect the monitor's power cable and turn it on. A light on the front should show that it has power. After you have verified that the monitor is getting power, turn on the PC and make sure the monitor works.

To take full advantage of your new monitor, you may want to change the video mode that you use in Microsoft Windows. I explain how to do that, as well as how to make adjustments for a new video card, in this afternoon's session.

# Connecting a New Printer

After unpacking the new printer, you may need to prepare it in one or more ways. Read the documentation that came with the printer. Depending on the model, you may have to:

✿ Remove cardboard or plastic inserts or protectors from inside the printer.

✿ Install a toner or ink cartridge or print ribbon in the printer. (Pay close attention to the printer's documentation; every printer's toner or ink installs a little differently.) See the sidebar "Installing Ink or Toner" for some help.

✿ Attach any knobs or stickers that were packaged separately from the main unit.

✿ If possible, print a test page. The printer's documentation should explain exactly how to perform this test. On some printers, for example, you hold down a certain button on the front of the printer while you turn on the power. Turn the printer power off when you are finished printing a test page.

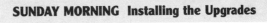

## INSTALLING INK OR TONER

All printers have a slightly different method for installing ink or toner, but some generalizations are possible.

For a laser printer, you will need to install a toner cartridge. Depending on the model, you may also have to install some sort of drum cartridge, which might look like a big metal roller. On a toner cartridge, there is usually a plastic strip that you need to pull away before inserting the cartridge into the printer; that strip holds the toner (which is essentially powdered ink) in the cartridge during shipping. The toner cartridge may also come with a felt strip on a plastic piece that fits somewhere in the printer to clean the printer's transfer wire. On a laser printer, you install toner while the printer is *off*.

For an ink-jet printer, in contrast, you are usually supposed to install the ink cartridge with the power *on*. In some printers, you must turn the printer on and press a button to move the cartridge holder into view. *Read the directions!* Most ink cartridges have some sort of plastic sticker that you need to pull off before installing. But pay close attention, because many of them have *two* plastic labels—one that you need to remove, and one that you *must not* remove. They are usually clearly marked, but pay attention to your documentation.

Some ink-jet printers require a few minutes to charge up the ink delivery system the first time you insert an ink cartridge. It may whir and make all sorts of noises. Do not turn the printer off during this process, or you could damage it. Wait until the printer has completed any kind of initialization or self-test before you turn it off.

 **NOTE**  Some printers don't have any mechanism for printing a test page except through Windows. If that's the case, you'll need to run the setup software for the printer in Windows (see this afternoon's session), and then use the Print Test Page utility from there.

Next, you'll need to hook up the printer to the computer. If you already had a working printer, you do not even have to touch the back of the PC. Instead, you just disconnect the printer cable from the old printer and connect it to the new printer.

The printer cable attaches to the printer with two wire loops. To disconnect the old printer, push the loops *away* from the plug, as shown in Figure 4.3. Then gently pull the plug away from the printer. To connect the cable to the new printer, plug the connector into the new printer, and then push the wire loops toward the connector until they snap into place.

**NOTE**

Most printers do not come with printer cables. If you did not have a printer before, you will probably need to buy a cable. They cost less than $10 at most computer stores.

If you did not have a printer before, you will need to attach the other end of the printer cable to the back of your computer. Just find the socket that matches the end of the printer cable (25 holes for its 25 pins) and plug it in. Then secure the connector to the PC with the screws built into the connector. (On most newer cables, you can turn the screws with your fingers.)

You probably also have some software to install. Most printers come with either an installation program or a set of drivers to use in DOS and

Wire loop

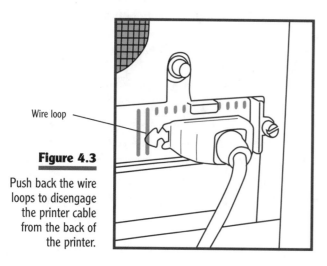

**Figure 4.3**

Push back the wire loops to disengage the printer cable from the back of the printer.

Windows programs. This afternoon's session explains how to install the drivers that enable your printer to work with your software.

## Connecting an External Modem

An external modem comes with a power supply and a telephone cord. It may or may not come with a serial cable (which you need). Figure 4.4 shows the connections you need to make.

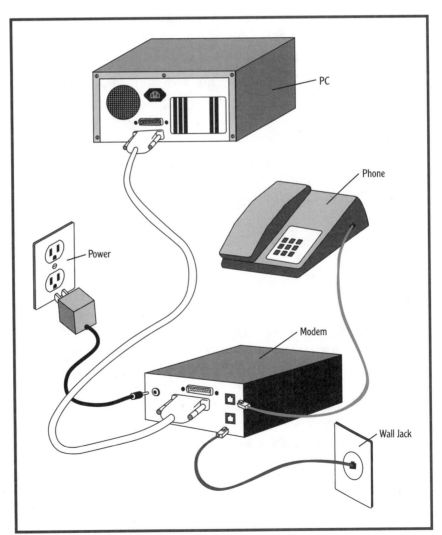

**Figure 4.4**

The correct connections for an external modem.

- Plug one end of the power supply cable into the wall outlet and the other end into the modem.
- Plug one end of the serial cable into the computer's serial port and the other end into the modem.
- Plug one end of the telephone cord into your telephone jack and the other end into the modem.
- (Optional) Plug the cable for your telephone into the modem.

One glitch you may run into is that the serial port in the back of the computer may have the wrong number of pins. Serial ports come in two varieties: 9 and 25 pins. Older computers have one of each size; newer computers only have 9-pin ports.

The serial cable that came with the modem probably expects a 9-pin port on your computer and probably plugs into a 25-pin port on the back of the modem. If all you have free on your computer is a 25-pin serial port, you can do one of these things:

- Decide to unplug the device that is currently using the nine-pin serial port. If it's a device you don't use very often, like a scanner, that approach may work just fine. If, however, you plug your mouse into that port, you are out of luck.
- Buy a 9 to 25 adapter. This connector converts an incoming 9-pin signal to pass through a receiving 25-pin socket. An example appears in Figure 4.5.

**CAUTION**   Be sure you are buying the right adapter for your situation. If the cable has 9 holes on the computer end and you want to plug into a 25-pin port on your computer, make sure the adapter you buy has 9 pins on one end and 25 holes on the other, *not* 9 holes and 25 pins. Check what you need—then check it again—before you go to the computer store. I have a drawer full of adapters that I can't use because I didn't heed my own advice in past upgrade jobs.

You can use 9-to-25 adapters, 25-to-9 adapters, or any combination on any serial port. If the serial cable came with the modem, the modem end will already be correct but the computer end may need adapting. If, on the other hand, you bought the serial cable separately from the modem, you might

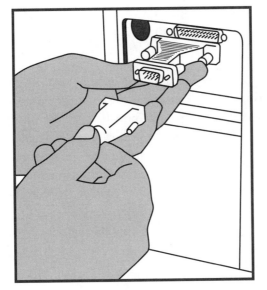

**Figure 4.5**

Use a 9-to-25 adapter to connect a 9-pin serial cable to a 25-pin port on your computer.

need an adapter on either or both ends. If you bought the cable separately and it has the wrong connections, returning the cable and getting one with the right pins on each end will be cheaper and easier than fiddling with adapters.

Another possible glitch involves plugging in the phone line. Make sure you plug the incoming telephone line into the hole in the back of the modem that is labeled *LINE*. If you put it in the hole labeled *PHONE*, it may not work. (Some modems are picky about this; others aren't.)

After you connect the modem, you will probably need to run an installation program to complete the setup. After the initial installation, external and internal modems work the same way, so refer to this afternoon's session on software setup for details about modems in general.

## Connecting a Parallel Port Device

Nowadays you can buy devices that share the parallel port with your printer. This arrangement not only saves you from having to take the cover off your computer and install a circuit board but also saves an IRQ (an interrupt) in the computer's operating system (see the Friday Evening session).

These devices are not particularly fast, but they work well and are a low-cost alternative to pricier models. Scanners work especially well as parallel-sharing devices.

Your computer probably has only one parallel port, so you will have to use the device-sharing adapter that came with your new component. The device plugs into your computer's parallel port (in place of your printer) and has a special offshoot connector for the printer cable. The adapter then regulates the traffic on the parallel port to ensure that the scanner (or whatever it is) and the printer do not try to use the line at the same time. Some devices have a built-in pass-through feature that lets you simply plug another parallel-port device straight into them without a separate adapter. Figure 4.6 shows the connections you need to hook up a parallel-sharing device.

1. Unplug the printer cable from the back of the computer. Depending on the cable type, you may be able to unscrew the connectors with your fingers or you may need a screwdriver.

2. Plug the new device's adapter into the parallel port on the computer.

3. Plug the printer cable into the extra connector on the device adapter.

4. Plug the power cord for the new device into the wall outlet and plug the other end into the device adapter.

When you are finished with the physical installation, you must run the installation software that came with the new device to install the program that manages the port sharing. (See this afternoon's session for software installation.)

## Removing the Cover

If your upgrade isn't one of the ones covered so far, you probably will have to take the cover off your PC. You will definitely have to take it off if you have to install any of the following components:

- Hard disk drive
- Floppy disk drive
- CD-ROM drive
- Sound card
- Video card

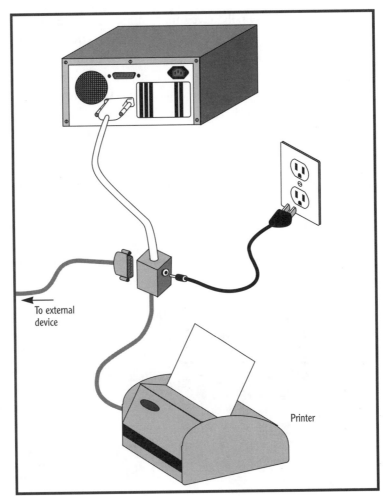

**Figure 4.6**

Connect an external device that shares the parallel port.

To external device

Printer

- Internal modem
- Memory
- Motherboard

My brother-in-law Garry claims that taking the cover off (and putting it back on) is the hardest part of working on a computer. I disagree, but some case designs seem like they were built specifically to cause the user grief in removing and replacing them. The screws are screwed in too tight, the grooves don't line up easily, and so on. Nevertheless, removing the cover is a necessary step in performing the upgrade.

Computers generally have one or more screws (usually Phillips) holding the cover in place, but the location of those screws varies. Most of the time they're in back, along the edges, but sometimes (especially on slim cases) they're on the sides. Figure 4.7 shows some likely locations. Remove the screws and put them somewhere safe. (If you're really lucky, you've got one of the new cases that has levers or a door to let you in . . . but most of the computers that have these nifty cases are too new to need much upgrading.)

**TIP**

I usually bring a soup bowl from the kitchen into my work area and put all the screws I remove into it. That way I don't have to wonder where I put them.

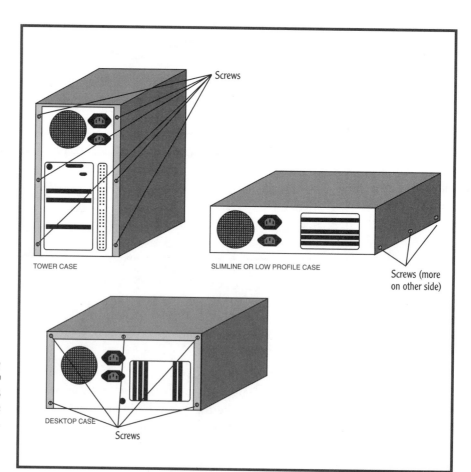

**Figure 4.7**

Look for the screws that secure the computer's case.

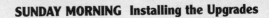
After the screws are out, the cover slides either forward or backward, depending on the case. Figuring out which way it goes is a simple matter of physics:

- ✿ If a metal lip on the cover wraps around the back of the computer, the cover probably slides toward the back of the PC.

- ✿ If the cover is one solid piece of metal or plastic that includes a plate covering the front of the computer, you can guess that the cover slides toward the front.

Remove the cover completely and set it aside.

**NOTE**  Some cases slide back or forward a few inches and then lift straight off. If the cover slides a few inches and then stops, try lifting up.

# A Look Inside a PC

Before you start taking things out or putting things in, you should familiarize yourself with what's already inside your PC. Figure 4.8 shows the layout of a typical system. See if you can find these same parts inside your own PC.

**NOTE**  If you have a low-profile or "slimline" case, the expansion slots and installed circuit boards may not look like those in the computer in Figure 4.8. The slimline case might have a single expansion board plugged into the motherboard, with one card plugged into it. That card, in turn, contains four or more other expansion slots. Circuit boards are mounted onto that card, so they sit parallel to the motherboard rather than at a 90-degree angle to it.

When you take that first look, you probably won't be able to see all the parts because the hard disk or some cables may be covering many of the important parts. Figure 4.9 shows a bare motherboard, with all the drives, circuit boards, and cables removed, so you can see what you're missing. After you know where to look for the components in Figure 4.8, you should be able to peek around the cables and drives on your own system to locate them.

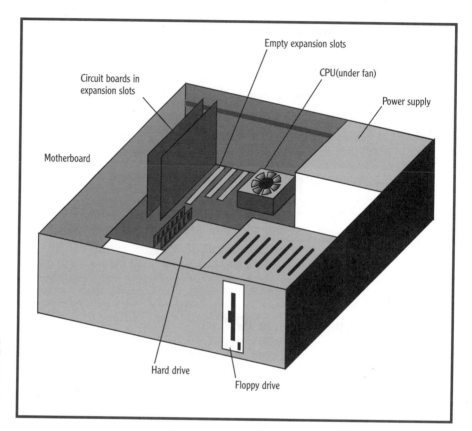

**Figure 4.8**

Here's what you might see when you remove the cover.

Labels in figure: Empty expansion slots · Circuit boards in expansion slots · CPU(under fan) · Power supply · Motherboard · Hard drive · Floppy drive

Figure 4.9 shows a Pentium-class motherboard with PCI bus slots. Your motherboard might be slightly different. You may not have any DIMM slots (or you may have more than one), and you may have a different number of SIMM slots. You may not have any PCI bus slots, and you may have one or two VLB slots instead. (VLB slots look like ISA ones with an extra brown socket at the far end.) Your CPU may be hiding under a fan or a heat sink (a porcupine-looking plastic thing).

## What to Touch—and What to Avoid

While you're looking around inside your PC, touch the power supply before touching anything else. This touch grounds you, preventing static electric shock to the other parts.

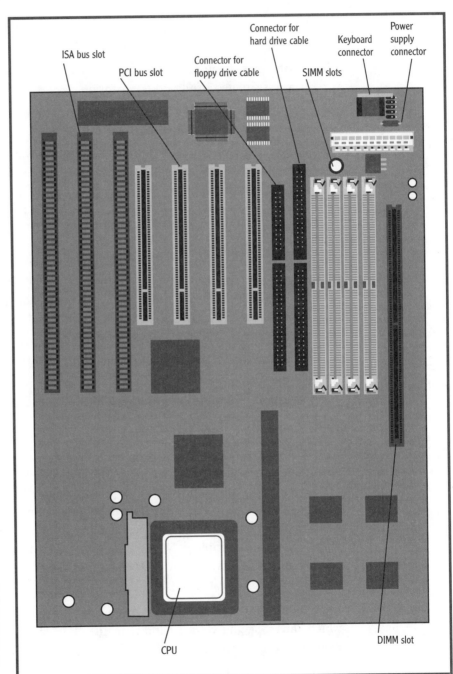

**Figure 4.9**

A typical motherboard underneath all the components that sit on top of it.

If something isn't working right, you might check to make sure all the connectors are firmly seated. Check these things:

○ Gently press down the edge of each circuit board, making sure the board is situated firmly in its expansion slot.

○ Gently press the ends of the ribbon cables into their sockets, making sure they are firmly connected.

○ Place a finger on top of each SIMM and try to wiggle it gently in its socket. If it wiggles, it's not properly seated. Reinstall it (you learn how later in this session).

○ Make sure all other cables that plug into the motherboard are firmly connected.

Here are some things *never* to do while looking at a motherboard:

○ Never touch any part of any circuit board or memory module except the edge. Especially avoid touching any resistors or capacitors soldered to the board.

○ Never drop your tools or screws on the motherboard. If you do so inadvertently, be sure to use a nonmagnetic tool to retrieve them.

○ Never touch any part of the PC when its power is on. Especially do not install or remove components while the power is on.

# DIP Switches and Jumpers

As part of your upgrade, you may have to change one or more DIP switches or jumpers. Your motherboard probably has several of these, and if you are installing a new drive or expansion board, you might find switches or jumpers on it, too. These switches and jumpers enable a component to be used in different ways. For example, if your motherboard can accept several types of processors, the DIP switch or jumper settings tell the motherboard which type of processor is installed.

Internal modems also often employ jumpers or DIP switches to determine which interrupt and device address to use. For example, a modem may require different settings to use IRQs 2, 3, 4, 5, or 7.

## Setting DIP Switches

DIP switches are small switches, like light switches, on a circuit board, as shown in Figure 4.10. They are usually white on an orange or red plastic block. Like a light switch, each one has only two positions: on and off. Compared to jumpers, DIP switches are more expensive to manufacture and are not as commonly used on the most modern hardware. The documentation that came with your new component (or your motherboard) will specify the correct DIP switch settings for a particular configuration.

Here's some practice reading and setting DIP switch settings. Suppose your motherboard has four DIP switches. The documentation has a chart like this that shows you how to set these switches:

| Processor | On |
| --- | --- |
| Intel 486SX | 1234 |
| Intel 486DX | 123 |
| Intel 486DX2 | 12 |
| Intel 486DX4 | 1 |
| AMD 486DX | 13 |
| AMD 486DX2 | 14 |
| AMD 486DX4 | 23 |
| Cyrix 486SX | 24 |
| Cyrix 486DX | 2 |
| Cyrix 486DX2 | 3 |
| Cyrix 486DX4 | 4 |
| UMC 486 | 34 |
| Intel P24T | none |

**Figure 4.10**

DIP switches are small on/off switches.

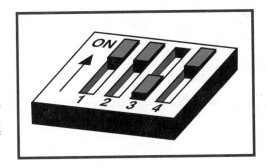

Now suppose you have an Intel 486SX processor and the DIP switches look like Figure 4.11. Your new processor is a Cyrix 486DX4. Consulting the chart, you realize that the new switch positions need to be Off-Off-Off-On. Therefore, you must move switches 1, 2, and 3 to the Off position. You can do this with anything small and pointed; many people use the leadless metal tip of a mechanical pencil. With your new settings in place, the switches would resemble Figure 4.12.

**CAUTION**

◆◆◆◆◆◆◆◆◆◆◆◆◆◆◆◆◆◆◆◆◆◆◆◆◆◆◆◆◆◆◆◆◆◆◆◆◆◆◆◆◆◆◆◆◆◆◆◆

Be careful not to use a needle-sharp instrument to move the DIP switches; it might damage their plastic. Conversely, do not use anything soft (like a lead pencil tip) that might break off during use.

◆◆◆◆◆◆◆◆◆◆◆◆◆◆◆◆◆◆◆◆◆◆◆◆◆◆◆◆◆◆◆◆◆◆◆◆◆◆◆◆◆◆◆◆◆◆◆◆

**Figure 4.11**

All four DIP switches in this block are set to the On position.

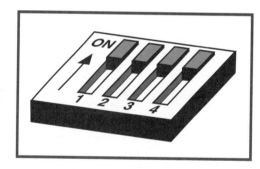

**Figure 4.12**

The new switch positions match the documentation's directive for the new component.

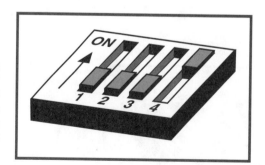

## Setting Jumpers

Jumpers are small plastic blocks that fit over two or more pins that stick up from a circuit board (see Figure 4.13). Jumpers and DIP switches perform the same function, but jumpers are cheaper to manufacture.

| IRQ | Jumper |
|-----|--------|
| 3 | 1–2 |
| 5 | 2–3 |
| 7 | 3–4 |
| 9 | None |

The jumper in Figure 4.13 is currently set for IRQ 5. If you needed to change your modem to IRQ 7 (perhaps to avoid conflicting with other devices in your system), you would lift up the jumper cap and gently push it down over pins 3 and 4.

**CAUTION**  ◆◆◆◆◆◆◆◆◆◆◆◆◆◆◆◆◆◆◆◆◆◆◆◆◆◆◆◆◆◆◆◆◆◆◆◆◆◆◆◆◆

If you need to set a jumper to None, do not remove the jumper cap completely; you might misplace it. Instead, attach it to only one pin. For example, put one hole over pin 1 and let the other hole hang off. This arrangement has the same effect as removing the jumper cap completely.

◆◆◆◆◆◆◆◆◆◆◆◆◆◆◆◆◆◆◆◆◆◆◆◆◆◆◆◆◆◆◆◆◆◆◆◆◆◆◆◆◆

**Figure 4.13**

Jumpers provide another way to configure a device.

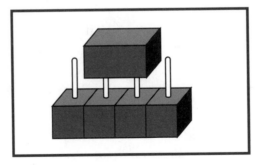

# Take a Break

Before you start the installation itself, take a moment to center yourself and admire the workspace you've created and the tools you've assembled so far. Remember, you're learning to do it the *right* way in this book. Review what you've learned about the inside of your PC and the jumpers and DIP switches you might need to set. Then start the next section refreshed and with a clear head.

# Installing a Processor Upgrade

A processor upgrade is like a brain transplant, but not nearly as gory and complicated. The difficulty depends a lot on your present system. You learned all about the various types of processors on Saturday, when you were deciding what to buy. Now it's time to make the switch from old processor to new.

## Tools Needed

If you are replacing a processor that is not in a zero-insertion-force (ZIF) socket, the upgrade processor will come with a chip-pulling tool. You don't need any other tools (assuming you have already removed the cover from the PC). You might also want an antistatic wrist strap.

## Precautions

Watch out for these things when upgrading a processor:

○ Triple-check that you bought the right model *before* you rip open the package.

○ Read the instructions *before* you take the new processor out of its protective bag. Make sure that this processor will work with your computer.

○ Read all the instructions from start to finish *before* you begin.

○ Don't force the new processor into the socket. If it doesn't fit in easily, you are probably not putting it in the right way.

○ Check your computer's manual to see whether you need to change any DIP switch or jumper settings.

## Possible Issues

The most important thing to remember when installing a new processor is to follow the instructions that came with it. Upgrade or OverDrive processors usually have very good instructions.

## Heat Sinks and Fans

Some newer processors require either heat sinks or fans to help them stay cool. A heat sink, as you learned earlier, is a porcupine-like plastic square that sits on top of the chip and conducts heat away from it. A computer fan is a small plastic device that spins whenever the computer is on, keeping it cool.

Usually when you buy a processor, it comes with the appropriate heat sink or fan, but occasionally it may not. Read the instructions for the processor carefully. If the instructions recommend a heat sink or fan, but none is provided, buy one separately and install it according to its directions. Heat sinks are usually glued or otherwise permanently fastened to the processor; fans are typically clipped or screwed into place with some kind of bracket. Some fans have two pieces that sandwich the processor. The instructions should explain the installation.

**CAUTION**

Different chip classes require different sizes of cooling fans. The cooling fan for 486-type chips will not work with Pentium chips, and vice versa. Both the Pentium Pro and Pentium II chips also require their own specific size and type of fan. If you must buy a fan separately, make sure you get the right kind.

Most fans have power connectors that must be hooked into the computer's power supply. The exception is the Intel OverDrive processors; these come with built-in fans that take their power from the processor socket so they don't require a separate power supply connection. Depending on the motherboard, there may be some pins on the motherboard that the fan's power cord fits down on, or you may need to plug the fan directly into a power supply plug.

If you have to buy a fan separately, buy a good one. The best ones cost from $20 to $30 and use ball-bearing motors. You can find cheaper fans for $10 or less, but they wear out more quickly than more expensive units. Fans usually stop working without any warning; your computer continues to function until the processor gets so hot that it destroys itself and the computer comes to an abrupt halt. That's why you shouldn't hesitate to spend the extra money for a reliable fan.

## Jumper Settings

With replacement processors (that is, new processors that happen to be better than what you have), you need to make sure the jumpers on the motherboard are set correctly for the new processor. With an upgrade or OverDrive processor, you may not need to change the jumpers, because the new processor will be "tricking" the motherboard into thinking it is the old one.

For example, the motherboard manual may have a line like this:

> JP14 Open:<=33MHz Closed:>33MHz

That statement means that jumper 14 should be open (that is, the jumper cap should *not* be across the two pins) if you are using a processor that runs at 33MHz or less but closed (with the jumper cap spanning the pins) with a processor that runs at more than 33MHz. You might have to set more than one jumper on the motherboard—for example, one jumper might determine the chip speed and another the chip manufacturer (AMD, Cyrix, Intel, and so on).

## Voltage

Motherboards vary in the voltage of the processor they will accept. Processors of different voltages have different numbers of pins and fit into different sizes of sockets. Some motherboards require 3-volt processors; others take 5-volt.

Other motherboards have sockets with extra pin holes so they can accept processors with varying numbers of pins. On such motherboards you must usually set a jumper to indicate which voltage of processor you have installed.

## Pin Numbers and Positions

Most older motherboards have a specific number of holes in their processor socket, which means that only one kind (the proper kind) of processor can fit into it. This design prevents someone from accidentally putting the wrong processor in a motherboard.

Nowadays, however, upgrade chips enable you to mix chips and motherboards. For example, you can now put a 5x86 upgrade chip into a 486 motherboard.

If your motherboard has a ZIF socket, it is probably large enough to accommodate the upgrade chip (even if it has a greater number of pins than the original chip). However, if your motherboard's socket does not have the right holes, you can install an *interposer* to correct the problem. An interposer is like a converter, and it solves the pin incompatibility problem; you plug the new chip into it, and then you plug the interposer into the motherboard socket. Most upgrade chips that are designed to work in older motherboards come with an interposer, just in case you need it. Some upgrade processors, like the Intel Pentium OverDrive, have a built-in interposer, so you do not even have to think about it.

## Special Software Required

Some processor upgrade chips require you to run a software installation program after you install the new processor. This program adds drivers to your startup files that help the new processor do its job.

Make sure you have a bootable disk handy before you perform the upgrade so that you can restart your system if the software installation bombs. Follow the installation instructions that came with the upgrade processor to install its drivers.

The drivers take up some of your computer's memory, so after installing the processor upgrade, try to run all your normal applications to make sure that the computer can still run them with its decreased amount of memory. (Insufficient memory is more of an issue for DOS program users; Windows programs can use extended memory, so a minor decrease in conventional memory is not likely to stall them.) If you encounter problems, contact the upgrade processor's manufacturer to see whether the technical support team can help.

## Procedure

Follow these steps to remove the existing processor and install a new one:

1. Read the instructions that came with the new processor. Read the entire document.

2. Check your computer's manual for any information about using a different or upgrade processor.

3. Turn off your computer and unplug it. Remove the cover.

4. If you are going to use an antistatic strap, attach it to the PC's case to ground yourself.

5. Locate the processor on the motherboard. Take note of which way the lettering faces. (You will need to make sure the lettering on the new processor faces the same way.) If a heat sink or fan is installed on top of the current processor, find some other landmark (such as a notch or fan cable) to note.

6. Determine whether a cooling fan is attached to the current processor. If so, unplug the fan's power cable, and, if possible, remove the fan.

7. Determine whether the current processor is removable; if so, remove it:

   ✿ If it is in a low-insertion-force socket, gently pry the current processor out using the CPU-removal tool provided with the upgrade. Apply even, gentle pressure on each side until you wiggle it far enough out of its socket to lift it out.

◆◆◆◆◆◆◆◆◆◆◆◆◆◆◆◆◆◆◆◆◆◆◆◆◆◆◆◆◆◆◆◆◆◆◆◆◆◆◆◆◆

**CAUTION** If you do not have the right tool for removing the processor, you can use one of the removable metal panels from the back of the PC if you are extremely careful with it. The main thing to avoid is having any of the little pins break off in the motherboard's socket, rendering the socket unable to accept the new processor.

◆◆◆◆◆◆◆◆◆◆◆◆◆◆◆◆◆◆◆◆◆◆◆◆◆◆◆◆◆◆◆◆◆◆◆◆◆◆◆◆◆

   ✿ If the old processor is in a ZIF socket, lift the handle next to it and then lift out the old processor.

8. Set any jumpers or DIP switches required to accommodate the new processor.

9. Straighten any bent pins on the bottom of the new processor. Be very careful and use a nonmagnetic tool such as a small screwdriver from your computer tool kit—not one of the ones that picks up screws for you.

10. Install any fans, heat sinks, and needed adapters that came with the processor if they are not already installed. Refer to the instructions that came with the processor or the fan.

**11.** Insert the new processor into the socket, being careful to place it in the same direction as the old.

**TIP**

Look for a notch on one corner of the new processor. This notch should match up with the corner of the socket that doesn't have a hole—usually the corner where the handle joins the socket on a ZIF socket. If the processor doesn't have a notch, look on the underside of the processor for a small line running out of one corner, or for a square solder point; either of these indicators can show which corner should match up with the different corner of the socket.

**12.** Do one of the following:

- If the processor is in a ZIF socket, lower the handle to secure it.
- If the processor is in a LIF socket, gently press the pins into the holes, alternately pressing on each side until the processor is completely seated.

**13.** Double-check that you have set the jumpers or DIP switches correctly.

**14.** Plug the new processor's fan (if it has one) into a power cable from the power supply. Power cables are white plastic plugs with four colored wires. You can use any available plug that fits—all plugs are the same.

**15.** Plug in everything and start the computer (without replacing the computer cover). Watch the opening screen carefully to see whether the new processor information appears.

**16.** Do one of the following:

- If the computer appears to start correctly, turn it off and replace the cover. You're done.
- If the computer does not work correctly, review this procedure and the instructions that came with the processor to find out what is wrong. If you have done everything correctly, you may have a defective part. (See this afternoon's session to learn how to return parts.)

# Installing an Expansion Card

Lots of upgrades involve expansion cards. A card can be an internal modem, a sound card, a new video card, an adapter for some other device (like a circuit board that you plug a drive or scanner into), an FM radio tuner, or any of dozens of other components.

**NOTE** The terms *expansion board, expansion card, circuit card,* and so on are all interchangeable. They all refer to a circuit board that fits into an expansion slot on your motherboard.

Depending on the upgrade, installing the card may be the only thing you need to do, or it may be one step of a larger procedure. For example, if you're installing an internal modem, you basically just install the card and go. On the other hand, if you're installing a card to function as an adapter for a CD-ROM drive, you must not only install the card but also install the drive and run a cable between them. Refer to the instructions that came with your upgrade for complete information.

## Tools Needed

To install a card, you need a small Phillips-head screwdriver. In addition, if you have an antistatic wrist strap, you will want to wear it. If you need to set jumpers or DIP switches, you may need a pointed object to move the switches or some tweezers to help you grab the jumper caps.

## Precautions

Here's what to watch for when installing a circuit board:

○ Read the instructions that came with the board before you begin the upgrade.

○ Handle circuit boards only by their edges.

○ Do not attempt to straighten anything sticking up out of a circuit board that looks bent. You will only make things worse.

○ Do not try to force a card into an expansion slot. If the card doesn't seem to fit, check to make sure you are putting it in a slot of the right size.

# Possible Issues

Installing a card is fairly straightforward; you should not have problems as long as you set the jumpers or switches correctly and firmly seat the card into the right kind of expansion slot.

## Jumpers and Switches

Many circuit cards have jumpers or DIP switches, but the settings usually do not need to be changed (see Figure 4.14). They come from the factory with default settings that work for most situations. Read the instructions carefully to determine whether you need to make any changes.

If you do need to change some settings, do so before you install the card. The controls are much easier to see when you can hold the board in your hands; after it is installed, you might not be able to reach the controls. More than once I have installed a card without reading the directions only to have to remove it to fiddle with the jumpers.

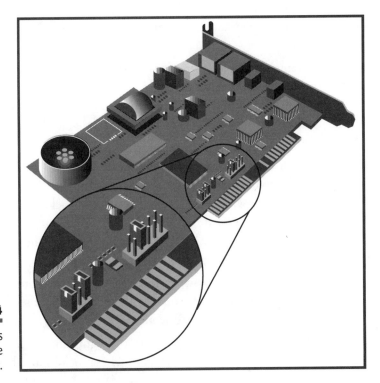

**Figure 4.14**

Set the jumpers on the card before you install it.

If the card you are installing was advertised as "Plug and Play–capable," and yet it has jumpers on it that seem to indicate a particular COM port or IRQ, check the documentation to see if you should remove them. Some devices (notably modems) can operate in either Plug and Play or non–Plug and Play modes, depending on the status of certain jumpers.

## Slot Selection

All the expansion slots with the same connector work equally well; you can pick any of them. That being the case, you should pick a slot that will be convenient for you. Consider these factors:

- If you think you might have to change the jumper settings after installation, install the card in a slot with plenty of room on that side so you can get your fingers in without removing the card.

- If the cables you need to connect to that card (outside the PC) are short, install the card in the slot that is closest to the other cable end. When you're dealing with a cable that is two inches too short, the card position can make the difference between usable and unusable. You can buy a new cable at a computer store, but it will likely be the same length.

- If some slots in your motherboard have two kinds of connectors, avoid using these slots until you have filled up all the slots. (For example, my motherboard has two dual slots with both ISA and PCI connectors.) That way, you will have an available slot for whatever kind of card you buy next.

- If your computer has some 8-bit and some 16-bit ISA slots (in other words, some slots that have only one black canal and others that have two of them end to end), use the smallest socket that can accommodate the card you are installing. That way if you ever need to install another card, you will not have to move the smaller card to the smaller socket to make room.

- If the card you are installing has two sections of connectors, do not put it into a too-short slot. You don't want the second section of connectors to be socketless. The card won't work that way, trust me.

- Make sure the card is going into the right kind of slot. PCI cards go in those short white PCI sockets. These sockets are shorter than ISA

sockets. Although you can force a PCI card into an ISA socket, the device won't work. You need to be sure that the length of the connector on the card matches the length of the socket.

## Slot Seating: Is It In?

After you've selected the socket, you have to place the card into it. This step is not a zero-insertion-force activity; you really need to apply some pressure. The fit is intentionally tight so that the card won't fall out.

The best way to put a card in a slot, I have found, is to see-saw it. Start with one corner and push firmly on the top edge of the card until you feel the slot give way slightly. Then push on the other end's edge until it goes in slightly. (Never touch the card except on the edge.) Keep pushing one end and then the other until the card is completely seated.

How do you tell when the card is in as far as it will go? Check out the metal plate at the back of the PC. When a card is fully seated, the top lip of its metal plate will rest on the PC's bracket (see Figure 4.15), and you can attach

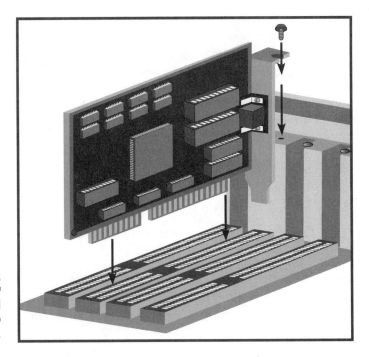

**Figure 4.15**

Push the card completely into the slot.

its mounting screw. If the lip is not resting there, the card is not completely seated.

## Procedure

Follow these steps to install any expansion card:

1. Turn off the PC and remove the cover.

2. Wear an antistatic wrist strap or touch the power supply to discharge static.

3. Locate the slot into which the new card should be placed.

4. Do one of the following:

   ⚙ If you are replacing an old card (for example, replacing the video card), remove the screw holding the old card in place and gently pull it out of the slot. Set it aside.

   ⚙ If you are installing a new card (not replacing an old one), remove the screw holding the metal plate over the selected slot's access panel at the back of the PC.

   ⚙ If you are replacing an old card with a new card that goes in a different kind of slot, remove the old card. Then remove the metal cover plate for the new slot, and install that cover plate over the hole left when you removed the old card.

◆◆◆◆◆◆◆◆◆◆◆◆◆◆◆◆◆◆◆◆◆◆◆◆◆◆◆◆◆◆◆◆◆◆◆◆◆◆◆◆◆◆◆

**CAUTION** Do not throw away the metal plate that you remove in Step 4. You will need it again if you ever remove this expansion card.

◆◆◆◆◆◆◆◆◆◆◆◆◆◆◆◆◆◆◆◆◆◆◆◆◆◆◆◆◆◆◆◆◆◆◆◆◆◆◆◆◆◆◆

5. Check to make sure that any jumpers or DIP switches on the new card are set correctly for your system.

6. Align the new card with the new slot and confirm that the slot is the right size.

7. Insert the card into the slot, pressing firmly in a see-saw action until the card is completely seated.

8. Attach the new card to the PC with the screw that you removed when you removed the metal cover plate.

9. Install any other parts for your new upgrade (for example, a drive), as described elsewhere in this session.

10. Follow the instructions that came with the upgrade to complete the installation. This step might include running an installation program, as explained in this afternoon's session.

# Installing a Drive

As with expansion cards, dozens of types of drives are available, each with a different purpose. Fortunately, they all install approximately the same way. You slide the drive into an empty drive bay and then connect the drive to a controller and to a power supply. Then you usually have to use the computer's BIOS setup program to tell the computer that the new drive exists.

Some of the types of drives you can install include:

- Hard drives
- Floppy drives
- Tape backup drives
- Removable mass storage (Jaz, ZIP, and so on)
- CD-ROM drives (regular, DVD, or writable)

## Tools Needed

To install a drive, you will need a Phillips-head screwdriver for the screws and possibly a small flat-head screwdriver (or something similar) to pry off the plastic plate from the front of the drive bay.

If you need to set jumpers on the drive, you might want a pair of tweezers to help you grasp and pull off the jumper caps, although some people (especially those with small hands) can do this task with their fingers.

## Precautions

Watch out for these pitfalls when installing a drive:

- Wear an antistatic wrist strap or ground yourself frequently by touching the power supply.

   ✿  Make very sure the computer's power is off before plugging or unplugging any cables inside.

   ✿  Be careful not to cut your fingers while working. The drive bays in some low-quality computer cases may have sharp metal edges.

   ✿  Handle a drive only by its metal casing. If you see a circuit board on one side of the drive casing, do not touch it.

# Possible Issues

Lots of things can go wrong when installing a drive; it's one of the more complicated and fumble-prone upgrade activities. You need to fiddle with cables and connectors, align a lot of holes, and tighten many screws. The following information prepares you for some of these potential headaches and helps you avoid them.

## Removing the Bay Cover from the Case

If you have an open external drive bay, it probably has a plastic plate covering it in the front of your PC. The plate keeps the dust out of that empty hole and makes your PC look good. When you are ready to install a new drive in that bay, you must first remove the plastic plate.

**NOTE**   External drive bays are bays that open to the front of the PC when you remove a plastic panel. Internal drive bays are bays that have no front access. Internal drive bays are used primarily for hard disks, which you do not need to access from the outside.

You remove plates from the inside. If the plates are attached to the computer cover, work from the inside of the removed cover. If the plates are attached to the PC itself, work from the inside of the drive bay. The plates usually have some kind of lip or edge that holds them in place; sometimes you can pull these back with your fingers and then push the plate through the hole. Other times you have to apply gentle pressure with a flat metal object such as a flat-head screwdriver.

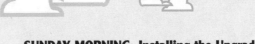
## Wrong Kind of Drive Bay Available

A computer case can house two kinds of drive bays: internal and external. Your PC has a certain number of internal drive bays, which hold a drive but have no front access. These are for hard disks. If you have a hard disk in an externally accessible drive bay, you are wasting that bay. (An exception is a case that has only external bays, which you might find in some older systems.) Using an external bay for a hard disk doesn't really matter until you need to use that bay for something else; then you will want to move the hard disk into one of the internal bays, freeing up the external spot.

External bays are available in two sizes. Most floppy and hard drives are 3.5" drives. (That measurement refers to their width.) They fit in the smaller drive bays in a PC's case. Most CD-ROM and tape backup drives are 5.25" drives. They fit in the larger drive bays.

You can't put a large drive in a small bay, obviously, but the reverse does work. If you don't have a large enough bay available, check your existing drives and make sure that none of them are small drives sitting in large bays. If you have any of those, you can switch them with the new equipment so all drives are in their correct bay size.

If you have a small drive to install but only a large bay free, it's not a big problem. You can buy a mounting kit from your local computer store that will provide the supports needed to center the smaller drive in the larger hole, as shown in Figure 4.16. Follow the directions that come with the kit to install it. Some good-quality drives even come with their own mounting rails and hardware for this purpose, so you don't have to buy a kit separately.

## Metal Plate Blocking the Drive Bay

On some systems you remove the plastic plate over an available drive bay only to find . . . another plate. Yes, some case manufacturers, in their infinite wisdom (cough, cough), put an additional barrier between the inside of the drive bay and the outside world. This inner plate, if present, is usually metal and is held in place by screws.

If you have such a plate blocking your progress, don't panic. Examine it and determine how it is held in place. Then unscrew or otherwise manipulate the plate so that it comes out.

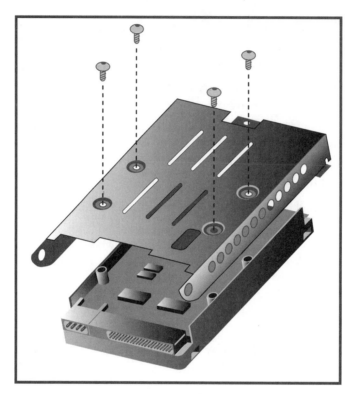

**Figure 4.16**

If you need to mount a small drive in a large bay, install a mounting bracket around the drive to hold it in place.

## Can't Reach the Screws

When you mount a drive into a bay, you secure it to the inside of the PC with two screws on each side. Some case designs make it very hard for you to reach the far side with a screwdriver. You then have two choices: You can say "forget it" and secure the drive as well as possible with screws on only one side, or you can go to the trouble of removing other components until the screw holes are accessible. I recommend the latter, even though it's more work.

## Not Enough Power Supply Plugs

See the colorful wires coming out of the power supply, in sets of four? These are the power plugs, and each drive must have one plugged into it. (The motherboard has two of them plugged in, which is how the expansion cards get their power.) An average-size power supply has at least eight power plugs, so you should have plenty.

If your system already has many drives, though, you may be out of power plugs. An easy work around is to buy a splitter, which is like an extension cord. It plugs into a single plug and has two or more outlets.

However, stop for a moment and think. Why do you suppose your power supply has a finite number of plugs? Perhaps because it has a finite amount of power to give out. If all the plugs are in use, the power supply is probably close to its limit. If you plug in more devices with a splitter, you might overload it. When a power supply overloads, it usually just shuts down, but sometimes it causes damage to the devices connected to it.

In reality, the chance of a single splitter causing damage to your computer is remote. If you just need one more power plug than your power supply provides, you are probably OK buying and installing a splitter. However, to be on the safe side, you might consider replacing the power supply with a larger one or perhaps replacing the entire case with one with more bays *and* a larger power supply.

In addition to the sheer number of plugs, you also need to consider the sizes. A power supply typically has both large and small plugs. The large size gets the most use; almost all devices connect to these large plugs. The small plugs are for floppy drives. Figure 4.17 shows the difference. If you need another small plug but have only large ones available, you can buy an adapter that will convert a large plug to a small one. There's no need to hesitate, because using such an adapter will not overload the power supply.

**Figure 4.17**

Power supplies have two connector sizes to accommodate devices with differing power requirements.

## Ribbon Cable Going in the Correct Direction?

When I install a new drive and it doesn't work, the first thing I check is the direction of the ribbon cable. The ribbon cable connects the drive to the controller. The controller can be built into the motherboard, or it can be a separate circuit board installed in an expansion slot.

Newer cables and devices have a notch in the connector that makes it fit only one direction in a socket. The notch prevents you from plugging in the connector incorrectly. However, older connectors do not have this notch, and you must rely on another method for deciding which way the connector goes.

All ribbon cables have a stripe on one edge (usually red). This edge should plug into pin 1 at both ends of the connection. The pins that the cable plugs into are numbered, 1 through whatever. On most devices, if you look very closely at the pins, you will see a tiny 1 printed next to one end. You need to make sure that the striped edge of the cable plugs into pin 1.

The ribbon cable for a floppy drive has a notch on the top of the cable, which forces it to fit in the correct orientation. The ribbon cable for an IDE drive has a prominent red stripe down the edge to indicate where pin 1 should go.

## Master/Slave Relationships between IDE Drives

IDE drives (and ATA, ATA-2, EIDE, and so on all fall into this category) run on an IDE controller. This controller is built into the motherboard on newer computers; on older computers an IDE interface card in an expansion slot controls them. Each IDE interface can control a maximum of two drives. (Most motherboards today have two IDE interfaces, so they can support a total of four drives.) Drives of this type include IDE hard disks and some CD-ROM drives and ZIP drives.

Because each IDE controller can have two drives, it needs a way to distinguish between them. One drive is designated the *master,* and the other the *slave.* The master drive is the one that the PC talks to directly; it receives all the instructions from the controller, and then passes along to the slave drive any instructions that are meant for it.

The interface cable runs from the controller to one disk to the next in a chain fashion. On most systems, which drive is plugged into which connector doesn't matter. The disks rely on jumpers that you set for one of the following messages:

⚙ The drive is the only drive on that controller and is therefore, by default, the master.

⚙ The controller has two drives, and this drive is the master.

⚙ The controller has two drives, and this drive is the slave.

You might see an additional setting on some drives called Single. It is used, if available, as an alternative to Master when the drive is the only drive on the controller.

Some newer systems use CSEL, which stands for cable selection. With such systems the drive's position in the cabling determines whether it is the master or the slave. For example, suppose you have a cable that starts at the controller, runs to disk 1, and then runs to disk 2. Disk 1 is the master because it is connected first. If you wanted disk 2 to be the master, you would simply swap the connectors plugged into the drives.

Let's look at an example. Suppose you see the jumpers shown in Figure 4.18 on the back of your new CD-ROM drive.

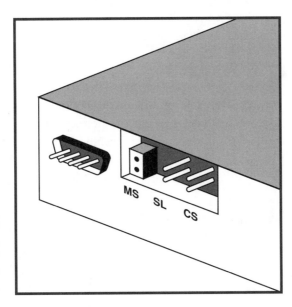

**Figure 4.18**

These jumpers control whether the drive is master or slave.

*MS* stands for "master," *SL* for "slave," and *CS* for "cable select." If this drive is the only drive on the controller, or the primary drive on it, you can leave the jumper set to MS, as shown in Figure 4.18. If it is going to be the slave (for example, on the same cable as your bootable hard disk), you should move the jumper over to the SL pins. If you are using cable select, you need to move it to the CS pins.

Some drives have jumpers that are not so self-explanatory. They might not have any labeling on them. In that case you need to refer to the instructions that came with the drive. The jumpers also might not be on the back of the drive; they might be somewhere else, for example, on the circuit board on the side of the drive. Look carefully.

If you are adding a second drive to the controller, you may also need to change the jumpers on the existing drive. For example, suppose you are adding a CD-ROM drive to a controller cable that already runs your hard disk. You would set the jumpers on the CD-ROM drive to slave, of course. But then you would need to check the hard disk's jumpers. Some hard disks require different settings for being the master all alone and being the master with a slave.

**TIP**

If you no longer have the instructions for your original hard disk and you aren't sure whether you need to change the jumpers, you can call the manufacturer and ask. Have your drive model number and capacity ready. You can also get jumper information for drives at many manufacturer Web sites on the Internet.

Using the correct jumper settings is extremely important. If two drives are both set for master, or both set for slave, neither one will work. Similarly, if your primary hard disk is set for "Master, No Slave" and you add a slave, the drive won't know that the slave is there. Carefully study the documentation that came with both drives to determine the correct settings.

## SCSI Termination on SCSI Drives

If you are adding a SCSI drive, some special rules apply. SCSI devices run on a SCSI interface (which is probably a circuit card in one of your expansion

slots). If you already have a SCSI interface card, you don't need to add another one; a single SCSI card can support up to seven devices. (Some SCSI cards can support more than that.) However, if this is your first SCSI device, you should have already installed the new interface card as explained earlier in this session.

SCSI devices work in a chain fashion. A cable runs from the controller card to the first device. Another cable runs from the first device to the second device. If you have more devices, cables run from one to the next, and so on. Each device has a single-digit ID number (which is just an identifier; it does not necessarily reflect its place in the chain). The controller sends a message down the cable, along with the device number that the message is for, and the appropriate device listens to the message. All other devices ignore it.

The last device in the chain needs to be *terminated,* meaning that a stopper prevents the signal from going any further. The stopper reflects the message back to the controller: Your message has reached the end of the line.

As you can imagine, it is very important that each device be assigned a unique ID number and that the last device be terminated. (It's also important, of course, that no devices be terminated other than the last device; otherwise, the signal would go no further, and subsequent devices would never receive any messages.)

You set the SCSI ID on a device with DIP switches, jumpers, or some other special control. Some devices have really nifty little windows and buttons. Every time you press the button, a different number appears in the window, indicating the device's new ID number.

Termination varies according to the device. On some internal SCSI devices such as circuit cards, you have to install a special resistor (which comes with the device, along with specific instructions on how to use it). External SCSI devices usually have some type of plug that plugs into the socket where the cable would go to the next device if you had one. Or you might get some of the really modern ones, which have an "auto-terminate" setting—if they have anything plugged into the outgoing plug, they know they're not the end of the line; if the outgoing plug is empty, a built-in terminator takes effect. Check the documentation to see what you have.

As you do with all upgrades, carefully read the instructions that come with your new device. They should explain how this SCSI device handles addressing and termination.

## BIOS Setup

The newest systems detect the new drive automatically when you turn on the system, and you don't have to do anything special. However, on most older computers, you must let the BIOS setup program know that you have installed a new drive. Some BIOS setup programs can automatically detect the type of new drive you have when asked to do so; others require you to enter a string that includes the new drive's number of sectors, landing zone, and other specifications.

Floppy drives are easy to set up in the BIOS setup program because the BIOS typically supports only five or six floppy types. IDE CD-ROM drives are easy, too, especially if your BIOS setup program has AutoDetect or Auto-Configure as a selectable drive type. You learn how to handle this setup in this afternoon's session, but it's really no big deal. Some BIOS setup programs automatically detect CD-ROMs without your making any changes to the settings at all.

However, if you are installing a new hard drive, you need to prepare for later BIOS dealings by jotting down all the specifications for the drive. You will find them in the instructions for the drive and also on the sticker on the drive itself. Don't wait until you have installed the new drive and can't read the sticker anymore to verify the specs. You may need the specs or you may not, but it never hurts to be safe and have them ready.

## Special Cables to Attach

Almost all drives require you to attach two cables: the power cable (which runs to the power supply) and the interface cable (a ribbon cable that runs to the controller or to the motherboard). With a few drives, however, you might have an additional cable or two:

○ For CD-ROM drives, you may have a cable to run from the drive to your sound card. This cable enables you to play audio CDs through your sound card's speakers.

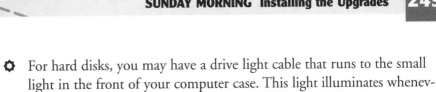

✿ For hard disks, you may have a drive light cable that runs to the small light in the front of your computer case. This light illuminates whenever the hard disk reads or writes. This light is not necessary, strictly speaking, but it is handy and not very difficult to hook up.

If you have either of these drive types, take a look at the instructions that came with the drive to see how to connect the special cable you need.

**NOTE** If you buy a CD-ROM drive, it probably will not come with the audio cable you need to attach to the sound card. This cable looks like a cluster of three or four colored wires bound together with small white connectors on each end. A sound card is more likely to include such a cable, but some cheaper models and brands omit it to cut costs. If you find yourself without the proper cable, you can pick one up at a computer store for less than $10.

## Procedure

To install a drive, follow these steps:

1. Set any necessary jumpers, switches, or settings on the new drive.

✿ If this is a floppy drive, no adjustments are necessary.

✿ If this is an IDE drive, set the jumpers to designate whether the drive is to be a master, slave, or cable selected.

✿ If this is a SCSI drive, make sure it is terminated—or not—as the situation requires. (Read the instructions.)

✿ If this is a SCSI drive, make sure that a unique SCSI ID number is set on the new device. Check the ID numbers of all existing devices in the chain to make sure you don't have any duplicates.

**TIP** If you're ever faced with unlabeled jumpers on a SCSI device, use the following rule to determine the device's setting: There should be 3 vertical sets of two pins, and jumpers cover at least one set. The leftmost set is 1, the middle set is 2, and the rightmost set is 4. To determine the SCSI ID, add up the numbers of the covered pins. For example, if there are jumpers over the middle and right sets, that's 2 plus 4, or SCSI ID number 6.

2. Set any necessary jumpers, switches, or settings on any existing drives that will share a cable with this drive.

   ⚙ If installing the new drive to a SCSI chain, make sure the correct device is terminated and that none of the others are.

   ⚙ If installing the new drive to the same IDE controller as an existing drive, make sure that no jumpers need to be set on the old drive to tell it that it now has a slave.

3. If you are installing an externally accessed drive (like a floppy or CD-ROM), remove the plastic cover plate over the drive bay into which you want to install the new drive.

4. Slide the new drive into the bay to make sure it fits. Then remove it. Install mounting rails or spacers if needed for a proper fit. (Refer to the instructions that came with the drive.)

5. Slide the new drive into the bay from the back, so that you can see and reach where the power and interface cables need to be connected.

6. Plug the power cable into the power socket on the drive. The power socket has four rather thick pins. Notches on either side of the socket prevent the connector from going in the wrong way.

7. Plug the ribbon cable (the interface cable) into the interface socket on the drive. Make sure that the striped edge goes to pin 1 and that it is firmly seated in place (see Figure 4.19).

**NOTE** Some floppy drives have pins into which you plug a many-holed connector; other floppy drives have a protrusion with metal stripes on it into which you plug a trench-like connector. The two connector types work the same way. Most floppy drive cables have both kinds of connectors, so they can accommodate either type of floppy drive.

Also, as I noted earlier, floppy drives usually have a smaller power connector socket than the other drives in your system. Instead of the regular socket shown in Figure 4.19, you might see four small metal prongs sticking out of a white piece of plastic. You plug the smaller power supply cable shown in Figure 4.17 into these prongs.

8. Plug any special cables into the drive as needed (for example, a cable from the CD-ROM drive to the sound card). Refer to the directions that came with the drive.

9. Attach the other ends of the cables (the interface cable and any special cables) to the proper places if necessary. For example, attach the interface cable to the controller (either on the motherboard or the controller card) and attach a sound cable to the sound card.

10. Slide the drive into its final location in the bay. If the drive is externally accessible, align its front with the front panel of the PC. If it is a hard disk, align the screw holes in the drive with those in the bracket.

11. Use the screws provided with the drive to fasten the drive in place.

12. Check that no cable connections have worked loose while you were sliding the drive.

13. Start up the computer (don't put the cover on yet) and test the new drive's operation. Set it up in the BIOS setup program as needed. Refer to this afternoon's session for details.

The setup that follows the installation depends on the drive type. For floppy drives, you simply tell the BIOS program about the new drive, and you're off and running. For a CD-ROM drive, you set it up in BIOS (if it's an IDE model) and then run an installation program that came on a disk with the drive. For a hard disk, you must inform the BIOS of its presence (if it's IDE) and possibly partition and format the drive, depending on

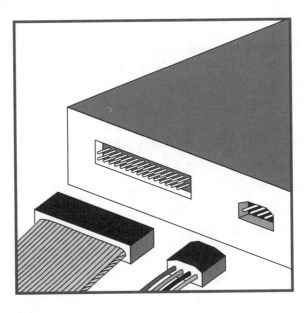

**Figure 4.19**

Most drives require two connections on the back.

whether those things have already been done or not. You learn all about these post-installation steps this afternoon.

# Some Drive Installation Scenarios

Drive installation has so many variables that it is easy to get lost in general instructions like the ones just given. Here are a few specific situations, with advice for handling each.

## Tips for Installing a Floppy Drive

To install a floppy drive, just physically place the drive in the open bay and tighten. Connect the floppy drive interface cable (making sure pin 1 is in the right place) and the power supply. Then turn on the computer and enter the BIOS setup program. (Watch the screen as the computer boots; often it will say something like Press F1 To Enter Setup. Follow the instructions.) Tell the BIOS program about the new floppy (explained this afternoon) and then exit the BIOS setup program. The drive should work perfectly.

You can have two floppy drives in most systems. If you already have one floppy drive, you should see an extra connector or two on its cable. That's the cable to use for the interface. (If both the drives are 3.5", you may need to buy an adapter to convert one of the large power supply connectors into the smaller type required by the second 3.5" floppy.)

If you want to have more than two floppies, you will need to install an input/output (I/O) expansion card. These fairly inexpensive cards (available at a computer store) enable you to attach extra floppy and IDE drives, above and beyond the two floppies and four hard drives that most systems support.

## Tips for Installing Any IDE Device

With an IDE device, the most important thing is to get the jumpers for master/slave set correctly. This process can be a little confusing.

Say your system has two IDE interfaces, each of which can handle two devices, and the only IDE device you have installed so far is a hard disk. You now want to add a second IDE device (perhaps a hard disk, or perhaps a CD-ROM).

You have two choices. One is to put the new drive and the old drive on the same cable, and make the new one the slave. You then have a primary master and primary slave. The alternative is to put the new drive on a new cable and run that cable to the secondary IDE interface in your system. The new device is then the master of that cable. Your system has a primary master, a secondary master, and no slaves.

If you want to make the new device a secondary master, you must locate the secondary IDE connector on your motherboard (or I/O expansion card) and plug an IDE cable from it to the new device.

After you have installed a new IDE device, you tell the computer about your new configuration in two ways: by setting the jumpers and by informing the BIOS. (The exception is an IDE CD-ROM drive; you might not need to inform the BIOS about it.)

## Tips for Installing a CD-ROM Drive

Some CD-ROM drives come with their own interface cards. You need to pay close attention to that card. One type of card is a standard IDE interface card. Such cards are optional—you need one only if your system's IDE interfaces are all full. Another type of card is a SCSI interface card. It is also optional; use it only if you do not have a SCSI card or if all the addresses are in use on the one you have. The final type of card looks like SCSI but is proprietary— in other words, it uses its own format. You need this kind of card to run the CD-ROM drive because the drive expects that interface and only that one. Read the instructions that came with the drive to determine what kind of interface card you are dealing with.

If you have a sound card in your system and you want to be able to play audio CDs, you must install a cable between the sound card and the CD-ROM drive. It is usually a thin round cable with small connectors on each end. Some sound cards have more than one connector for such plugs so that you can play sounds from more than one CD-ROM drive.

On some computers you must tell the BIOS that a CD-ROM drive is installed on one of the computer's built-in IDE interfaces. (The BIOS setup program may refer to it as an *ATAPI device*.) On other computers the computer detects the drive automatically. A SCSI CD-ROM drive (or any

CD-ROM drive that runs off a separate interface card) requires no BIOS modification.

All CD-ROM drives come with a setup program on disk, which you may or may not have to run. If you are using Windows 95/98, the system might detect the new drive automatically. If it doesn't, you can run the setup program.

**TIP** If you are running Windows 95/98 and you can avoid running the CD-ROM drive's setup program, do so. Some setup programs load drivers in the computer's startup files (AUTOEX-EC.BAT and CONFIG.SYS) that are redundant with Windows' own drivers for the device. At best, the files take up space in the computer's memory unnecessarily; at worst, they can force Windows into running in Compatibility mode, which decreases its performance.

This tip applies only to Windows 95/98 users; users of DOS/Windows 3.1 systems always need to run the CD-ROM drive's setup program.

# Installing RAM

Remember yesterday, when I made such a big deal out of picking the correct RAM for your system? That was necessary. If you don't have the right RAM, it won't work. Some systems are extremely picky about the RAM they will accept. As you learned yesterday, RAM modules come in different sizes (72-pin SIMMs, 30-pin SIMMs, 168-pin DIMMs, and so on), different amounts (1MB, 4MB, 16MB, and so on), different types (FPM, EDO, and parity), and different speeds (80ns, 70ns, and 60ns). You must have the right combination of all these factors for your system. One of the most common reasons that new RAM doesn't work is that the user has bought the wrong type, so double-check the type you bought right now, before you start installing it.

RAM can be a really easy upgrade if everything goes well. On most newer systems, assuming you have the right type of RAM, you simply plug it in and go. The system detects the new amount of RAM automatically. On older systems, you may have to do one or both of the following:

✪ Set jumpers on the motherboard to tell it how much RAM it has.

⚙ Enter the new amount of RAM in the BIOS program or at least enter the BIOS program so that it redetects the RAM itself.

## Tools Needed

You don't need any special tools to install RAM. (Well, you need a Phillips-head screwdriver to remove the computer's cover, but you've probably done that already.) Some people also like to wear an antistatic wrist strap, as an added precaution.

## Precautions

RAM can't hurt you, but you can hurt it. Take these steps to avoid RAM-ruining hazards:

⚙ Leave the RAM in its antistatic bag until you are ready to install it; otherwise you risk exposing it to static electricity zaps.

⚙ When installing SIMMs or DIMMs into their banks on the motherboard, don't force them. If you break off the little clips that hold the RAM in place on the motherboard, you have ruined your whole motherboard (unless you can find someone to repair the clip for less than a new motherboard would cost).

⚙ Handle RAM the same way you handle any circuit board: by the edges only.

## Possible Issues

What can go wrong when installing RAM? Plenty, especially in older PCs. Before you install, read about the following issues.

### Putting the Right RAM in the Right Banks

Remember that chart you looked at yesterday that told what capacity of RAM module should go in each bank? Haul it out again, because you'll need it to determine where to put the new RAM.

Each bank must have only one kind of memory in it; for example, you can't mix a 4MB and a 16MB SIMM in the same bank. In most 486 systems a bank can consist of either four 30-pin SIMM slots or one 72-pin SIMM slot.

Pentium systems always have two 72-pin SIMM slots per bank, but 168-pin DIMM slots each stand alone as a bank. You don't have to remember this, though—the chart that came with the computer will show the possible combinations.

Return for a moment to the 486 system example from yesterday. Suppose you currently have 8 megabytes of RAM in your system and the memory chart in your computer manual shows the following valid RAM installation options:

| Memory Size | Bank 2 (30 pin) | Bank 0/2 (72 pin) | Bank 1/3 (72 pin) |
|---|---|---|---|
| 8MB | 1Mx4 | 4Mx1 | — · |
| 8MB | 1Mx4 | — · | 4Mx1 |
| 8MB | — · | 4Mx1 | 4Mx1 |
| 8MB | — · | 8Mx1 | — · |
| 8MB | — · | — · | 8Mx1 |

You look at your current system and see that you have four 30-pin 1MB SIMMs installed in bank 2 and one 4MB 72-pin SIMM installed in bank 0/2. You have just bought a single 16MB 72-pin SIMM to install. Looking at the 16MB lines in the chart, you see this:

| Memory Size | Bank 2 (30 pin) | Bank 0/2 (72 pin) | Bank 1/3 (72 pin) |
|---|---|---|---|
| 16MB | 4Mx4 | — · | — · |
| 16MB | — · | 16Mx1 | — · |
| 16MB | — · | — · | 16Mx1 |

From this table you see that you can put the 16MB SIMM in either of the 72-pin banks but that you must remove all the old SIMMs from all the banks. But wait—suppose you want to reuse some of the old memory. You look through the chart and find the following lines that would allow you to use your new 16MB SIMM along with some of the old memory:

| Memory Size | Bank 2 (30 pin) | Bank 0/2 (72 pin) | Bank 1/3 (72 pin) |
|---|---|---|---|
| 20MB | 1Mx4 | 16Mx1 | — · |
| 20MB | 1Mx4 | — · | 16Mx1 |
| 24MB | 1Mx4 | 4Mx1 | 16Mx1 |
| 24MB | 1Mx4 | 16Mx1 | 4Mx1 |

As you can see from the preceding chart, you can reuse all of your old RAM and have 24MB. Bank 2 can stay the same; you don't have to remove it. And because the chart says that the 16MB and the 4MB SIMMs can be in either of the two 72-pin banks, you can also leave the 4MB SIMM in place and just install the new 16MB SIMM.

In this example the 72-pin banks are interchangeable. This situation is not true on every PC. You need to pay close attention to the chart and make sure that the RAM you end up with in the system is one of the valid combinations shown on the chart. Otherwise, it won't work at all (at worst), or it will work but not recognize some of the RAM (at best).

## Inserting the RAM Correctly

After you get the hang of inserting and removing RAM, it's not difficult. However, beginners often fumble with it simply because the pieces are small.

SIMMs can fit into their banks facing in only one direction; if you try to put one in the wrong way, it won't stand upright. SIMM modules have small notches in their circuit boards that must be aligned correctly for the SIMM to be inserted (see Figure 4.20). DIMM modules, on the other hand, can go either way into their banks.

Small clips (usually metal) hold SIMMs in place; DIMMs have clips (usually plastic) that push down over their tops. To install most SIMMs, you slide them into the slot at a 45-degree angle to the motherboard, and then push them upright into a 90-degree angle (see Figure 4.21). DIMMs, in contrast, drop straight down into their 90-degree slots. (DIMM sockets are found only

**Figure 4.20**

Make sure the notch at one end of the SIMM matches the notch in the SIMM holder on the motherboard.

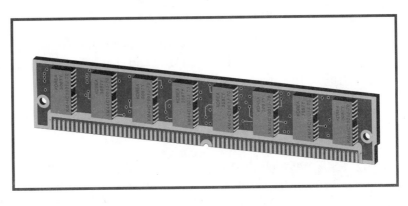

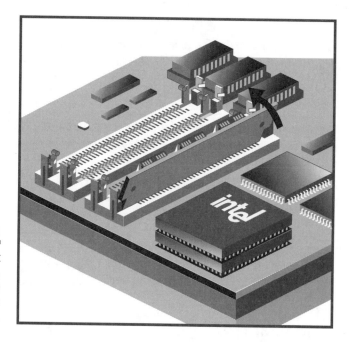

**Figure 4.21**

Insert the SIMM at a 45-degree angle, and then push it up perpendicular to the motherboard.

on newer computers, so if you are upgrading an old system, you probably won't have them.)

**CAUTION**

◆◆◆◆◆◆◆◆◆◆◆◆◆◆◆◆◆◆◆◆◆◆◆◆◆◆◆◆◆◆◆◆◆◆◆◆◆◆◆◆◆◆◆

If you are inserting a DIMM, you may have to press it down very hard to get it into a tight DIMM slot. This can be scary, pressing so hard on something so expensive! Just remember to press only by the edge and not to touch any of the circuitry or chips. You'll know when the DIMM is fully inserted because the retaining clips will hold it in place. If you can lift either end of the DIMM out of the slot with your fingers, it's not in all the way.

◆◆◆◆◆◆◆◆◆◆◆◆◆◆◆◆◆◆◆◆◆◆◆◆◆◆◆◆◆◆◆◆◆◆◆◆◆◆◆◆◆◆◆

Removing a SIMM is harder than inserting it. To remove a SIMM, you must pull back the metal tabs on each end that hold the SIMM in place, and then pivot the SIMM back to its 45-degree angle. From there, you lift it out. To remove a DIMM, just pull back the clips that hold it in place and lift it out.

## Setting Jumpers

On some motherboards (486 and lower), you must set jumpers or DIP switches to tell the system how much RAM is installed. If this is the case on

| Memory size | Bank 1 | Bank 2 | SW1 | SW2 | SW3 | SW4 |
|---|---|---|---|---|---|---|
| 2M | 2x1M | —- | Off | Off | Off | Off |
| 4M | 2x1M | 2x1M | Off | Off | Off | On |
| 8M | 2x4M | —- | Off | Off | On | On |
| 10M | 2x4M | 2x1M | Off | On | On | On |
| 16M | 2x4M | 2x4M | Off | Off | On | Off |
| 16M | 2x8M | —- | Off | On | On | Off |
| 18M | 2x8M | 2x4M | On | On | On | Off |
| 24M | 2x8M | 2x4M | Off | On | Off | Off |

**Figure 4.22**

Systems that require jumper or DIP switch changes include this kind of information in a table in the manual.

your system, you will have extra columns in the RAM chart, or a separate chart, that show the proper switch settings, as shown in Figure 4.22.

If you do not have the manual for the computer and the new RAM doesn't work, you might need to set jumpers or DIP switches for it. Call the PC manufacturer and ask the technical support person to look up the motherboard settings for you. If the manufacturer is out of business, try to identify the motherboard manufacturer and call that company. If that fails, try the Internet; look for an archive that contains pictures of generic motherboards. You might be able to match your board to a picture and get the settings that way. Realistically, however, if your motherboard is old enough to require jumper changes for different amounts of RAM, you might be better off getting a whole new PC or at least a new motherboard.

## Making the BIOS Recognize the New RAM

Don't worry too much about the BIOS right now; your primary concern is to get that RAM physically installed. However, I wanted to let you know what to expect later, when it comes time to deal with the BIOS setup program.

On very few systems, when you install new RAM, you must enter the BIOS setup program and tell it how much RAM it now has. On many other systems, when you start the PC with new RAM, you will see some sort of memory error and a message about pressing some key to enter the setup program. When you do so, the BIOS setup program automatically detects and displays the new RAM amount. You then exit from the BIOS setup program, saving your changes, and the new RAM is ready to go.

The newest systems do not require you to interact with the BIOS setup program at all. When you start the computer, it automatically detects and uses all the available RAM.

## Procedure

Ready to install RAM?

1. Remove the cover of the PC, if it is not already off, and take a look at the existing RAM. Note which banks it is in and which direction it faces.

2. Consult the computer's documentation and determine your RAM plan: Will you be removing the old RAM? Will you be reinstalling the old RAM in a different bank?

3. Remove the old RAM if necessary.

   ✿ To remove a SIMM, place a thumb on each of the two clips holding the RAM's ends, and then pull those clips away from the RAM. Then with your index fingers, gently push the RAM backward to a 45-degree angle. Then slide and lift the RAM out of the bank at that same 45-degree angle.

   ✿ To remove a DIMM, use your thumbs to push the retaining clips away from the ends of the DIMM, and then lift it out of its bank.

4. Install the new RAM:

   ✿ To install a SIMM, slide the SIMM into the bank at a 45-degree angle. Make sure it is seated in the slot; then gently pull it forward to stand it up at a 90-degree angle. The clips should snap around its ends; if they do not, the SIMM is not properly seated. Remove the SIMM and try again.

   ✿ To install a DIMM, make sure the retaining clips are pulled back and drop the DIMM into its bank. Push it firmly straight down, and then with your thumbs push the retaining clips up over the top.

**TIP** SIMMs have a notch on one end that aligns with an indent on the SIMM holder on the motherboard, so they can only go in one way. Similarly, DIMMs have a break in the edge along the bottom that aligns with a break in the slot, so you can only insert a DIMM facing in the correct direction.

5. Change jumpers or DIP switches on the motherboard if necessary.

6. Plug everything in and start the computer (don't replace the cover yet). Deal with the BIOS program as needed (see this afternoon's session).

Sometimes RAM installation does not go right the first time. Perhaps your PC now shows that you have a different amount of RAM than you actually have, or perhaps it does not start at all. If you hear a steady beep-beep-beep from the PC, that's a sign that the new RAM is defective, that the new RAM is improperly installed, or that the jumpers are not set correctly. You learn more about troubleshooting in this afternoon's session.

# Replacing a Battery

All PCs have a battery (somewhat like a watch battery) that keeps the memory chips in the ROM-BIOS charged. This battery enables the computer to keep track of the current date and time and to remember what kind of drives it has when the power is off.

These batteries typically last at least two years, but after that, they begin weakening. You can tell when a battery is dead (or dying) when the computer forgets the date and time or forgets that it has a certain kind of disk drive. You can enter the BIOS setup program and remind the computer of these facts as a stopgap measure, but the only way to permanently correct the problem is to replace the battery.

## Tools Needed

If your battery is not failing, but you want to test it to see if it will last a lot longer or not, you will need a digital multimeter. (Try Radio Shack.) If your battery is already failing, you can obviously ignore this test.

Batteries vary in how they are connected to the motherboard. Some of them have a Velcro strap; others are held in by a metal clip. If your battery uses some sort of clip or fastener, you may need nonmagnetic needle-nose pliers or some similar tool to undo the fastener.

## Precautions

Watch these things when replacing a battery:

✪ Before you remove or disable the old battery, make sure you enter the BIOS setup program and jot down all pertinent settings. You will need to set them up again after the installation, because when you remove the battery, all of your settings vanish.

 **TIP** It's a good idea to have such information written down somewhere even if you're NOT replacing a battery. On some systems, you may be able to press Shift+Print Screen to get a printout of the BIOS settings in the BIOS setup program; on other PCs, that doesn't work and you must copy down the information manually. Some utility programs are available that can print this data for you too.

✪ Some batteries are permanently soldered onto the motherboard. Before you try to pull the battery off, check to make sure it is not soldered down.

## Possible Issues

Here are some of the problems and dilemmas you may have when replacing a battery.

### Locating the Battery

Computers use several different types of PC batteries, and most of them don't look like any batteries you have ever seen before. Therefore, they are hard to locate inside your computer! Here are some things to look for:

✪ The battery is usually along one edge of the motherboard rather than in the middle.

- Some batteries look like little barrels or oil drums on their sides. These are usually encased in a plastic sheath with writing on them such as 3/V60R.

- Some batteries are flat metal discs lying flat against the motherboard, like a battery in a watch. A metal clip over the top sometimes holds them in place.

- Some batteries look like flat metal disks held at a 90-degree angle to the motherboard by two fasteners (one on either side).

- Some batteries look like any other microchip on the motherboard but with some special writing on them to indicate their battery function. (Such batteries seldom go bad, so you should not have to replace this kind of battery.)

If you have your computer's documentation, it should show where the battery is located and give directions for replacing it. If you have such documentation, follow it rather than the instructions given here.

## What If It's Soldered in Place?

On some motherboards the battery is soldered into place. (What were the manufacturers of these boards thinking, I'd like to know?) With such systems you can't remove the old battery. If the old one goes dead, you must buy an external replacement battery. The replacement battery comes in a plastic-encased pack, with a three- or four-hole connector that plugs onto pins on the motherboard.

If you must buy an external replacement battery for your computer, your computer's manual should explain how to install it. At minimum it should tell you which pins on the motherboard a replacement battery's connector should plug into.

After installing an external battery, you may need to set some jumpers on the motherboard to tell it to use the external battery rather than the old soldered one. Again, you'll need to check your computer's manual to find out what jumpers to set.

If you are stuck—that is, if you don't have any documentation for the motherboard and the battery is soldered in place—then you might consider just scrapping the whole motherboard and buying a new one. I know that sounds extreme, but soldered batteries are uncommon except on old systems, and if your system is old anyway, you may have found a good excuse to upgrade to a better motherboard and processor.

**NOTE** Some technicians don't like to leave an old battery soldered to the motherboard; they are afraid that the battery might leak and cause acid damage. The possibility is remote, but if you want to be on the safe side, you can remove it. After you have installed and successfully tested the new external battery, you can remove a soldered-down battery by breaking it off forcibly (with pliers). Be aware, however, that a clumsy hand can damage other parts of the motherboard with the pliers, and the chance of doing so is greater than the chance of acid damage from an old battery.

## Checking the Battery's Remaining Life

You can check the battery with a multimeter if you are curious about how much life it has left. To do so, set the multimeter to DCV (direct current voltage) and place the red probe on the positive side (look for a + sign) and the black probe on the negative side. Compare the voltage readout to the voltage listed on the battery. Most PC batteries are 3.6 volt. If the measured voltage is not at least 80 percent of the listed voltage, you should replace the battery. For example, a 3.6-volt battery should measure at least 2.88 volts. If it doesn't, you should replace the battery.

Some systems have multiple-battery packs or batteries mounted in holders. It's hard to check the voltage on these. If you have such as system, check the date on the battery pack. If the date is more than three years old, you should replace it while you have the case open anyway.

## Installing the New Battery

The procedure for installing a new battery depends heavily on the type of battery.

Barrel-type batteries are held in by friction; simply pull them out, like you would pull out the batteries from a portable radio or other device. Then wedge the new battery in place between the two connectors.

With a coin battery, release the clip holding it in place and lift the old battery out. Then place the new one in its spot, making sure the plus side is up.

With an external battery pack, the procedure is a little trickier. You must locate the connector on the motherboard that an external battery pack plugs into and then orient the connector properly over the pins. As a general rule, the red (positive) wire should always be furthest from the power supply. Some batteries have a tiny + or – printed next to one of the pins to help you identify them. You must also locate the jumper on the motherboard that tells it to rely on the external battery, and you must fasten the battery to the motherboard with the Velcro strip provided.

## Procedure

Follow these steps to replace the battery:

1. Make notes of your BIOS setup settings so you can restore them after the replacement. Then turn off the PC's power and unplug the machine.

2. Remove the PC's cover if it's not already off and figure out what kind of battery you have (and what kind you need).

   If you must use an external battery as a replacement, check the computer documentation to figure out how to install such a battery.

3. Remove the old battery by following the instructions in the computer's documentation for doing so.

4. Install the new battery. If you are replacing an old battery with the same kind, make very sure that you orient it the exact same way as the old one. If you are installing an external battery pack, make sure that you set the motherboard jumpers correctly and plug the pack's connector over the appropriate pins on the motherboard.

5. Restart the PC and check the BIOS setup program. If the old settings are still intact—great. Otherwise, reenter the information about your drives and other devices as needed. (See this afternoon's session for help.)

**TIP** If you replace the battery and the PC boots perfectly sometimes and refuses to boot other times, you probably installed the battery backwards or inserted the external battery pack's connector upside down.

# Installing a Motherboard

Motherboard installation is the big Kahuna of upgrades. Don't attempt it lightly! If you are not comfortable working with your PC's innards, do yourself a favor: Take your machine to a friendly local repair shop, where techies will cheerfully install the new motherboard for you. I work on PCs a lot, and motherboard installations still make me nervous.

## Tools Needed

To replace the motherboard, you will need a Phillips-head screwdriver. You should strongly consider an antistatic wrist strap for this upgrade too, even if you have to go out and buy one.

You may also need a small pair of pliers (to remove plastic standoffs from the old motherboard) and some tweezers or a pointed object (to set jumpers or DIP switches).

## Precautions

There are many precautions with a motherboard installation:

✪ Handle the motherboard only by its edges.

✪ Make sure you install paper washers on both sides of the motherboard wherever you put metal screws that will touch the board. The washers prevent electrical current from passing through the screws. The washers should come with the new motherboard.

✪ Make sure the black wires go toward the center when you plug in the power connectors to the motherboard!

✪ Make sure the jumpers and DIP switches are set correctly on the motherboard before you mount it in the case. The switch or jumper

settings may vary according to the type of processor, the amount of memory installed, and the cache installed on the motherboard. These adjustments are much easier to do when the motherboard has not yet been attached to the case.

# Possible Issues

Here is some information about the trickier aspects of a motherboard transplant.

## Removing the Old Motherboard

Your old motherboard probably has at least two different pieces holding it in place: one or more metal screws and one or more plastic standoffs. To remove the old motherboard, you must remove all metal screws holding it down. The plastic standoffs do not have to be removed, but you have to slide the motherboard a few inches in one direction to allow the flared bottoms of the standoffs to clear the channels they are in.

On some cases the motherboard is mounted to a removable panel instead of to the fixed floor of the case. On such systems you remove the screws holding the panel to the case, and then pull the motherboard and panel out the bottom. You can remove the motherboard from the panel much more easily than you could remove one from a full case. Figure 4.23 shows a case with a removable panel.

Remove these screws

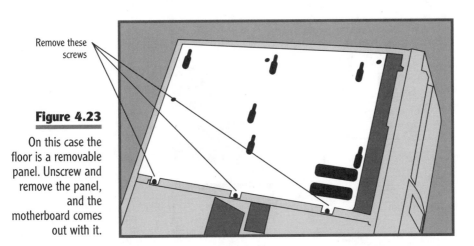

**Figure 4.23**

On this case the floor is a removable panel. Unscrew and remove the panel, and the motherboard comes out with it.

## Installing Standoffs

Standoffs are the supports (some plastic and some brass) that hold the motherboard off the floor of the case. (They make the motherboard "stand off" the floor.)

When you removed the old motherboard, the plastic standoffs probably came with it. You don't have to remove them from the old motherboard unless the new motherboard didn't come with its own (in which case you have to reuse the old ones). To remove a standoff, you must squeeze the top with pliers to collapse the umbrella-like tip (as shown in Figure 4.24), and then pull it out of the hole from the bottom. Fortunately, most new motherboards come with a bag of screws and standoffs, so you should not have to bother with removing the old ones.

The brass standoffs remained in the case when you removed the old motherboard. Take a close look at one of them. They screw into the case, and they have holes on top that allow other screws to fit into them.

Place the new motherboard into the case and note where the screw holes in the new motherboard fall. If they fall directly over the existing brass standoffs—great. If not, pull the motherboard back out and unscrew any brass standoffs that do not match up. Then reposition the standoffs to match the

**Figure 4.24**

If you need to remove the old standoffs from the old motherboard, pinch the top with needle-nose pliers to make the standoff fit through the hole.

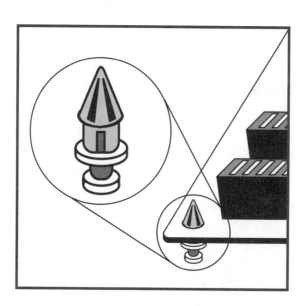

screw holes in the motherboard. The case should have several sets of screw holes to accommodate various motherboard designs.

After you get the brass standoffs in the right places, place paper washers over their tops. Your motherboard's little bag of screws and standoffs should contain at least six paper washers. Don't discard them—they are very important! Wherever metal touches the motherboard, the possibility for an electrical short exists. To avoid trouble, you must install these paper washers. You will also place washers between the metal screws that you install later and the motherboard.

The next step is to install the plastic standoffs in the case. To do so, note which holes in the motherboard align with standoff canals in the case. Then in each of those canals, slide a standoff into place.

Place the motherboard into the case so that the holes in the motherboard align with the tips of the plastic standoffs. Press the motherboard down so the umbrella tips of the standoffs poke through, holding the motherboard in place.

■ ■ ■ ■ ■ ■ ■ ■ ■ ■ ■ ■ ■ ■ ■ ■ ■ ■ ■ ■ ■ ■ ■ ■ ■ ■ ■ ■ ■ ■ ■ ■ ■ ■ ■ ■ ■ ■ ■
You will probably have trouble keeping the paper washers atop the brass standoffs as you press the motherboard down and lock it to the plastic standoffs. One way to keep the washers in place is to tape the paper washer to the brass standoff with a tiny piece of clear tape. Another is to apply the barest amount of glue from a glue stick to each side of them. (Don't use bottled glue—you'll get it on too thick. It needs to hold only for a few minutes.)
■ ■ ■ ■ ■ ■ ■ ■ ■ ■ ■ ■ ■ ■ ■ ■ ■ ■ ■ ■ ■ ■ ■ ■ ■ ■ ■ ■ ■ ■ ■ ■ ■ ■ ■ ■ ■ ■ ■

Finally, place paper washers over each hole in the motherboard that corresponds to a brass standoff and then tighten a screw into the hole. The paper washer prevents the metal screw from touching any metal on the motherboard that might cause it to short out. Figure 4.25 shows all the connectors and pieces for this upgrade job.

## Figuring Out Where to Connect the Pieces

When you unplug parts from the old motherboard, make sure to label everything and pay close attention as you work. I like to stick a loop of masking tape on each end of each cable and write on the tape where that connector

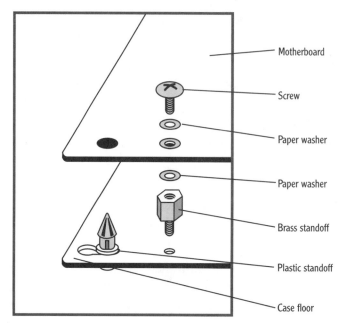

Motherboard

Screw

Paper washer

Paper washer

Brass standoff

Plastic standoff

Case floor

**Figure 4.25**

Use these connectors to attach the motherboard firmly to the case.

was plugged in. Sometimes I also indicate how it was plugged—for example, black wire toward back.

However, even with precise labeling and meticulous notes, you still may have a question or two about what goes where. In some cases the connectors and sockets on the new and old motherboards may not look the same.

No matter what the cause of your confusion, the solution is to look at the manual that came with the new motherboard for a diagram that tells what's what. Rather than one comprehensive diagram, you will probably find a simple diagram with codes and letters on it and a series of corresponding tables and charts. For example, the diagram may show a grouping of three pins labeled J7. A table on the next page tells you that J7 is the spot where you plug in the connector that runs to the power light on the front of the case.

## Connecting the Power Supply Cables

Two special-purpose connectors on the power supply connect to the motherboard. They supply power to the processor, the memory, and all the expansion boards. These connectors are designed to fit only one way, so you can't put them on backwards, but each will fit equally well on either the right or the left. You are looking at a dangerous situation. Putting the connectors in the wrong position can ruin your motherboard.

**NOTE** Figure 4.26 shows the situation for an AT motherboard and power supply. On an ATX motherboard and power supply, the connector that connects to the motherboard is a single long piece, eliminating the danger for error.

When connecting the power connectors to the motherboard, *the black wires must go toward the middle*, as shown in Figure 4.26. If you connect them the other way, with the black wires on the outside, the results can be disastrous.

## Procedure

Follow these steps to replace your motherboard.

1. Make a detailed drawing of your current motherboard that includes every cable connected to it and what that cable is for.

2. Put a piece of masking tape on every cable and write yourself a note describing where that cable was connected and in which orientation.

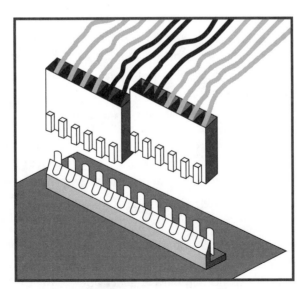

**Figure 4.26**

Make sure you get the power connectors oriented with the black wires in the middle!

For example, for the floppy disk drive cable, you might write "FD—stripe toward center" to remind yourself that the striped wire on the ribbon cable pointed toward the center of the drive.

3. Unplug all the external connectors from the back of the PC, including the power cable.

4. Trace the small ribbon cables that run from the PC's serial and parallel ports to the motherboard (or to an expansion card) and unplug them from the motherboard.

5. Remove all cables that run from expansion cards to anywhere else in the computer.

6. Carefully unscrew all the screws holding the expansion cards into place and pull each card from the motherboard. Put the screws aside in a safe place.

7. Unplug all the power supply connectors from the drives and from the motherboard itself.

8. Remove all remaining cables from inside the PC. Each cable should have a masking tape label on each end telling where it comes from and where it goes.

9. Take out any drives that look like they will be in the motherboard's way when you are ready to remove it. Unscrew the mounting screws holding them in place, and they should slide out easily.

**TIP** On some systems, multiple drives are mounted in a single metal frame, called a *cage.* You may be able to remove that metal frame by detaching its retaining screws. If so, you can then lift out all the drives in that frame as a group.

10. Unplug any wires that lead from the motherboard to the lights on the front of your PC. These are typically tiny black connectors, plugged into a cluster together on the edge of the motherboard.

11. Check to make sure that nothing else is plugged into the motherboard.

12. If the motherboard is mounted to a removable plate on the bottom of the case, remove the screws holding the plate to the case and pull the plate (with the motherboard attached) out of the case.

13. Locate the metal screws (you should find at least two) that hold the motherboard to the case (or the plate). Remove the screws with a non-magnetic screwdriver and put them somewhere safe.

14. Slide the motherboard a few inches to the side to release its plastic standoffs from the case (or plate). Then lift out the motherboard.

15. Clean the empty case with a damp cloth (just damp, not wet!) or some computer-cleaning towelettes. Avoid touching any connectors or wires.

16. Read every word of the new motherboard's manual and make sure that all the jumpers and DIP switches are set correctly. Change settings if necessary.

17. Install the new processor (if needed), as you learned earlier in this session.

18. Install the new memory, as you learned earlier in this session. (Remove the memory from the old motherboard if you are planning to reuse it in the new one.)

19. Check the positioning of the brass standoffs that remain in the case against the holes on the new motherboard. Reposition the standoffs as needed.

**CAUTION** ◆◆◆◆◆◆◆◆◆◆◆◆◆◆◆◆◆◆◆◆◆◆◆◆◆◆◆◆◆◆◆◆◆◆◆◆◆◆◆◆◆◆◆◆◆

Do not leave any brass standoffs in spots where the new motherboard does not have holes. The metal will touch the bare motherboard. Brass is not particularly conductive but it could still conceivably cause an electrical short.

◆◆◆◆◆◆◆◆◆◆◆◆◆◆◆◆◆◆◆◆◆◆◆◆◆◆◆◆◆◆◆◆◆◆◆◆◆◆◆◆◆◆◆◆◆

20. Place the new motherboard in the case (or on the plate) and note which holes in the motherboard align with standoff canals in the case.

21. Remove the motherboard from the case again, and install plastic standoffs in the case in spots that match holes in the motherboard.

22. Place paper washers over each brass standoff. Secure them with tiny pieces of clear tape if desired.

23. Place the motherboard in the case, being careful not to knock off the paper washers from the brass standoffs. Make sure the tips of the plastic standoffs align with holes in the motherboard.

24. Gently press down on the motherboard, forcing the umbrella-like tips

of the plastic standoffs through the holes and locking them into place. Be careful not to slide the motherboard from side to side, as this may knock the paper washers off the brass stand-offs.

**25.** Place paper washers over each screw hole on top of the motherboard; then insert and tighten the screws. Make sure you select appropriate screws from the bag that came with the motherboard; a too-small screw will be loose, whereas a too-large screw will not screw in all the way or will damage the motherboard if you force it.

**26.** Reconnect everything (aren't you glad you labeled all those wires and connectors?) and reinstall all drives and expansion cards:

    ✿  Reconnect the power supply cables to the motherboard and to each device.

    ✿  Reinstall all expansion cards and reattach their screws to hold them in place.

    ✿  Reconnect the ribbon cables between the drives and their controllers. Make sure you get the stripe on the cable aligned with pin 1.

    ✿  Connect any special cables (such as an audio cable between the sound card and the CD-ROM drive).

◆◆◆◆◆◆◆◆◆◆◆◆◆◆◆◆◆◆◆◆◆◆◆◆◆◆◆◆◆◆◆◆◆◆◆◆◆◆◆◆◆◆◆◆

**CAUTION**  You've seen this warning before, but it's important enough to repeat: *If your power supply connects to the motherboard using two connectors (rather than a single one), you must attach the two power supply connectors so that the black wires are in the middle.*

◆◆◆◆◆◆◆◆◆◆◆◆◆◆◆◆◆◆◆◆◆◆◆◆◆◆◆◆◆◆◆◆◆◆◆◆◆◆◆◆◆◆◆◆

**27.** Turn on the system. If it works, you're in business! If not, see the troubleshooting section in this afternoon's session.

# Other Installations

I'll end this chapter by giving you some pointers on a few less common upgrades that you might face. In most cases, these upgrades are either very easy or very much like an upgrade that I have already explained in this session.

# Setting Up a Peer-to-Peer Network

To set up a simple home network, you need network cards, a hub, and some network cabling. Network cards are just normal circuit cards. After you put them in both computers, you run cables from each of them to the hub, and plug the hub's power cable into the wall. That's all there is to it! Installing the physical hardware for a peer-to-peer network is easy. The hard part comes when you have to configure Windows 95/98 to recognize it! You'll learn how to do that in this afternoon's session.

# Changing Keyboards

In most cases, you can simply unplug your old keyboard and plug in your new one. The only glitch might be that you have the wrong kind of plug on the new keyboard. AT-style motherboards have 5-pin, AT-style keyboard plugs, while ATX-motherboards have 6-pin, PS/2 style. If you get your new keyboard home only to find that you have the wrong type, you can either return it or buy an adapter like the one shown in Figure 4.27. Adapters are relatively inexpensive (under $10), and allow you to use a different keyboard type.

# Connecting a Scanner

Scanner hookup varies depending on the type you have bought. Some are parallel port devices, discussed earlier in this session. Others are SCSI devices

**Figure 4.27**

A keyboard adapter can let you use an AT-style keyboard with a PS/2 style motherboard, or vice-versa.

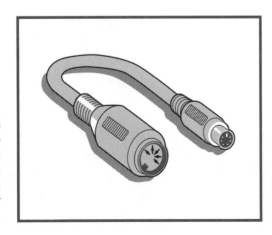

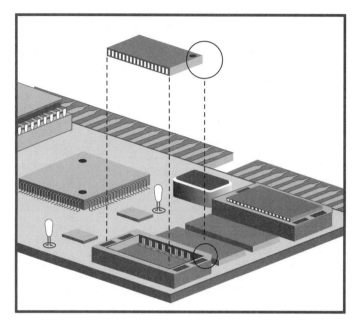

**Figure 4.28**

Adding RAM to a video card is as simple as pressing in a new chip.

that come with their own interface boards you install and then plug into with the cable provided.

## Upgrading Your Video Card's RAM

If you have bought a memory upgrade for your video card, it probably came on a rectangular chip with little metal legs. You plug it into an empty socket on your video card, as shown in Figure 4.28. You will probably want to remove the video card from the PC and place it on a flat surface before doing this, because you might have to push on it moderately hard.

## Summary

Is it lunchtime yet? You've made great progress this morning, and now your new device is physically installed in the computer. But physical installation is only half the battle for some upgrades; you still need to set up the BIOS and run the installation software. That's what you learn in this afternoon's session—along with what to do if the upgrade doesn't work properly the first time.

# Testing and Troubleshooting

- ✪ Working with the BIOS Setup
- ✪ Troubleshooting Startup Problems
- ✪ Figuring Out Why a Device Isn't Working
- ✪ Protecting Your Warranty Rights
- ✪ Returning Defective Merchandise

Now comes the moment you have been waiting for—or perhaps dreading. It's time to see whether you (1) bought the right part and (2) installed it properly. This session shows you how to configure your new device in the BIOS setup and how to run the setup software. If it works—great. If it doesn't, the troubleshooting information included at the end of this session can help you figure out why.

# All about the BIOS

Part of your upgrade installation may include configuring your BIOS setup program to recognize the new device. The background information in the following section will help you understand what's going on with your BIOS.

## What Is the BIOS, Anyway?

When you start the computer, it loads its operating system (such as DOS or Windows 95/98). But what tells the computer to perform the task of loading the operating system? The BIOS tells it. The BIOS (which stands for basic input/output system) is in charge of the low-level startup routine that tells the computer how to load the operating system. When you start up the computer, a typical BIOS checks these things:

- Is a working processor installed?
- Is the BIOS information uncorrupted?
- Is memory installed?
- Is a working video card installed?

- ❖ Is a keyboard installed?
- ❖ What ports does the computer have?
- ❖ How fast does the processor run?
- ❖ Is the memory without defect?
- ❖ Is a working floppy disk drive installed?
- ❖ Is a working hard disk drive installed? What kind is it?

The BIOS is an automatically executed startup routine that runs these tests (and others) before loading the operating system. This program is stored on a Read-Only Memory (ROM) chip mounted on the motherboard. Some people refer to this program as the *ROM-BIOS,* which is its full name. The essential parts of the BIOS routine are hard-coded into the chip so that they are never lost.

Several major brands of BIOS chips are available. AMI, Award, and Phoenix are among the most popular. If you were building a PC from scratch, you could get the BIOS brand you wanted by selecting a motherboard with that particular brand of chip, but most people don't care too much one way or the other. All brands have approximately the same BIOS features.

## The BIOS Setup Program

Most systems have a setup program built into the BIOS. This setup program displays the BIOS settings and enables you to customize them.

Here's how it works: The BIOS settings are permanently stored on the ROM-BIOS chip and can't be changed. Think of the BIOS settings as the "house rules." Nevertheless, sometimes you will have a good reason to break a rule, and sometimes you will need to change the original settings. For example, the default BIOS might specify that the system has one floppy drive, but your system actually has two.

Using the BIOS setup program, you can enter overrides to the BIOS rules. As the system starts up, it first reads the original BIOS settings to get the baseline, and then it reads the overrides to make any needed changes. For example, the override message "There are two floppy drives" would override the original BIOS message "There is one floppy drive."

These overrides are stored on a special microchip called a CMOS chip. (CMOS stands for Complementary Metal-Oxide Semiconductor.) This chip is volatile, like regular RAM; in other words, a CMOS chip requires power to sustain its memory. But unlike regular RAM, the CMOS chip requires only a tiny amount of electricity to maintain itself. The computer's battery provides all the power that the CMOS needs. Some people call the BIOS setup program *CMOS setup.*

**NOTE** When your computer battery dies, you lose all the information on the CMOS chip, including the correct date and time and the types of floppy and hard disks installed on the computer. In the absence of CMOS data, the BIOS reverts to a set of default settings, so the computer may be able to start even when the battery is dead. However, the drives often behave strangely (you may be unable to access one of your floppies or portions of your hard disk) if the default settings do not match the actual system. In this morning's session I explained how to replace a dead battery.

From a user perspective, the BIOS setup program is the most visible difference among various brands of BIOS. Different brands have different setup programs, which vary in their ease of use.

# Making BIOS Changes for Your Upgrade

Now that you understand the BIOS settings, how do you know whether you need to change them? You'll need to consult the instructions that came with the upgrade to be sure, but here are some hints:

- **Hard disk**. If you are installing an IDE drive attached to one of the built-in IDE controllers on your system, you will have to configure it in the BIOS setup program. If your new hard disk is either a SCSI drive or an IDE drive attached to its own separate controller card, you probably won't have to set it up in BIOS.

- **CD-ROM drive**. If you are installing an IDE drive attached to the computer's built-in IDE controller, use the BIOS setup program to configure it (in most cases). If your new CD-ROM drive runs on a SCSI controller, a sound card controller, or a separate IDE controller, you do not need to set it up in BIOS. A few BIOS setup programs do

not require CD-ROM setup; you might try starting the PC first without entering the setup program to see if it recognizes the CD-ROM drive on its own.

- ⚙ **Replacement floppy**. If you are installing a replacement floppy drive that is the same type as an old one you've removed, you do not have to set it up in BIOS. If it is an additional drive or a different type from what you had, you do.

- ⚙ **New memory**. If you are installing new memory, you may or may not need to do anything in the BIOS setup program, depending on your system. The older the system, the more likely you will have to work with the BIOS setup.

- ⚙ **Internal modem**. If you are installing an internal modem, you may want to disable one of your system's built-in COM ports to avoid an IRQ conflict. I explain this problem in more detail later in the session.

- ⚙ **Removable hard disk** or **tape backup unit**. If you are installing a ZIP or Jaz drive or a tape backup unit, you do not have to set it up in BIOS. This rule is true even if the device is an IDE device connected to your computer's built-in IDE controller.

In the end, you should let the instructions that came with the new device be your guide. Each device is different—you may be installing some special kind of drive that does not need BIOS setup, or that needs to be set up in a certain way.

◆◆◆◆◆◆◆◆◆◆◆◆◆◆◆◆◆◆◆◆◆◆◆◆◆◆◆◆◆◆◆◆◆◆◆◆◆◆◆◆◆◆

Make sure you read the instructions carefully as they pertain to BIOS setup! I once made a big mistake on a system by not following this advice. I had installed lots of drives in the past, so when I encountered a system with an IDE ZIP drive, I thought I knew just what to do. I figured that a ZIP drive was a lot like a hard disk, so I asked the BIOS setup program to use its AutoDetect feature to set the appropriate settings for the new drive. Sure enough, the BIOS detected the device as a ZIP drive, and I thought everything was fine. But shortly after that, the computer began locking up frequently for no reason.

When I reread the ZIP driver's documentation, it clearly stated that you should not let the BIOS setup program autoconfigure the drive. Instead, you should leave it completely out of the BIOS program. Sheepishly, I made that change, and the computer has been working fine ever since.

◆◆◆◆◆◆◆◆◆◆◆◆◆◆◆◆◆◆◆◆◆◆◆◆◆◆◆◆◆◆◆◆◆◆◆◆◆◆◆◆◆◆

# Starting the BIOS Setup Program

Different systems have different ways of starting the BIOS setup program. On newer systems (486 and above, usually) as the computer starts you can see a message like this:

```
Press F1 to enter Setup
```

The message may show a different key to press (Del and Esc are popular); just do whatever it says. Be quick, though, because you can enter setup only as long as that message appears, and the message goes away after a few seconds. If you miss it, just restart the computer (by pressing its Reset button or pressing Ctrl+Alt+Del).

On some older systems you may not be able to enter the BIOS setup program at startup. Some systems came with a special disk that contained a Setup program to run, and other systems enabled you to enter BIOS from the DOS prompt by pressing a certain key combination (such as Ctrl+Alt+Esc). On such systems you must read the computer documentation to find out how to enter BIOS Setup, because you will probably not be able to find the entryway by trial and error.

# Finding Your Way Around

Once you've made it into the BIOS Setup program, you will see its opening screen. Every BIOS has a different setup program, and even different versions from the same company have different controls. Depending on the BIOS your system has, you may see either a text-based or graphics-based display. Figures 5.1 and 5.2 show examples.

There are hundreds of different BIOS setup programs, made by dozens of companies. This session shows two examples: one text-based and one graphical. Chances are good that yours will be different, but it will probably be similar to one or the other of these.

You can't really see it in Figure 5.1 because this book is in black-and-white, but on a color monitor, some items have a blue description and a black value, while others use blue for both entries. What's the difference? The items with the value in black are changeable; the items where the value appears in blue are for information only. In Figure 5.1 everything from Video Mode to the bottom is blue. The information about Video Mode, Mouse, Base Memory, Extended Memory, and BIOS Version is strictly FYI; you can't change it.

Chances are good that your computer's BIOS program resembles one of these examples. You should be able to figure out the significance of any differences after you learn about the programs in Figures 5.1 and 5.2.

**TIP** Somewhere on the screen the BIOS program tells you how to get help. In Figure 5.1, for example, you press F1 (notice F1 Help in the right column); in Figure 5.2 you press Alt+H for Help (notice Alt+H: Help in the lower-right corner). Press the designated key or combination to display instructions for your BIOS setup program. The instructions given in this book are general and do not apply to every situation.

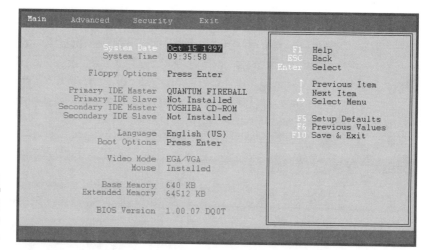

**Figure 5.1**

Here's a text-based BIOS setup program.

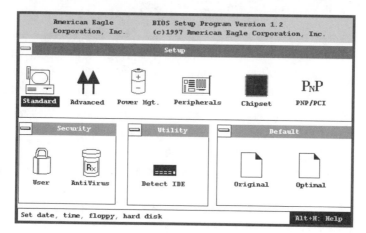

**Figure 5.2**

This BIOS setup program has a graphical interface.

## Moving among Menus

Most BIOS setup programs do not display all their options on the screen at the same time. For example, in Figure 5.1 the word *Main* is brighter than the other three words across the top. In this case Main is selected, and the options you see are the Main options.

If you look at the instructions on the right side of the screen in Figure 5.1, you'll see a horizontal double-headed arrow next to Select Menu. That symbol tells you to press right arrow and left arrow to move through the menus. Press right arrow from the screen shown in Figure 5.1 to open the Advanced menu; press right arrow again to open the Security menu. Almost all text-based BIOS setup programs use these arrow keys to move from menu to menu.

In a graphical BIOS setup program like Figure 5.2, you may see a series of icons in boxes, instead of menu names across the top. Each icon represents a menu. Just double-click on an icon to view a menu's options. Figure 5.3 shows a window that might open when you double-click on a Standard icon like the one shown in Figure 5.2.

## Choosing a Menu Command

Notice in Figure 5.1 that the System Date command is selected. You can tell because its title appears in white (instead of gray) and its current value appears in a black block. By checking the right side of the screen, you see that pressing up arrow and down arrow will let you move among items. So, for example, to select the System Time in Figure 5.1, you would press down arrow one time.

When a command is highlighted, you can usually press Enter to select it. For example, if you press Enter in Figure 5.1, with the System Date field

**Figure 5.3**

In a graphical BIOS setup program, new windows open when you double-click on some icons.

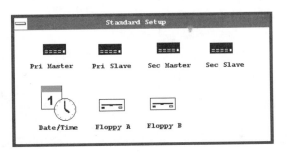

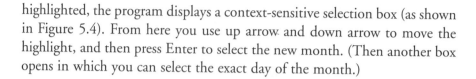
highlighted, the program displays a context-sensitive selection box (as shown in Figure 5.4). From here you use up arrow and down arrow to move the highlight, and then press Enter to select the new month. (Then another box opens in which you can select the exact day of the month.)

**NOTE** Not all BIOS setup programs work the same way. For some commands in some setup programs, pressing Enter has no effect. Instead, you change the value of the highlighted field by pressing Page Up or Page Down.

A graphical BIOS setup displays icons for each menu command. You double-click on the command you want, and controls appear allowing you to change the setting. For example, in Figure 5.5 the BIOS setup program displays a list of drive types, and you must click on the button next to the type that is connected to your system.

## Getting Out

In almost all BIOS setup programs, you can return to the previous screen by pressing Esc.

Many programs display exiting instructions on the screen. For example, you press F10 to save and exit from the program in Figure 5.1. Different BIOS

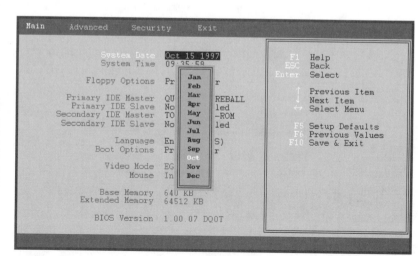

**Figure 5.4**

To change a setting in a text-based program, highlight a setting and press Enter. You might make the actual change in a selection box as shown here.

**Figure 5.5**

Graphical BIOS
setup programs use
dialog boxes with
controls similar to
those found in
Microsoft Windows.

```
┌─────────────────────────────┐
│ ▭        Floppy A            │
│                             │
│  ☐  Not Installed           │
│  ☐  360  KB 5 1/4           │
│  ☐  1.2  MB 5 1/4           │
│  ☐  720  KB 3 1/2           │
│  ☑  1.44 MB 3 1/2           │
│  ☐  2.88 MB 3 1/2           │
└─────────────────────────────┘
```

programs have different exit routines. If your program doesn't display instructions for exiting, try pressing Esc at the main screen.

As you exit, you will be asked whether or not you want to save your changes. If you have made changes you want to keep, select Yes; if you were just browsing, or have made changes you regret, select No.

## BIOS Setup for New RAM

The procedure for setting up RAM in the BIOS setup program depends heavily on the age of the system.

In the newest systems you do not have to do anything in the BIOS setup program. The system detects its new RAM automatically. When installing new RAM, try starting the system normally first. If it works and the startup screen counts up the new RAM, great! You're all set. (If it counts up the new RAM incorrectly or doesn't see it at all, see the troubleshooting information later in this session.)

In some middle-aged systems (usually 486s), when you start the computer after installing RAM, you see a scary-looking error message, something like "Memory error" or "Invalid RAM checksum." It is usually followed by a message like "Press F1 to enter setup." Press the appropriate key to enter the BIOS setup program. Once in there, check out the reported amount of RAM. (If you have a text-based BIOS setup program, the value should be obvious, as it is at the bottom of Figure 5.1; if you have a graphical setup program, you may have to double-click on the Standard icon to display this information.) The setup program should reflect the new RAM amount. (If it doesn't, check that there are no jumpers on the motherboard that need to be set differently.) Now just exit the BIOS setup program (saving your changes—even though you didn't do anything yourself but look at a number) and let the computer restart itself. Done deal!

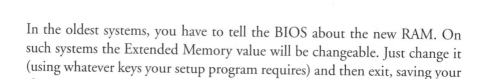

In the oldest systems, you have to tell the BIOS about the new RAM. On such systems the Extended Memory value will be changeable. Just change it (using whatever keys your setup program requires) and then exit, saving your changes.

 **NOTE** As I've mentioned before, a megabyte of memory is not exactly one thousand bytes; it's a little more. One megabyte is actually 1024K of memory. That means 4 megabytes is 4096 and so on, adding an extra 24K for every extra megabyte. If you have to manually enter the amount of RAM in the system, don't forget to take these extra bits into account.

## BIOS Setup for IDE Hard Drives

This BIOS change is the most common type and, unfortunately, also one of the most complicated to do. (Don't panic; I'll walk you through it.)

First, a bit o' history. Back in the old days (the 1980s), the computer industry used only about 40 types of hard disks. Because the types were limited, the BIOS setup program could maintain a list of all possible hard disk types; when you installed a new drive, you simply selected the type from the list. A *type* of hard disk is a specific combination of the following factors: number of cylinders, number of heads, and number of sectors per track. These factors combine to determine the hard disk's capacity.

Then hard disks started getting bigger and having more features, and the BIOS setup programs couldn't keep up. To avoid problems, BIOS programmers began allowing a type of drive called *User Defined,* in which the user could manually enter the cylinders, heads, and sectors. This option enabled the BIOS to support new drives that were created many years after the setup program was written.

As time went by, users complained about the difficulty of setting up new drives manually with the User Defined drive type. Typing a wrong number could result in a drive not working properly or losing data, so the stakes were high. Users also complained that sometimes they did not have the needed information handy, especially with used drives. Clearly, something had to change.

As a result of the public outcry, BIOS setup programmers began including either an AutoConfigure drive type or a drive configuration utility, depending on the brand of BIOS. Both of these features have the same result: They query the drive about its optimal settings and then automatically enter the information in the appropriate spots in the BIOS setup program.

## Using the BIOS AutoConfigure Drive Type

If your BIOS has an AutoConfigure (or just Auto) selection on the list of drive types, you're in luck. Choose this option as the hard drive type, and the BIOS setup program will make all the choices for you.

For example, to add a primary slave drive to a system that has a text-based BIOS setup program like the one shown in Figure 5.1, here's what I would do:

1. Press the down arrow until you highlight the phrase *Not Installed* next to Primary IDE Slave.

2. Press Enter to display the Primary IDE Slave screen. The first line is IDE Device Configuration, and it is highlighted and set to Not Installed.

3. Press Enter to display the available drive types. Among them is Auto Configured.

4. Press the down arrow until you highlight the phrase *Auto Configured.* Then press Enter to select it. At this point the BIOS setup program queries the installed hard disk and reports its settings onscreen, as shown in Figure 5.6.

From looking at Figure 5.6, you probably can't tell that the individual settings for the drive (the heads, sectors, and cylinders) are not editable when Auto Configured is the drive type. However, when Auto Configured is the drive type, its settings are in control.

## Using the BIOS Drive Detection Program

In the preceding example the drive detection program was built right into the drive selection screen. In some other BIOS setup programs, drive detection is a separate routine. (The latter case is more prevalent in the graphical BIOS programs, whereas the all-in-one detection and selection is more common with text-based BIOS programs.)

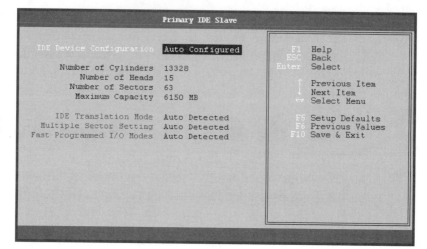

**Figure 5.6**

The BIOS setup program determined these settings when I chose Auto Configured as the drive type.

For example, in Figure 5.2 you run the drive type detection program by double-clicking on the Detect IDE icon in the Utility window. When you do so, a brief message says that the check is in progress, and then you see a list of all the drives that the system detected, as shown in Figure 5.7.

**NOTE** Some BIOS programs detect each of the four positions separately (Primary Master, Primary Slave, Secondary Master, and Secondary Slave), and you must press Enter or some other key between each detection. The onscreen directions should be clear.

Notice in Figure 5.7 that you can change three of the settings: PIO, Block, and LBA. (See the following section to learn more about these.) The program determines the rest of the settings automatically.

**Figure 5.7**

In this example the detection program found one hard disk and one CD-ROM drive.

|  | Type | Cyl | Hd | WP | Sec | Size(MB) | PIO | Block | LBA |
|---|---|---|---|---|---|---|---|---|---|
| Pri Master: | User | 4970 | 16 | 0 | 63 | 2446 | 4 | On | On |
| Pri Slave: | Not Detected | | | | | | | | |
| Sec Master: | CDROM | | | | | | | | |
| Sec Slave: | Not Detected | | | | | | | | |

Auto Detection Status

After you run Auto Detect, the BIOS setup program may ask whether it should transfer the new settings to the BIOS's setup for that drive. You should answer Yes. However, most BIOS setup programs automatically transfer the settings for you. If you go into the Standard setup screen and display the settings for the drive you just Auto Detected, the correct settings will be there.

## Manually Configuring a Hard Disk

If your BIOS program does not automatically detect the hard disk type, or does not detect it correctly, you must configure it manually. This method requires you to know a little more about the drive you're installing than you would normally need to know. Before you start, consult the drive's documentation (or the label on the outside of the drive casing) to determine the correct settings for the following factors:

- **Type**. The type of the drive. If this drive is one of the older drive types, it will have a type number from 1 to 46. If you have this number, you do not need any of the other settings described below. Most likely, though, your drive will not have a type number.

- **Cylinders (Cyl)**. The number of cylinders that the drive has. It should be a number in the thousands for most modern drives; my 2.4-gigabyte drive has 4790 cylinders. A sticker on the drive should list the number of cylinders, heads, and sectors to use.

- **Heads (Hd)**. The number of read-write heads that the drive has. This value is a single- or double-digit number. My 2.4-gigabyte drive has 16.

- **Sectors (Sec)**. The number of sectors per track on the disk.

Depending on the BIOS program, you may also be asked about these features:

- **Landing zone**. This setting is nearly obsolete on newer drives; it's the position where the heads rest when the drive is off. On all modern drives it is 65550.

- **PIO**. New enhanced IDE drives support fast data transfer with Programmed I/O (PIO) modes. If your drive supports this feature, you should use the highest mode it supports (0 through 4). Don't use too

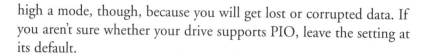

high a mode, though, because you will get lost or corrupted data. If you aren't sure whether your drive supports PIO, leave the setting at its default.

◆◆◆◆◆◆◆◆◆◆◆◆◆◆◆◆◆◆◆◆◆◆◆◆◆◆◆◆◆◆◆◆◆◆◆◆◆◆◆◆◆◆◆

Don't change the PIO mode for a drive that is already installed and working fine. Doing so could introduce new problems in your system.

◆◆◆◆◆◆◆◆◆◆◆◆◆◆◆◆◆◆◆◆◆◆◆◆◆◆◆◆◆◆◆◆◆◆◆◆◆◆◆◆◆◆◆

- ✿ **Translation**. Translation converts the physical disk locations into logical addressable units. If your drive is over 504MB, it probably uses some extended translation method, such as Logical Block Addressing (LBA). You may also see this method referred to as Extended Cylinder Head Sector (ECHS) or just plain Large. In contrast, a translation type of Normal refers to the standard Cylinder Head Sector (CHS) translation.

- ✿ **Block mode**. Not all BIOS programs ask about Block mode, but some do. If it's enabled, the computer can transfer data to and from the drive in blocks rather than in bytes, so it can perform better. Enable this mode only if you are sure that your drive supports it. (If your drive uses Large, LBA, or ECHS translation, it is a safe bet that it also supports Block mode.)

- ✿ **32-bit mode**. This setting allows 32-bit access to the drive through the BIOS. Most IDE drives support this setting, but you can use it only if your motherboard has a local bus (PCI or VLB).

From your BIOS setup program and with your drive information in hand, follow these steps for a manual configuration:

1. Select the interface on which the drive is installed (Primary Master, Secondary Master, Primary Slave, or Secondary Slave). Its current setting is probably Not Installed.

2. Select User Defined (or just User in some programs) as the drive type. The setup program opens some sort of box through which you can enter the settings.

3. Enter the settings in the appropriate fields. Different BIOS setup programs handle the entry in different ways. In text-based programs you

typically just type the value into the first field and then press Enter or the down arrow to move to the next field, as shown in Figure 5.8. Some graphical programs provide an onscreen numeric keypad in which you use mouse clicks to enter the numbers, as shown in Figure 5.9.

4. Exit from the BIOS setup program, saving your changes.

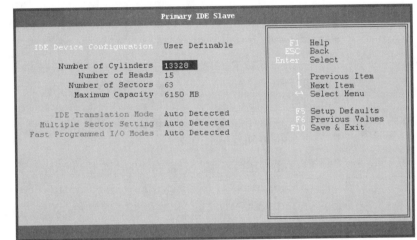

**Figure 5.8**

Text-based BIOS programs typically have simple fields, for example, Number of Cylinders and Number of Heads, for you to fill in.

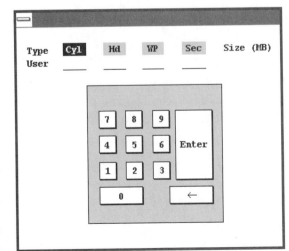

**Figure 5.9**

Some BIOS programs provide an onscreen keypad that you use to enter numbers.

# BIOS Setup for CD-ROM Drives

You have to set up your new CD-ROM drive in the BIOS setup program only if it is an IDE device attached to the computer's built-in IDE controller. BIOS setup doesn't need to know about the drive if it's attached to its own interface card or to a SCSI card. In addition, not all BIOS setup programs require you to configure a CD-ROM in them; on some computers you can just plug in your CD-ROM drive and it works perfectly without making any BIOS changes. On such systems, trying to configure the BIOS with CD-ROM information actually makes the drive *not* work. Therefore, you should test the newly installed drive to see if it works without BIOS changes first.

You set up a CD-ROM drive the same way as a hard drive, except you don't have to enter any numbers. If your BIOS has auto detection, just ask it to Auto Detect, the same as you did in the preceding section with the hard disks. (Refer to that section if you need to.) If the BIOS doesn't support Auto Detect, follow these steps:

1. In your BIOS setup program, select the interface on which the CD-ROM is installed (Primary Master, Secondary Master, Primary Slave, or Secondary Slave). The interface is probably currently set to Not Installed.
2. Select CD-ROM for drive type.
3. Exit from the BIOS program, saving your changes.

If your BIOS program does not have CD-ROM as a drive type, exit from the BIOS program without making changes. Then run the CD-ROM setup software and give it a try without BIOS configuration; it may work fine anyway.

If the drive does not appear to work without BIOS setup, and you can't set it up in BIOS, you have two choices. You can box it up and return it to the store where you bought it, hoping you can exchange it for a model that comes with its own interface card, or you can buy an IDE interface card for your PC and try running the CD-ROM drive with it.

# BIOS Setup for Floppy Drives

If you are replacing a defective floppy with the same type (for example, replacing one high-density 3.5" drive with another), you don't have to configure

anything in BIOS. Just take the old drive out of the computer and put the new one in, as you learned this morning, and everything should be fine.

On the other hand, if you are adding a floppy drive or changing from one type to another, you may need to tell the BIOS about the new unit. Some detect floppy drives automatically; some do not.

Most BIOS programs list the floppy drives either in the Standard section or in their own section. If you'll look back at Figure 5.1, you see a Floppy Options line, with Press Enter next to it. Use down arrow to highlight that line and then press Enter; you'll see a Floppy Options screen like the one in Figure 5.10.

What you do next depends on the BIOS setup program. In Figure 5.10, for example, if you were installing a second floppy, you would follow this procedure. (These steps are just for the BIOS setup program shown in Figure 5.10; your situation will probably be a little different.)

1. Press the down arrow to move the highlight to the Floppy B line.

2. Press Enter to view the available values. The available values for that field are Installed and Not Installed.

3. Press the down arrow once to switch from Not Installed to Installed; then press Enter to select it.

4. Back at the Floppy Options screen, press down arrow two times to highlight the Floppy B: type line. Its current value is Disabled.

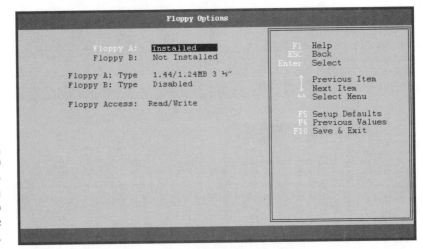

**Figure 5.10**

You may have to jump to a screen like this one to configure the floppies.

5. Press Enter to display the available values for the field. They are Disabled, 360KB, 1.2MB, 720KB, 1.44MB, and 2.88MB (see Figure 5.11).

6. Press the down arrow until you highlight the appropriate value. (Most floppy drives sold today are 1.44MB.) Then press Enter.

7. Press Esc to return to the main screen. Then exit the program and save your changes.

In other text-based BIOS setup programs, instead of selecting from a list (as you do in Figure 5.11), you highlight the field you want and then press Page Up or Page Down to toggle through the available values.

In a graphical BIOS setup program, you will probably find Floppy A and Floppy B icons in the Standard Setup window. Double-click on the icon for the floppy drive you want to configure, and you will see a list of floppy options, as shown in Figure 5.12. Click on the type you want, and then press

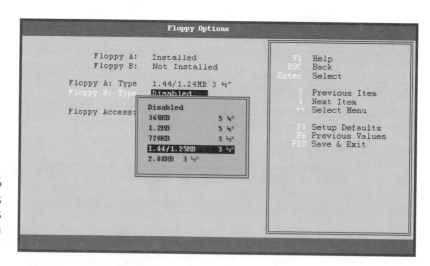

**Figure 5.11**

When the field is highlighted, press Enter to display a box of choices.

**Figure 5.12**

In a graphical BIOS setup program, you may see a box of choices; click on what you want.

Esc or click on the minus sign in the window's upper-left corner to close the window.

No matter what kind of BIOS setup program you have, after you make the change, exit from the program. Be sure to say Yes if you are asked whether you want to save your changes.

# BIOS Setup for an Internal Modem

In theory, you shouldn't have to change anything in your BIOS setup for an internal modem. Your computer's BIOS supports two internal COM ports: COM1 and COM2. When you install an internal modem, it is usually configured as COM3 or COM4, so you shouldn't have a conflict. However, if installing an internal modem were as simple as that, I wouldn't be writing this section. Unfortunately, some things don't work in reality as well as they work in theory, and internal modem installation is one of them. If you can stick with me through a bit of techno-explanation, you'll understand the situation.

**NOTE**  If you have Windows 95/98 and a Plug-and-Play modem, you should not have to do any BIOS setup or set any COM ports for it. Windows should automatically determine the best setting for it. However, if you are having trouble with your modem in Windows 95/98 due to an IRQ conflict (see the troubleshooting section at the end of this session), it might help to disable either COM1 or COM2 in your BIOS, as explained shortly, to free up one of them for the modem.

## All About COM Port IRQs

Each device that communicates directly with the processor has a base address and an interrupt request (IRQ) number. The base address is a hexadecimal code that refers to the memory location in which the device's information is contained. For example, COM1's base address is usually 2F8H, and COM2's is usually 3F8H. Each device (including each COM port) must have its own unique base address.

IRQs are communication lines between the device and the processor, and most systems have 15 of them. Generally speaking, each device has its own, but some devices share a single IRQ. Two IRQs are set aside for COM ports:

IRQ3 and IRQ4. If the system has more than two COM ports, they must share. Odd-numbered COM ports (COM1 and COM3) share IRQ4, and even-numbered COM ports (COM2 and COM4) share IRQ3.

IRQ sharing usually works OK, but if both devices try to talk to the processor at once over the same IRQ line, the messages get garbled and the devices have problems. For example, if you have your mouse on COM1 and your internal modem on COM3, your mouse might stop working every time your modem sent or received data. For this reason, you should avoid IRQ sharing if at all possible.

## Developing Your IRQ Strategy

To avoid IRQ sharing, you need to look at which COM ports are already being used and which ones are idle. From there, you can decide which COM port number would be the best choice for your new modem.

Look on the back of your PC and see which COM ports are in use. You might have a serial mouse, for example, plugged in. The COM ports should be labeled COM1 and COM2; if they're not, check the PC's user manual to determine which is which.

Armed with that information, check out Table 5.1 to find out what to do next.

Here's the action plan:

1. Set a jumper or DIP switch on the modem to set its COM port number if necessary.

**NOTE** Most internal modems allow you to specify their COM port. On some modems you use DIP switches or jumpers to do so; others require special software that comes with the modem. One way or another, you can probably select any COM port, 1 through 4, for the modem. Read the instructions that came with the modem.

2. Install the modem.
3. Disable one of the internal COM ports in the BIOS setup program if necessary.

| **TABLE 5.1 ACTION PLANS FOR AVOIDING IRQ SHARING** | |
|---|---|
| **If:** | **Then plan on this:** |
| COM1 is used but COM2 is free. | Disable COM2 in the BIOS setup program and set the modem to COM2. |
| COM2 is used but COM1 is free. | Disable COM1 in the BIOS setup program and set the modem to COM1. |
| Both COM1 and COM2 are used and a mouse is plugged into COM1. | Set the modem to COM4. Whatever device is plugged into COM2 will probably be used less than the mouse. Or, if your system has an unused PS/2 port, buy an adapter that will enable your mouse to plug into that port. |
| Both COM1 and COM2 are used, and a mouse is plugged into COM2. | Set the modem to COM3. (Same explanation as COM1 mouse.) |

**4.** If the modem's COM port number is set with setup software, run it and set the modem to the correct number.

Steps 1 and 2 were covered in this morning's session, and Step 4 depends on your particular modem (read the directions). The following section explains Step 3.

## Disabling a COM Port in BIOS Setup

Somewhere in your BIOS setup program, you'll find a place to control the COM ports. The exact path to it varies; in the preceding text-based BIOS setup program, you would display the Advanced options and then select Peripheral Configuration.

When you find the list of COM ports, select the one you want to disable and press Enter. A drop-down menu explains your choices, as shown in Figure 5.13. Select Disabled from the list and press Enter. Then exit from the BIOS setup program, saving your changes.

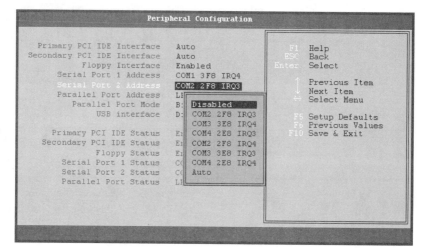

**Figure 5.13**

In a text-based BIOS setup program, the Peripheral Configuration is usually a full-screen display.

 **CAUTION** Be careful not to disable a COM port that is in use! If you disable the COM port that your mouse is attached to, for example, the mouse won't work anymore. A PS/2 mouse is not using a COM port, so you don't have to worry about accidentally disabling it.

In the sample graphical BIOS setup program, double-click on the Peripheral icon in the Setup window. A window appears in which you can set the COM and LPT (parallel) port configuration. From there you double-click on the line for the COM port you want and make your selections from the small pop-up box, as shown in Figure 5.14. Then press Enter to close the window.

 **NOTE** Some BIOS programs use the term *Onboard Serial Port,* rather than COM port. It's the same thing.

# Running Setup Software

Most upgrades come with some sort of setup software. Usually, running this software completes the upgrade installation by copying the needed driver

```
         American Eagle        BIOS Setup Program Version 1.2
         Corporation, Inc.     (c)1997 American Eagle Corporation, Inc.

                                  Setup

              Peripheral Setup                    Options                 P

         Onboard FDC              : Auto          Auto              PCI
         Onboard Serial Port 1    : 3F8h          Disabled
           Serial Port 1 IRQ      : 4             3F8h
         Onboard Serial Port 2    : 2F8h          2F8h
           Serial Port 2 Mode     : Normal        3E8h
           Serial Port 2 IRQ      : 3             2E8h
         Onboard Parallel Port    : 378
           Parallel Port Mode     : Normal
           Parallel Port IRQ      : 7
         Onboard IDE              : Both          Original    Optimal


         Set peripheral options                          Alt+H: Help
```

**Figure 5.14**

In this graphical
BIOS setup
program, you select
which ports to
enable or disable
from a pop-up box.

files to your hard disk and adding lines in the PC's startup files so that the
drivers load every time you turn on the computer.

Again, your best bet is to refer to the instructions that came with the device.
They should thoroughly explain the setup process.

**TIP**

Sometimes you may not have to install everything that came with the upgrade. For example, if you get a new modem, in addition to its own setup program, it probably comes with
startup kits for all the popular online services. Don't confuse this extra software with the
modem's setup disk. The setup disk should be clearly labeled as such with the name of the
modem on it.

The upgrade may also come with some programs that provide a helpful service but are not
essential for the device to work. For example, a modem may come with a communications
and faxing program. You don't have to use it if you already have something better, but it's
there, and it's free, if you need it.

Lay out all the disks that came with the upgrade. Find the ones that have the
name of the device on them plus the word *Installation* or *Setup*. Those are
the ones you need. Refer to the instructions if in doubt.

> ### HARD DISK SETUP DISKS
>
> Most hard disks come with a setup disk, but in most cases you do not have to use it. I recently bought a hard disk that came with a Windows-based setup program. It was designed for systems that already had a hard disk with Windows installed, with the assumption that the new drive was in addition to the old one and not replacing it. It was a cool idea, but unfortunately I didn't get to use it, since the new hard drive was replacing one that died.
>
> Some hard disks come with setup programs that provide BIOS extensions that enable older BIOS setup programs to recognize and configure a new, high-capacity drive properly. You don't have to use such a program if your PC's BIOS autodetects the new drive correctly or allows you to enter its correct parameters as a User Defined type. Read the documentation that came with the new hard drive if you are not sure how to proceed.

One of the disks probably says DISK 1. Pop that one into your floppy disk drive. Then use one of the following procedures to run the setup program:

- If you have DOS only, obviously you should run the setup program from DOS.

- If you have DOS and Windows 3.x, check the instructions that came with the upgrade. If it says to run the setup program from within Windows, do so; otherwise, run it from the DOS prompt.

- If you have Windows 95/98, run the setup program from there if possible. (More on this later.)

## Running a Setup Program in DOS

Most devices include a DOS-based setup program, because not everyone has Windows 95 or 98. Even if the device works with Windows 3.x, its setup program will probably be DOS based. The program copies the appropriate Windows 3.x drivers through DOS so that the next time you start Windows 3.x, it will recognize your device.

To run a setup program from DOS, follow these steps:

1. Put the setup disk in your floppy drive.

2. Switch to the floppy drive by typing **A:** and pressing Enter. (If your floppy drive is B:, substitute B: for A: throughout these instructions.)

3. Consult the instructions to find out what to type to run the setup program. If you can determine it from the instructions, skip to Step 6. If you can't, go on to Step 4.

4. Type **DIR /W** and press Enter to get a list of the files on the disk.

5. Look on the screen for a file that is likely to be the setup program. Look for names like INSTALL.EXE, INSTALL.COM, INSTALL.BAT, SETUP.EXE, SETUP.COM, SETUP.BAT, or any name with *SETUP* or *INSTALL* in it—for example WPSETUP.COM—or an instructive name like RUNME.BAT.

6. Type the name of the file that you think is the setup program and press Enter. If the setup program doesn't start, repeat Steps 3 and 4 and try another file.

7. Follow the onscreen instructions to install the device's software.

# Running a Setup Program in Windows 3.1

If the instructions say to run the setup program from within Windows 3.1, follow these steps:

1. Put the setup disk in your floppy drive.

2. Start Windows 3.1, if it is not already started, by typing **WIN** and pressing Enter at the DOS prompt.

3. Double-click on the Main program group to open it.

4. Double-click on the File Manager icon.

5. Double-click on the A: drive icon near the top of the screen to display a list of the files on the A: drive.

6. Consult the instructions to find out what to type to run the setup program. If you can determine it from the instructions, skip to Step 8. If you can't, go on to Step 7.

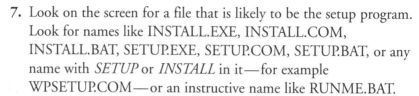

7. Look on the screen for a file that is likely to be the setup program. Look for names like INSTALL.EXE, INSTALL.COM, INSTALL.BAT, SETUP.EXE, SETUP.COM, SETUP.BAT, or any name with *SETUP* or *INSTALL* in it—for example WPSETUP.COM—or an instructive name like RUNME.BAT.

8. Double-click on the name of the file that you think is the setup program. If the setup program doesn't start, return to Step 7 and try a different file.

9. Follow the instructions on the screen to install the device's software.

**TIP** If you know the name of the file to run, you can bypass File Manager and choose File, Run from Program Manager. Type the path and name for the program and click OK to run it.

# Running a Setup Program in Windows 95 or 98

Windows 95/98 offers a somewhat different situation for hardware installation because it supports Plug and Play. If you have a Plug and Play–compatible BIOS and your new device supports Plug and Play, then when you start your computer for the first time after installation, Windows 95/98 automatically detects the new device and sets it up for you. Pretty nifty, eh?

Unfortunately, Plug and Play doesn't always work. Sometimes it works imperfectly, sometimes not at all. The following scenario examines the ideal situation—after which I tell you how to overcome some common stumbling blocks.

## Scenario 1: Everything Works Fine

Here is how Plug and Play is supposed to work:

1. Physically install the hardware, as described in this morning's session.

2. Turn on the computer and Windows 95/98 starts. Windows detects the new device and installs drivers for it.

3. Test the new device to make sure it works. If it doesn't, try Scenario 3.

## Scenario 2: Windows Prompts for a Setup Disk

Sometimes Windows detects something new but needs a little help deciding whether or not to install a driver for it:

1. Physically install the hardware, as described in this morning's session.

2. Turn on the computer and Windows starts. Windows detects the new device and asks you if you want to install a driver for it. The dialog box includes a Have Disk button.

3. Insert the floppy that came with the device and click on Have Disk. Windows reads the driver from the disk and installs the device.

4. Test the new device to make sure it works. If it doesn't, try Scenario 3.

## Scenario 3: You Have a Setup Program

If Windows 95/98 didn't detect the device at startup, but you have a setup disk that came with the device, now would be a good time to run that setup software. Follow these steps:

1. Place the disk or CD into the appropriate drive on your computer.

2. Double-click on the My Computer icon on your desktop and then double-click on the icon for the drive containing the disk you just inserted.

3. Look on the screen for a file that is likely to be the setup program. Look for names like INSTALL.EXE, INSTALL.COM, INSTALL.BAT, SETUP.EXE, SETUP.COM, SETUP.BAT.

4. Double-click on the file that runs the setup program. The setup program runs.

5. Follow the on-screen instructions to complete the setup program's work. If asked whether you want to restart the computer, click on Yes (or Restart or whatever the button is called).

6. Test the new device to make sure it works. If it doesn't, try Scenario 5.

## Scenario 4: You Must Tell Windows to Detect the Device

Sometimes, for whatever reason, Windows 95/98 doesn't immediately notice the new device. If you don't have a setup program—or you have one and running it didn't make the device work—here's how to prompt Windows into noticing the new device. (If you ran the setup program in Scenario 3 and it still isn't working, this technique is not likely to do any good, but it's worth a try.)

1. Physically install the hardware, as described in this morning's session.

2. Turn on the computer and Windows starts. Nothing unusual happens.

3. Double-click on My Computer and then double-click on Control Panel.

4. Double-click on Add New Hardware. The New Hardware Wizard opens.

5. Click on Next to continue.

6. If you are using Windows 98, it informs you that it will look for Plug-and-Play devices. Click on Next to let it do so. If it finds the new device—great. Follow the on-screen prompts to continue the installation.

   If Plug-and-Play detection fails to find the device, you're asked whether you want to search for a device that is not Plug and Play–compatible (see Figure 5.15). Click on Yes and then click on Next.

7. Read the warning message, and click on Next again to begin.

8. Wait for the progress indicator to reach 100% and for another dialog box to appear. It may take several minutes.

   If Windows finds the new hardware, you see a dialog box like the one

**Figure 5.15**

Let Windows try to detect the hardware before resorting to manual configuration.

in Figure 5.16; otherwise, you see the dialog box in Figure 5.17.

If Windows detects the hardware (see Figure 5.16), continue to Step 9. If not, skip to Scenario 5.

9. Click on the Details button to see what Windows found.

10. Do one of the following:

   ✪ If the device on the list is the device you are installing, great. Click on Finish to finish the installation.

   ✪ If the device on the list is not the device you installed, Windows did not detect it correctly. Click on Cancel. Then repeat Steps 1 to 5. When you get to Step 6, click on No and then jump to Step 2 of Scenario 5.

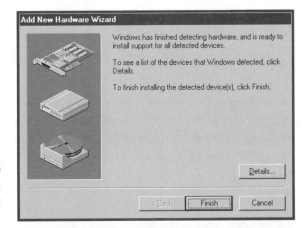

**Figure 5.16**

Windows was able to identify the new hardware.

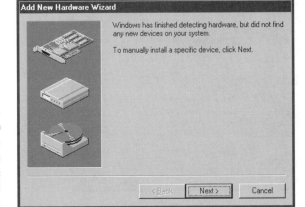

**Figure 5.17**

If Windows fails to detect the hardware, you're stuck with manual configuration.

## Scenario 5: Windows Failed to Detect the Device

If you're reading this section, you've just completed Scenario 3 or part of Scenario 4 and Windows wasn't able to find your device. Starting from Figure 5.17 (the screen where Windows reports that it couldn't find your hardware), follow these steps to install the device's driver manually:

1. Click on Next. The Add New Hardware Wizard displays a list of hardware types, as shown in Figure 5.18.

2. Click on the device type you are installing (for example, Modem) and then click on Next.

3. If you are installing a modem, a box appears offering to search for the modem. (You won't see this box with any other device type.) Click on the "Don't select my {device type}; I will select it from a list" check box; then click on Next.

   A list of manufacturers and models appears for that device type. The list for modems is shown in Figure 5.19.

**NOTE**
In Step 3 you are bypassing the automatic detection because you came here from Scenario 3, where detection failed. There's no reason to think that detection will work now when it failed earlier.

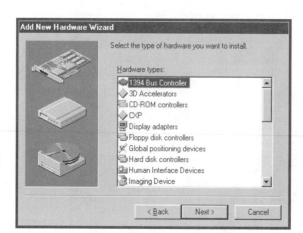

**Figure 5.18**

Choose the type of hardware you are trying to install from this list.

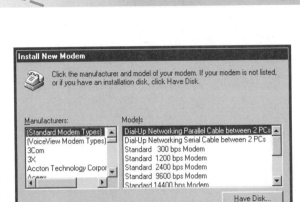

**Figure 5.19**

You can choose your device's make and model from a list of devices that Windows supports.

4. Do one of the following:

   ✪ If the device came with a setup disk, place it in your floppy drive and click on Have Disk. In the Install from Disk dialog box, confirm the drive letter for the floppy (A:\ is the default) and click on OK. Windows finds the driver and installs it. If the disk contains drivers for more than one device model, Windows displays a list of model names; double-click on the name of the model you have.

   ✪ If you do not have a setup disk or you have one but it does not contain the right files (perhaps you have tried the first suggestion and it didn't work), select the device's manufacturer from the list. Then select the model number from the list on the right. Click on Next to continue.

5. If you are installing a device that requires you to select a port, a new dialog box asks you to do so. For example, Figure 5.20 shows the dialog box for a modem. If you see such a box, do one of the following:

   ✪ If the port that the device is connected to appears on the list, click on the port and then click on Next to continue.

   ✪ If the port that the device is connected to does not appear on the list (for example, if you have a new internal modem set for COM3 but COM3 does not appear), click on Cancel and go to the appropriate troubleshooting section later in this chapter.

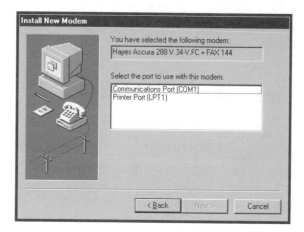

**Figure 5.20**

For some devices,
such as modems,
you must specify
a port.

❖ If you see some other kind of information request other than port, click on whatever setting is appropriate and click on Next to continue.

6. Click on Finish when Windows tells you that your device has been set up successfully. If Windows asks whether to restart the computer, click on Yes (or Restart, or whatever the button says).

7. Test the device to make sure it works. If it doesn't, go to the appropriate troubleshooting section later in this chapter for the type of device you are installing.

## Installing the Extra Software

After you get the device set up, you may want to run the setup programs for any extra software that came with the device. For example, if your new modem came with a communication program, you might want to install it.

Whether you install the extra software is strictly your call. Personally, I seldom install the software that comes with a new modem because it duplicates the capability already built into Windows 95/98. If you are using Windows 3.1, you might find it more useful. On the other hand, I almost always install the software that comes with a sound card because it usually includes a cool audio CD player with fancy controls and a sound or video editing program that is fun to play with.

# Backing Up Your Setup Disks

If the setup disks were necessary to get your new device running, you may want to make a backup copy of them. (If you didn't end up using them, don't worry about it; just file them away.) Here's how to make a backup copy from DOS and from Windows 95/98.

## Copying a Disk in DOS

If you are a Windows 3.1 user, exit from Windows (File, Exit) so you are at the DOS prompt. Then follow these steps:

1. Locate some blank disks or disks that don't contain anything you want to keep. Make sure they're the same type of disk as the disks you want to copy.

2. Place the disk that you want to copy in your floppy drive (usually A:). If your floppy drive is B:, substitute B: for A: in the following steps.

3. Type **DISKCOPY A: A:** and press Enter. You're prompted to place the disk in drive A:, but you've already done that.

4. Press Enter to continue. DOS reads the source disk.

5. Remove the original disk from the drive when prompted and insert the disk that will hold the copy.

6. Press Enter to continue. DOS places the copied files on the disk.

7. Type **N** when DOS asks whether you want to make another copy.

8. Do one of the following when DOS asks if you want to copy another disk:

   ✿ If you have another disk to copy, place the new original in the drive, type **Y,** and return to Step 4.

   ✿ If you are finished, type **N.**

## Copying a Disk in Windows 95/98

If you have Windows 95 or 98, you can copy a disk right from My Computer without typing any commands. Follow these steps:

1. Place the disk to be copied in your floppy drive.

2. Double-click on the My Computer icon on your desktop.

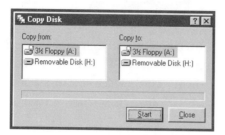

**Figure 5.21**

Use this box to copy a disk in Windows 95/98.

**3.** Right-click on the drive icon for the floppy drive and click on Copy Disk on the shortcut menu that appears. The Copy Disk dialog box appears (see Figure 5.21).

**4.** Make sure the correct drive is selected on the Copy From and Copy To lists. (You can select the same drive for both; Windows will prompt you to switch disks when needed.)

**5.** Click on Start. The copying process begins. A progress indicator reports that it is reading the source disk.

**6.** Remove the original disk when prompted and insert the disk to contain the copy. Then click on OK to continue.

**7.** Do one of the following when the copy is finished:

✪ If you are finished, click on Close.

✪ If you have another disk to copy, place the next original disk in the drive and then return to Step 4.

# Configuring Windows 95/98 for Peer-to-Peer Networking

After you install a network card in your computer, you must do several things in Windows 95/98 to share files among your computers:

✪ Install the driver for the network card.

✪ Install the Windows Networking drivers needed.

✪ Set the Access Control for the PC to log on to the network.

✪ Share individual drives and printers.

# Installing the Network Card Drivers

Your first step is getting Windows to recognize the network card. If the card supports Plug and Play, Windows may do this automatically. You will probably be prompted for a setup disk; use the one that came with the network card. Refer back to the procedures I explained earlier in this chapter for installing drivers for new hardware.

# Installing Windows Networking Drivers

Next, you must install the necessary drivers in Windows to enable network support. These are:

- ⚙ Client for Microsoft Networks
- ⚙ Client for Netware Networks
- ⚙ IPX/SPX-Compatible Protocol
- ⚙ NetBEUI

To check to see if any or all of these are already installed, go to the Control Panel and double-click on the Network icon. On the Configuration tab of the Network dialog box, look for the listed drivers (see Figure 5.22).

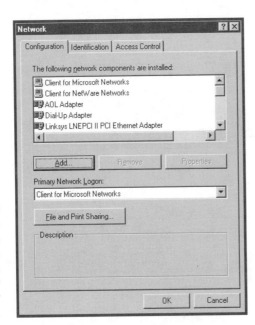

**Figure 5.22**

You must have the necessary Windows network drivers installed to share files among your PCs through your network card.

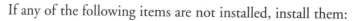

If any of the following items are not installed, install them:

✿ **Client for Microsoft Networks**. Click on Add, and then click on Client and then on Add again. A list of client manufacturers appears. Click on Microsoft in the left pane, and then double-click on Client For Microsoft Networks in the right pane (see Figure 5.23).

✿ **Client for Netware Networks**. This is the same as installing the Client for Microsoft Networks, except you choose a different item from the right pane. (As you can see in Figure 5.23, they are both considered Microsoft clients.)

✿ **IPX/SPX-Compatible Protocol**. Click on Add, and then click on Protocol and then on Add again. A list of protocols appears. Choose Microsoft as the manufacturer, and double-click on IPS/SPX-compatible Protocol on the list.

✿ **NetBEUI**. Same as IPX/SPX-compatible Protocol except you choose NetBEUI instead. NetBEUI is also a protocol, and it is also under Microsoft.

You will probably be prompted to restart your computer at least once during all this. Whenever you see the prompt, click on Yes or OK. After you have restarted with all the needed drivers in place, go on to the next section, "Setting Up Access Control."

**Figure 5.23**

Client for Microsoft Networks is a client found under Microsoft.

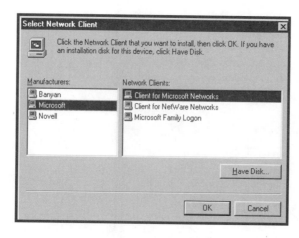

# Setting Up Access Control

Now you are ready to enable network access for your computer. To do so, follow these steps:

1. Open the Control Panel and double-click on the Network icon.

2. On the Configuration tab, open the Primary Network Logon drop-down list and choose Client for Microsoft Networks.

3. Click on the Identification tab.

4. Type the name you want to give your PC in the Computer Name box. Make up a name that is unique from the other computers you are going to include on your network.

5. Type the name of your workgroup in the Workgroup box. This can be anything, but the name you type should be the same for all PCs on your network. This name is case sensitive.

6. Enter a description of your PC in the Computer Description box (see Figure 5.24).

7. Click on the Access Control tab.

8. Make sure that Shared-level Access Control is selected.

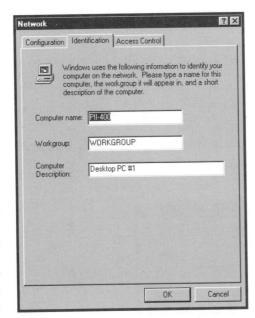

**Figure 5.24**

Enter the information that your PC will provide to identify itself to others on the network.

9. Click on OK. If prompted, insert your Windows CD and click on OK.

10. When prompted to restart your PC, click on Yes.

11. When your PC restarts, a Logon window appears requiring a username and password. Make up a user name and password, enter them, and click on OK. Do not click on Cancel, or you won't be able to log into the network.

# Sharing a Drive or Printer

The final step in configuring networking is to share a drive or printer with other computers. If you don't do this, other computers on your network won't be able to use this computer's resources (disks and printers).

To set up sharing for the first time on a computer, do the following:

1. In the Control Panel, double-click on the Network icon.

2. Click on the Configuration tab.

3. Click on the File And Printer Sharing button. The File And Printer Sharing window appears.

4. Click on both check boxes to enable both file and printer sharing (see Figure 5.25). Then click on OK.

5. When asked if you want to restart your computer, click on Yes.

To share the files on a drive with other computers on the network, follow these steps:

1. Double-click on the My Computer icon. A window of available disk drives appears.

2. Right-click on a drive that you want to share, and choose Sharing. The drive's Properties dialog box appears with the Sharing tab displayed.

**Figure 5.25**

Choose to share
both files
and printers.

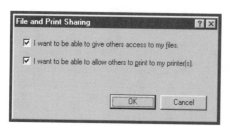

3. Click on the Shared As option button.

4. Type a name by which this drive should be known on the network in the Share Name box.

5. Choose an Access Type: Read-Only (can read but not change), Full (can both read and change), or Depends On Password (see Figure 5.26).

6. If you chose Read-Only or Full, type the password to use in the Read-Only Password or Full-Access Password text box.

7. Click on OK.

8. Repeat these steps for each drive you want to share.

To share a printer, the procedure is somewhat the same:

1. Open the My Computer window, and then double-click on the Printers icon.

2. Right-click on the printer you want to share, and then choose Sharing from the shortcut menu.

3. On the Sharing tab that appears, click on the Shared As option button.

4. Enter a name that the printer should be known by in the Share Name box.

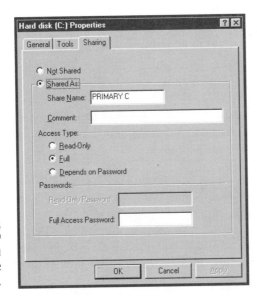

**Figure 5.26**

Choose how you want to share the files on this disk.

5. (Optional) If you want to assign a password to use the printer, enter it in the Password box.

6. Click on OK.

Now, repeat all this on each PC in the network, and that's all there is to it! You are now ready to share your files on your network. To access files on another computer, use the Network Neighborhood icon on your desktop, or when browsing for files in an application, choose Network Neighborhood from the list of drives.

# General Troubleshooting

I wish things always worked right the first time, but unfortunately they don't. I have been installing computer hardware for years, but every installation seems to have at least one problem. But you know what? It's usually due to my own carelessness. Perhaps I didn't firmly seat an adapter, or I forgot to set a jumper. The computer is rarely at fault.

If you are having video, modem, or sound problems in Windows 3.1 or 95/98, skip to the specific troubleshooting sections later in this chapter for those issues. Otherwise, start your troubleshooting journey here.

Turning on the computer is your first test. If the computer starts normally and DOS (or Windows) appears as usual, you've done something right and can skip down to the section titled "PC Starts but New Device Doesn't Work." If not, use the following troubleshooting information to identify the problem.

## Blank Screen

The hardest problems to troubleshoot are those in which you don't see any information on the screen. Without that, it's hard to know where to start. Here are some hints.

### Blank Screen, No Fan

SYMPTOM: The screen is blank, and you hear absolutely nothing from the PC, not even a fan.

EXPLANATION: The computer is not getting power, or the power supply is defective.

**SOLUTION:** Check the following:

- ✪ Is the computer plugged into an electrical outlet?
- ✪ If the computer is plugged into a surge protector or power strip, is its power switch on?
- ✪ Is the power cable plugged firmly into the back of the computer?
- ✪ If you replaced the motherboard, did you remember to plug the power supply cables into the motherboard? Did you plug them in properly—with the black wires toward the center?
- ✪ Is the wall outlet working? Try another appliance such as a lamp in the outlet, to see if it works.

If all the connections are OK and you still don't get any power, the PC's power supply may need to be replaced or the power cord to the computer may be faulty.

If you need to replace the power supply, you might as well buy a whole new computer case with a built-in power supply if you can afford it. The cases available today are more compact and have better designs that keep the processor cooler than the cases made only a few years ago.

## Blank Screen, No Disk Activity

**SYMPTOM:** The screen is blank, and you hear nothing except the power supply fan. There is no disk activity.

**EXPLANATION:** Something is wrong with the motherboard or the processor, or you do not have the video card installed correctly. (The system checks for a video card as one of its first tests, and if it doesn't find one, it refuses to go on.)

**SOLUTION:** If you installed a new motherboard, check these things:

- ✪ Have you connected all the cables correctly? Refer to the manual that came with the motherboard.
- ✪ Have you installed a video card in an appropriate slot on the motherboard? Is it seated firmly?

- Have you set any jumpers on the motherboard that needed to be set?
- Did you install paper washers wherever metal screws touch the motherboard to prevent electrical current from passing through the screws?
- Is the right kind of memory installed in the right banks?
- Are the appropriate switches and jumpers set on the motherboard for the processor and memory you are using?

If you installed a new processor, check the following items:

- If the new processor requires a cooling fan, is it installed and operating?
- Have any needed jumpers on the motherboard been changed to tell the motherboard about the new processor?
- Is the processor firmly seated in its socket and facing the right direction?
- Did you install whatever adapters or interposers that may be necessary to give the new processor and the motherboard's processor socket the same number of pins?

If you installed a new video card or put your old video card into a new motherboard:

- Is the card firmly seated in its slot?
- Is the card in the right kind of slot?

If you are still having a problem, your new motherboard, processor, or video card is probably defective. Return it for a replacement or refund.

## Blank Screen, Beeps

**SYMPTOM:** You see a blank screen and hear a series of beeps.

**EXPLANATION:** The memory is not installed correctly, it is defective, or some other kind of motherboard error exists.

**SOLUTION:** If you installed memory, check these items:

- Have you installed the memory in the correct banks?
- Have you set any needed switches or jumpers?

**TIP**

If you have another computer available that uses the same kind of memory, swap out the SIMMs or DIMMs one at a time to try to determine whether one of them is faulty.

If you have not installed memory or you have checked the memory and determined that it is not faulty, refer to the Appendix, "Post Error Beep Codes," to see whether you can interpret the beep code you are hearing.

**NOTE**

Even though the beep error codes can tell you what's wrong with your system, they probably can't help you fix it unless you're an electronics whiz. For example, if you determine from the beep codes that the built-in I/O controller on the motherboard is bad, you still must return it for a replacement. The only thing that the beep codes offer you is assurance that the device is truly broken and that the problem is not related to your installation.

## Blank Screen, Single Beep, Disk Activity

**SYMPTOM:** You see a blank screen, and you hear a single beep. The floppy disk light lights briefly, and you hear the hard disk spinning.

**EXPLANATION:** The computer is starting normally, but the monitor isn't displaying it.

**SOLUTION:** Try to figure out where the disconnect is between the monitor and the computer, or why the monitor isn't working:

- Is the monitor getting power? Check to make sure it is plugged in and turned on. A light should illuminate on its front when it has power.

- Is the light on the front of the monitor solid green? If so, that's good. If it's amber or blinking, the monitor is in standby mode, which could indicate one of two things:

  - The monitor is working fine but not receiving any signal from the computer.

  - The monitor has set itself in standby mode. Some monitors have a standby button on the front; try pressing all the buttons on the front to see whether any of them change the light to solid green.

- Are the monitor contrast and brightness controls set appropriately? If the brightness is turned all the way down, the screen might appear to be blank.
- Is the monitor firmly plugged into the video card?
- Is the video card firmly seated in its slot?
- Is the video card in the correct kind of slot?

# BIOS Information Followed by Error Message

If the system passes its basic startup tests, you see a BIOS message on the screen. It reports the brand and serial number of the BIOS, how much memory the computer has, and perhaps some other information. After that, if all goes well, the operating system loads and you see a DOS prompt or a Windows screen. If all doesn't go well, you see an error message instead.

## Floppy Disk Fail, Continuous Light

SYMPTOM: You see the BIOS identification onscreen, followed by a message that the floppy disk drive has failed. The light on the floppy drive stays on constantly.

EXPLANATION: Your floppy drive cable is plugged in backwards at one or both ends.

SOLUTION: Unplug the ribbon cable from the floppy drive and plug the cable in the other direction, so the stripe on the cable aligns with pin 1.

If you are sure it is already correctly oriented, check the other end of the ribbon cable, where it plugs into the motherboard or the I/O controller card. On the motherboard or card, you should see a tiny 1 next to one end of the socket. Make sure the stripe on the ribbon cable plugs into that end.

## Floppy Disk Fail, No Light

SYMPTOM: You see the BIOS identification onscreen, followed by a message that the floppy disk drive has failed. The floppy drive does not light at all.

EXPLANATION: You may have a defective floppy drive or a defective floppy

drive cable. Or the floppy drive cable may be plugged in backwards at one or both ends.

**SOLUTION:** Check to make sure that the stripe on the ribbon cable is aligned with pin 1 on both ends, as explained in the preceding symptom section.

Also make sure that the connector on the ribbon cable is connected to all of the pins on the motherboard or I/O card, not just to one row of them. You might have to inspect carefully—sometimes other cables get in the way.

If you are sure that the cable is on correctly, you may have a bad floppy drive or a bad cable. If you have another working computer, you can use the floppy disk from that system to troubleshoot. (Otherwise, all you can do is take the unit to a repair center or buy a new floppy just to check it out.)

If you have a second computer available, follow these steps to track down the problem:

1. Turn off both computers.
2. Remove the cover from the working computer and detach the floppy drive cable at both ends.
3. Replace the nonworking computer's floppy drive cable with the cable that works.
4. Restart the nonworking computer. If it now works, you have a bad cable; buy a new one at any computer store.
5. If the nonworking computer still doesn't work, remove the floppy drive from the working computer.
6. Set the removed floppy drive near the nonworking computer so that a power supply cable and the floppy drive ribbon cable can reach it.
7. Plug the two cables into the removed floppy drive so that it is temporarily a part of the nonworking system.
8. Restart the nonworking computer:
   - If it works, you have a bad floppy drive; either buy a new one or return the bad one for a replacement if it is still under warranty.
   - If the nonworking computer still doesn't work, check the following items again: Is the floppy drive cable's stripe aligned with pin 1 on each end? Is the floppy drive properly configured in BIOS?

✪ If the answer to each of these last two questions is Yes, you may have a defective I/O controller. If it is a controller card in a slot, you may be able to buy a replacement at a computer store; if the ribbon cable plugs directly into the motherboard, you may need to replace the whole motherboard. Contact the PC manufacturer to see if it can offer any additional troubleshooting ideas or send a replacement.

## Hard Disk Fail

SYMPTOM: You see the BIOS identification onscreen, followed by the message Hard Disk Fail.

EXPLANATION: The hard disk is not physically working. The drive is probably experiencing a mechanical failure or is not connected correctly.

SOLUTION: Check the following:

✪ Is the hard disk correctly connected with the stripe on its ribbon cable plugged into pin 1 at both ends?

✪ If the motherboard or I/O card has two IDE controller sockets, is the drive plugged into the Primary socket? In many cases a system with only one hard disk won't work if the disk is plugged into the Secondary socket.

✪ Is the power supply cable firmly plugged into the back of the hard disk?

✪ If the I/O controller is a separate circuit board, is it firmly plugged into the motherboard?

✪ If you are using the Cable Select method of establishing a drive's slave or master status, is the drive using the correct connector on the ribbon cable for its status?

If all these items check out, your drive probably has a mechanical failure. Return it for a refund or exchange. If that doesn't solve the problem, you might have a bad I/O controller. If it's built into the motherboard, you can either buy a replacement I/O controller board (and disable the onboard one in BIOS) or replace the motherboard. If the I/O controller is a separate card, simply replace it.

# Can't Boot from a Floppy

**SYMPTOM:** Your hard disk isn't working, so you are trying to boot from a bootable floppy, but the system won't recognize the floppy. The system keeps asking you to insert a bootable floppy and press Enter, even though a disk is already in place.

**EXPLANATION:** Your BIOS is not aware of the floppy drive, or the BIOS has been set so that it doesn't boot from the floppy drive, or doesn't boot from it first.

**SOLUTION:** Follow these steps:

1. Enter the BIOS setup program and confirm that the floppy drive is set up correctly there.

2. Check the boot sequence in the BIOS setup program. This command is probably in the Advanced section of the BIOS options. For example, Figure 5.27 shows the boot sequence in the sample graphics-based BIOS program. Make sure that the first boot device is set to A: (or Floppy) and that the second is set to C: (or IDE-0, which means the first IDE device).

3. Exit the BIOS program, saving any changes you made.

If the problem persists, you may have a bad floppy drive or floppy cable. If you have another working system, swap these parts (one at a time), as explained in the preceding symptom section. (If not, taking the unit to a repair center may be your only recourse.) If you can't get a floppy drive to work, contact the PC manufacturer for help.

**Figure 5.27**

In most BIOS programs you can choose which drives are bootable and in what order.

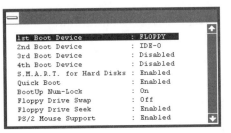

## Hard Disk Isn't Bootable

SYMPTOM: You see the BIOS startup screen and then a message about No Operating System or No Command Processor, or perhaps a message prompting you to insert a disk with startup files.

EXPLANATION: Your hard disk does not contain the startup files needed to start the computer.

SOLUTION: First things first: You need to be able to start the PC, so you can figure out what's wrong. If you have a bootable floppy disk (your original DOS installation disk will do nicely), place it in your floppy drive and restart the computer. If the computer starts and you see the A:\> prompt, you know that the hard disk needs help. If you don't have a bootable floppy, you need to get one; ask a friend with a working PC to make one for you or buy a copy of the latest version of MS-DOS.

**NOTE** Refer to this morning's session if you need to make a bootable disk. Of course, if your computer is not working, you will have to make this bootable disk on some other computer and then take the disk to the nonworking one.

From the A:\> prompt, do the following:

1. Type **C:** and press Enter.

2. Do one of the following:

   ✿ If you see C:\>, you know that the hard disk is partitioned and formatted and merely needs to have the system files transferred to it. Continue to Step 3.

   ✿ If you see Invalid Drive Specification or something about the drive not being readable, skip to the section "Hard Drive Not Formatted" later in this chapter.

3. Type **DIR A:** and press Enter. A list of files on the A: drive appears. If you see the file SYS.COM, you can continue to Step 4. Otherwise, buy a copy of MS-DOS or have a computer-savvy friend make you a boot disk containing those files.

◆ ◆ ◆ ◆ ◆ ◆ ◆ ◆ ◆ ◆ ◆ ◆ ◆ ◆ ◆ ◆ ◆ ◆ ◆ ◆ ◆ ◆ ◆ ◆ ◆ ◆ ◆ ◆ ◆ ◆ ◆ ◆ ◆ ◆ ◆

When you make a bootable disk, it copies the hidden startup files for that version of the operating system to the floppy. Then when you start a PC with that floppy, that particular version of the operating system is in control (for example, DOS 5 or DOS 6.2).

All the files on your bootable disk must be from the same DOS version as those hidden start-up files. You can't have a boot disk made with DOS 5, for example, on which you have copied SYS.COM from DOS 6.2. Although each version of DOS contains programs with the same names, the programs are different versions that work only under their specific version of DOS.

◆ ◆ ◆ ◆ ◆ ◆ ◆ ◆ ◆ ◆ ◆ ◆ ◆ ◆ ◆ ◆ ◆ ◆ ◆ ◆ ◆ ◆ ◆ ◆ ◆ ◆ ◆ ◆ ◆ ◆ ◆ ◆ ◆ ◆ ◆

4. Type **SYS C:** at the A:\> prompt and press Enter. The system files are copied to your C: drive.

5. Remove the floppy disk from the PC when you see the System Transferred message and restart the computer. It should boot from the hard disk this time.

## Hard Drive Not Formatted

**SYMPTOM:** You cannot access the C: drive. When you type **C:** at the DOS prompt, you get an Invalid Drive Specification message or some other message indicating that the drive is unreadable.

**EXPLANATION:** If you have just installed a new hard disk, you may need to partition and format it. If you already had this hard disk and suddenly it doesn't work, you may have hooked it up incorrectly when you were reassembling the system.

**SOLUTION:** If an existing hard disk is suddenly not working, check all the cables and connectors and verify that you have not inadvertently disabled the drive in the BIOS setup program.

The following procedure wipes out everything on the hard disk, so you should not do it if the drive contains important information. In such a case you should call a computer professional to help you make your old drive work again.

If you are working with a brand-new drive or you have abandoned hope of salvaging anything from your existing drive, follow these steps:

1. Boot from a floppy that contains the following files: SYS.COM, FORMAT.COM, and FDISK.EXE. You can copy these files from the DOS directory of the computer on which you made the bootable disk. If you made your bootable disk with the Windows 95/98 Startup Disk feature, your disk already has these files.

2. Type **FDISK** at the A:\> prompt and press Enter. The FDISK screen appears. Figure 5.28 shows the Windows 95 version; other versions look very similar.

● ● ● ● ● ● ● ● ● ● ● ● ● ● ● ● ● ● ● ● ● ● ● ● ● ● ● ● ● ● ● ● ● ● ● ● ● ● ● ●

If you see a message about enabling large hard disk support, type **Y** or **N**. (You get this message only with the Windows 95/98 version of FDISK.) Choose N if you have old DOS-based utility programs that you would like to continue to use; otherwise choose Y. Choosing Y enables 32-bit file system support, which is more efficient and modern; choosing N forces the drive to use the 16-bit file system for backward compatibility.

Don't confuse 16 and 32-bit file systems with 16- and 32-bit programs. The file system is the underlying structure that determines how your disk stores files. It doesn't have anything to do with the programs that are stored there or how they run.

● ● ● ● ● ● ● ● ● ● ● ● ● ● ● ● ● ● ● ● ● ● ● ● ● ● ● ● ● ● ● ● ● ● ● ● ● ● ● ●

3. Type the number for the Display Partition Information option (it's 4 in Figure 5.28) and press Enter.

4. Do one of the following:

   ● If you see partition information that indicates that drive C is partition 1, then the drive has already been partitioned. Press Esc to return to the FDISK main menu and then press Esc again to exit the FDISK program. Then skip to Step 9.

   ● If you see a message that says there are no partitions, press Esc if needed to clear that message. Then from the main menu (Figure 5.28), type **1** to choose Create DOS Partition or Logical Disk Drive. Press Enter.

5. Type **1** to choose Create Primary DOS Partition; then press Enter. If you see the message "Primary DOS partition already exists," press Esc

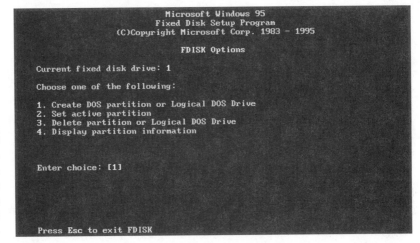

**Figure 5.28**

Use FDISK to examine the current drive partitions.drives are bootable and in what order.

twice to exit from the FDISK program. Otherwise FDISK checks the disk and creates the partition.

This message appears:

```
Do you wish to use the maximum available size for a Primary DOS
partition and make the partition active (Y/N)?
```

6. Type **Y** and press Enter. FDISK verifies the partition. Then you see a message like this:

```
You MUST restart your system for your changes to take effect.
Any drives you have created or changed must be formatted AFTER
you restart.
```

7. Press Esc to exit FDISK.

8. Restart the PC again, still using your boot disk. Now that you're back at the DOS prompt with a newly partitioned drive, you need to format it.

9. Type **FORMAT C:** and press Enter. A warning message tells you that formatting deletes all data on the drive.

10. Type **Y** to continue.

11. Wait for the progress indicator to show 100% formatted. It may take several minutes. When it is finished, you will be prompted for a volume label.

12. Type a volume label if you want and press Enter, or just press Enter to bypass this step. The DOS prompt returns.

13. Type **C:** and press Enter to try accessing the hard disk. If you see C:\>, the formatting worked.

14. Make the hard disk bootable by following the procedure explained in "Hard Disk Isn't Bootable" earlier in this session.

If your drive is still not accessible, it's time to call a computer-techie friend.

## Memory Error

**SYMPTOM:** You see the BIOS identification message onscreen, followed by a memory error message.

**EXPLANATION:** If you are starting your PC for the first time after installing new memory, this message may be normal. It's just a signal that you need to enter and exit the BIOS setup program, as explained earlier in this chapter.

If you have entered and exited the BIOS setup program once already since installing the new memory and you're still getting the message, your system's memory is faulty or improperly installed. Or the jumpers or DIP switches on the motherboard are set incorrectly for the amount of memory you have.

**SOLUTION:** Assuming you have already done the in and out of BIOS setup once, you need to figure out why the system is rejecting the memory. Older systems can be extremely finicky about the memory they will accept and the way it must be installed.

Check the following:

○ Have you chosen the correct type of memory, as indicated in the computer's manual?

○ Have you installed the memory in the correct bank or banks, according to the chart in the manual?

○ Is the memory firmly locked into each bank and held in place with clips at both ends?

○ Have you set any necessary DIP switches or jumpers on the motherboard?

**NOTE** Some 486 motherboards have a little quirk: To use more than 16 megabytes of RAM, you must disable the internal cache. Disabling the cache makes the system run slower, partially canceling out the performance benefit of the extra RAM. If you are having trouble getting the computer to notice the new RAM, check your computer's manual to determine whether you must disable the internal cache.

If you are still getting a memory error at startup, perhaps the memory itself is bad; contact the vendor for a replacement.

## PC Starts but New Device Doesn't Work

If the PC appears to work properly but your new upgrade doesn't function, maybe you have installed it wrong or forgotten to install the drivers. Maybe it has an address or IRQ conflict, or maybe it's just plain broken. You never know until you check it out.

Check the following items first:

- ✪ Did you carefully read and follow the installation instructions? Read them again to make sure you didn't miss something.
- ✪ Is the physical installation correct? Check all cable connections and make sure all circuit boards are pressed completely into their slots.
- ✪ Did you remember to run the installation software that came with the device?
- ✪ Is this device compatible with your other hardware? Look on the box that the new device came in for the system requirements, such as 486 with 8MB of RAM and Windows 3.1 or 95. If your system doesn't meet the requirements, you may not be able to use the new device.

If everything on the list appears to be in order, jump to the troubleshooting section that deals with your operating system and the type of device you are installing.

## Troubleshooting Video Problems

If you recently installed a new video card or monitor, getting it to work optimally can be a real challenge. The following sections can help.

# Monitor Problems

Many people who think they have video problems are embarrassed to find out that they simply needed to make some minor adjustment on the monitor. So before you launch into a full-fledged troubleshooting expedition, read through the following material.

## Image Doesn't Fill Entire Monitor, or Is Off-Center

SYMPTOM: The DOS prompt looks OK, but when you start a program with a background color other than black, a noticeable black ring appears around the edges.

or

The screen image appears off-center or has noticeable black space on one or more sides. Part of the screen image may be cut off.

EXPLANATION: Your monitor's image controls need to be adjusted.

SOLUTION: Refer to your monitor's manual to find out how to adjust it.

The first adjustment you make should be to center the image onscreen. Use these controls:

○ **Vertical position**. This controls the position of the image relative to the top and bottom of the screen. Increase the vertical position setting to move the image up (turn the knob or wheel to the left); decrease it (turn the knob or wheel to the right) to move the image down.

○ **Horizontal phase**. This controls the position of the image relative to the sides of the screen. Increase this setting to move the image to the right; decrease it to move the image to the left.

After the image is centered, expand it to fill the entire screen. Use these controls:

○ **Vertical size**. This stretches or contracts the image vertically. If you have black space at the top and bottom, increase the vertical size. If the image is cut off at both top and bottom, decrease it. (If the image is wrong on only one end, top or bottom, adjust the vertical position first.)

- **Horizontal size.** This stretches or contracts the image horizontally. If you have black space on both sides, increase the horizontal size. If the image is cut off on both sides, decrease it.

**TIP**

In Windows 95 and 98 you can change the refresh rate for your display. Changing the refresh rate often throws off your carefully set image size and position adjustments, so if you are planning to change the refresh rate, do it before you spend a lot of time adjusting the monitor controls.

Some monitors also offer fine-tuning controls like these:

- **Trapezoid.** This controls how wide the image is at the top versus the bottom of the screen. If you have more black space on the sides near the top of the monitor than near the bottom, or vice versa, adjust this setting to even it out.

- **Pincushion.** This controls how wide the image is near the vertical center of the image compared to the top and bottom. If your image looks like it has a waistline drawn in near the middle of each side, reduce this setting; if it bulges in the middle, increase it.

- **Rotation.** This controls the tilt of the image. If you have more black space on the top of the image near one end and more black space at the bottom near the other, adjust the rotation to square it up.

## Monitor Picture Is Too Dark or Light

**SYMPTOM:** The monitor's picture lacks contrast or is too dark or light.

**EXPLANATION:** You need to adjust the contrast or brightness settings on the monitor.

**SOLUTION:** *Contrast* refers to the amount of difference between the lightest and darkest parts of the image; *brightness* refers to the overall lightness or darkness of the image. Refer to your monitor's manual to find out how to adjust these. Almost all monitors have contrast and brightness settings. These may be simple knobs or wheels, or your monitor may have digital controls where you specify a numeric value (0 through 100) for each setting.

# DOS Video Problems

Here are a couple of commonly encountered DOS video issues.

## Picture Is Scrambled

**SYMPTOM**: When you turn on the computer, the monitor displays something, but you can't tell what it is because the letters are scrambled like a bad TV signal.

**EXPLANATION:** Your monitor is broken.

**SOLUTION:** You can't do much for a broken monitor. It is so expensive to have one repaired, and so cheap to buy a new one, that most people just throw away a broken monitor.

I recently had a monitor with this very problem. Here's what I learned when I went looking for a repair shop to repair it:

○ Only 4 of the 10 local stores I surveyed repaired monitors.

○ Three of those stores wanted $100 or more to repair the monitor but had new monitors on sale for about $150. One clerk tried vigorously to talk me out of having mine repaired.

○ The one remaining store that offered monitor repair for a reasonable cost ($60 was the estimate) kept my monitor for three weeks and then told me it was not repairable.

If your monitor isn't working in Windows or works only in certain programs, the trouble is usually something simple like a driver problem. But if it won't even show the BIOS startup information and the DOS prompt, it's all but dead.

## Certain DOS Programs Don't Look Right

**SYMPTOM:** Your monitor works at the DOS prompt but scrambles the image when you start a certain DOS-based application.

**EXPLANATION:** Many DOS-based programs come with special drivers for various kinds of video cards so that they can display the program at a high resolution. If you had one kind of video card before and now you have a new kind, the old video driver is probably still loaded and sending out the old signals to

the video card. Unfortunately, the new video card doesn't speak the same language as the old one, and so it interprets the instructions as gibberish.

**SOLUTION:** To correct this problem, rerun the installation program for the DOS-based software. When asked to choose a video card, choose your new model.

♦ ♦ ♦ ♦ ♦ ♦ ♦ ♦ ♦ ♦ ♦ ♦ ♦ ♦ ♦ ♦ ♦ ♦ ♦ ♦ ♦ ♦ ♦ ♦ ♦ ♦ ♦ ♦ ♦ ♦ ♦ ♦ ♦ ♦ ♦ ♦ ♦ ♦ ♦ ♦

If your card isn't listed, choose VGA. All video cards produced in the last several years accept that setting. Do not assume that a model with a name similar to your video card's will work the same way.

If the video card you just installed is new, it probably conforms to the VESA standard, which is format for high-performance video. If your DOS-based application does not have your specific video card listed but it does have VESA as one of the video card choices, choose VESA.

♦ ♦ ♦ ♦ ♦ ♦ ♦ ♦ ♦ ♦ ♦ ♦ ♦ ♦ ♦ ♦ ♦ ♦ ♦ ♦ ♦ ♦ ♦ ♦ ♦ ♦ ♦ ♦ ♦ ♦ ♦ ♦ ♦ ♦ ♦ ♦ ♦ ♦ ♦ ♦

# Windows 3.1 Video Problems

Windows 3.1 works with almost any video card, so not much can go wrong with its video performance. As long as your system's display works in DOS, it will probably work in Windows 3.1. But just in case it doesn't, refer to the following points.

## Picture Is Scrambled

**SYMPTOM:** Your display is fine at the DOS prompt, but when you start Windows 3.1 the screen is a scrambled mass of colors.

**EXPLANATION:** You are using the wrong video driver for your video card, or your video driver is corrupted.

**SOLUTION:** When you install a new video card, if you were using the ordinary VGA driver in Windows 3.1, everything will still work fine. But if you were using a video driver specific to that old video card, you will need to change to a different driver for the new card.

Follow these steps to work it out:

1. Locate the driver disk that came with your new video card.

2. Pop it in your floppy drive and type **DIR A:** at the DOS prompt. Read through the list of the files on the disk.

3. Examine the names of any files on the list that end in EXE to determine whether they are installation files. When you find a file called SETUP.EXE or INSTALL.EXE or something like that, type its name to run the program.

4. If you were able to run a setup program in Step 3, restart the computer and try entering Windows 3.1 again. If not, or if you ran the program but it still displays scrambled video in Windows, go to Step 5. Otherwise, you solved the problem.

5. Type **CD\WINDOWS** at the DOS prompt and press Enter. Then type **SETUP** at the C:\WINDOWS\> prompt and press Enter. A DOS-based setup screen appears for Windows 3.1.

6. Press the up arrow until the Display line is highlighted. Then press Enter to see a list of video displays.

7. Press the down arrow until VGA is highlighted, as shown in Figure 5.29.

8. Press Enter to accept VGA. You return to the opening screen.

9. Press Enter to accept the current configuration.

10. Do one of the following:

    ✪  If prompted to insert a Windows 3.1 installation disk, do so and press Enter.

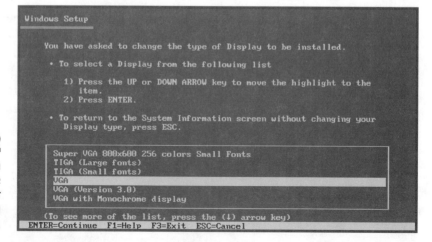

**Figure 5.29**

Choose VGA from the list to remove the video driver that is scrambling your screen.

☼ If informed that the VGA driver is already on your hard disk, press Enter to accept its use.

☼ If prompted to press Enter to exit, do so. (You may not see this prompt; the system may jump directly to the DOS prompt after installing the driver.)

**11.** Try restarting Windows 3.1; your video should be OK. You can continue using this generic VGA driver, or do the following to install your own video card's driver from disk:

**12.** Repeat Steps 1 to 6.

**13.** Press the down arrow until "Other display (Requires disk from OEM . . . )" is highlighted and then press Enter.

**14.** Insert your driver disk in your floppy drive when prompted; then press Enter to return to the main menu.

**15.** Press Enter to choose Accept The Current Configuration and exit the program.

## Stray Lines or Color Patches Onscreen

**SYMPTOM:** Windows 3.1 shows colored stripes or colored patches on-screen, or when you move a dialog box or icon, remnants of it remain behind in the old location.

**EXPLANATION:** One of the following is probably happening:

☼ The video driver is slightly incompatible with the video card, or the driver is corrupted.

☼ The video card is not completely seated in its slot.

☼ The monitor connector is not plugged tightly into the video card.

**SOLUTION:** Do the easy checks first: Ensure that the monitor is snugly plugged into the video card and that the video card is firmly seated in the motherboard. If that doesn't help matters, reinstall the video driver, as explained in the preceding section, "Picture Is Scrambled."

**NOTE** If the colors on the screen look funky, or of you aren't seeing all the colors, make sure that the monitor cable is firmly plugged into the video card, and the power cable is firmly plugged into the monitor. If either are loose, odd video anomalies may appear.

# Windows 95/98 Video Problems

With Windows 95/98, you don't have the scrambled video problem. Because Windows 95/98 has Plug-and-Play capability, it detects the absence of the old video card and removes its drivers. If Windows can also identify your new video card, it automatically installs drivers for it; otherwise, Windows installs a generic VGA video driver for the new card.

The video problems in Windows 95/98 are more a matter of quality. The generic VGA driver won't give you the image quality or system performance that you would receive from video drivers designed specifically for your video card. The following sections explain some problems you might encounter and how to correct them.

## Windows Fails to Detect New Card

**SYMPTOM:** Windows 95/98 detects your new video card as Generic VGA.

**EXPLANATION:** Windows cannot figure out what kind of video card you installed. Perhaps your PC's BIOS does not support Plug and Play, or perhaps the new card does not.

If possible, you should install drivers for your specific video card, even if the system appears to be working with the generic drivers. You will get maximum video performance by using drivers designed specifically for your video card.

**SOLUTION:** Install a driver specific to your new card.

One way to do this is to run the installation program that came with your video card, if you have one. This is the best way.

If you do not have an installation program, you can try to tell Windows what kind of card you have. Maybe it will have a driver for it.

1. Right-click on the desktop and choose Properties from the shortcut menu that appears.
2. Click on the Settings tab.
3. Click on Advanced. (The button is called Advanced Properties in Windows 95.) The Advanced Display Properties dialog box appears.
4. Click on the Adapter tab if it is not already on top.

5. Note the adapter type on the first line. If it does not match your actual video card, click on Change.

6. If you are using Windows 95, skip to Step 7.

   If you are using Windows 98, the Update Device Driver Wizard opens. Click on Next to continue. Then choose one of the following:

   ✿ If you have a disk that came with your video card, put it in your floppy drive and choose "Search for a better driver than the one your device is using now." Even if the disk did not contain an installation program, it might contain an information file that Windows can use.

   ✿ If you do not have any disk for your video card, choose Display a list of all the drivers in a specific location, so you can select the driver you want.

   After making your selection, click on Next.

   If you chose to search for a driver, Windows (hopefully) finds it on the floppy and installs it. If the disk has more than one driver, Windows opens an extra box where you can choose among them. Follow the prompts to finish up.

   If Windows can't locate the driver on that floppy, or if you chose to display a list, go on to Step 7.

7. Click on the Show All Hardware (or Show All Devices, in Windows 95) option button (see Figure 5.30).

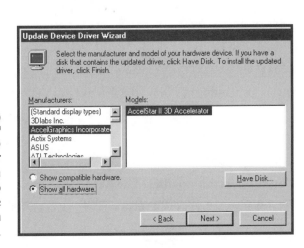

**Figure 5.30**

Choose your video card manufacturer and model from the list if you do not have an installation disk for it.

8. Do one of the following:

   ✿ *If have a disk that came with your video card,* put it in your floppy drive if it's not already in there and click on Have Disk. The Install From Disk dialog box opens. Click on OK to accept the A: drive. Windows locates the driver. If the disk has more than one driver, Windows opens an extra box where you can choose among them. Choose the driver that matches your video card and click on OK.

   ✿ *If you do not have the disk,* locate your video card's manufacturer from the list on the left and then locate the model from the list on the right (see Figure 5.30). Click on OK.

◆ ◆ ◆ ◆ ◆ ◆ ◆ ◆ ◆ ◆ ◆ ◆ ◆ ◆ ◆ ◆ ◆ ◆ ◆ ◆ ◆ ◆ ◆ ◆ ◆ ◆ ◆ ◆ ◆ ◆ ◆ ◆ ◆ ◆ ◆ ◆ ◆ ◆ ◆ ◆ ◆

If your model does not appear on the list in Step 7, do not use an alternative model. Even though the names may be similar, the drivers may be very different. Instead, click on Cancel. Then visit the video card manufacturer's Web site and download the driver you need, or telephone the manufacturer and ask someone to send you a driver disk.

◆ ◆ ◆ ◆ ◆ ◆ ◆ ◆ ◆ ◆ ◆ ◆ ◆ ◆ ◆ ◆ ◆ ◆ ◆ ◆ ◆ ◆ ◆ ◆ ◆ ◆ ◆ ◆ ◆ ◆ ◆ ◆ ◆ ◆ ◆ ◆ ◆ ◆ ◆ ◆ ◆

## Display Flickers Noticeably

**SYMPTOM:** Ever since you installed the new video card or monitor, the video display flickers, causing eyestrain.

**EXPLANATION:** The refresh rate is not set as high as it should be. Two factors jointly determine the refresh rate: the maximum capability of the video card and the monitor. If either is set for a generic model in Windows 95/98, the refresh rate used will be low.

**SOLUTION:** Make sure Windows 95/98 knows what model of video card and monitor you have. To do so, follow these steps:

1. Right-click on the desktop and choose Properties from the shortcut menu that appears.

2. Click on the Settings tab.

3. Click on Advanced Properties. The Advanced Display Properties dialog box appears. (In Windows 98, the button is just labeled "Advanced.")

4. Click on the Adapter tab if it is not already on top.

5. Determine whether your correct adapter is listed; if not, click on Change and install a new driver for it, as explained in the preceding section.

6. Click on the Monitor tab.

7. Determine whether your correct monitor is listed; if not, click on Change and specify it, as you did for the video driver. (Just as with the monitor, Windows 98 opens a Wizard that tries to detect it; Windows 95 opens a list of models to choose from immediately.)

8. After selecting the correct monitor, click on Close to close the dialog box. A new dialog box informs you that Windows is going to change your refresh rate. Click on OK.

9. Windows asks whether you want to keep the new refresh rate. If you click on Yes, the change takes effect. If you click on No or do nothing for 10 seconds, Windows reverts to your old refresh rate. (This step prevents a new refresh rate from taking hold and scrambling the display.)

 The monitor you choose determines the refresh rate, but little else. If you do not see your exact model number on the list, it is usually OK to choose a similar model because it probably has approximately the same refresh rate.

 Some video cards come with their own utility programs for Windows 95/98. For example, I have an STB Nitro video card that came with a program called STB Vision. I can use this program in Windows 95/98 to set a specific refresh rate.

# Troubleshooting Modem Problems

I have had more clients call for help with modem problems than with any other kind of troubleshooting request. There's just so much that can go wrong with them! Installing the modem properly is only the first step. In addition,

## ONE TECHIE'S OPINION ON MODEMS

I have some very definite prejudices when it comes to modems. For installation by a beginning computer user, I prefer external modems to internal, and I prefer regular modems to Winmodems.

Some people may tell you that you should always use an internal modem because external ones occupy one of your two precious built-in COM ports, but as you learned earlier in this chapter, you should disable one of the internal COM ports when you have an internal modem to avoid conflicts. So that disadvantage cancels out the perceived benefit.

External modems are less prone to problems caused by address conflicts because the COM port (COM1 or COM2) is built into the system and preassigned an address. To assign a COM port to an internal modem, you have to set jumpers or run special software. And it doesn't always work very well.

The address problems are further compounded when the modem is a Windows-only model, because the address must be set in two places—with a DOS-based configuration utility (or jumpers on some models) and within the Windows driver software. Especially in Windows 3.1, this requirement can be a never-ending nightmare. I had a client once whose modem changed its own base address every time he restarted the computer, sometimes to an address already taken by some other device.

If you are a beginner struggling with an internal Winmodem and none of the troubleshooting methods described in the following sections work, don't bang your head against the wall. Do yourself a favor—repackage the thing, return to the store, and trade it for a nice non-Windows-only external model like a US Robotics Sportster 56K.

Windows must be set up for the modem (if it is a Winmodem), the address and IRQ must be set correctly (if it is an internal model), the phone line must be connected properly, and you must have your communication software set up to recognize it. That's a lot to expect from a beginning computer user.

# General Modem Problems

Some modem problems happen to all kinds of users, regardless of the operating system in use. You look at this type of problem first.

## Modem Makes Endless Connection Noises

**SYMPTOM:** The modem appears to dial and connect with the remote site, but instead of connecting, it keeps making static noises and beeping, over and over, until the remote modem finally gives up and hangs up on it.

**EXPLANATION:** Your modem string is not set correctly in your communication program, or your phone line is very bad.

**SOLUTION:** First, check to see whether this problem happens in every communication program. For example, if it's happening with America Online, get a CompuServe or Prodigy startup kit and try connecting to that service. (You don't actually have to sign up for the service—if you can just get to the initial connection, you'll have your answer.) If the problem occurs with only the one service, then the modem setup string is wrong for that service. Call the online service's technical support line for help.

If the problem happens with all connections, your phone line is probably extremely bad. This situation happens when a household has bad phone service to begin with and then installs a second line that runs over the same wires. The already weak phone line, when split in two, becomes unsuitable for modem connections. Compared to humans, modems are much more demanding of clear phone lines. If you have a second phone line in your house, try the modem on the other phone line. If that clears up the problem, call the phone company and have it check the line that is causing the problems.

## Modem Won't Stay Connected

**SYMPTOM:** The modem dials and connects, but then hangs up after a few seconds. Repeated attempts almost always have the same result.

**EXPLANATION:** The setup string that the program is sending to the modem is inappropriate for that modem. Different modems require different setup strings in the form of *Hayes commands*. Each setup string begins with AT for

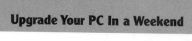
attention, followed by a series of two-character codes that turn on or off certain modem features. When you install a communication program such as the America Online software, it asks what kind of modem you have. This is important because the America Online software knows what strings to send to what modems. If you tell it that you have the wrong type of modem, it will send the wrong string. Even though it may be able to connect briefly, it won't be able to stay connected.

**SOLUTION:** Make sure you have chosen the correct modem type in the communication program. If it is correct, check the modem manual; the modem manufacturer may suggest certain setup strings to use for certain online services.

The procedure for checking the setup string varies from program to program. For example, in America Online you choose Setup from the sign-on screen and then click on Modem Commands. Call the technical support phone number for the online service you are using if you cannot figure out how to access its setup string.

## No Dial Tone

**SYMPTOM:** Your modem appears to be installed correctly, but you get a message that there is no dial tone when you try to use it.

**EXPLANATION:** You do not have a working telephone line plugged into the correct jack on the modem.

**SOLUTION:** You do not have to turn off your computer to troubleshoot this problem. Check the back of the modem. You should see two telephone jacks. One is for the incoming line, and the other is for an outgoing phone. Make sure that you have the incoming line plugged into the correct jack. If the jacks are not labeled, switch the lines and try the modem again.

If that doesn't help, try plugging a telephone directly into the line that is feeding into the modem. Do you hear a dial tone? If not, your telephone line is the problem.

If you heard a dial tone through the telephone, unplug the line from the telephone and plug it back into the modem. Then plug the telephone into the

other jack in the modem (the outgoing one, probably labeled PHONE). Do you still hear a dial tone? If so, the telephone dial tone is passing through the modem successfully and should be detected.

If you still keep getting a No Dial Tone message when trying to use the modem, you may have an address problem; see "Windows 3.1 Modem Problems" or "Windows 95/98 Modem Problems," depending on which version of Windows you have.

## DOS Modem Problems

If you are one of the few people left who uses a DOS-based communication program, follow these steps to make the modem work with it:

1. Start the communications program. You probably see a blank screen (indicating that you are in Terminal mode). If you see some sort of dialog box or menu, press Esc or whatever key is needed to enter Terminal mode. (Consult the program's documentation if needed.)

2. Type **ATZ** and press Enter. This command says to the modem, "Hello? Are you there? Please reset yourself." If the modem is working and the program recognizes it, the modem will respond "OK." If not, you will see either nothing or an error message.

3. If you did not see "OK," check the program's documentation to find out how to specify which COM port the program listens to. The information may be under Communications Settings. When you find a box that lets you choose between COM1, COM2, COM3, or COM4, you've struck gold—choose the COM port on which your modem is installed and return to Step 2.

4. If your modem still doesn't work, call the technical support line for the modem manufacturer and ask for help.

 **NOTE** If you can't make the modem work with your DOS program, check the modem's box and documentation to be sure that you did not buy a model that requires Windows to operate.

# Windows 3.1 Modem Problems

It's hard to tell in Windows 3.1 whether your modem is working correctly because Windows 3.1 does not have built-in modem support the way Windows 95/98 does. One of my clients, for example, had his modem for over a year before he got around to installing the software to sign up for America Online (AOL). When he ran the AOL installation software, it told him that it couldn't detect his modem. That's when he realized he had a problem.

Your first clue that your modem doesn't work will come when you try to use it, so if you have a new modem, try it out right away. Sign up for one of those free online service offers, or dial into your current Internet provider or your computer at work. Any test will do as long as it involves connecting to some remote computer over the phone lines.

The first test I always do in Windows 3.1 is to dial a number with the Terminal program that comes with Windows. If that works, then I try the online service or Internet connection.

## Online Service Program Doesn't See Modem

**SYMPTOM:** While installing software for an online service like America Online, the setup program reports that it can't detect any modems attached to your computer.

**EXPLANATION:** As far as Windows 3.1 is concerned, your modem isn't there.

**SOLUTION:** If you have an internal modem, check the address and IRQ to make sure that it is not conflicting with anything. The modem should have come with some kind of diagnostic program that checks this situation; it was probably copied to your hard disk when you ran the modem installation software. Follow these steps to run it.

1. Exit Windows. You'll see the DOS prompt.

2. Change to the directory where the modem's files are stored. (For example, if they're in a directory called MODEM, type **CD\MODEM**.) This directory was created when you ran the modem's setup program. (You did run it, didn't you? If not, do it now.)

3. Type **DIR \*.EXE** and press Enter to find out what programs you can run in that directory.

4. Look through the list of programs for one that might be a configuration program. (For example, TPDIAG.EXE might be a diagnostic program for a Telepath modem.)

5. Type that command at the DOS prompt and press Enter. If a DOS-based setup program doesn't start or you see the message "This program requires Windows to run," try another name until you find the setup program. Or read the modem's documentation to find out what to use.

6. Check the current IRQ and address settings and confirm that no conflicts exist between the modem and any other devices. (Each setup program is different, so I can't tell you specifically how to do it.)

7. Write down the address and IRQ that you just set and then exit the configuration program.

NOTE  If you have changed modems rather than installed your first one, you may already have online service software installed. If so, use its Setup feature to change the modem type. Call the online service technical support line if you need help doing this.

Next, if it is a Windows-only modem, you must tell the Windows software about the modem's address and IRQ. Follow these steps:

1. Restart Windows.

2. Confirm that you have installed the needed Windows software for the modem. If you have not run the modem's setup program yet from the disk that came with it, do so.

3. Find the program group containing the modem programs and run the configuration program to tell Windows 3.1 the modem's settings. Make sure that the address and IRQ set there match the settings you made in the DOS-based setup program.

Now, regardless of the modem type, you are ready to test it. You can test it with Windows 3.1's Terminal program. Just follow these steps:

1. Open the Windows 3.1 Accessories program group and double-click on the Terminal icon. Terminal opens.

2. Depending on whether Terminal has been used before on this com-

**Figure 5.31**

The first time you start Terminal, it asks what COM port your modem uses.

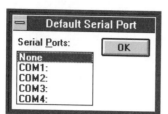

puter and whether it detects a modem on a COM port, one of the following happens:

✪ If this is the first time Terminal has been run on this computer, a box pops up asking for your serial port (see Figure 5.31); choose it and click on OK. If you choose the wrong COM port or your modem is not installed properly, Terminal reports that it is wrong and does not permit you to choose that COM port; instead it redisplays the box in Figure 5.31, asking you to make another selection.

✪ If you have used Terminal before but with a modem on a different COM port, the program displays an error message and asks you to specify a different port. Click on the port you are using and click on OK.

3. Type **ATZ** at the blank Terminal screen and press Enter. If "OK" appears on the screen (a response from the modem), the modem is working properly. If you see nothing, the modem may not be working or you may have chosen the wrong COM port.

4. If the modem did not work in Step 2, open the Settings menu and choose Communications. The Communications dialog box appears.

5. Click on a different COM port in the Connector area of the dialog box to see whether you chose the wrong COM port for the modem. Then click on OK. If no error message appears, try Step 3 again.

If the modem still doesn't work, try its diagnostic program again. Then call the manufacturer's technical support line to see if anyone can offer troubleshooting suggestions for your particular model.

# Windows 95/98 Modem Problems

After you get a modem up and running in Windows 95/98, it is usually trouble free. It's getting it going in the first place that can be a challenge.

Windows 95 and 98 feature Plug and Play, which is supposed to automatically detect your hardware and install the correct drivers. However, computer cynics often refer to this feature as "plug and pray"—and rightly so. It doesn't always work right. The following sections will help you figure out why your modem isn't working as it should in Windows 95/98.

# Windows Doesn't See the Modem

SYMPTOM: Windows did not detect the modem and does not know it is there.

EXPLANATION: Perhaps the modem or your BIOS is not Plug and Play–compatible, or perhaps you need to run an installation program that came with the modem.

SOLUTION: Look through the disks that came with the modem and see whether they include an installation program that you did not run. If so, read the part of the instructions that pertain to Windows 95/98 and then run it.

If the modem does not include an installation program, manually install the modem in Windows, as you learned earlier in this session.

## The Modem Doesn't Work

SYMPTOM: Windows detected the modem when you installed it, but the modem doesn't seem to work.

EXPLANATION: The modem probably has an address or IRQ conflict with another device.

SOLUTION: Follow these steps to troubleshoot the modem problem:

1. Open the Windows Control Panel and double-click on the System icon.
2. Click on the Device Manager tab.

3. Click on the plus sign next to Modem to display the list of modems installed. Your modem should appear on the list. If a yellow circle with an exclamation point appears next to the modem, as shown in Figure 5.32, the modem is not working properly. (If your modem is not on the list, or if there is no Modem entry, look for an Other Device entry. If your modem appears under that category, see the section titled "Windows 95/98 Sees Modem as 'Other Device'" later in this chapter.)

4. Click on the modem and then click on Properties. A Properties dialog box appears for the modem.

5. Check the Device status area. You should see the following message: "The device is working properly." If not, click on the Resources tab.

6. Check the Conflicting device list. If a conflict is listed, note whether it is an Input/Output Range conflict or an IRQ conflict.

7. Click on the Use Automatic Settings check box to deselect it.

8. Open the Setting Based On drop-down list and choose a new configuration. Keep trying different configurations until you find one that says "No Conflicts" in the Conflicting Device list (see Figure 5.33).

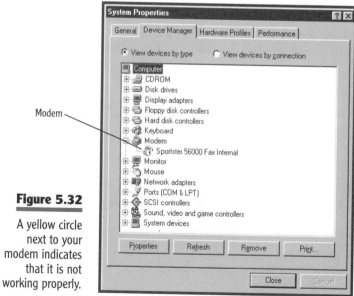

**Figure 5.32**

A yellow circle next to your modem indicates that it is not working properly.

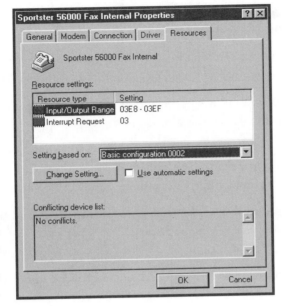

**Figure 5.33**

In this case Configuration 0002 has no conflicts, so I'll use that one.

9. Click on OK to close the dialog box.

10. Try using your modem again. It should work now.

**NOTE** In rare cases all the configurations on the list (in Step 8) have a conflict. If you face this situation, you can try changing the Interrupt Request and the Input/Output Range separately. Keep choosing configurations from the Setting Based On list until you find a configuration with only one conflict. Make a note of what it is (Interrupt Request or Input/Output Range.) Then click on the matching line in the Resource settings list. Next, click on Change Setting. One of two things may happen: You may see a message that the setting cannot be modified, or you may see a box containing alternate settings. If you see the latter, try a different setting. Repeat this procedure until you find a setting that produces no conflicts.

If Windows 95/98 tells you that the setting cannot be modified, you have one last remedy to try. In the Conflicting Device list, note the device that is the other half of the conflict. Then try modifying the settings for that device so that it no longer conflicts with your modem.

Another possible remedy is to go into your BIOS program and disable another COM port, freeing up another IRQ and address that your modem could use.

## Windows 95/98 Sees Modem as "Other Device"

SYMPTOM: When you look for your modem in the Device Manager list, the modem appears under Other Devices rather than under Modem.

EXPLANATION: Windows partially detected the new device but couldn't figure out that the device was a modem.

SOLUTION: This problem usually occurs when the modem comes with its own drivers that need to be installed. Assuming you have a driver disk from the modem manufacturer, follow these steps:

1. Click on the Device Manager tab, your modem, and then Properties. The Properties dialog box opens.

2. Click on the Driver tab.

3. Click on Update Driver. The Update Device Driver Wizard dialog box appears.

4. Place the disk containing the modem driver in your floppy drive (or CD-ROM drive if it is on CD.)

5. Click on Next.

6. If you are using Windows 95, jump to Step 8. In Windows 98, choose "Search for a better driver than the one your device is using now" and then click on Next.

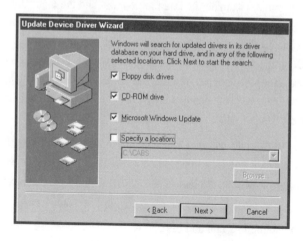

**Figure 5.34**

Windows 98 can search for the driver in various locations.

7. Make sure the check box is marked for the drive containing the modem driver disk. And if you want to use Windows Update to see if a better driver is available online, click on the Windows Update check box too (see Figure 5.34). Then click on Next.

8. Wait for the wizard to find the new driver.

9. Click on Finish. The new driver is installed and your modem moves to the Modem list in Device Manager.

10. Close the Device Manager dialog box, and restart your computer. (This may not be necessary in all cases but it doesn't hurt.)

11. Try your modem again. It should work now.

# Troubleshooting Sound Problems

Lack of sound isn't usually critical to a program—but it's annoying to pay good money for a sound card and not have it work, or work with only some of your programs. The following sections explain how to troubleshoot a lack of sound.

## General Sound Troubleshooting

If you aren't getting sound, you need to figure out whether the sound card isn't working at all or just in certain programs. Narrow it down and then check the appropriate section in this session.

- Do you have speakers plugged into the sound card? If the speakers have a power switch, is it on? Are the speakers plugged into an electrical outlet (if they're the kind that run on AC current rather than batteries)? Or do they have the appropriate batteries installed?

- Have you installed the driver software that came with the sound card? Most sound cards won't work unless you do so.

- Have you run the diagnostic program that came with the sound card? This program can tell you whether the sound card is working at all. If you get no sound from the diagnostic program, see "No Sound in Any Programs" later in this session. If the problem is related to certain programs, see "Sound Doesn't Work in a Specific Program."

✿ Does the sound work in DOS programs, but not in Windows? If so, see "Sound Card Doesn't Work in Windows 3.1" or "Windows 95/98 Sound Problems."

# No Sound in Any Programs

No sound at all? Check out the solution that pertains to your situation.

## No Sound, Diagnostic Program Reports Failure

**SYMPTOM:** The sound card does not work at all, even in its own diagnostic program. The diagnostic program reports that the sound card is not functioning.

**EXPLANATION:** The sound card is either defective or improperly installed.

**SOLUTION:** Check the installation instructions that came with the sound card to make sure you performed the installation as directed. Make sure you ran the installation software and that you restarted your computer afterward.

The sound card diagnostic program should check the IRQ that it is using to make sure that it doesn't conflict with any other devices. Pay attention to this test; specify a different IRQ and base address if needed.

Check Device Manager and make sure the sound card is not installed as "Other Device." If it is, follow the steps in the preceding section to correct it.

Finally, check that the sound card is completely seated in its socket. Still no luck? The sound card may be defective. Return it for an exchange or refund.

## No Sound, Diagnostic Program Thinks It's Fine

**SYMPTOM:** The diagnostic program acts like everything is fine, but you don't hear any sound.

**EXPLANATION:** Something is probably wrong with your speakers.

**SOLUTION:** Check the following:

✿ Are the speakers plugged into an electrical outlet if necessary?

- ✪ Are the speakers plugged into the correct socket on the sound card? Is the connection firm?
- ✪ Do the speakers have a power switch? Is it turned on?
- ✪ Is the volume turned up?

If all of the above checks out, you may have a defective speaker. (One speaker is usually the "leader" and the other one just plugs into it, so if the lead speaker is the faulty one, neither may work.)

## Sound Doesn't Work in Specific Program

**SYMPTOM:** You hear sound in some programs, but in one particular program (perhaps a DOS-based game) the sound does not work.

**EXPLANATION:** Today's DOS-based games are typically very sophisticated, with lots of sound and music. But unlike Windows-based programs, DOS-based programs cannot rely on the operating system handling the sound, so they must provide their own special drivers. Most games support at least three or four different sound cards, but if you don't have one of the supported cards, you're out of luck.

The most popular brand of sound card is SoundBlaster (and its variants, SoundBlaster Pro and SoundBlaster 16), so most off-brand cards try to offer SoundBlaster compatibility. They do so, however, with varying degrees of success. Even though your sound card is supposed to be completely SoundBlaster compatible, it may have a few little quirks that prevent it from working in all situations where a true SoundBlaster card would work.

**SOLUTION:** If you still have the installation disks for the program, reinstall it. You may be given a choice of sound cards during installation.

If that doesn't work, look in the same directory as the program's files for a configuration program. (Hint: Look for something about CONFIG in the name, and it probably ends in EXE, COM, or BAT.) If you find such a program, run it; maybe it will let you specify what sound card you have.

Still no luck? Check the manual that came with the sound card. Look for tips for making your sound card perform in SoundBlaster-compatible mode.

Your last recourse is to contact the game's manufacturer to see whether the company can provide a patch to make the game work with your sound card.

If you strike out on all counts and this game is really important to you, consider buying a different sound card. You can buy a genuine SoundBlaster card for less than $100 if you get a no-frills model. (The SoundBlaster 16 Value is a good choice.)

# Sound Doesn't Work in Windows 3.1

**SYMPTOM:** At least one of your DOS-based programs works with your sound card, but you can't get any sound out of it in Windows 3.1.

**EXPLANATION:** You probably do not have the Windows 3.1 drivers installed for your sound card.

**SOLUTION:** Find the driver installation disks that came with your sound card and rerun the installation program. If you are given a choice of DOS or Windows driver installation, choose Windows. (Actually, if one of the choices is Both, that's the best choice of all.) After the installation program has finished, restart your computer and reenter Windows; you should have sound.

To test your sound card in Windows 3.1, follow these steps:

1. Start in the Main program group and double-click on Control Panel.
2. Double-click on the Sound icon. The Sound dialog box opens, as shown in Figure 5.35.
3. Make sure that the Enable System Sounds check box is marked.
4. Check the Files and Events lists. If they are grayed out (unavailable), the driver is not installed correctly; click on Cancel and check the sound card's documentation to find out how to install the Windows drivers.
5. Click on any sound file in the Files list.

**Figure 5.35**

You can test your sound card in Windows 3.1 from here.

6. Click on Test. The sound should play. If you hear it, Windows 3.1 is successfully set up for sound. If you don't hear it, turn to "No Sound, Diagnostic Program Thinks It's Fine" earlier in this session.

# Windows 95/98 Sound Problems

Windows 95/98 is supposed to detect your sound card automatically with Plug and Play, but it doesn't always work right. Here's how to get your sound card in working order under Windows 95 or 98.

## Windows Doesn't See Sound Card

SYMPTOM: When you install a sound card and then start Windows, it does not detect any new hardware.

EXPLANATION: Maybe your system doesn't support Plug and Play, or maybe the sound card doesn't.

SOLUTION: Windows gives you two ways to install sound card drivers: You can either follow the Add New Hardware Wizard prompts or run an installation program that came with the sound card. If the sound card's installation program is Windows-sensitive, it's the better of the two options. Generally speaking, you would use the Add New Hardware Wizard method only if the sound card is old (pre-1996).

Running the installation program that came with the sound card is easy—just pop the disk in your floppy drive and run the setup program. You can browse for the filename in My Computer, or you can follow these steps to have Windows detect and run the setup program:

1. Place the floppy disk in the drive.
2. Open the Control Panel and double-click on Add/Remove Software.
3. In Windows 95, click on Install. Windows looks for the installation program, finds it on the floppy, and begins the installation.

   or

   In Windows 98, click on No, I want to select the hardware from a list in the Add New Hardware Wizard dialog box and then click on Next. In the next panel, choose the type of hardware (Sound, Video, And Game Controllers) and click on Next again. At this point, you can either choose a manufacturer and model or click on Have Disk to install the drivers from the diskette.

If you don't have a setup program on disk for the sound card, you can use the Add New Hardware Wizard to install a driver for the card. Follow these steps:

1. Open the Control Panel and double-click on Add New Hardware. The Add New Hardware Wizard opens.

2. Click on Next to begin. If you are using Windows 98, it will perform a search for Plug-and-Play devices, after which you must click on Next again.

3. Click on No when Windows asks whether it should search for your new (non–Plug-and-Play) hardware. Then click on Next to continue.

4. Click on Sound, Video And Game Controllers on the Select The Type Of Hardware You Want To Install list. Then click on Next.

5. Select the sound card manufacturer from the left side of the screen and then select the model from the right side (see Figure 5.36). (If your model isn't listed, check the documentation for the name of a compatible model.) Then click on Next.

**TIP** If your sound card is not listed in Step 5 and you don't have any documentation, choose Creative Labs as the manufacturer and Creative Labs SoundBlaster as the model. Many generic sound cards are compatible with this card. It's worth a try.

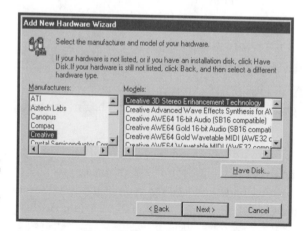

**Figure 5.36**

Choose the sound card's manufacturer and model.

6. If Windows asks you to insert the Windows CD-ROM, do so. Wait for the wizard to install the correct driver.

7. Click on Yes to restart the computer when prompted.

When Windows restarts, the sound card drivers should be installed. The next three steps check to make sure that Windows sees the sound card.

8. Open the Control Panel and double-click on the System icon.

9. Click on the Device Manager tab.

10. Click on the plus sign next to the Sound, Video And Game Controllers entry. One or more drivers for your sound card should be listed under that category, indicating the drivers are successfully installed, as shown in Figure 5.37.

If this procedure doesn't work, contact the sound card manufacturer for more troubleshooting ideas. If the sound card appears on the list but it has a yellow circle with an exclamation point next to it, see the following section, "Windows 95/98 Sees Card but No Sounds Heard."

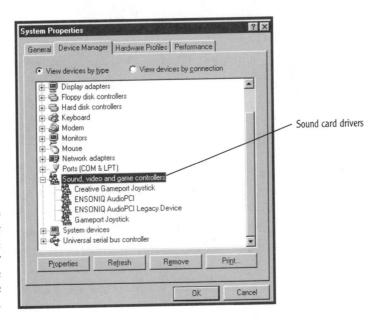

**Figure 5.37**

Look for your sound card on the Device Manager list to make sure its drivers are installed.

 If more than one driver appears in the Device Manager list under the category of sound, video, and game controllers, Windows does not necessarily think you have more than one sound card. In many cases this type of entry simply indicates that more than one driver is required. For example, Figure 5.37 shows four drivers listed for a single sound card—and the card uses all of them. (The Gameport Joystick driver is included in that count because the joystick port is on the sound card.)

## Windows 95/98 Sees Card but No Sounds Heard

**SYMPTOM:** Your sound card was detected by Windows and appears on the Device Manager list, but you can't hear any sound.

**EXPLANATION:** Perhaps your speakers are not working or your volume is too low. If a yellow circle appears next to the sound card on the Device Manager list, perhaps an address conflict exists.

**SOLUTION:** Check the easy things first:

- ✪ Are the speakers turned on and working?

- ✪ Does the Device Manager see the sound card as "Other Device"? If so, jump to "Windows Sees Sound Card as 'Other Device'" later in this session.

- ✪ Is the volume turned up in Windows? If you're not sure, double-click on the speaker icon in the lower right corner of the Windows screen to open a dialog box where you can adjust the volume.

 If you do not have a speaker icon (or some other volume control icon) near the clock in the lower right corner of the Windows screen, here's how to turn on the display: From the Control Panel, double-click on the Multimedia icon. The Multimedia Properties dialog box appears. Click to place an X in the Show Volume Control On The Taskbar check box; then click on OK.

If you still do not have sound, follow these steps:

1. Open the Control Panel and double-click on the System icon.

2. Click on the Device Manager tab.

3. Select the entry for your sound card. (Click on the plus sign next to Sound, Video And Game Controllers if needed).

4. Click on Properties. A Properties dialog box for the sound card appears.

5. Check the Device Status area. You should see the following message: "The device is working properly." If you don't, click on the Resources tab.

6. Check the Conflicting device list. If a conflict is listed, note whether it is an Input/Output Range conflict or an IRQ conflict.

7. Click on the Use Automatic Settings check box to deselect it.

8. Open the Setting Based On drop-down list and choose a new configuration. Keep trying different configurations until you find one that says No Conflicts in the Conflicting Device list.

9. Click on OK to close the dialog box.

10. Try using your sound card again. It should work now.

• • • • • • • • • • • • • • • • • • • • • • • • • • • • • • • • • • • • • • • •

In rare cases all the configurations on the list (in Step 8) have a conflict. In this situation you can try changing the Interrupt Request and the Input/Output Range separately. Keep choosing configurations from the Setting based on list until you find a configuration with only one conflict. Make a note of what it is (Interrupt Request or Input/Output Range.) Then click on the matching line in the Resource settings list. Next, click on Change Setting. One of two things may happen: You may see a message that the setting cannot be modified, or you may see a box containing alternative settings. If you see the latter, try a different setting. Repeat this process until you find a setting that produces no conflicts.

If Windows tells you that the setting cannot be modified, you have one last remedy to try. In the Conflicting Device list, note the device that is the other half of the conflict. Then try modifying the settings for that device so that it no longer conflicts with your sound card.

• • • • • • • • • • • • • • • • • • • • • • • • • • • • • • • • • • • • • • • •

## Windows Sees Sound Card as "Other Device"

**SYMPTOM:** Windows automatically detects your sound card, but it doesn't work, and on the Device Manager list the sound card appears in the Other Device category.

**EXPLANATION:** Your sound card requires you to run its own setup software, and you have not done this yet. Some sound cards do not work correctly when merely detected by the Windows Plug and Play feature; they need their own special drivers to operate.

**SOLUTION:** Run the installation program that came with the sound card.

In some cases, the sound card may not have come with a full-fledged installation program. Instead it may simply have a disk with a driver on it (perhaps a file with a DRV or a DLL extension and maybe a file called OEMSETUP.INF). To install the driver for your sound card from such a disk, follow these steps:

1. Open the Control Panel and double-click on the System icon.
2. Click on the Device Manager tab.
3. Locate and double-click on the line for your sound card, opening its Properties dialog box.
4. Click on the Driver tab.
5. Click on Update Driver. The Update Driver Wizard dialog box opens.
6. Place the floppy disk in your floppy drive.
7. If you are using Windows 95, make sure Yes is selected and click on Next. Then skip to Step 10. In Windows 98, click on Next to begin a Plug-and-Play search, and then click on Next again when it doesn't find anything.
8. Make sure the Search For option is selected on the next screen, and then click on Next.
9. On the list of places to search, make sure Floppy Disk Drives is marked. Then click on Next.
10. Wait for the wizard to find and install the driver.
11. Click on Yes if prompted to restart your system with the new driver in place.

# Troubleshooting Windows 95/98 Network Problems

I'm going to stick with Windows 95/98 networking issues in this book, because that's the operating system that by far most people will be working with. (If you've gone to the expense of buying networking equipment, it's a good bet that you've upgraded to Windows 95 or 98 too!)

## Windows Can't Locate the Drivers for Network Installation

**SYMPTOM:** Windows prompts you to insert your Windows 95/98 CD, but it can't find the files it is looking for.

**EXPLANATION:** You may have installed Windows from installation files on your hard disk instead of from the CD, or you may be running Windows 98 but using a network setup program that is looking for Windows 95. (The setup program that came with your network card may predate the release of Windows 98.)

**SOLUTION:** Try inserting the Windows 95/98 CD in your CD-ROM drive and pointing the installation program to it, rather than trying to use the Windows setup files on your hard disk.

If that doesn't work, try pointing the installation program to the floppy disk that came with the network card.

If that doesn't work, use the Windows Find command (Start, Find) to search your system and see if the needed file is already on your system somewhere. If you locate it, make a note of the location (perhaps Windows\System) and point the installation program to that location.

## The Logon Screen Doesn't Appear

**SYMPTOM:** You are never prompted to log onto your network.

**EXPLANATION:** It could just be a fluke, or it could be that networking has not been installed properly.

SOLUTION: First try logging on again. In Windows 95, try choosing Start, Shut Down, Close All Programs And Logon As A Different User. In Windows 98, try choosing Logoff {yourname} from the Start menu.

If that doesn't work, return to the installation procedure for networking earlier in this chapter and make sure that your Primary Network logon in the Network properties dialog box is set for Client For Microsoft Networks.

# You Cannot Choose Shared Level Access on the Access Control Tab

SYMPTOM: The Shared Level Access option is grayed out.

EXPLANATION: You previously had your primary network logon set to Client For Netware Networks.

SOLUTION: In the Control Panel, double-click on the Network icon. On the Configuration tab, make sure that your primary network logon is set to Client For Microsoft Networks. Then restart the PC.

# You Cannot See Any Other Computers in Network Neighborhood

SYMPTOM: No other computers appear in your Network Neighborhood window.

EXPLANATION: The other PCs are not sending your PC their information.

SOLUTION: Check to make sure that you have configured the other PCs for networking, same as this one. Make sure that the cables are all securely in place, and the power to the hub is plugged in.

# In Network Neighborhood, You See Other PCs but Not Yourself

SYMPTOM: Other PCs appear, but not your own PC, and other computers can see each other but not you.

EXPLANATION: Your network card may not be set up properly, or you may not have enabled file and printer sharing.

**SOLUTION:** Confirm that you have completed all the steps for setting up your network connection (both hardware and software). Make sure that you have enabled file and printer sharing in particular.

# New Device Works but System Crashes Frequently

Now look at a slightly different problem: Your new device is installed, and it works like a charm, but other odd things have started to happen. Perhaps your system locks up for no reason more often now than it did before, or perhaps some other device doesn't work anymore. These events are the thorniest problems to troubleshoot because the cause of the problem is not obvious. Is it the new device, or is it an old device's reaction to the new device? Here are some things to check:

- If the system locks up when you try to use two devices at the same time (for example, if it locks up when you move your mouse but only when the modem is in use), you probably have a device conflict. Turn back to the sections on modems and sound cards earlier in this chapter if you need help tracking down a conflict.

- Perhaps the driver for one or more devices became corrupted. Try reinstalling all your drivers (by running the setup programs that came with the devices).

- Check manufacturer Web sites for driver updates. Perhaps you can fix a known problem with a certain driver by downloading an update.

- If all else fails, reinstall all your software. This remedy sounds extreme, and it may take you several hours, but compared to how many hours you will probably waste in the future trying fruitlessly to track down the reason for the problem, it may be the best solution in the long run. To reinstall, back up everything important and then reformat your hard disk and start over, reloading your operating system (DOS or Windows 95/98) and then all your drivers and applications. Ask a techie friend to help you if you're a beginner.

- If your system still crashes after a complete reinstall, suspect the hardware itself. Perhaps you need to install a *firmware update* (a BIOS update that affects only a single device) for a particular device, or

maybe the computer has some bad memory. (A memory chip with a tiny flaw in it can sometimes cause system problems, although it appears to work normally most of the time.) The best thing to do in this case is to contact the PC manufacturer and ask for ideas. Be persistent. If you bug the company enough, it will eventually figure out your problem or send you a replacement computer.

 **NOTE** True story: I had been having problems with intermittent crashes and lockups ever since I got my new computer six months ago. Finally I talked to a technical support representative who suggested that I download a firmware revision for my hard disk. I did so, and the problems went away.

# Getting Help from the Manufacturer

Throughout this chapter I have advised you to contact the manufacturer quite a few times. In this section I explain the best ways to get results.

## By Phone

Your upgrade probably came with some sort of instructions, and those instructions probably included a section about how to get technical support. In addition, computer magazines have contact information for some manufacturers. The best companies have toll-free numbers, but smaller companies may require you to pay for the call.

There are two schools of thought on the best time to contact technical support:

- Some people say to call during the day because the most experienced tech support people usually work the day shift.
- Some people say to call in the middle of the night because you probably won't have to wait on hold as long.

My own philosophy is a mixture of these two: If I have a simple question, I usually call at night; if I have a difficult problem and want to talk with a real expert, I call during the day and find something to do (like a crossword puzzle) while I'm on hold.

Before placing a call to tech support, have the following information at your fingertips:

- The name of the store you purchased it from and the date of purchase
- The complete model number
- The serial number

You also need to make sure you can clearly describe what's wrong with the device or what your dilemma or difficulty is. The better you can explain what you want, the easier it will be for the technical support person to help you.

An automated system will probably answer your call. Listen carefully to the choices provided and punch the appropriate buttons. Then, depending on the company and the time of day you call, you will probably wait on hold for at least five minutes (and maybe as long as a half hour. (Waiting on hold is a much bigger deal if the manufacturer does not provide a toll-free number.)

After you get through to a real person, immediately ask for his or her name and extension so that you can talk to the same person later if you need to (or are disconnected). Then explain your problem as clearly and concisely as possible.

**TIP** If you think you have gotten someone who doesn't know much more than you do, don't be shy about (politely) asking to speak with someone else. Most good technical support people, however, will realize by themselves when they are in over their heads and will send you to a more experienced person before you have to ask.

# By Internet

I almost never call technical support phone numbers anymore because I've discovered that I can find the answers to 99 percent of my problems on the Internet. (Of course, if it's your modem that isn't working, this method is not for you.)

If you used the Internet for comparison shopping before you bought your upgrade, you already have the address for the manufacturer's Web site; just return to it and look for a technical support area.

If you haven't visited the manufacturer's Web site yet, here are some ways to find the address:

- ✿ Check the documentation that came with the device. Most companies proudly put the address on their boxes or in their documentation.

- ✿ Check computer magazines for major companies and their contact information, including Web sites in most cases.

- ✿ Use a search engine like Lycos (**http://www.lycos.com**), Excite (**http://www.excite.com**), or Yahoo! (**http://www.yahoo.com**) to search for the company's name.

- ✿ Guess. Most large companies have predictable Web page addresses. For example, Microsoft is **http://www.microsoft.com** and Creative Labs is **http://www.creativelabs.com**.

The Web-based technical support offerings vary from company to company, but you may find databases of technical information, a message board where people like you have posted questions and company representatives have posted answers, and a mechanism for sending your particular problem via e-mail to a technical support representative.

# Protecting Your Warranty Rights

Today's hardware is better than ever before, but it still breaks. Consequently, you should understand your warranty rights and do everything in your power to keep them in force.

## Fill Out the Registration Card

In the excitement of the new installation, you may have forgotten about your warranty registration card, but don't throw it away. After your hardware is installed and you're happy with it, take a few moments and fill out and mail that card.

**CAUTION**    Don't fill out the warranty card until you are sure you want to keep the new device. You cannot usually return a nondefective device if the warranty card is marked up because then the vendor cannot resell it.

When you mail in the registration card, you get various benefits, depending on the manufacturer. The biggest benefit is that your date of purchase is registered in the manufacturer's database, so if you need service or replacement during the warranty period, the manufacturer can verify that your device is indeed still under warranty. Other benefits might include sweepstakes entries, free gadgets, or newsletter subscriptions.

Some installation programs include online registration options. When the installation program terminates, it runs a program that enables you to fill in your information onscreen and send it via modem (usually with a toll-free number) to the manufacturer. Online registration saves you a stamp and the bother of filling out the card and taking it to a mailbox. Online registration is also good from the manufacturer's point of view because more people are likely to register this way than through the mail.

## Keep Your Receipt

File away the receipt for your purchase in a safe place and do not throw it away until after the warranty period has expired. If you ever need warranty service on the device, you will need the receipt as proof of your purchase date. You will also need it if you want to return or exchange your purchase (typically within the first 30 days).

## Save the Warranty Information

You should also save the warranty certificate that came with the device—the piece of paper that explains the warranty terms and conditions. I usually staple the purchase receipt to this card and file them together.

## Keep the Boxes and Packing Materials

For the first 30 days that you have a device, keep everything, including the box and all the packing materials, the installation instructions, the user manual—the whole package. Most manufacturers give you 30 days to return a defective device to the store. Returns go much more smoothly if you can return the device in its original box and packing—and customer service people are likely to ask a lot of questions if you try to return the item, for example, loose in a crumpled paper sack.

## Write Down the Serial Number and Model Number

If you ever need to contact technical support, the first things the representative will ask for are your model and serial number. Have these handy! I usually write them on the inside cover of the user manual that comes with each device. Then I keep a special folder in my file cabinet for all the user manuals.

## Defective Merchandise: What to Do?

I hope you're not reading this section—that is, I hope you aren't *having* to read it. Buying something that doesn't work is a frustrating experience.

The procedure for dealing with a defective device depends on how long ago you purchased it. Within the first 30 days, you can return it to the vendor and get a replacement. After 30 days most vendors won't accept it, and you have to deal with the manufacturer.

If you have to return the device to the manufacturer, check the warranty terms and conditions (aren't you glad you saved that information?) to find out what needs to be done. Then call the company and ask for an RMA number. *RMA* stands for return material authorization. You write this number on the outside of your package so that the manufacturer knows what the package is when it arrives and how to deal with it.

Some companies are better than others about handling returns. One company that I dealt with actually sent me a postage-paid label for my package, and UPS came to my house and picked it up at no charge to me. That was great! Other companies make you pay for shipping and might even ask you to pay for package insurance. In that case, if the product you are returning is relatively inexpensive, your cheapest option could be to just buy a new device and throw the old one away.

## Summary

Hey, congratulations! You made it through the weekend! I hope that you had some fun doing your upgrade and that you learned a bit about your computer in the process. If you want to tell me about your upgrade experience, drop me a line at **fwempen@iquest.net**. Thanks for sharing the weekend with me—and see you next time!

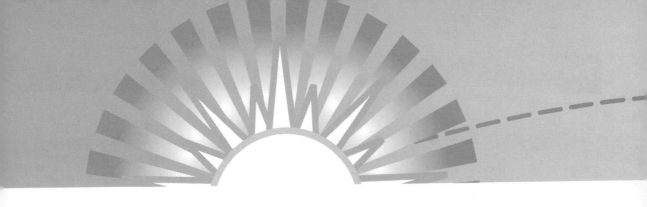

# Post Error Beep Codes

If you hear a single beep when you start up your computer and then the computer starts normally, the beep is simply telling you that the speaker is working.

However, if you hear one or more beeps and the computer does not start normally, it may be trying to tell you that something is wrong. When the computer can't start up enough to display a message on the monitor, it taps out its problem in a kind of beeping Morse code. For example, if your AMI BIOS system beeps five times, it may be telling you that your processor has a problem.

These audio codes are not usually all that helpful for a beginner, because most of them indicate a physical failure on the motherboard. There's not much you can do about it other than send it back to the vendor for an exchange. However, codes can help in some situations when you are not sure what's wrong and you need to know which part to return. For example, the beep codes might help you distinguish a computer that won't start because of a dead processor from one that won't start because of faulty memory.

# Award BIOS

According to the Award Bios Web site (**http://www.award.com**), its BIOS produces only one beep code: a single long beep followed by two short ones. This signal indicates that a video error has occurred and that the BIOS cannot initialize the video screen to display any additional information. If you are receiving any other beeps with an Award BIOS, you probably have defective, incompatible, or incorrectly installed memory.

# AMI BIOS

Table A.1 lists the beep codes for most AMI BIOS systems, along with a bit of explanation about them.

# Phoenix BIOS

The Phoenix BIOS sends a complex sequence of beeps that precisely describe the point at which the system got hung up on its way to starting. The codes are represented in Table A.2 by series of numbers and dashes; for example, 1-1-2 means "one beep, pause, one beep, pause, two beeps." Therefore, if you were getting a 1-1-2 error, you would hear a total of four beeps.

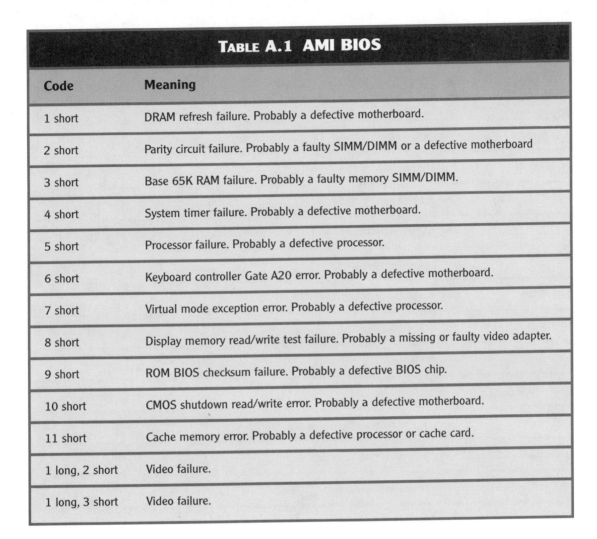

## TABLE A.1 AMI BIOS

| Code | Meaning |
|---|---|
| 1 short | DRAM refresh failure. Probably a defective motherboard. |
| 2 short | Parity circuit failure. Probably a faulty SIMM/DIMM or a defective motherboard |
| 3 short | Base 65K RAM failure. Probably a faulty memory SIMM/DIMM. |
| 4 short | System timer failure. Probably a defective motherboard. |
| 5 short | Processor failure. Probably a defective processor. |
| 6 short | Keyboard controller Gate A20 error. Probably a defective motherboard. |
| 7 short | Virtual mode exception error. Probably a defective processor. |
| 8 short | Display memory read/write test failure. Probably a missing or faulty video adapter. |
| 9 short | ROM BIOS checksum failure. Probably a defective BIOS chip. |
| 10 short | CMOS shutdown read/write error. Probably a defective motherboard. |
| 11 short | Cache memory error. Probably a defective processor or cache card. |
| 1 long, 2 short | Video failure. |
| 1 long, 3 short | Video failure. |

### TABLE A.2 PHOENIX ROM BIOS PLUS AND PHOENIX BIOS A286/A386/A486 VERSION 1.xx

| Code | Meaning |
|------|---------|
| 1-1-3 | The motherboard is bad. |
| 1-1-4 | The BIOS is bad. |
| 1-2-1 | The motherboard is bad. |
| 1-2-2 | The motherboard is bad. |
| 1-2-3 | The motherboard is bad. |
| 1-3-1 | The motherboard is bad. |
| 1-3-3 | The motherboard is bad. |
| 1-3-4 | The motherboard is bad. |
| 1-4-1 | The motherboard is bad. |
| 1-4-2 | Some of the memory is bad. |
| 2-1-1 | Some of the memory is bad. |
| 2-1-2 | Some of the memory is bad. |
| 2-1-3 | Some of the memory is bad. |
| 2-1-4 | Some of the memory is bad. |
| 2-2-1 | Some of the memory is bad. |
| 2-2-2 | Some of the memory is bad. |
| 2-2-3 | Some of the memory is bad. |
| 2-2-4 | Some of the memory is bad. |

**TABLE A.2 PHOENIX ROM BIOS PLUS AND PHOENIX BIOS A286/A386/A486 VERSION 1.XX (CONTINUED)**

| Code | Meaning |
|------|---------|
| 2-3-1 | Some of the memory is bad. |
| 2-3-2 | Some of the memory is bad. |
| 2-3-3 | Some of the memory is bad. |
| 2-3-4 | Some of the memory is bad. |
| 2-4-1 | Some of the memory is bad. |
| 2-4-2 | Some of the memory is bad. |
| 2-4-3 | Some of the memory is bad. |
| 2-4-4 | Some of the memory is bad. |
| 3-1-1 | The motherboard has a defective chip. |
| 3-1-2 | The motherboard has a defective chip. |
| 3-1-3 | The motherboard has a defective chip. |
| 3-1-4 | The motherboard has a defective chip. |
| 3-2-4 | The keyboard controller has failed. |
| 3-3-4 | The video card is missing or bad. |
| 3-4-1 | The video card isn't working. |
| 3-4-2 | The video card isn't working. |
| 4-2-1 | The motherboard has a defective chip. |
| 4-2-2 | Either the keyboard has a problem or you have a bad motherboard. |

## PHOENIX ROM BIOS PLUS AND PHOENIX BIOS A286/A386/A486 VERSION 1.XX (CONTINUED)

| Code | Meaning |
| --- | --- |
| 4-2-3 | Same as 4-2-2. |
| 4-2-4 | One of the expansion cards is bad or the motherboard is bad. |
| 4-3-1 | The motherboard is bad. |
| 4-3-2 | The motherboard is bad. |
| 4-3-3 | The motherboard is bad. |
| 4-3-4 | Either the battery or power supply is bad. |
| 4-4-1 | One of the serial ports is malfunctioning. |
| 4-4-2 | The parallel port is malfunctioning. |
| 4-4-3 | The math coprocessor is malfunctioning. |

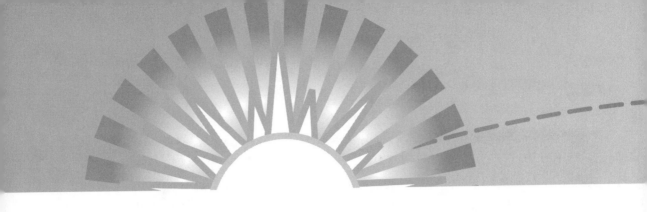

# GLOSSARY

**6x86MX**. Cyrix's MMX technology processor, which competes with the Pentium MMX.

**Accelerated Graphics Port**. See *AGP*.

**AGP**. Stands for Accelerated Graphics Port. A new, very fast technology for connecting a video card.

**Aperture grille**. A monitor technology that uses an array of stretched wires to create images. Compared to *Dot trio shadow mask* monitors, aperture grille monitors have superior brightness and contrast, but their poorer horizontals make them less suited for displaying text.

**AT motherboard**. A motherboard in which the card interface slots run parallel to the narrow edge of the board. Compare to *ATX motherboard*.

**ATA-2**. See *IDE*.

**ATX motherboard**. A motherboard in which the card interface slots run parallel to the wide edge of the motherboard. Compare to *AT motherboard*.

**AUTOEXEC.BAT**. A startup file that processes its batch of commands whenever the computer starts.

**Average access time**. A hard disk performance measurement: the time it takes for the drive head to reach and read the average bit of data. It's measured in milliseconds (ms). The lower the number, the faster the drive.

**Basic input/output system**. See *BIOS*.

**Beep codes**. Patterns of beeps produced by a nonworking PC when it starts up—designed to help a technician diagnose the problem.

**BIOS**. Stands for basic input/output system. The low-level startup routine that tells the computer how to load the operating system.

**BIOS setup program**. A built-in program in a PC that enables you to configure the PC's base-level settings. See *BIOS*.

**Block mode**. A data transfer scheme (set in the BIOS) that enables a computer to transfer data to and from the drive in blocks rather than in bytes, so it can perform better.

**Boot**. To start up a computer.

**Boot disk**. A disk (hard or floppy) that contains the startup files needed to boot a computer.

**Cable modem**. A device that interfaces with a PC and a cable TV system to permit Internet access if the cable company provides it.

**Cable select**. A mechanism by which a hard disk or other IDE device can tell whether it is the master or the slave according to its connection position on a multi-device cable. See *Master* and *Slave*.

**Case**. The metal box that holds the computer's internal parts.

**CD-ROM drive**. A drive that reads CD-ROM discs. Most programs come on CD-ROM these days, so a CD-ROM drive is almost a necessity for any computer. Some CD-ROM drives have extra features such as the ability to play DVD movies or hold more than one disc at a time.

**CHKDSK**. A command run at the DOS prompt to check for errors on a disk.

**Clock speed**. The speed, in MHz, at which a processor's internal clock operates. For example, some of the newer Pentium II processors operate at 400MHz.

**CMOS**. Stands for Complementary Metal Oxide Semiconductor. A microchip on the motherboard that stores the BIOS setting changes you make with the BIOS setup program.

**Complementary Metal Oxide Semiconductor**. See *CMOS*.

**CONFIG.SYS**. A startup file that lists the drivers and system settings the PC should load when it starts. This is important with DOS-based systems—less so with Windows 95/98 systems.

**Convergence**. A measurement of how well the three "guns" inside the monitor—red, blue, and green—align to paint the color onto each dot. If one of the guns is misaligned, the colors will not be true.

**Cooling fan**. A small round fan that straps onto a processor to keep it cool.

**Data transfer rate**. A measurement of how quickly data moves from the hard disk to memory. The higher the number, the faster the rate.

**Defragment**. To reorder the data on a disk so that all files are stored contiguously, rather than in multiple noncontiguous pieces (fragments).

**Digital camera**. A camera that saves images in electronic format and feeds them into your PC instead of putting the images on conventional film.

**Digitize**. To scan an image or record it with a digital camera so that it becomes a computer file.

**DIMM**. Stands for Dual Inline Memory Module. A newer kind of memory (RAM) for PCs that is faster and better than the older SIMM type. The most popular type is *S-DRAM DIMMs*.

**DIP switches**. Small switches, like light switches, on a circuit board, that control low-level settings (much as *jumpers* do).

**Disk Operating System**. See *DOS*.

**DOS**. Stands for Disk Operating System. For many years, the definitive operating system for PCs. The most popular brand is MS-DOS. Newer systems that use Windows 95 or Windows 98 do not rely on a DOS user interface.

**Dot matrix**. A printer technology that works by striking the paper with a series of little pins against a ribbon (like a typewriter ribbon). In many ways a dot matrix printer is like an automated typewriter except that, instead of letter-shaped hammers, a group of small pins changes position to form each letter.

**Dot pitch**. The measurement of how far apart the dots are that make up the picture in a dot trio shadow mask monitor. Lower is better.

**Dot trio shadow mask**. The most common monitor technology. Three colored guns (red, green, and blue) shine light through a screen of round holes to form the picture. These monitors deliver clean edges and sharp diagonals, which is important for showing text onscreen. See *Aperture grille*.

**DoubleSpace**. See *DriveSpace*.

**DriveSpace**. A program that compresses your hard disk so you can store more files on it. Called DoubleSpace in DOS 6.20, but renamed DriveSpace in DOS 6.22 when the program's compression algorithm was changed in response to a lawsuit.

**Drum**. The big metal cylinder inside a laser printer that transfers the image onto the paper.

**Dual Inline Memory Module**. See *DIMM*.

**DVD drive**. A type of super CD-ROM drive, which can read special DVD discs that can hold as much as 8.5 gigabytes on each side. DVD drives can also function as regular CD-ROM drives.

**EDO memory**. An improved type of non-parity memory (compared to FPM, or *Fast Page Mode,* memory). Many Pentium-class systems use it.

**EIDE**. See *IDE*.

**Extended Data Out**. See *EDO memory*.

**Fast Page Mode memory**. Generic memory. It works in just about any system that requires "non-parity" memory and doesn't mention anything about EDO. Look for a *32* in the specifications for this, as in 16×32-60ns.

**FAT**. A system chart stored on your hard disk that keeps track of what files are using which physical spots on the disk. Accessible only by the operating system.

**File Allocation Table**. See *FAT*.

**FM Synthesis card**. A type of sound card that does not include *wavetable* support.

**FPM memory**. See *Fast Page Mode memory*.

**Hard drive**. A fixed storage drive inside your PC where you can store program and data files. A hard disk consists of a series of stacked metal platters with a read-write head that reads them like a phonograph needle reads a record or a laser reads a CD.

**Hard drive type**. Older hard disks have a type number from 1 to 46. Hard disks manufactured in the last several years, however, do not use this typing scheme, relying instead on your BIOS's AutoDetect Hard Disk utility to determine the type.

**Heat sink**. a grid of black spikes like porcupine quills mounted on top of a processor to keep it cool. Heat sinks are common on newer 486 and older Pentium systems.

**IDE**. The most popular type of hard disk interface. Each motherboard has two IDE interfaces that can each support two devices. Other devices that can be plugged into an IDE interface include some CD-ROM drives and ZIP drives. Enhanced versions of the IDE specification include EIDE and ATA-2.

**Ink-jet**. A type of printer that works by squirting tiny blobs of ink onto the paper with an ink nozzle.

**Interlacing**. A display monitor scheme that refreshes every other line on the screen rather than every line in order to create acceptable video performance on cheap hardware. Interlacing can cause eyestrain, and the inability to display in noninterlaced mode is the mark of an old or poor-quality monitor.

**Internet**. A vast network of computer networks all over the world.

**Interrupt Request**. See IRQ.

**IRQ**. Stands for Interrupt Request. A path from the processor to a device on the motherboard. Each system has 16 IRQs (0 through 15), and each device should be assigned its own IRQ. Under certain circumstances, devices can share IRQs, but this often causes problems.

**ISA**. Stands for Industry Standard Architecture. One of the 8- or 16-bit slots on a motherboard that can accept ISA expansion cards. ISA is old technology; a newer kind of slot is *PCI*.

**Jumpers**. Small plastic blocks that fit over two or more pins that stick up from a circuit board to change a low-level setting on it (such as its IRQ or its operating mode). Like DIP switches, but cheaper to manufacture.

**K6**. An AMD (Advanced Micro Devices) brand processor that competes with the Pentium.

**K6-2**. An AMD (Advanced Micro Devices) brand processor that competes with the Pentium II. The K6-2 has a built-in 3-D technology called 3DNow! that supposedly gives it an edge over a Pentium II.

**Laser printer**. A printer that prints by fusing toner onto a page using a drum and transfer wires, much like a photocopier. Laser printers provide superior-quality images to ink-jets, but print only in black except for a few very expensive color models.

**LCD monitor**. A very thin, high-quality monitor found mostly on laptop computers. Some manufacturers are beginning to use LCD in large desktop monitors with stunning results.

**Line in** and **line out**. Jacks on a sound card. A line in jack provides a way to route sound from another amplifier such as your home stereo system or a boom box headphone jack. The line out jack provides a way to route the sound card output to an amplifier such as your home stereo system.

**Local bus**. Expansion slots on a motherboard that have high-speed connections to the processor for fast performance. Types of local buses include *VLB*, *PCI*, and *AGP*.

**Low-insertion force (LIF) socket**. A processor socket in which the processor's pins are wedged into little corresponding holes and held in by the tension. An older technology; *zero-insertion force (ZIF)* is newer.

**LQ**. Stands for letter quality. Generically, any printout that is as good or better than that achievable with a typewriter. Also refers specifically to the output of the 24-pin kind of dot matrix printer.

**Master**. The IDE device that controls the device chain. Each IDE port on a motherboard can support two devices. The primary device is the master; it talks directly to the processor. The secondary device is the slave; its orders come from the processor through the master device. IDE devices usually have jumpers that determine master or slave status.

**Memory (RAM)**. The workspace in which your computer operates. The more memory you have, the more and bigger programs you can run at the same time. If you don't have enough memory, your programs may run more slowly or not at all. Physically, memory consists of chips or small circuit cards installed on the motherboard. The most common types are *SIMMs* and *DIMMs*.

**MIDI input**. This port enables you to plug in a keyboard or other instrument to put sounds into the computer for manipulating or saving.

**M-II**. Cyrix's Pentium II equivalent processor.

**MMX**. Stands for Multimedia Extensions. A capability of some processors to handle multimedia processing better than others. Built into most newer Pentiums and all Pentium IIs. Lacking in the Pentium Pro.

**Modem**. A device that allows you to communicate with other computers through phone lines by translating digital data (PC) to analog (sound) and then back again on the other end.

**Motherboard**. The big circuit board inside the case that everything else plugs into. The motherboard you have determines the processor (or processors) you can use, the type and amount of memory, the video card type, and more.

**MS-DOS**. See *DOS*.

**Multimedia Extensions**. See *MMX*.

**Multimedia**. A "multimedia system" usually has a sound card, speakers, and a CD-ROM drive.

**NLQ**. Stands for near letter quality. A description of output quality of a 9-pin dot matrix printer. The "near" means it is not quite as good as the output from a typewriter.

**Non-interlaced**. See *Interlacing*.

**PCI**. Peripheral Connection Interface, a very popular type of local bus slot on newer motherboards.

**Pentium II**. An improved Pentium with both MMX capability and features from the Pentium Pro. It is a good choice for Windows 95/98 and Windows NT power users.

**Pentium Pro**. The original successor to the Pentium. It fits in a different size socket from the one the regular Pentium uses, so you need a new motherboard if you want to switch to a Pentium Pro. It is optimized for 32-bit operating systems like Windows NT; if you are an NT user, the Pro will boost your system's performance. However, this chip has been phased out and is no longer being produced because the Pentium II is better.

**Pincushion**. A monitor adjustment that controls how wide the image is near the vertical center of the image compared to the top and bottom. If your image looks like it has a waistline drawn in near the middle of each side, increase this setting; if it bulges in the middle, reduce it.

**PIO**. Stands for Programmed I/O. A scheme of enhancing data transfer on a hard disk. There are five available PIO modes (0 through 4), which can be set in the BIOS setup.

**Plug and Play**. A method of identifying and configuring new hardware. If your motherboard and the new device are both Plug and Play–compatible, when you add your upgrade components to the system, Windows 95/98 detects and configures them automatically.

**Processor**. The "brain" of your computer. The types produced by Intel include 286, 386, 486, Pentium, Pentium Pro, and Pentium II. (Competing products generally refer to a specific Intel model to define their place in the market.) Your processor has a speed—given in megahertz (MHz)—at which it operates.

**PS/2**. An obsolete type of IBM PC that introduced the PS/2 port. Even though the computers are no longer produced, PS/2 ports have become the standard for mouse and keyboard connections in almost all new PCs made today.

**Pull**. A piece of equipment that has been removed from an old system. Buying one is like buying a car part from a junkyard—it's cheap and it may work perfectly, but then again it may not.

**Refresh rate**. Refers to how often the video card sends updated instructions to the monitor. If you have ever seen a videotape of someone working at a computer and the computer screen seemed to be blinking or flickering, the computer screen's refresh rate was lower than the videotape's frame rate. Both monitors and video cards can be bottlenecks to improving refresh rates.

**Resolution**. The number of pixels (dots) that make up a display on a monitor. Common resolutions are 640×480 and 800×600.

**ROM-BIOS**. See *BIOS*.

**Scandisk**. A utility program that runs in DOS 6.0 or higher or in Windows 95/98 to check a disk for errors. Replaces the older *CHKDSK*.

**Scanner**. A device for digitizing pictures so that you can use them in your computer. Some scanners also come with optical character recognition (OCR) software, which allows you to scan text and then translate the picture of the text into real text in a word processor.

**SCSI**. Stands for Small Computer System Interface. A type of device interface that runs a variety of devices such as hard disks, scanners, and CD-ROM drives. Its primary benefit is that you can plug up to 7 devices into a single chain, without using separate IRQs. (A newer device called "wide SCSI" allows for 15 devices.) SCSI is common on high-end systems and servers, but has not caught on in the mainstream PC market because it requires buying a special interface card into which to plug the SCSI devices.

**S-DRAM DIMMs**. This newer, faster kind of memory comes in a 168-pin DIMM package. The performance is great, but the cost per megabyte may be higher than it is for non-parity EDO SIMMs.

**Shadow mask**. See *Dot trio shadow mask*.

**SIMM**. A type of memory found in 486 and some Pentium systems. SIMMs were the standard type of memory for many years, but are now being superceded by *DIMMs*.

**Single inline memory modules**. See *SIMM*.

**Slave**. The secondary device in a two-device IDE chain. See *Master*.

**Slot mask**. A hybrid type of monitor that integrates features of both shadow mask and aperture grille technologies.

**Slot pitch**. A measurement, like *dot pitch*, of the quality of a slot mask type monitor. Smaller is better.

**Socket 1**. A long, thin slot on a motherboard designed for a Pentium II cartridge.

**Socket 7**. A square processor socket on a motherboard designed for 486 or Pentium CPUs or their competitors.

**Sound card**. An interface card that plugs into the motherboard and enables you to hear sound through speakers (typically sold separately). If you don't have a sound card, you miss out on the sound effects associated with most games and also on the audible warnings your computer issues from time to time.

**Standoffs**. The supports (some plastic and some brass) that hold the motherboard off the floor of the case. (They make the motherboard "stand off" the floor.)

**Swap file**. A portion of the hard disk set aside to be used as a temporary holding tank for information that won't fit in the computer's memory as it operates.

**System resources**. Generically, this means the memory available for running the operating system and your programs. In Windows, it also includes virtual memory created with a swap file.

**Termination**. In a SCSI device chain, the switch, plug, or other indicator on the last device that tells the PC that there are no more devices in the chain.

**Thrashing**. Continual hard disk spinning caused by the PC accessing its swap file. This can indicate that the PC could benefit from more memory being added.

**Toner**. The dry ink used by laser printers.

**Trapezoid**. A monitor adjustment that controls how wide the image is at the top versus the bottom of the screen. If you have more black space on the sides near the top of the monitor than near the bottom, or vice versa, adjust this setting to even it out.

**True parity memory**. A type of memory for systems that require parity memory. Many older 486 systems require true parity memory.

**UART**. A chip in a serial port or an internal modem that controls the throughput. If you want to use a high-speed serial device, you may want to buy a high-speed serial port interface card that contains the top-of-the-line UART, which is the 16750.

**Universal Serial Bus**. See *USB*.

**USB**. Stands for Universal Serial Bus, a new kind of connector that PC manufacturers began including on their systems in mid-1997. You can plug up to 128 USB devices into a single USB port (chaining them together) and you don't have to do any special configuring for them. The later releases of Windows 95 supported USB, as do all releases of Windows 98.

**Video card**. The interface between your PC and your monitor. The card interprets the PC's instructions and sends codes that tell the monitor which pixels (dots) to light up with which colors.

**Video driver**. A file that tells your operating system (such as Windows 98) how to work with your video card.

**Video RAM**. Memory built into your video card.

**VLB**. Stands for VESA local bus, an older kind of local bus slot found on 486 computers. See *Local bus*.

**Wavetable cards**. Interface cards (usually sound cards) that have prerecorded, built-in sounds, such as the sounds of different instruments playing different notes. Regular FM synthesis sound cards don't have wavetables; they simulate these notes instead, which doesn't sound as good.

**Zero-insertion force (ZIF) socket**. A type of processor socket newer 486 computers and all Pentiums and Pentium-equivalent computers have. The processor appears to be sitting on a small platform (usually white) with a handle alongside it. You lift the handle, and the chip then lifts easily out of the socket.

# INDEX

## A

**Accelerated Graphics Port slots.** *See* AGP slots
**Adobe Photoshop,** 8
    3-D features, 115
**advertising**
    mail-order vendor ads, 160
    name-brand parts, 157
    Web site ads, 160-162
**AGP slots,** 8, 30
    determining, 47-49
**AMD K6/K6-2 processors,** 93, 106
**America Online,** 346
**AMI BIOS beep codes,** 372-373
**antistatic wrist straps,** 202
**aperture grille monitors,** 118
**Apple computers DIMMs,** 96
**ATAPI devices,** 253
**AT/ATX motherboards.** *See* motherboards
**ATI All In Wonder Pro,** 151
**AuctionWeb,** 184-185
**auction Web sites,** 180-183
    consumer-to-consumer sites, 183-185
    Onsale.com, 181, 183
**audio.** *See* sound cards
**AUTOEXEC.BAT files,** 24
    removing lines with REM, 28
**Award Bios beep codes,** 372

## B

**backing up**
    setup disks, 311-312
    system files, 205
**.BAK files, deleting,** 39
**batteries**
    CMOS chip and, 281
    external batteries, 263-264
    installing new battery, 264-266
    locating, 262-263
    replacing, 261-266
    soldered on batteries, 263-264
    testing, 261, 264
    upside down installation, 266
**bay covers, removing,** 240
**beep codes, BIOS,** 372-376
**Better Business Bureau,** 178
**Bigfoot drive, Quantum,** 130
**BIOS,** 248, 280-281, 283
    AMI BIOS beep codes, 372-373
    AutoConfigure drive type, 289
    Award Bios beep codes, 372
    battery information, 262
    beep codes, 372-376
    CD-ROM drives, setup for, 294
    changing settings for upgrade, 281-282
    commands, 285-286

**BIOS** *(continued)*

COM ports, disabling, 299-300

description of, 279-280

drive detection program, 289-291

exiting from setup program, 286-287

firmware updates, 365-366

floppy drives, setup for, 248, 282, 294-297

hard drive, setup for, 248, 288-293, 381

help for, 284

IDE devices, setup for, 288-293, 381

internal modems, setup for, 297-300

landing zone position, 291

memory (RAM)

recognizing, 259-260

setup for, 282, 287-288

menus in setup program, 285-286

modems, setup for internal, 282, 297-300

navigating in, 283-287

Onboard Serial Port, 300

Phoenix BIOS beep codes, 373-376

Plug-and-Play flash BIOS, 109

**blank screen**

beeps, 320-321

no disk activity, 319-320

quiet blank screen, 318-319

single beep, disk activity, 321-322

**Block mode,** 292

**.BMP files, deleting,** 39

**boot disks,** 205-208, 326-327

**boxes, saving,** 369

**brass standoffs,** 269, 273

**bus speed,** 109

## C

**cables**

drives, attaching cables for, 248-249

motherboard, connecting power supply cables to, 270-271

**cache feature,** 108-109

**cages,** 272

**calibration controls on monitors,** 120

**Canon printers,** 140

**capacitors on circuit boards,** 205

**cases,** 4, 110-112. *See also* drive bays

inside computer, view of, 221-222

removing cover, 218-221

sizes and types of, 111

slimline cases, 221

**catalogs, mail order,** 172

**CD-R drives,** 127

**CD recorders,** 57

**CD-ROM drives,** 4

adding, 57

audio CDs, 11

BIOS setup for, 248, 294

BIOS setup program for, 381-382

cables, attaching, 248, 249

changers, 127

compatibility, 125-126

IDE connections for, 124-125, 253

interfaces for, 124-125

internal/external decision, 126

recordable C, 127

SCSI drives for, 124, 126

sound cards supporting, 135

speed features, 123-124

tips for installing, 253-254

two-speed drives, 124

upgrading, 122-126

for Windows 95/98 programs, 7

**CD-RW drives,** 127

**CDW,** 178

**Chkdsk, running,** 17, 50

**.CHK files, deleting,** 39

**circuit boards.** *See also* expansion cards

electronics, 204-205

seating of, 224

touching, 224

unpacking components, 209

**clean back monitors,** 120

**Client for Microsoft Networks,** 313, 314

**Client for Netware Networks,** 313, 314

**clock doubling,** 85

**CMOS chips,** 281

**COAST,** 109

**cold temperatures,** 204

**colors**
 printer capabilities, 142
 scanners, 147
 video cards displaying, 114
 in Windows 3.1, 31
 in Windows 95/98, 34-36
**commercial auction Web sites.** *See* auction Web sites
**compatibility mode for Windows 95/98,** 37
**components**
 instructions, reading, 209-210
 lack of, 57
 unpacking, 209
**COM ports,** 59-60
 disabling in BIOS setup, 299-300
 IRQs (interrupt addresses), 297-300
**COM1 ports,** 59-60
**COM2 ports,** 59-60
**compressing hard disk,** 40-42
**Compression Agent,** 42
**Computer Discounters, Inc.,** 186
*Computer Shopper,* 160, 172
 NetBuyer Web site, 180
**CONFIG.SYS files,** 24
 removing lines with REM, 28
**Connectix camera,** 149
**consumables,** 13
**consumer-to-consumer auction sites,** 183-185
**conventional memory,** 9
**convergence, checking,** 121
**cooling fans,** 229
**copiers, printers with,** 141
**cordless mouse,** 150
**covers.** *See* cases
**crashing system,** 365-366
**Create Disk command,** 206
**Creative Labs SoundBlaster,** 53, 133-134, 136, 356
 compatibility with, 358
 Web site, 161
**cross-linked files,** 15
**CSEL (cable selection) system,** 245
**CTX monitors,** 121
**customer support,** 157
**Cylinder Head Sector (CHS),** 292

**Cyrix processors,** 93
 6X86MX/M-II processors, 106
 upgrade chips, 88

**D**

**.DAT files,** 39
**defective merchandise,** 370
**DEFRAG command,** 20, 79
**defragmenting hard drive,** 18-22, 79
**DejaNews.** *See* USENET newsgroups
**deleting files from hard disk,** 39-40
**DELOLDOS command,** 39
**DEO DIMMs,** 101
**department stores,** 168
**desktop cases,** 111
**Diamond video cards,** 115
**Digital Alpha 21164/21664PC processors,** 106
**digital cameras,** 11, 54, 57, 149
**DIMMs.** *See* dual inline memory modules (DIMMs)
**DIP switches,** 224-227
 expansion cards, installing, 235-236
 for memory (RAM), 259
 setting, 225-226
**DIR command,** 50
**discount stores,** 168-169
**Disk Cleanup program,** 40
**disk compression programs,** 40-42
**Disk Contents Changed, Restarting message,** 22
**Disk Defragmented,** 21-22
**.DLL files,** 39
**Doom,** 115
**DOS, older versions**
 boot disks in, 207-208
 Chkdsk, running, 17
 compatibility mode, 37
 freeing conventional memory in, 26-30
 setup programs, running, 302-303
 startup files, trimming, 25-26
 unneeded files, deleting, 39
**DOS 6.x**
 boot disk in, 207-208
 compatibility mode, 37
 compressing hard disk with, 40-41

**DOS 6.x** *(continued)*
    defragmenting with, 20
    disk errors, checking for, 15-17
    emergency startup disk, creating, 23-25
    freeing conventional memory in, 26
    hardware limitations, 80
    modem problems, 345
    scrambled picture, 334
    setup disks, copying, 311
    setup programs, running, 302-303
    upgrading, 78-79
    video problems, troubleshooting, 334-335
**dot matrix printers,** 138
    memory, 145
**DoubleSpace,** 34
**DRAM,** 116
**drive bays,** 62
    covers, removing, 240
    internal/external drive bays, 240
    metal plates blocking, 241
    mounting drive into, 242
    wrong bays, dealing with, 241
**drives, tape backup drives.** *See also* CD-ROM drives;
        floppy disks; hard drives
    BIOS setting, 248
    cables, attaching, 248
    cages, multiple drives mounted on, 272
    installing, 239-254
    peer-to-peer networking, sharing for, 316-318
    power plugs, lack of, 242-243
    procedure for installing, 249-252
    removable mass storage, 132-133
    ribbon cable, 244
    SCSI termination, 246-248
    tools for installing, 239
**DriveSpace,** 42
    in DOS 6.0, 79
    swap files with, 34
**.DRV files,** 39
**dual inline memory modules (DIMMs),** 96, 97, 101. *See*
    *also* memory (RAM)
    clips for, 257-258
    in Pentium/Pentium II computers, 256
    seating in slot, 258
    swapping out, 321

**Dutch font,** 144
**DVD drives,** 126-127
**dye sublimation printers,** 137

## E

**ECP/EPP parallel ports,** 108
**Edlin,** 25
**EDO RAM,** 113
**EDO SIMMs,** 101
**EIDE drives**
    for hard drives, 129
    interfaces, 108
**electronics on circuit boards,** 204-205
**emergency startup disk, creating,** 23-25
**enhanced (EMS) memory,** 44
**Epson printers,** 140
    Stylus Color 600 printer, 146
    Stylus Color 850 printer, 146
    Stylus Photo 700 printer, 142
**Evergreen processors,** 93
**Evergreen upgrade chips,** 88
**exchanges, store policies,** 192
**expansion cards,** 48
    DIP switches, setting, 235-236
    installing, 234-239
    I/O expansion cards, 253
    jumpers, 235-236
    procedure for installing, 238-239
    seating in slot, 237-238
    selecting slot for, 236-237
    tools for installing, 234
    upgrades requiring, 58
**Extended Cylinder Head Sector (ECHS),** 292
**extended data out (EDO) memory,** 96
**extended (XMS) memory,** 24, 44
**external drive bays,** 240
**external modems.** *See* modems
**eyestrain,** 12

## F

**factory refurbished equipment,** 181
**fans,** 229
**Fast Page Mode (FPM) memory,** 95, 100, 101
**fax machines, printers with,** 141

**FDISK program,** 328-329

**File Allocation Table (FAT),** 14-15

**firmware updates,** 365-366

**586 computers.** *See also* Pentium/Pentium II computers
    upgrading, 91-92

**flash BIOS,** 109

**flatbed scanners,** 148

**floppy drives**
    BIOS setup for, 248, 282, 294-297
    boot from floppy, failure to, 325
    cable connector types, 250
    continuous light, floppy disk fail with, 322
    no light, floppy disk fail with, 322-324
    power connector socket for, 250
    ribbon cable for, 244
    system files, backing up, 205
    tips for installing, 252

**fonts**
    adding, 12
    printer fonts, 143-145

**footprint of monitors,** 120

**form factor of motherboard,** 104

**486 computers**
    BIOS setup for new RAM, 287-288
    clock speeds, 85
    processor upgrades for, 90-91
    single inline memory modules (SIMMs) in, 95
    upgrading, 84

**fragmented files,** 19
    defragmenting hard drive, 18-22, 79

**free fixes,** 13-14

**friends, information from,** 165

**FrontPage 98,** 11

**full-height hard drive,** 130

**full parity memory,** 63

**G**

**game controllers,** 151-152. *See also* joysticks

**game pads,** 8, 151

**games,** 7-8
    CD-ROM speed and, 123
    computers for playing, 68
    3-D feature support, 115

**Gateway monitors,** 122

**generic parts,** 156-158

**graphical BIOS setup program,** 285, 286

**graphics-intensive programs,** 8-9

**H**

**half height hard drive,** 130

**hard drives,** 4
    AutoConfigure drive type, 289
    average access time, 130
    BIOS setup for, 248, 288-293, 381
    Block mode, 292
    cables, attaching, 248
    capacity decision, 130
    compressing hard disk, 40-42
    costs of, 63
    cylinders of, 291
    data transfer rate, 131
    defragmenting, 18-22
    drive detection program, 289-291
    dying, 15
    error message, Hard Disk Fail, 324
    errors on, 14-15
    full hard drives, 49-50
    heads of, 291
    increasing capacity of, 40-42
    interfaces for, 129-130
    manually configuring, 291-293
    nonbootable hard drive, 326-327
    not formatted message, 327-330
    performance, evaluating, 130-131
    physical size of, 130
    PIO modes, 291-292
    replacing, 129-131
    SCSI hard drives, 129-130
    sectors of, 291
    setup disks, 302
    translation, 292
    unneeded files, deleting, 39-40
    as weak link, 56

**Hayes commands,** 343-344

**heat sinks,** 229

**help**
    BIOS help, 284
    manufacturer's help, 366-368

**Hewlett Packard**
    laser printers, 147
    PhotoRET, 143
    printers, 140, 147
**home business computers,** 68-69
**HotDog Pro,** 11
**hot temperatures,** 203-204
**hybrid printers,** 141

## I

**IDE devices**
    AutoConfigure drive type, 289
    BIOS setup for, 288-293, 381
    drive detection program, 289-291
    hard drives, 129
    manually configuring hard drive, 291-293
    master/slave relationships, 244-246
    for monitors, 124-125
    tips for installing, 252-253
**Industry Standard Architecture slots.** *See* ISA slots
**ink cartridge, installing,** 212, 213
**ink-jet printers,** 138-140
    color printouts, 142
    memory, 145
    photo-quality, 142
**input devices,** 149-151
**Insight,** 178
**instructions, reading,** 209-210
**Intel OverDrive,** 88
    fans for, 229
    interposers, 231
    for Pentiums, 92
    sockets, 87, 88
**Intel processors,** 93. *See also* Intel OverDrive
**interfaces**
    for CD-ROM drives, 124-125
    for hard disk, 129-130
    MIDI interface, 134
    motherboards, EIDE interfaces for, 108
    scanners, 148
    TV cards, 151
**interlacing,** 118-119
**internal drive bays,** 240
**internal modems.** *See* modems

**Internet.** *See also* Web sites
    adequacy of connection, 54-55
    computers for using, 69-70
    connecting to, 10-11
    manufacturer's help on, 367-368
    motherboards, obtaining information on, 86
    purchasing on, 197
    Windows 98 on, 75
**interposers,** 231
**I/O expansion cards,** 253
**Iomega's ZIP and Jaz drives,** 132-133
**IPX/SPX-compatible Protocol,** 313, 314
**IRQs (interrupt addresses),** 59
    DIP switches, 224
    modems and, 297-300
    for printers, 61
    sound problems and, 361
    strategy for using, 298-300
**ISA slots,** 47, 48
    selecting, 236-237
    trend to, 58

## J

**J. C. Penney,** 168
**Jaz drives,** 132-133
**joysticks,** 8, 57, 151-152
    sound cards with ports, 135
**JTS hard drives,** 131
**jumpers,** 224
    batteries, external, 263-264
    drives, installing, 249-250
    expansion cards, installing, 235-236
    memory (RAM), setting for, 258-259
    original instructions for, 246
    processors, settings for, 230
    setting, 227

## K

**Kensington ExpertMouse,** 150
**keyboards,** 149
    changing, 275
    special keyboards, 150-151
**Kingston processors,** 93
**K-Mart,** 168

**Kodak Photo CD,** 126

## L

**landing zone position,** 291
**laptop computer PS/2 ports,** 60
**laser printers,** 140-141
   for business, 146-147
   memory, 145
**LCD monitors,** 118
**legacy programs,** 7
**LIF sockets,** 82, 233
**light pens,** 150
**Local Block Addressing (LBA),** 292
**local bus slots,** 8, 30-31
   determining type of, 48
   video cards and, 8, 113
**locally owned computer stores,** 166-167
**Logitech**
   PageScan Color scanner, 60-61
   TrackMan Marble, 150
**lost cluster,** 15
**low-insertion force (LIF) sockets,** 82, 233

## M

**magazines**
   information in, 158-160
   mail-order shopping from, 172
**Mag Innovision monitors,** 121
**magnets,** 203
**mail-order vendors,** 169-170
   best prices, finding, 172-177
   checking on, 171-172
   for monitors, 121
   multiple-vendor shopping sites, 175-177
   reliability of, 178
   restocking fees, 177
   return policies, 177-178
   shipping terms, checking on, 177
   telephones
      call to vendors, 173
      ordering by, 196
   vendor ads, 160
   warranty policies, 177-178
   Web sites, 173-177

**manufacturers**
   direct buying from, 169
   help from, 366-368
   literature from, 160
**Marshall Fields,** 168
**master/slave relationships, IDE drives,** 244-246, 290
**math coprocessors,** 89
**Matrox video cards,** 115
**Maxim Technology refurbished equipment,** 186
**Maxtor hard drives,** 131
**MDRAM,** 113
**MEM command,** 43-45
**memory (RAM),** 3-4. *See also* printer memory; video cards
   banks for, 255-257
   BIOS
      recognizing RAM, 259-260
      setup for, 282, 287-288
   checklist for, 103
   computer using, 24
   costs of, 63-64
   diagnosing problem, 10
   DIP switches for, 259
   documentation, checking on, 98-101
   for graphics-intensive programs, 8
   improving memory, 94-102
   increasing, 9
   inserting RAM, 257-258
   installing, 254-261
   jumpers, setting, 258-259
   megabytes of memory, 288
   memory error message, 330-331
   motherboards, 97-98, 106-107
   procedure for installing, 260-261
   protecting RAM, 255
   tools for installing, 255
   types of RAM, 95-96
   unpacking components, 209
   as weak link, 55-56
   Windows 95/98 and, 77
   for Windows 95/98 programs, 7
**menus, BIOS setup program,** 285-286
**microphones,** 135
**Microsoft Natural keyboard,** 151
**Micro Warehouse,** 178

**MIDI interface**, 134
    sound cards with MIDI input, 135
**MMX,** 92
    processors, 8
**model numbers,** 370
**Modem Doctor,** 54
**modems,** 10-11
    adequacy, determining, 54-55
    BIOS setup for, 282, 297-300
    COM port IRQs, 297-300
    cost of, 64
    dial tone, lack of, 344-345
    DIP switches, 224
    disconnecting modems, 343-344
    endless connection noise problem, 343
    external modems
        adapters for, 216
        connecting, 215-217
        preference for, 342
    Modem Doctor, 54
    online service program not detecting, 346-348
    troubleshooting problems, 341-353
    voice modems, 11
    as weak link, 57
    WMPLUS utility, 55
**monitors,** 4
    adequacy of, 49
    adjustment controls, 120
    with aperture grilles, 118
    brightness problems, 333
    clean back monitors, 120
    contrast problems, 333
    convergence, checking, 121
    costs of, 64
    darkness/lightness problem, 333
    dot trio shadow mask, 118
    eyestrain and, 12
    footprint of, 120
    glare problems, 12
    for graphics-intensive programs, 9
    horizontal phase control, 332
    horizontal size control, 333
    image problems, 332-333
    interlacing, 118-119

    mail-order vendors, 121
    maximum resolution of, 117
    new monitor, connecting, 211-212
    off-center image problem, 332-333
    pincushion control, 333
    plugging in, 211-212
    refresh rate, 118-119
    rotation control, 333
    size of, 116-117
    technology of, 117-118
    trapezoid control, 333
    troubleshooting problems, 332-333
    upgrading, 116-122
    vertical position control, 332
    vertical size control, 332
    as weak link, 56
**Mopier printer,** 141
**MORE command,** 27
**motherboards,** 4
    AT/ATX motherboards, 104-105
        case style and, 111
        keyboards for, 275
        power supply for, 270-271
    brass standoffs, 269, 273
    bus speed, 109
    cache feature, 108-109
    cages, 272
    case style and, 111
    clock speeds, 85
    cost of, 64
    documentation, obtaining, 86
    ECP/EPP parallel ports, 108
    EIDE interfaces, 108
    expansion slots, 58
    installing, 266-274
    jumper settings, 230
    local bus slot types, 48
    math coprocessor sockets, 89
    memory (RAM) and, 97-98, 106-107
    orientation of, 104-105
    paper washers on standoffs, 269
    for Pentium Pro, 92
    permanently attached to processor, 82
    pin numbers, 230-231

Plug and Play flash BIOS, 109
ports supported, 108
power supply cables, connecting, 270-271
procedure for replacing, 271-274
processor-motherboard connection, 81
removing old motherboard, 267
replacing, 102-110
shopping checklist, 110
size of, 104-105
slots supported, 108
standoffs, installing, 268-269
support for processors, 105-106
tools for installing, 266
view of, 223
voltages, 230
**mouse,** 149
types of, 150
**MPC-3 standard,** 125
**MS-DOS Editor,** 25-26
**multimedia,** 4
adequacy, determining, 52-53
input devices, 149-150
MMX, 92

**N**

**name-brand parts,** 156-158
advantages of, 157
**national chain stores,** 167-168
**NEC slot mask monitors,** 118
**NetBEUI,** 314, 313
**NetBuyer Web site,** 180
refurbished equipment, 186
**network cards,** 275
drivers, installing, 313
**networking.** *See* peer-to-peer networking
**newsgroups.** *See* USENET newsgroups
**nonflash BIOS,** 109
**Norton Utilities,** 19

**O**

**OfficeJet printer,** 141
**office supply stores,** 168
**Onboard Serial Port,** 300
**online service program not detecting modem,** 346-348

**Onsale.com,** 181, 183
**operating systems,** 73-74
**optical character recognition (OCR) software,** 147
**OS/2 Warp,** 74
**Out of Memory messages,** 9
**OverDrive.** *See* Intel OverDrive
**overstock equipment, places to buy,** 186-187

**P**

**packing materials, saving,** 369
**paper washers on standoffs,** 269
**Paradise video cards,** 115
**parallel ports,** 60-61
connecting devices on, 217-218, 219
ECP/EPP parallel ports, 108
*PC Computing,* 159
**PCI slots,** 8, 30
determining, 47-49
selecting slot, 236-237
trend to, 58
*PC Magazine,* 159
*PC Novice,* 159
**PC Tools,** 19
*PC World,* 159
**PC Zone,** 178
**peer-to-peer networking,** 78
access control, setting up, 315-316
configuring Windows 95/98 for, 312-318
drivers
installing, 313-314
troubleshooting problems, 363
logon screen, failure to appear, 363-364
network card drivers, installing, 313
other computers, failure to see, 264
setting up, 275
shared level access, problems with, 364
sharing drive or printer, 316-318
troubleshooting, 363-365
your own computer, failure to see, 364-365
**pen plotter printers,** 137
**Pentium/Pentium II computers,** 8
DIMM slots per bank, 256
fans, 229
motherboards supporting, 105-106

**Pentium/Pentium II computers** *(continued)*
    pipeline burst cache, 108-109
    single inline memory modules (SIMMs) in, 95, 256
    Socket 7, 83
    upgrades for, 92-93
**Pentium Pro computers,** 92
    fans, 229
    motherboards supporting, 105-106
    pipeline burst cache, 108-109
**Peripheral Connection Interface slots.** *See* PCI slots
**permanent swap files,** 32-34
**Phillips screws,** 220
**Phoenix BIOS beep codes,** 373-376
**PhotoRET, Hewlett Packard,** 143
**photo scanning.** *See* scanners
**pin numbers,** 230-231
**PIO modes,** 291-292
**pipeline burst cache,** 108-109
**Plug-and-Play,** 304
    compatibility, 76
    flash BIOS, 109
    modems, BIOS setup for, 297
**PostScript fonts,** 143, 144
**power plugs,** 63
    lack of, 242-243
**power supply**
    capacity, 111
    replacing, 319
    turning off, 204
**PriceWatch Web site,** 175, 176
    cheapest products, searching for, 179
**Primary Master position,** 290
**Primary Slave position,** 290
**Princeton monitors,** 121
**printer cables,** 214
**printer memory,** 9, 145
    laser printers, 52, 140
    professional printouts and, 12
**printers.** *See also* dot matrix printers; ink-jet printers; laser printers
    adequacy, determining, 51-52
    colors, 142
    cost of, 64
    fonts, 143-145

    hybrid printers, 141
    IRQs (interrupt addresses) for, 61
    letter quality printers, 143
    new printer, connecting, 212-215
    paper handling, 145-146
    parallel ports for, 61
    peer-to-peer networking, sharing for, 316-318
    quality of, 136-137, 143
    replacing, 136-147
    software, installing, 214-215
    speed of, 141-142
    technologies, 137-141
    test page, 212, 213
    toner/ink cartridge, installing, 212, 213
    as weak link, 57
**processors,** 3
    adequacy, determining, 50-51
    brands of, 93
    cost of, 64
    current processor, examining, 81-83
    diagnosing speed problem, 10
    fans, 229
    heat sinks, 229
    improving, 81-94
    installing upgrade, 228-233
    jumper settings, 230
    low-insertion force (LIF) sockets, 82
    MMX-capable processors, 8
    motherboard-processor connection, 81
    nonremovable processor, upgrading, 89
    notch on, 233
    procedure for installing, 231-233
    removable processor, upgrading, 87-88
    replacement processors, 83-85
    shopping tips, 93-94
    software for upgrades, 231
    upgrade processors, 85-87
    as weak link, 55
    for Windows 95/98 programs, 7
    zero-insertion force (ZIF) sockets, 82-83
**professional printouts,** 12-13
**PS/2 ports,** 60
**pull equipment,** 186

# Q

**Quake,** 115
**Quantum**
    Bigfoot drive, 130
    hard drives, 131

# R

**Radio cards,** 151
**RAM.** *See* memory (RAM)
**Read-Only Memory (ROM),** 280
**receipts, keeping,** 369
**recordable CD-ROM drives,** 127
**refresh rate**
    changing, 333
    eyestrain and, 12
    for monitors, 118-119
    video cards supporting, 114
**refurbished equipment,** 181, 183
    places to buy, 186-187
**registration card,** 368-369
**REM, removing lines with,** 28
**removable hard drives,** 132-133
    BIOS setup program for, 282
**removable mass storage,** 132-133
**removable processor, upgrading,** 87-88
**resistors on circuit boards,** 205
**resolution**
    monitors, maximum resolution of, 117
    scanners, 147
    video cards, 114
    Windows 3.0/3.1, color resolution for, 31
**restocking fees,** 177
**retail stores,** 187-193
    information-gathering at, 189
    salespeople, talking to, 190-193
    strategy for shopping, 188-189
**returns, store policies,** 192
**ribbon cable,** 244
**ribbon for printer,** 12-13
**RMA numbers,** 370
**ROM-BIOS,** 280

# S

**salesclerks, talking to,** 164-165, 190-193
**ScanDisk,** 14
    DOS version, running, 16, 79
    Windows 95/98 programs, 17-18
**scanners,** 11, 54, 57
    colors, 147
    connecting, 275-276
    interfaces, 148
    Logitech PageScan Color scanner, 60-61
    parallel ports for, 61
    printers with, 141
    replacing, 147-148
    resolution, 147
    types of, 147-148
**screwdrivers,** 203
**screws from case, saving,** 220
**SCSI devices,** 58
    for CD-ROM, 124, 126
    CD-ROM drive, 253-254
    hard drives, 129-130
    jumpers, unlabeled, 249
    removable hard drives, 132-133
    for scanners, 148
    terminating SCSI devices, 246-248
**SCSI ID,** 247
**S-DRAM,** 101
**S-DRAM DIMMs,** 96, 97, 101
    compatibility issues, 107
    memory configuration chart, 99
**Seagate hard drives,** 131
**Search hyperlink,** 185
**Sears,** 168
**Secondary Master position,** 290
**Secondary Slave position,** 290
**self-powered hub,** 62
**serial numbers,** 370
**serial ports,** 59-60
**setup disks, backing up,** 311-312
**SGRAM,** 63, 113
**sheet-fed scanners,** 148
**shipping costs,** 183

**shopping.** *See also* mail-order vendors; retail stores
  comparison of sources, 170
  deep-discount shopping, 179-187
  at locally owned computer stores, 166-167
  making the purchase, 195-197
  monitors, mail-order shopping for, 121
  places to shop, 165
  process, 155-156
  for processors, 93-94
  Web sites, 180-183
  for Windows 95/98, 79-80
**SIMMs.** *See* single inline memory modules (SIMMs)
**single inline memory modules (SIMMs),** 95. *See also* memory (RAM)
  clips for, 257
  converters, 98
  memory configuration information, 100-101
  notches on, 261
  in Pentium/Pentium II computers, 95, 256
  removing SIMM, 258
  silver or gold colored, 102
  swapping out, 321
  30-pin SIMM, 96
**slimline cases,** 221
**slot mask monitors,** 118
**Socket 6,** 87
**Socket 7,** 83, 87-88
**software**
  extra software, installing, 310
  printer software, 214-215
  for processor upgrades, 231
  refresh rates, support for, 119
  reinstalling software, 365
  setup software, running, 300-302
  upgrades, 5-6
**Sony monitors,** 121
**sound cards,** 4
  adequacy, determining, 52-53
  auxiliary input, 135
  bits, number of, 134
  for games, 8
  input/output jacks, 135
  IRQ problems, 361
  line in/line out jack, 135

  no sound in any program, 354-355
  replacing, 133-136
  specific program, no sound in, 355-356
  troubleshooting sound problems, 353-362
  wavetable cards, 134
  Windows 3.0/3.1, no sound in, 356-357
  Windows 95/98, no sound in, 357-362
**Sparq,** 132-133
**speaker icon, turning on,** 360
**speakers**
  monitors with, 120
  sound card with output jack, 135
**splitters,** 63, 243
**standoffs, installing,** 268-269
**startup disk, creating,** 23-25
**startup files, trimming,** 25-26
**static electricity,** 202
**STB Nitro video cards,** 46, 115, 341
**STBVision,** 341
**stripe pitch,** 118
**SuperDisk,** 53
**SuperDrives (LS-120),** 132
**super floppies,** 62, 132
**SVGA Generic Video Driver,** 32
**SVGA monitor,** 45
**swap files**
  defined, 33
  Windows 3.1, creating for, 32-34
**Swiss font,** 144
**.SYS files,** 39

## T

**tape backup drives,** 53, 133
  BIOS setup program for, 282
**Target,** 168
**telephones.** *See also* mail-order vendors
  magnets in, 203
  manufacturer's help on, 366-367
**temperature extremes,** 203-204
**temporary swap files,** 33
**Texas Instruments MicroLaser Pro 600 printer,** 141
**thermal wax transfer printers,** 137
**third height hard drive,** 130
**30-pin SIMM,** 96

**32-bit file system**
  BIOS setup and, 392
  converting to, 42
  Windows 98, 76
**3-D features,** 115
**386 computer upgrades,** 89-90
**tips**
  any key, meaning of, 27
  batteries, incorrect installation, 266
  BIOS
    information, 252
    program help, 284
  boot disks in DOS, 207, 208
  CD-ROM
    installing, 253-254
    Windows 95/98, running drive setup program
      in, 254
  Compression Agent, 42
  DIMMS, swapping out, 321
  Disk Defragmented, 22
  floppy drives, installing, 250
  hard drives, jumpers for, 246
  IDE devices, installing, 252-253
  jumpers
    for hard drives, 246
    unlabeled jumpers, 249
  magazines, 159
  mail-order vendors
    advertising, 160
    phone calls to vendors, 173
    prices, 171
  manufacturers Web sites, 169
  memory (RAM)
    problems, 10
    trade in allowance for, 107
  Modem Doctor, 54
  modems
    Modem Doctor, 54
    WMPLUS utility, 55
  monitors
    from Gateway, 122
    plugging in, 211
    refresh rates, support for, 119
    size of, 117

  motherboard cages, 272
  power supply, replacing, 319
  printers, self-test mode, 52
  processors
    notch on, 233
    performance measurements, 91
    speed problems, 10
  refresh rate, changing, 333
  replacement processors for 486 machines, 84
  screws from case, saving, 220
  Search hyperlink, 185
  SIMMs
    notches on, 261
    swapping out, 321
  software, installing, 301
  sound cards, no documentation for, 358
  speaker icon, turning on, 360
  standoffs, washers on, 269
  technical support people, help from, 367
  VER command, 40
  video cards with Windows 95/98 utility programs, 341
  Windows 3.1/3.11, finding, 80
**.TMP files, deleting,** 39
**toner,** 12-13
  cartridge, installing, 212, 213
**Tool Management Console,** 39
**Tool/Reskit folder,** 39
**tools**
  assembling, 208-209
  batteries, replacing, 261
  drives, installing, 239
  expansion card, installing, 234
  memory (RAM), installing, 255
  motherboards, installing, 266
  for processor upgrade, 228
**touchpads,** 150
**trackballs,** 57, 150
**translation,** 292
**Trinitron monitors,** 118
**troubleshooting**
  BIOS
    beep codes, 372-376
    information with error message, 322-331

**troubleshooting** *(continued)*

blank screen, 318-322

crashing system, 365-366

memory error message, 330-331

modem problems, 341-353

monitor problems, 332-333

peer-to-peer networking, 363-365

sound problems, 353-362

upgrade not functioning, 331

video problems, 331-341

**true color mode,** 114

**true parity memory,** 95

**TrueType fonts,** 143, 144, 145

**TSR (terminate-and-stay-resident) programs,** 24

**TV cards,** 151

# U

**uninstalling programs,** 36-37

**Universal Serial Bus.** *See* USB ports

**unpacking components,** 209

**upgrade processors,** 85-87

**upper memory,** 24

**USB ports,** 58, 61-62

monitors with connectors, 120

scanners connecting to, 148

**USENET newsgroups,** 163-164

mail-order vendor information, 178

# V

**vendor refurbished equipment,** 181

**Ventura Publisher for DOS,** 144

**VER command,** 40

**Vesa Local Bus.** *See* VLB slots

**VGA monitor,** 45

**video cameras,** 57

**video capture,** 149

**video cards,** 4, 45. *See also* local bus slots

color displays, 114

costs of, 64

DOS video problems, 334-335

evaluating, 112

for games, 8

input, 53-54

local bus connection, 8, 113

memory (RAM), 46-47, 113-114

upgrading, 276

refresh rate, 114

resolution, 114

3-D feature support, 115

upgrading, 112-114

as weak link, 56

Windows 3.0/3.1

improving performance, 31-32

troubleshooting, 335-337

Windows 95/98 video problems, 338-341

**ViewSonic**

monitors, 121

Web page, 161, 162

**virtual reality gloves/helmets,** 152

**VLB slots,** 30

determining, 47-49

video card connections, 8

**voice modems,** 11

**voltage for motherboards,** 230

**VRAM,** 113, 116

# W

**Wal-Mart,** 168

**warranties**

mail-order vendors, 177-178

name-brand parts, 157

protecting warranty rights, 368-370

for refurbished equipment, 181

retail store policies, 192

**washers on standoffs,** 269

**wavetable cards,** 134

**Web sites,** 180-183

AuctionWeb, 184-185

creating, 11

mail-order vendors, 173-177

manufacturers Web sites, 169

multiple-vendor shopping sites, 175-177

NetBuyer Web site, 180

purchasing on, 197

shopping at, 160-162

**Western Digital hard drives,** 131

**Windows 3.0/3.1,** 6. *See also* video cards
   color patches onscreen, 337
   color resolution for, 31
   finding, 80
   hardware limitations, 80
   improving performance in, 30-34
   modem problems, 346-348
   online service program not detecting modem, 346-348
   scrambled pictures, 335-337
   setup programs, running, 303-304
   sound problems, 356-357
   stray lines onscreen, 337
   swap files, creating, 32-34
   upgrading to, 77-78
**Windows 95/98,** 6-7. *See also* peer-to-peer networking; Plug-and-Play
   amount of memory, determining, 43-45
   boot disks in, 206-207
   CD-ROM drive setup program in, 254
   compatibility mode for, 37
   compressing hard disk with, 41-42
   defragmenting with, 21-22
   detecting device, prompting for, 304-307
   Disk Cleanup program, 40
   disk errors, checking, 17-18
   disk version of, 77
   display, simplicity of, 34-36
   drawbacks, 76-77
   failure to detect device, 308-310
   fine-tuning performance, 37-39
   flickering display, 340-341
   hardware limitations, 80
   improving performance, 34-39
   IRQs (interrupt addresses) and modems, 351
   legacy programs, 7
   modem problems, 349-353
   need for RAM, determining, 96-97
   other device
      modem seen as, 352-353
      sound card seen as, 362
   port, installing device and selecting, 309-310
   refresh rates, changing, 333
   setup disks
      copying, 311-312
      prompt for, 305
   setup programs, running, 304-310
   shopping for, 79-80
   sound problems, 357-362
   32-bit file system, converting to, 42
   uninstalling programs, 36-37
   upgrading to, 74-77
   video problems, 338-341
**Winmodems,** 342
**WMPLUS utility,** 55
**word processing, computer for,** 67-68
**WRAM,** 113
**wrist straps, antistatic,** 202

# X

**XA standard,** 126

# Y

**Yahoo!, refurbished equipment on,** 186

# Z

**zero-insertion force (ZIF) sockets,** 82-83, 231
   processors, installing, 233
**ZIP drives,** 53, 57, 132-133
   parallel ports for, 61

# OTHER BOOKS FROM PRIMA TECH
## A Division of Prima Publishing

| ISBN | Title | Price |
|---|---|---|
| 0-7615-1363-9 | Access 97 Fast & Easy | $16.99 |
| 0-7615-1412-0 | ACT! 4.0 Fast & Easy | $16.99 |
| 0-7615-1348-5 | Create FrontPage 98 Web Pages In a Weekend | $24.99 |
| 0-7615-1294-2 | Create PowerPoint Presentations In a Weekend | $19.99 |
| 0-7615-1388-4 | Create Your First Web Page In a Weekend, Revised Edition | $24.99 |
| 0-7615-0428-1 | The Essential Excel 97 Book | $27.99 |
| 0-7615-0733-7 | The Essential Netscape Communicator Book | $24.99 |
| 0-7615-0969-0 | The Essential Office 97 Book | $27.99 |
| 0-7615-1396-5 | The Essential Photoshop 5 Book | $34.99 |
| 0-7615-1182-2 | The Essential PowerPoint 97 Book | $24.99 |
| 0-7615-1136-9 | The Essential Publisher 97 Book | $24.99 |
| 0-7615-0967-4 | The Essential Windows 98 Book | $24.99 |
| 0-7615-0752-3 | The Essential Windows NT 4 Book | $27.99 |
| 0-7615-0427-3 | The Essential Word 97 Book | $27.99 |
| 0-7615-0425-7 | The Essential WordPerfect 8 Book | $24.99 |
| 0-7615-1008-7 | Excel 97 Fast & Easy | $16.99 |
| 0-7615-1534-8 | FrontPage 98 Fast & Easy | $16.99 |
| 0-7615-1194-6 | Increase Your Web Traffic In a Weekend | $19.99 |
| 0-7615-1191-1 | Internet Explorer 4.0 Fast & Easy | $19.99 |
| 0-7615-1137-7 | Jazz Up Your Web Site In a Weekend | $24.99 |
| 0-7615-1379-5 | Learn Access 97 In a Weekend | $19.99 |
| 0-7615-1293-4 | Learn HTML In a Weekend | $24.99 |

| ISBN | Title | Price |
|------|-------|-------|
| 0-7615-1295-0 | Learn the Internet In a Weekend | $19.99 |
| 0-7615-1217-9 | Learn Publisher 97 In a Weekend | $19.99 |
| 0-7615-1384-1 | Learn QuickBooks 6 In a Weekend | $19.99 |
| 0-7615-1251-9 | Learn Word 97 In a Weekend | $19.99 |
| 0-7615-1296-9 | Learn Windows 98 In a Weekend | $19.99 |
| 0-7615-1193-8 | Lotus 1-2-3 97 Fast & Easy | $16.99 |
| 0-7615-1420-1 | Managing with Microsoft Project 98 | $29.99 |
| 0-7615-1382-5 | Netscape Navigator 4.0 Fast & Easy | $16.99 |
| 0-7615-1162-8 | Office 97 Fast & Easy | $16.99 |
| 0-7615-1186-5 | Organize Your Finances with Quicken Deluxe 98 In a Weekend | $19.99 |
| 0-7615-1786-3 | Organize Your Finances In a Weekend with Quicken Deluxe 99 | $19.99 |
| 0-7615-1405-8 | Outlook 98 Fast & Easy | $16.99 |
| 0-7615-1677-8 | Prima's Official Companion to Family Tree Maker 5 | $24.99 |
| 0-7615-1513-5 | Publisher 98 Fast & Easy | $19.99 |
| 0-7615-1787-1 | Quicken 99 Fast & Easy | $16.99 |
| 0-7615-1699-9 | SmartSuite Millennium Fast & Easy | $16.99 |
| 0-7615-1328-0 | Web Advertising and Marketing, 2nd Edition | $34.95 |
| 1-55958-738-5 | Windows 95 Fast & Easy | $19.95 |
| 0-7615-1006-0 | Windows 98 Fast & Easy | $16.99 |
| 0-7615-1007-9 | Word 97 Fast & Easy | $16.99 |
| 0-7615-1316-7 | Word 97 for Law Firms | $29.99 |
| 0-7615-1083-4 | WordPerfect 8 Fast & Easy | $16.99 |
| 0-7615-1188-1 | WordPerfect Suite 8 Fast & Easy | $16.99 |

# TO ORDER BOOKS

Please send me the following items:

| Quantity | Title | Unit Price | Total |
|---|---|---|---|
| —————— | ———————————————————————————— | $———————— | $———————— |
| —————— | ———————————————————————————— | $———————— | $———————— |
| —————— | ———————————————————————————— | $———————— | $———————— |
| —————— | ———————————————————————————— | $———————— | $———————— |
| —————— | ———————————————————————————— | $———————— | $———————— |

|  |  |
|---|---|
| Subtotal | $———————— |
| **Deduct 10% when ordering 3–5 books** | $———————— |
| 7.25% Sales Tax (CA only) | $———————— |
| 8.25% Sales Tax (TN only) | $———————— |
| 5.0% Sales Tax (MD and IN only) | $———————— |
| Shipping and Handling* | $———————— |
| TOTAL ORDER | $———————— |

*Shipping and Handling depend on Subtotal.

| Subtotal | Shipping/Handling |
|---|---|
| $0.00–$14.99 | $3.00 |
| $15.00–29.99 | $4.00 |
| $30.00–49.99 | $6.00 |
| $50.00–99.99 | $10.00 |
| $100.00–199.99 | $13.00 |
| $200.00+ | call for quote |

Foreign and all Priority Request orders:
Call Order Entry department for price quote at 1-916-632-4400

This chart represents the total retail price of books only (before applicable discounts are taken).

**By telephone:** With Visa, Mastercard, or American Express, call 800-632-8676 or 916-632-4400. Mon.–Fri. 8:30–4:00 PST.

**www.primapublishing.com**

**By E-mail:** sales@primapub.com

**By mail:** Just fill out the information below and send with your remittance to:

**PRIMA PUBLISHING**

P.O. Box 1260BK
Rocklin, CA 95677-1260

Name_____ Daytime Telephone_____

Address _____

City _____ State _____ Zip _____

Visa /MC# _____Exp. _____

Check/Money Order enclosed for $_____ Payable to Prima Publishing

Signature _____